MORE PRAIS...
*WHY ARE ALL THE ...*
*SITTING TOGETHER IN THE CAFETERIA*

"When I began my own journey of anti-racism, Beverly Daniel Tatum's *Why Are All the Black Kids Sitting Together in the Cafeteria* was the first and most instructive work I discovered. Its anniversary edition—with timely new research, revisited institutional issues, and personal examples so fresh they seem to have come from the headlines—is the book that everyone in America needs to read right now. With clarity and grace, Tatum chronicles how our country has become so racially polarized— how the methods and signifiers may have changed, but the world has not, sustaining inequities for people of color in terms of school segregation, law enforcement, economic obstacles, and voting rights. From the spate of police shootings to the challenge to Affirmative Action, from the rise of the Black Lives Matter movement and the parallel swell of hate crimes based on race, this updated version of a classic is the clearest illustration I've found of how fear and anxiety in the declining White population of the United States has created a living environment of fear and anxiety for people of color. We don't talk about race in America, but we must start if we are going to heal this broken country—and Tatum's book is exactly the conversation opener we should be using."

—Jodi Picoult, #1 *New York Times* bestselling author of *Small Great Things*

"*Why Are All the Black Kids Sitting Together in the Cafeteria* was a landmark publication when it appeared in 1997. Twenty years later this updated edition is as fresh, poignant, and timely as ever. Bias, explicit and implicit, limit options, produce deadly encounters, and gnaw away at the fabric of our social contract. Racism, prejudice, and discrimination remain active characteristics of life in our society, notwithstanding the prominence of African Americans, Latinos/as, Asian Americans, and Native peoples in the media, entertainment, sports, politics, and many domains of business. Beverly Daniel Tatum reminds us that against this backdrop individuals sometimes seek out others like themselves because it secures their sense of self in a world that often makes them feel insecure. As a result, group congregation becomes a means of flipping the power dynamics and affirming oneself in a social context. If you somehow missed this book in its original form, I recommend this revised edition to you. It remains a must-read."

**—Earl Lewis, president, Andrew W. Mellon Foundation**


"Beverly Daniel Tatum answers the question posed in the title of her book in a brilliant synthesis informed by history, developmental psychology, and great wisdom. Stereotypes, omissions, and distortions—each rooted in our nation's history of slavery—cause each of us to breathe the 'smog of racism.' It is little wonder that Black adolescents rely on one another for social support as they navigate identity development. In the twenty years since Tatum first published her classic book, Black people have been disproportionately affected by the economic crisis of 2008, mass incarceration, and a backlash against affirmative action. In this revision, Tatum finds a way to remain hopeful as today's youth lead movements exposing racial hierarchies, race and class privilege, and seemingly invisible systems of oppression. This book should be required reading for every American."

**—Kathleen McCartney, president, Smith College**

"We read the original version of this book twenty years ago and learned a great deal about race, racism, and human behavior. This updated version provides even more insights about the racial, ethnic, and cultural challenges we face in American society, and particularly in higher education. What makes these insights so valuable is the author's ability to look at our problems from different perspectives and to challenge us to look in the mirror as we think about who we are and whom we serve. She gives excellent examples of leaders who succeeded during times of crisis, and of others who struggled. Any American leader wanting a deeper understanding of these issues should read this book."

—Freeman A. Hrabowski III, president, University of Maryland, Baltimore County

"Set today against the backdrop of a highly divisive and still persistently racialized societal landscape, this newly revised and updated publication is still a must-read classic. Tatum unpacks with moving narratives, the psychology that drives us all, as we grow up in largely homogenous communities, schooled in the nuances of difference that define too starkly our racial identities, even as we strive to learn how to embrace rather than distance [ourselves] from the many others that define our world. Just as this experienced psychologist and wise educational leader reminds us here that we cannot talk meaningfully about racial identity without talking about racism, so too must we learn from her words about how to talk and teach and dialogue across those boundaries, in the hopes of better realizing the potential of our diverse democracy."

—Nancy Cantor, chancellor, Rutgers University-Newark

"In 1997, *Why Are All the Black Kids Sitting Together in the Cafeteria?* changed the conversation about race and racism in our nation. Twenty years later, this new edition is sure to do the same, this time with thoroughly updated information about the growing ethnic, racial, cultural, and religious diversity that now characterizes the United States, as well as important insights about persistent barriers to authentic integration and shrinking opportunities for many segments of the population. Given the current sociopolitical context in which we find ourselves, a context too often defined by exclusion and the stubborn persistence of bigotry and racism, this new edition couldn't have come soon enough!"

> —Sonia Nieto, Professor Emerita, University of
> Massachusetts, Amherst

"In the face of setbacks economically, socially, and racially, Beverly Daniel Tatum's work is ever relevant. Spanning so very much history in recent decades and engagingly written, this book remains the go-to volume on identity groups and social exclusion, especially among college-aged people."

> —Roger Brooks, president and CEO, Facing History
> and Ourselves

# WHY ARE ALL THE BLACK KIDS SITTING TOGETHER IN THE CAFETERIA?

## And Other Conversations About Race

## Beverly Daniel Tatum

BASIC BOOKS
*New York*

Basic Books
Hachette Book Group
1290 Avenue of the Americas, New York, NY 10104
www.basicbooks.com

Printed in the United States of America

Originally published in hardcover and ebook by Basic Books in September 1997
Third trade paperback edition: July 2017

Published by Basic Books, an imprint of Perseus Books, LLC, a subsidiary of Hachette Book Group, Inc.

The Hachette Speakers Bureau provides a wide range of authors for speaking events. To find out more, go to www.hachettespeakersbureau.com or call (866) 376-6591.

The publisher is not responsible for websites (or their content) that are not owned by the publisher.

Some names and identifying details have been changed to protect the privacy of individuals.

Library of Congress Cataloging-in-Publication Data

Names: Tatum, Beverly Daniel, author.
Title: "Why are all the black kids sitting together in the cafeteria?" : and other conversations about race / Beverly Daniel Tatum.
Description: New York : Basic Books, 2017. | "Fully revised and updated"—Provided by publisher. | Includes bibliographical references and index.
Identifiers: LCCN 2017014766 (print) | LCCN 2017017216 (ebook) | ISBN 9781541616585 (ebook) | ISBN 9780465060689 (paperback)
Subjects: LCSH: African Americans—Race identity. | Whites—Race identity—United States. | African American children—Psychology. | African American youth—Psychology. | Whites—United States—Psychology. | Race awareness in adolescence—United States. | Intercultural communication—United States. | Communication and culture—United States. | Communication—Social aspects—United States. | United States—Race relations. | BISAC: SOCIAL SCIENCE / Ethnic Studies / African American Studies.
Classification: LCC E185.625 (ebook) | LCC E185.625 .T38 2017 (print) | DDC

305.800973—dc23

ISBNs: 978-0-465-06068-9 (2017 paperback); 978-1-54161-658-5 (ebook)

LSC-C

Printing 16, 2020

*In remembrance of my parents,*
*Robert and Catherine Daniel,*
*whose love and encouragement lives on*

When I dare to be powerful,
to use my strength in the service of my vision,
then it becomes less important whether or not I am afraid.

**—AUDRE LORDE**

# CONTENTS

# "Why Are All the Black Kids *Still* Sitting Together in the Cafeteria?" and Other Conversations About Race in the Twenty-First Century

WHEN I TOLD PEOPLE THAT I WAS WORKING ON A TWENTIETH-anniversary edition of my 1997 book, *"Why Are All the Black Kids Sitting Together in the Cafeteria?" and Other Conversations About Race,* the typical response came in the form of a question, or sometimes two: "Is that still happening? Are things getting better?" A quick glance across the cafeteria in the average racially mixed US high school or college will tell you that the answer to the first question is usually yes. What, if anything, does that tell us about the answer to the second question, "Are things getting better?" What does "better" look like? That is a more complicated question. What has changed, for better or worse, in the last twenty years? What is the implication for how we understand ourselves and each other in reference to our racial identities? And, if we are dissatisfied with the way things are, what can we do to change it?

I wrote the first version of this book in 1996, in the closing years of the twentieth century. Now, almost two decades into the twenty-first, it seems we are still struggling with what W. E. B. Du Bois identified in 1906 as the "problem of the color line," even though the demographic composition of that color line has changed quite a bit since then. In his provocatively titled 2016 book, *Brown Is the New White: How the Demographic Revolution Has Created a New American Majority,* author

Steve Phillips highlights the speed with which the American population is shifting. He writes, "Each day, the size of the U.S. population increases by more than 8,000 people, *and nearly 90 percent of that growth consists of people of color* [emphasis in original]," a consequence of differential rates of birth, death, and patterns of immigration. The numbers are pretty remarkable when you consider that in 1950 the total US population was nearly 90 percent White. But many members of that 1950s population are now elderly, and as the older White population is passing away, the White birth rate is not sufficient to replace them at the same population percentage. Add to this the fact of immigration. The majority of people immigrating legally to the US are people of color, coming from places like Asia, Africa, and Latin America, reflecting the fact that the majority of the world's population is of color. When immigration numbers are added to the net increase from births, "the bottom line is that each and every day, 7,261 people of color are added to the U.S. population, in contrast to the White growth of 1,053 people."[1] Indeed, the 2014 school year marked the first time in US history that the majority of elementary and secondary schoolchildren were children of color—Black, Latinx,[2] Asian, or American Indian.[3]

## New Faces, Same Places

Though much of what has historically been written about race relations in the United States describes the traditional Black-White racial binary—a function of the legacy of slavery, the African American struggle for civil rights, and the fact that in the twentieth century Blacks represented the largest minority group—it is important to note that in the twenty-first century, people of Latin American descent (referred to by the US Census Bureau as Hispanics) are the largest population of color in the nation. According to the Census Bureau, while Blacks compose 13 percent of the US population, Hispanics are now 17.6 percent.[4] Growing faster than the Hispanic population is the Asian American community. Less than 1 percent of the population in 1965, by 2011 the Asian population had grown to approximately 6 percent of the US population, now the fastest-growing racial group in the country. Within the broad umbrella category of Asian Americans, the six largest groups by country of origin are Chinese Americans, Filipino Americans, Indian Americans, Vietnamese Americans, Korean Americans, and Japanese Americans, together representing 83 percent of the total Asian population in the US.[5]

While Muslims cannot be accurately defined in terms of one racial or ethnic group, because Muslims come from many countries of origin and not just the Middle East, it seems fitting to include current statistics about the Muslim population because some of the dynamics we see regarding racial difference during the last two decades apply here as well. Certainly since the September 11, 2001, terrorist attacks, there has been an increase in anti-Muslim sentiment in the US that should not be ignored. The Pew Research Center estimates that there were approximately 3.3 million Muslims of all ages living in the United States in 2015, representing about 1 percent of the total US population. The Muslim population is expected to double by 2050, half of that projected growth the result of immigration.[6]

Also of note is the growth in the population described as multiracial. In the year 2000, the United States Census Bureau began allowing people to choose more than one racial category to describe themselves. Since then, the nation's multiracial population has grown significantly. The number of White and Black biracial Americans more than doubled, while the population of adults with a White and Asian background increased by 87 percent. According to a report of the Pew Research Center, "multiracial Americans are at the cutting edge of social and demographic change in the U.S.—young, proud, tolerant and growing at a rate three times as fast as the population as a whole." Indeed, the percentage of multiracial babies has risen from 1 percent in 1970 to 10 percent in 2013.[7]

Clearly our national diversity is growing rapidly, yet old patterns of segregation persist, most notably in schools and neighborhoods. More than sixty years after the *Brown v. Board of Education* Supreme Court decision, in every region of the country except the West, our public schools are more segregated today than they were in 1980, as measured by the percentage of all Black students who are attending schools that are "90–100% non-White," with the highest rates of school segregation in the Northeast. Though the South made rapid progress toward school desegregation in the late 1960s and 1970s, typically in response to court orders and other federal pressure, the Northeast did not budge much, and patterns of de facto segregation in the Northeast continue to rise slowly but steadily, such that today more than 50 percent of Black students in the Northeast attend schools that are classified as "90–100% non-White."[8] Nationwide, nearly 75 percent of Black students today attend so-called majority-minority schools, and 38 percent attend schools with student bodies that are 10 percent or less White. Similarly large numbers of Latinx students, approximately 80 percent, attend schools where students of color are in the majority, and more than 40 percent attend schools where the White population is less than 10 percent of the student body. Both Black and Latinx students are much more likely than White students to attend a school where 60 percent or more of their classmates are living in poverty, as measured by the percentage of students eligible for free or reduced-price lunch programs. Separate remains unequal as schools with concentrated poverty and racial segregation are still likely to have less-experienced teachers, high levels of teacher turnover, inadequate facilities, and fewer classroom resources.[9]

A series of key Supreme Court decisions during the three decades between 1974 and 2007 dramatically reduced the number of implementation methods available to communities engaged in school desegregation by eliminating strategies such as cross-district busing, dismantling local court supervision of desegregation plans, and limiting use of race-based admissions to ensure diversity in magnet school programs.[10] As these options for desegregation have been curtailed by court rulings, the number of intensely segregated schools with zero to 10 percent White enrollment has more than tripled.[11] Students are, once again, predominantly assigned to schools based on where they live, and to the extent that neighborhoods are segregated, the schools remain so.

When we talk about residential segregation, we inevitably find that we are talking about not only race but also class. Certainly income matters when you are looking for housing. But we can't overlook the way housing patterns have been shaped historically by race-based policies and practices, such as racially restrictive real estate covenants, racial steering by real estate agents, redlining, and other discriminatory practices by mortgage lenders. That history includes the use by many White homeowners' associations of physical threats and violence to keep unwanted people of color out of their neighborhoods.

In her 2014 book *Reproducing Racism: How Everyday Choices Lock In White Advantage*, legal scholar Daria Roithmayr succinctly reminds us of that exclusionary history. Describing practices that originated in Chicago in the first quarter of the twentieth century, she details how regional practices became national law and federal policy:

> In a crucial historical moment that would pave the way for the rest of the country, the [Chicago Real Estate Board] put in place an ethics code provision that prohibited brokers from selling to buyers who threatened to disrupt the racial composition of the neighborhood. The move was so effective that the National Association of Real Estate Boards (NAREB) adopted an identical provision. Now brokers would have to risk their careers to sell across racial lines—state commissions were authorized by state law to revoke the state licenses of those brokers who violated this provision.[12]

NAREB not only adopted the ethics code provision but also copied the Chicago use of the racially restrictive covenant, a legal instrument that served to prevent individual White homeowners from selling or leasing their property to Black residents, and spread the practice nationwide. For nearly three decades, these practices were not only legal but undergirded by federal policy.

The policies of the Federal Housing Authority (FHA), the Department of Veterans Affairs (VA), and the federal Home Owners' Loan Corporation (HOLC) all converged to establish redlining as a national practice. "The most important factor encouraging white suburbanization and reinforcing the segregation of blacks was the FHA requirement for an 'unbiased,' professional appraisal of insured properties, which naturally included a rating of the neighborhood."[13] Using a coding system originally created by the HOLC, Black neighborhoods received a score of four, the lowest rating, and were coded as red. Those areas deemed at risk of becoming Black neighborhoods received a rating of three and were labeled "hazardous." As a matter of policy, the FHA loans went toward the purchase of homes in the top two neighborhood rating categories, "new and homogeneous" and "expected to remain stable." In effect, the federal loans were issued to White families to buy homes in new suburban neighborhoods that were all White and in older White neighborhoods that were expected to remain homogeneous. Private lenders took on the same redlining practices of the federal government, making it very difficult for Black families to obtain loans for property in the neighborhoods to which they were being confined. "The lack of loan capital flowing into minority areas made it impossible for owners to sell their homes, leading to steep declines in property values and a pattern of disrepair, deterioration, vacancy and abandonment."[14] The racially restrictive covenants that served to keep Black people from moving into White residential neighborhoods were officially endorsed by the FHA in the late 1940s and maintained until 1950, even though the Supreme Court declared such covenants unconstitutional in 1948.[15]

The legacy of these policies and practices lives on in the present as past housing options enhance or impede the accumulation of home equity and eventually the intergenerational transmission of wealth. And though such policies are now illegal at the federal, state, and local levels, evidence suggests they haven't been eliminated in practice. In 2006 the National Fair Housing Alliance (NFHA) released the results of a multiyear, multicity investigation of real estate practices using paired teams of testers (White and African American, or White and Latinx) that were matched in terms of housing needs, financial qualifications, and employment history. Eighty-seven percent of the time the testers were steered to neighborhoods on the basis of race and/or national origin. In most cases, Whites were shown homes in primarily White neighborhoods, African Americans were shown homes in primarily African American neighborhoods, and Latinx buyers were shown homes in primarily Latinx neighborhoods.[16]

To the extent there is progress toward Black-White racial integration, it is most apparent in communities where the total Black population is relatively small and of relatively high socioeconomic status and there is a military base or university in the region.[17] My family and I lived in a place like that for twenty years—Northampton, Massachusetts. While these characteristics do not describe the communities where the majority of Black people live, it is worth noting that Black families have been moving out of the inner cities in large numbers. Demographer William Frey notes that by 2010, as the result of accelerated "Black flight," more Blacks lived in the suburbs than in the cities of the biggest metropolitan regions.[18]

Contemporary surveys of racial attitudes among Whites indicate that the larger the hypothetical Black population in an area, the more likely White respondents are to express discomfort about living in the same neighborhood.[19] The behavioral result of such attitudes is that in those cities that still have large urban Black populations—places like New York, Chicago, Detroit, Cleveland, Milwaukee—progress toward residential integration has been quite limited. According to the 2010 census tract data, roughly a third of all Black metropolitan residents live in extremely segregated, or what researchers call "hyper-segregated," neighborhoods.

A similar pattern is visible among Latinx families in the two largest Latinx communities—New York and Los Angeles—where nearly 20 percent are in hypersegregated neighborhoods. However, Latinx residential patterns do vary based on factors such as country of origin, recency of immigration, and skin color. New Latinx immigrants are likely to live in highly segregated communities, and those who are darker-skinned (many Puerto Ricans and Dominicans, for example) also tend to live in segregated neighborhoods, often in or adjacent to African American neighborhoods.[20] Those who are lighter-skinned (many Cubans and South Americans, such as Argentineans, for example) may self-identify racially as White and are more likely to live in areas with non-Hispanic Whites.

Discussing the housing patterns of American Indians and Alaska Natives is difficult because of the group's relatively small population and the fact that many still live on rural American Indian reservations and in Alaska Native villages. It is estimated that 34 percent of the 4.1

million American Indians and Alaska Natives (1.5 percent of the total US population) live outside metropolitan areas.[21] Of all groups of color, Asian Americans are the least segregated from Whites, though there is variation in that pattern as well. Recent immigrants are more likely to be concentrated in ethnic enclaves than those who have been in the US for several generations.[22] Not surprisingly, of all racial groups, Whites are the most isolated. They are the most likely to live in racially homogeneous communities and the least likely to come into contact with people racially different from themselves.[23]

What difference does it make now? For people of color, living in a hypersegregated community increases one's exposure to the disadvantages associated with concentrated poverty and reduces access to the benefits associated with affluent communities (e.g., higher rates of voting, more political influence, lower rates of crime and delinquency, greater involvement with cultural and educational institutions, healthier lifestyles), *regardless of your own socioeconomic status*. Sociologists Massey and Tannen conclude the following:

> Our focused analysis of neighborhood trends in hypersegregated areas further demonstrated the power of segregation not only to compromise the neighborhood circumstances of poor African-Americans but also to limit the ability of affluent Black residents to improve their geographic position in urban society. . . . Not only was the quality of neighborhoods inhabited by affluent Blacks lower in absolute terms compared to their affluent counterparts across metropolitan areas generally, but also their neighborhood circumstances improved little relative to those experienced by the very poorest of Whites. These findings confirm what social scientists have long known: *Residential segregation continues to be the structural linchpin in America's system of racial stratification.* [italics mine][24]

In everyday terms, Daria Roithmayr explains that racial segregation limits access to the helpful social networks needed for successful employment. Neighbors connect each other (or each other's children) to employment opportunities and other needed resources. Keeping groups separated means that community helpfulness is not shared across racial lines. Because of residential segregation, economic disadvantage and racial disadvantage are inextricably linked.[25]

Acknowledging the now centuries-long persistence of residential segregation and its consequence, school segregation, goes a long way toward explaining why the answer to the first question posed to me is still "Yes, the Black kids are *still* sitting together." The social context in which students of color and White students enter academic environments together (in those few places where they do) is still a context in which their lived experiences are likely to have been quite different from each other, and in which racial stereotyping is still likely to be an inhibiting factor in their cross-group interactions.

## Change You Can Believe In?

That said, isn't *anything* better? In his commencement address at Howard University on May 7, 2016, President Barack Obama offered an answer to that question. Speaking to a largely Black audience, he highlighted the ways the world has improved since his own college graduation in 1983, including in the area of race relations. Here's an excerpt of that speech: "In my inaugural address, I remarked that just 60 years earlier, my father might not have been served in a D.C. restaurant—at least not certain of them. There were no black CEOs of Fortune 500 companies. Very few black judges. . . . We're no longer only entertainers, we're producers, studio executives. No longer small business owners—we're CEOs, we're mayors, representatives, Presidents of the United States."[26]

Of course, President Obama was correct that there has been positive, meaningful social change in our lifetimes—certainly in the years since I was born in 1954—but if we focus specifically on the twenty-year period from 1997 to 2017, we must acknowledge some setbacks beyond just the stubborn persistence of neighborhood and school segregation. There are three I want to highlight here: the anti–affirmative action backlash of the late twentieth and early twenty-first centuries, the economic collapse of 2008 known as the Great Recession, and the phenomenon known as mass incarceration.

The first of these setbacks—the anti–affirmative action backlash of the late twentieth and early twenty-first century—has had significant impact on Black, Latinx, and American Indian access to the best-resourced public colleges and universities. The case of higher education in California is a telling example. In 1996 California voters approved an initiative, known as Proposition 209, that prohibited "preferential treatment" based on "race, sex, color, ethnicity or national origin" in employment, education, and contracting programs, effectively ending all state-run affirmative action programs. The California legislation inspired other states to place a ban on affirmative action in state-run programs. As of 2014, Washington, Florida, Michigan, Nebraska, Arizona, New Hampshire, and Oklahoma had done so.[27]

In the case of California, the Proposition 209 initiative, which took effect in 1998, had a devastating effect on the enrollment of Black and Latinx students at the two leading public universities in California, UCLA and UC Berkeley. African American undergraduate enrollment dropped at UCLA by more than 37 percent, from 5.6 percent of the freshman class to 3.5 percent. Almost two decades later, the proportion of African American freshman students enrolling at UCLA remains below the pre–Proposition 209 levels. At UC Berkeley, African American undergraduate enrollment has fluctuated between approximately 3 percent and 4 percent between 1998 and 2014, far below the pre–Proposition 209 level, which was approximately 6.5 percent. Similarly Latinx undergraduate enrollment also fell sharply in the wake of Proposition 209 at both institutions. At UC Berkeley, Latinx enrollment dropped from 16.9 percent of the freshman class to 8.2 percent—a staggering 52 percent decline—in the years between 1995 and 1998. Enrollment of American Indian students also plummeted. As of 2014, American Indian undergraduate enrollment at UCLA and UC Berkeley is still 45 percent lower than it was when Proposition 209 went into effect.[28] The decrease in students of color has led to a greater sense of isolation among those who do enroll.[29]

A similar impact was seen in Michigan following the passage of its own version of Proposition 209. Known as Proposal 2, the Michigan Civil Rights Initiative (MCRI) became law in 2006. As in California, the proposal banned all affirmative action programs that gave "preferential treatment" to people of color in state contracting, employment, and higher education. Before Proposal 2 took effect, underrepresented students of color made up 13 percent of the University of Michigan's total enrollment. By 2014, the overall percentage had dropped to 11.5 percent of total enrollment. The figures are even worse for African Americans, with undergraduate enrollment dropping more than a third, from 7 percent in 2006 to approximately 4.5 percent in 2014. Ironically, this decrease occurred even as the total percentage of college-aged Blacks in Michigan increased from 16 to 19 percent.[30]

The California and Michigan flagship institutions have found that without taking race in consideration, it is very difficult to achieve representative levels of diversity across the higher education landscape, despite the demographic changes of the twenty-first century. Recognition of that difficulty seemed to play a role in the most recent Supreme Court decision regarding affirmative action programs in higher education. On June 23, 2016, the court ruled on the case of *Fisher v. University of Texas at Austin,* which challenged UT Austin's use of race as one factor among many in a holistic review of applicants. To the surprise of many court watchers, the Supreme Court ruled on the side of the university. Writing the majority opinion for the court, Justice Anthony Kennedy praised Texas for having offered a reasoned, principled explanation of its policy, but also warned that the court's decision "does not necessarily mean the university may rely on that same policy without refinement" in the future, reminding us all of the still-unsteady ground on which current affirmative action programs stand.[31]

The second setback—the economic collapse of 2008—shook the ground for Americans of all racial and ethnic backgrounds, but it had a disproportionately disastrous effect for many Black and Latinx families. In their sobering 2009 *Huffington Post* essay titled "The Destruction of the Black Middle Class," Barbara Ehrenreich and Dedrick Muhammad wrote:

> After decades of being denied mortgages on racial grounds, African Americans made a tempting market for bubble-crazed lenders like

Countrywide, with the result that high income blacks were almost twice as likely as low income whites to receive high interest subprime loans. According to the Center for Responsible Lending, Latinos will end up losing between $75 billion and $98 billion in home-value wealth from subprime loans, while blacks will lose between $71 billion and $92 billion. United for a Fair Economy has called this family net-worth catastrophe the "greatest loss of wealth for people of color in modern U.S. history."[32]

Not only did many families of color lose their homes in the Great Recession, they also lost their jobs. Disparate unemployment rates continue, despite the national economic recovery. At this writing, in the third quarter of 2016, the White unemployment rate is 4.4 percent, but for African Americans it is 8.5 percent (4 percent for Asians and 5.8 percent for Latinxs).[33] "The racial wealth gap between whites and people of color is the highest it has been in 25 years; 2014 estimates by the Pew Research Center put the gap in net worth between African Americans and Whites at 1,300 percent and that between Whites and Hispanics at 1,000 percent."[34] The economic disparities translate into educational disparities as well. College access is much more difficult when families have had little opportunity to accumulate savings and have no real estate assets against which to borrow. According to data from the National Postsecondary Student Aid Study, the percentage of Black students whose families had nothing to contribute to their college education (in financial aid terms, an "expected family contribution of zero") went from 41.6 percent in 2008 to 60 percent in 2012.[35] For the Black elites that President Obama mentioned in his Howard University commencement speech, the last twenty years may have represented an improvement in their economic circumstance, but for the vast majority of Black and Latinx families it has been a downward slide.

It is worth noting that some White families have been sliding, too. The number of White families with "an expected family contribution of zero" went from 18.7 percent in 2008 to 29 percent in 2012.[36] The poverty rate among working-class Whites rose three percentage points, from 8 percent in 2000 to 11 percent in 2011, still less than half of the poverty rate of working-class communities of color (23 percent in 2011). Nevertheless, the gap between White and Black poverty is closing, due to the declining fortunes of Whites in that sector of the economy.[37] That fact is fueling both economic anxiety and anger among Whites, as evidenced among some of the White voters supporting Donald Trump's candidacy in the 2016 presidential election.

The third setback of the late-twentieth century and nearly two decades of the twenty-first century that we must acknowledge is the impact of mass incarceration. Historian Carol Anderson puts the phenomenon of mass incarceration in a particular context in her well-documented book *White Rage* when she makes the case that since the end of slavery in 1865, the prevailing White reaction to Black social and political gains has been an effort to push back those advances and regain social control. For example, following the end of the Civil War, there was a period of reformation in the South that included the establishment of the Freedmen's Bureau to help those newly released from bondage. Blacks were given the right to vote, and some were elected to Southern state governments. Many social reforms, including the establishment of public schools, were instituted during that period. However, there was also massive White resistance from the former Confederates, which became violent with the rise of the KKK. As Northern law enforcers eventually withdrew from the South (marking the end of Reconstruction), White supremacists reasserted control and "took back the South" through the institution of Jim Crow laws and the disenfranchisement of Black voters. Slavery was replaced with the system of exploitation known as sharecropping and the use of lynching as a means of social intimidation designed to enforce racial subordination.[38] More than four thousand racial-terror lynchings took place across twelve southern states between 1877 and 1950.[39] When, during the Great Migration (1915–1970), more than six million African Americans escaped the Jim Crow South, thereby threatening the southern economy so dependent on their cheap labor, White southerners used both legal and illegal means to try to stop their exodus.[40]

Similarly, the Supreme Court's landmark 1954 *Brown v. Board of Education* case was met with strenuous White opposition in cities across both the South and North until federal intervention in the 1970s brought change, most of which has now been undone by subsequent Supreme Court decisions. Likewise, the advances of the civil rights era, culminating in the Civil Rights Act of 1964 and the Voting Rights Act of 1965, evoked White resistance, particularly in the South, and triggered what has been called the "southern strategy," an effort by national politicians like Richard Nixon to court White voters (in both the South and the North) unhappy about Black gains not by making specific reference to race but rather by promising things like "law and order," "welfare reform," and "school choice," alluding to race by association without actually using racial language to "trigger Pavlovian anti-black responses."[41] Sometimes called "dog whistle politics," this use of coded language and images taps into and reinforces stereotypes. In the 1980s, during Ronald Reagan's tenure as president, the "War on Drugs" became the coded language, and young Black and Latinx men became the targets of aggressive stop-and-search policing and harsh mandatory sentences, even for first-time offenders. These policies and the criminal justice practices that followed from them escalated under Presidents George H. W. Bush and Bill Clinton.[42]

Michelle Alexander, author of *The New Jim Crow,* describes the result in powerful terms. She writes:

More African American adults are under correctional control today—in prison or jail, on probation or parole—than were enslaved in 1850, a decade before the Civil War began. . . . The clock has been turned back on racial progress in America, though scarcely anyone seems to notice. All eyes are fixed on people like Barack Obama and Oprah Winfrey, who have defied the odds and risen to power, fame, and fortune. For those left behind, especially those within prison walls, the celebration of racial triumph in America must seem a tad premature. More black men are imprisoned today than at any other moment in our nation's history. More are disenfranchised today than in 1870, the year the Fifteenth Amendment was ratified prohibiting laws that explicitly deny the right to vote on the basis of race. Young black men today may be just as likely to suffer discrimination in employment, housing, public benefits, and jury service as a black man in the Jim Crow era—discrimination that is perfectly legal, because it is based on one's criminal record. This is the new normal, the new racial equilibrium.[43]

And while Alexander highlights the plight of Black men, similarly disturbing statistics exist for Black women. Though many more men are in prison than women, the growth rate for female imprisonment between 1980 and 2014 exceeds that for male imprisonment by more than 50 percent. According to the Bureau of Justice statistics, Black women represent 23 percent of the 1.2 million women under the supervision of the criminal justice system, though only 13 percent of the female population overall. In 2014, the imprisonment rate for African American women (109 per 100,000) was more than twice the rate of imprisonment for White women (53 per 100,000), while Hispanic women were incarcerated at 1.2 times the rate of white women (64 per 100,000).[44]

This dramatic increase in incarceration is not due to a rising crime rate. Rather, it can be traced back directly to changes in drug sentencing laws and policies. Since the official beginning of the War on Drugs during the Reagan administration of the 1980s, the number of Americans incarcerated for drug offenses has skyrocketed, from forty-one thousand in 1980 to nearly a half million in 2014. Furthermore, tough sentencing laws such as mandatory minimums keep many people convicted of drug offenses in prison for longer periods of time. In 1986, people released after serving time for a federal drug offense had spent a little less than two years—an average of twenty-two months—in prison. By 2004, the average length of sentence had almost tripled, so that people convicted on federal drug offenses were expected to serve sixty-two months—more than five years—in prison. At the federal level, people incarcerated on a drug conviction make up half the prison population. At the state level, the number of people in prison for drug offenses has increased tenfold since 1980. Most of these people have no record of violent offenses and are not major players in the drug trade.[45]

The negative social, emotional, and economic impact on families torn asunder by mass incarceration cannot be underestimated. The number of parents of minor children held in the nation's prisons increased by 79 percent between 1991 and midyear 2007.[46] Black and Latinx children are especially impacted, since 90 percent of those admitted to prison for drug offenses in many states are Black or Latinx, despite the fact that the majority of illegal drug users and dealers in the United States are White. Alexander highlights the impact of this racial disparity in drug enforcement on Black families. She writes, "A black child born today is less likely to be raised by both parents than a black child born during slavery. The absence of black fathers across America is not simply a function of laziness, immaturity, or too much time watching Sports Center. Thousands of black men have disappeared into prisons and jails, locked away for drug crimes that are largely ignored when committed by whites."[47]

These statistics are depressing, and perhaps you are saying to yourself, as I say to myself, "Surely *something* has changed for the better in the last twenty years!" Indeed, if there is one thing that might suggest there has been a positive change in race relations in the twenty-first century, it *might* be the election of Barack Obama in 2008.

## The Election of President Barack Obama

I spent Election Night 2008 with hundreds of students gathered at Spelman College, along with faculty, staff, administrators, alumnae, and city leaders, to await the results of our historic presidential election. It was a remarkable evening in which we collectively reflected on the achievements of the past, the success of the present, and the hopes for the future. Civil rights icon Reverend Joseph Lowery spoke to the crowd and powerfully described the 2008 election process as a "transformational moment in which the United States is being reborn," a moment in which the politics of fear and division was giving way to the politics of hope and inclusion. When the announcement of Senator Barack Obama's victory came, the cheers and tears in the swell of the largely African American crowd at Spelman were mirrored in the faces captured by news broadcasters at the multiracial, multiethnic, and multigenerational gatherings in Grant Park in Chicago, in Times Square in New York, and at the gates of the White House in Washington. Surely it was a night to remember. The headline of the *Philadelphia Inquirer* captured the early sentiment: CHANGE HAS COME TO AMERICA![48] Regardless of political affiliation, for a moment at least we could relish the social significance of the success of President-Elect Obama, the first African American man to overcome the most symbolic of racial barriers, just forty years after Reverend Dr. Martin Luther King Jr. articulated his dream that one day his children—Barack Obama's generation—would be judged by the content of their character, not the color of their skin.

However, just after the 2008 presidential election I was asked to write an essay for an online publication called *Inside Higher Ed*, specifically in response to a series of ugly campus incidents that took place just before and after the election—incidents such as the hanging of an effigy of Barack Obama at the University of Kentucky, the appearance of a noose on a tree at Baylor University, the dumping of a dead bear plastered with Obama posters at Western Carolina University, and the postelection Facebook post by a University of Texas student that called for "all the hunters to gather up, we have a n——— in the white house." These four examples seemed perplexing among a generation of students that voted so enthusiastically, two to one, for Barack Obama.

My theory about this seeming paradox is rooted in my understanding of psychology. I know that a shifting paradigm can generate anxiety, even psychological threat, for those who feel the basic assumptions of society changing in ways they can no longer predict. According to a *USA Today* poll taken immediately after the 2008 election, 67 percent of Americans expressed pride in the racial progress the election represented, even if they did not vote for Barack Obama. Yet 27 percent of the poll respondents said the results of the election "frightened" them.[49] Some of that fear could have been connected to disagreement with Obama's policies or related concerns. But for some small segment, perhaps like those involved in the campus incidents, the fear might have been related to an unvoiced and maybe even unconscious recognition that the racial calculus of our society was being changed by the election, a change that could threaten the racial hierarchy that has advantaged White people for so long. Such a sense of threat can lead to irrational, potentially violent behavior, and of course, in 2008 the fear of such violence was underscored by the not-so-distant history of brutality and murder that accompanied the struggle for civil rights (including voting rights) in our nation. If, as Reverend Lowery said, America was being reborn, we might think of those campus incidents and others like them as a kind of birthing pains—painful contractions that no one wants, yet signs of something new emerging.

What *was* that new thing? One answer might be high voter turnout—particularly among young voters and voters of color. That was the secret to Barack Obama's successful campaign. A record voter turnout delivered President Obama a very decisive victory, winning the electoral college vote, 365 to 173, and 53 percent of the popular vote.[50] In 2008 President Obama garnered significant White support, more than the 2004 Democratic candidate, John Kerry, had received. But he also captured 66 percent of voters under thirty, 66 percent of the Hispanic vote, 62 percent of the Asian vote, and 95 percent of the African American vote. The turnout of Black voters was so high that for the first time in history, it nearly equaled that of White voters. His Republican opponent, Arizona senator John McCain, was only successful in capturing the majority of elderly White and evangelical Christian voters, a declining segment of the voting population. The growth in the electorate was driven largely by the rise in voters of color, of which only 8 percent identified as Republican.[51] "The demographics race we're losing badly," said Senator Lindsey O. Graham (SC), adding, "We're not generating enough angry White guys to stay in business for the long term."[52]

Certainly the election of 2008 and the reelection of President Obama in 2012 challenged a fundamental social narrative in American culture. That narrative has been replayed on television and in movies throughout most of American cinematic history. It can be summed up in this way: In a heroic struggle, after all the twists and turns of the plotline, the White guy (usually the blond) wins. The Black guy, if there is one, is usually eliminated from the story before the end. Surely the formula ending of that movie plot is familiar! Yet the presidential election of 2008, and subsequently of 2012, gave that story a new ending. It seemed that we could no longer predict the winner based on race. The possibility of an unpredictable ending makes for a much better story and a much better society. But, as noted, it also generates anxiety and, for some, a sense of threat.

History tells us that social change is hard and often resisted. One form that resistance has taken since 2008 has been the systematic effort on the part of Republican-controlled state legislatures to reduce voter participation among communities of color, a pattern that harkens back to the days of Jim Crow. Historian Carol Anderson writes, "Barack Obama's election was a catalyst for a level of voter suppression activities that had not been seen so clearly or disturbingly in decades. Nowhere was this more apparent than in the Supreme Court's 2013 gutting of the Voting Rights Act."[53]

This "Act to enforce the fifteenth amendment to the Constitution" was designed to ensure the voting rights of historically disenfranchised racial minorities and prohibits every state and local government from imposing any voting law that results in discrimination against these protected groups. It outlaws literacy tests and other requirements that were historically used to keep African Americans and other disenfranchised groups from voting, especially in the South. Because of that southern history, the Act contained special provisions that required certain jurisdictions (those with a long history of voter discrimination) to seek "pre-clearance" from the US attorney general or the US district court for DC before making any changes in their election laws, allowing the federal government to determine whether there would be any discriminatory impact.[54] In 2013, in a case involving Shelby County, Alabama (*Shelby County v. Holder*), the Supreme Court ruled in a 5–4 decision that, given the civil rights progress that had been made since 1965, the protection of the pre-clearance rule was no longer needed and indeed now placed an unfair burden on those jurisdictions whose past misdeeds had placed them under federal oversight.[55]

Freed from the pre-clearance requirement, state legislatures in Arizona, Arkansas, Florida, Iowa, Kansas, Mississippi, North Carolina, Texas, and Virginia lost no time in passing laws making it more difficult for people to vote. By 2014, thirteen more states had passed voter-restriction statutes.[56] Republican legislators argued that the more-restrictive laws were necessary to prevent voter fraud, yet research has shown repeatedly that there have been very few instances of voter fraud in modern US elections.[57] Rather than preventing nonexistent fraud, the impact has been to limit and/or frustrate voting among those with limited resources. For example, many states have imposed some form of voter-identification laws, the most stringent of which require a government-issued card with a photograph and expiration date. Someone with a current state-issued driver's license can easily meet this requirement, yet many students, elderly people, and low-income urban residents do not have one. Obtaining and renewing such an ID requires both time and money, thus becoming a poll tax by another name. Since the 2013 Supreme Court ruling, the only legal recourse is to challenge these new election laws in court, proving that they had a discriminatory impact after they went into effect, but that slow process leaves many eligible voters without protection in the meantime.[58]

This is exactly what happened in Texas in 2014. The Republican legislature in 2011 had passed Senate Bill 14, a highly restrictive voter ID law. A coalition of civil rights groups immediately sued the State of Texas. The case went to trial in 2014. The attorney general of Texas argued the law was necessary to prevent widespread voter-identification fraud. "Yet, out of ten million votes, he could produce only two documented cases of voter impersonation. On the other hand, it became clear that nearly six hundred thousand Texans, mainly poor, Black and Hispanic, didn't have the newly required IDs and often faced financial and bureaucratic obstacles in obtaining them."[59] The district court judge ruled the law was intentionally discriminatory, and the State of Texas appealed, arguing that a change in the law so close to the November 2014 midterm election would be disruptive. On October 14, 2014, the Fifth Circuit judge sided with the State of Texas and granted its request to keep the voter ID law in place. The civil rights groups, now aided by the US Department of Justice, rushed the case to the Supreme Court, seeking to overturn the Fifth Circuit ruling before the November 2014 election. The Supreme Court decided in favor of Texas without commentary. But Justice Ruth Bader Ginsburg wrote a dissenting opinion, saying there was not much risk of disrupting the election process. All Texas needed to do was to go back to the voter-identification process it had been using for many years prior to the passing of Senate Bill 14. She concluded, "The greatest threat to public confidence in elections is the prospect of enforcing a purposefully discriminatory law, one that likely imposes an unconstitutional poll tax and risks denying the right to vote to hundreds of thousands of eligible voters."[60] Yet in 2014 that is exactly what the US Supreme Court allowed to happen in Texas.[61]

The election of Barack Obama not only brought on intense voter-suppression activity, it also unleashed unprecedented attacks on the legitimacy of his presidency, particularly from political conservatives known as the Tea Party. "The fire that put many Tea Partiers into the streets in 2009 and into the voting booths in 2010 was fury at Obama himself— an opposition so deep it led many to firmly believe that Obama could not legitimately be president at all. An article of faith among Tea Partiers held that Obama was born outside the United States, and so was constitutionally barred from holding the presidency."[62] It is of course a fact that President Obama was born in Hawaii, as documented on his birth certificate. And his significant accomplishments in his first term as president of the United States earned him his reelection in 2012. Yet for some, the idea of a Black man in the White House was just too outside their frame of reference to accept.

To the extent that the election of Barack Obama disrupted the usual narrative of White victory, it represented unpredictability, and unpredictability creates anxiety. And during the last twenty years, we have seen the level of anxiety rise in our nation. It is not just the reality that a Black man could be the president of the United States that has threatened the status quo. It is also the collapse of the American economy in September 2008 and the financial threat that many felt in the waning months of George W. Bush's presidency; it is the ruptured sense of security brought on by the 9/11 terrorist attacks in 2001 and other, more recent attacks around the world and on American soil; it is the slow recognition that the United States might not always hold its position of prominence in the world; and perhaps especially it is the fact that White people will soon be in the numerical minority in the US. Each of these societal changes represents a challenge to a set of assumptions, deeply held, by many in our nation, and anxiety—even fear—is the result.

And how do we deal with fear? As human beings, like other animals, typically we either withdraw or attack. In the aftermath of the 2008 election, we could see evidence of both patterns. Withdrawal takes the form of "hunkering down"—pulling in and pulling away from those we feel threatened by. When we are afraid, we quickly begin to categorize people by "who is for me" and "who is against me." We start to think and act in terms of "us" and "them." We withdraw into our circles of safety, and we attack those we believe are outside that circle and who pose a threat.

Such behavior can help explain why there has been a sharp rise in hate groups and in racially and ethnically motivated hate crimes since 2008. Indeed, according to a *New York Times* report, Stormfront.org, America's most popular online White supremacist site, founded in 1995 by a former Klan leader, saw the biggest single increase in membership in its history on November 5, 2008, the day after President Obama was elected. Perhaps more surprising, 64 percent of the registered Stormfront users are under thirty.[63]

## The Myth of the Color-Blind Millennial

One of the young users of such internet hate sites was twenty-one-year-old Dylann Roof, charged with the 2015 murder of nine Black churchgoers in Charleston, South Carolina, after joining them for Bible study at the Emanuel African Methodist Episcopal Church. "You've raped our women, and you are taking over our country. . . . I have to do what I have to do," he said before he started shooting, leaving one survivor to tell what happened.[64] Following the horrific shooting, I read an NPR report by Gene Demby entitled "Dylann Roof and the Stubborn Myth of the Colorblind Millennial." The story opens with these lines:

The young age of Dylann Roof, who's charged with sitting alongside nine black churchgoers for an hour before standing up and shooting them dead, is sure to inspire some head-scratching in the wake of his attack. He's 21, which means he's a millennial, which means he's not supposed to be racist—so the thinking stubbornly (if disingenuously) persists, despite ample research showing that it's just not true.

Demby continues by citing the results of an MTV survey of young viewers regarding their racial attitudes. That 2014 survey of a nationally representative group of one thousand fourteen- to twenty-four-year-olds was the result of collaboration between MTV and David Binder Research to take an in-depth look at how the millennial generation thinks about issues related to bias.[65] Among the key findings was a widespread belief (91 percent) in equality and the idea that everyone should be treated equally. A corollary to that belief is that one should not acknowledge racial differences, with 48 percent believing it is wrong to draw attention to someone's race, even if you are doing so in a positive way. Seventy-two percent believe that their generation is more egalitarian than previous generations, and 58 percent believe that racism will become less and less of an issue as they take on leadership roles in our society. For 62 percent of them, electing a Black president in 2008 was evidence that race is no longer a barrier to opportunity for people of color.

White respondents and respondents of color, however, reported significantly different life experiences. Few White respondents, for example, reported feeling excluded at school or work because of race or ethnicity (10 percent) while 23 percent of respondents of color said they often felt excluded in those settings. Approximately one in eight (13 percent) White respondents said they had been treated differently by a teacher because of their race, compared to one in three (33 percent) respondents of color. Only 19 percent of Whites reported they were often asked about their ethnic background, while three times as many respondents of color (60 percent) indicated that this was a common experience for them. Only slightly more than one in four White respondents (28 percent) said they had been seriously affected by the cumulative effect of microaggressions (defined in the survey as brief and commonplace actions or words that are subtle examples of bias), compared to

...ly half (49 percent) of respondents of color. Despite the fact that White respondents reported fewer negative experiences with bias and 41 percent agreed that "I think that I have more advantages than people of other races," almost half (48 percent) also agreed with the survey statement, "Today, discrimination against White people has become as big a problem as discrimination against racial minority groups." Only 27 percent of the respondents of color shared that perception. Almost twice as many White millennial respondents (41 percent) agreed that "the government pays too much attention to the problems of racial minority groups" than did respondents of color (21 percent).

Despite these highlighted differences in experience and attitude, almost all millennials surveyed (94 percent) reported having seen examples of bias (defined by the survey as "treating someone differently—and often unfairly—because they are a member of a particular group"). Yet just 20 percent indicated that they were comfortable having a conversation with someone about bias. Most (73 percent) think we should talk openly about bias and that doing so would lead to prejudice reduction, but like many adults, they are hesitant to speak up. For 79 percent of them, their biggest concern about addressing bias is the risk of creating a conflict or making the situation worse.[66]

For me, one of the main conclusions from this survey is that neither my baby boomer generation nor theirs is living in a postracial, colorblind society. Instead we may be living in a color-*silent* society, where we have learned to avoid *talking about* racial difference. But even if we refrain from mentioning race, the evidence is clear that we still notice racial categories and that our behaviors are guided by what we notice.

Harvard professor Mahzarin Banaji has become internationally known for her research on unconscious bias—attitudes that influence our behavior sometimes below the level of our consciousness. According to Banaji and Anthony Greenwald, coauthors of *Blindspot: Hidden Biases of Good People,* there now exists a substantial body of evidence that a positive bias toward White people, what they call "automatic White preference," predicts discriminatory behavior even among people who fervently espouse egalitarian views.

Recent survey studies show that only 10 to 15 percent of Americans openly express prejudice against Black Americans. Yet as we have detailed . . . there is well-documented evidence of widespread acts of discrimination against Black Americans that have put them at a disadvantage in just about every economically significant domain of life. . . . *Implicit bias may operate outside of awareness, hidden from those who have it, but the discrimination that it produces can be clearly visible to researchers, and almost certainly also clearly visible to those who are disadvantaged by it.* [italics mine][67]

Those biases manifest themselves in ways that matter—whom we offer help to in an emergency, whom we decide to hire, whom we give a warning to instead of a ticket, or whom we shoot at during a police encounter.

Indeed, it is the latter example—police shootings and their aftermath—that has been the most glaring evidence that we are not living in a postracial world. The police shooting of Michael Brown in Ferguson, Missouri, in the summer of 2014 (just one of several highly publicized Black deaths at the hands of police since then) and the activism that followed, not just on the ground in Ferguson but around the nation and on college campuses, linked by the social-media–based movement Black Lives Matter, has awakened a new generation to the power of social protest.

## Black Lives Matter and Millennials in Motion

When a Black seventeen-year-old named Trayvon Martin was headed to his father's fiancée's home on February 26, 2012, in Sanford, Florida, talking on his cell phone to a friend as he walked, carrying only snacks purchased from a local convenience store, he did not know that he would have a fatal encounter with one of the neighbors, George Zimmerman, a neighborhood watch volunteer. Zimmerman, believing that Martin was an unwelcome intruder with criminal intentions, began following him in his car and called 911 to report his suspicions, saying,

"This guy looks like he's up to no good, or he's on drugs or something." Though told by the 911 operator to stay in his vehicle and leave the matter to the police, Zimmerman disregarded that instruction, got out of his car, and confronted Martin. An altercation between the two ensued, and in the struggle, Zimmerman shot and killed the unarmed teen. When the police arrived on the scene, they took Zimmerman to the police station for questioning but accepted Zimmerman's account that he had acted in self-defense and let him go. Though Martin was just a short walk away from where his father was staying, the police made no effort to determine if he was from the neighborhood, tagging his body as "John Doe." It was not until his father filed a missing-person report with the police the next day that Trayvon Martin's parents learned what had happened to their son.[68]

As the details of Trayvon Martin's murder became known through social media, it became a national news story. The fact that this young Black man was minding his own business, simply walking home, yet ended up dead because of someone else's unfounded suspicions was bad enough, but the fact that the killer had not yet been held accountable was cause for further outrage. Zimmerman is a Hispanic man. Certainly many felt that had the outcome of the altercation been different—if Martin had shot and killed Zimmerman in the struggle—the Black teenager would have been arrested immediately. Protests erupted across the country, with demands for Zimmerman's arrest. Under public pressure, forty-five days after the deadly encounter, the Sanford police arrested George Zimmerman and he was charged with second-degree murder. During the trial, the Zimmerman defense team worked to present Trayvon Martin as a "thug" who deserved Zimmerman's suspicions, and to portray Zimmerman as the innocent victim of Martin's aggression.

When the trial concluded with a "not guilty" verdict, again there was outrage, so much so that President Obama felt compelled to speak about it, saying, "I know this case has elicited strong passions. And in the wake of the verdict, I know those passions may be running even higher. But we are a nation of laws, and a jury has spoken. . . . We should ask ourselves, as individuals and as a society, how we can prevent future tragedies like this. As citizens, that's a job for all of us."[69] His words provided little comfort, particularly not to those young people of color who could easily imagine themselves in Trayvon Martin's hooded sweatshirt, possibly meeting a similar fate, or to their parents who feared for their own children's safety.

Indeed, the juxtaposition of the first Black president of the United States, arguably the most powerful man in the world, and the futility of his words to deliver justice for the young Black teen was salt in the wound for many young African Americans. Reflecting on that moment, Bree Newsome, a young Black activist explained, "To understand it, you have to go back to the election of Barack Obama in terms of what that symbolized in terms of the hope. We saw that as us turning a corner in the country. . . . And then what we saw through the Trayvon Martin case was that we haven't actually turned that corner. Honestly, Trayvon was the turning point. Trayvon Martin just had so many echoes of Emmett Till. It felt like something out of 1955."[70]

Expressing her own deep frustration in response to Zimmerman's acquittal, Alicia Garza, a community organizer based in Oakland, California, posted this message on Facebook: "I continue to be surprised at how little black lives matter. . . . Black people, I love you. I love us. Our lives matter." Garza's friend, Patrisse Cullors, a Los Angeles–based activist, shared the Facebook post and added the hashtag, powerful in its simplicity, #BlackLivesMatter. Opal Tometi, a social-justice activist living in New York City, reached out to Garza and offered to help build a digital platform that could mobilize action for meaningful change. In 2016, reflecting back to that 2012 moment, Garza said, "We wanted to connect people who were already buzzing about all this stuff and get them to do something, not just retweet or like or share. We thought, 'How do we get folks together and take that energy and create something awesome?'" The #BlackLivesMatter message resonated with many across the social media platforms of Facebook and Twitter, and with that amplification a rallying cry for the millennial generation was born.[71]

The importance of social media in spreading news and information about organizing cannot be overemphasized. As noted in a September

2016 *Smithsonian* magazine article appropriately titled "Black Tweets Matter," the phrase "Black Lives Matter" has been tweeted thirty million times since that first posting in 2012, and Twitter has completely changed the speed with which information can be conveyed, how organizing can be done, and who can participate and how.[72] The twenty-first-century omnipresence of cell phone cameras with video capacity has also had a tremendous impact. "No one knew who would be the next Trayvon Martin, but the increasing use of smartphone recording devices and social media seemed to quicken the pace at which incidents of police brutality became public."[73]

Though Martin's death was at the hands of a private citizen, the repeated capture of police violence against unarmed Black citizens on cell phone video compounded the anger and frustration of many. The death of Eric Garner on July 17, 2014, at the hands of Daniel Pantaleo, a White police officer who used a chokehold to restrain him on a New York sidewalk—allegedly because he was selling loose cigarettes—gained national attention when cell phone video of his death was captured by a bystander. Garner could be heard gasping "I can't breathe" eleven times as he was held down by several officers. Demonstrators across the nation, celebrity athletes among them, adopted the phrase "I can't breathe" as a slogan of protest.[74] Less than three weeks later, on August 5, 2014, a young African American man, John Crawford III, twenty-two, was shot and killed by a police officer at a Walmart store in Beavercreek, Ohio, after a White male shopper called 911, reporting there was a Black man walking around the store with a gun, pointing it at people. When the police arrived on the scene, they opened fire on the unsuspecting Crawford, who, as captured on store video, appeared to be alone in the store aisle talking on his cell phone, casually carrying by his side an unloaded air rifle he had taken from a store shelf, presumably with the intent of purchasing it. Within seconds, Crawford was dead. The officers involved in the shooting, Sean Williams and David Darkow, were not charged.[75]

Just four days later, on August 9, 2014, the shooting of Michael Brown in Ferguson, Missouri, became an especially powerful catalytic moment for the Black Lives Matter movement. Though the circumstances of the shooting by White police officer Darren Wilson remain in dispute—were Brown's hands up in surrender when Wilson shot the unarmed youth, as some witnesses reported, or was Brown lunging toward Wilson to attack, as the officer claimed?—what is indisputable is the inhumane treatment of Michael Brown's body, left to lie uncovered in the street where he was slain for four hours, lifelessly baking in the hot summer sun, his parents kept away at gunpoint and with police dogs. The disrespect continued. When residents spontaneously created a memorial of teddy bears and other mementos at the site of the shooting, a police officer with a canine unit allowed one of the dogs to urinate on it, and later a police cruiser drove by, crushing it and scattering the rose petals Lezley McSpadden, Michael Brown's mother, had arranged at the site. When she returned the next day, placing a dozen roses at the memorial, a police cruiser again came through and destroyed it. It was later that night that the Ferguson protest began.[76] "For reasons that may never be clear, Brown's death was a breaking point for the African Americans of Ferguson—but also for hundreds of thousands of Black people across the United States."[77]

The day after the shooting, what began as a peaceful protest march on a Sunday afternoon, led by local pastors with their congregations, quickly turned into a heated confrontation with the local police. "Night was close. The crowd continued shouting at the officers, who were shouting back. And as the church groups began to leave, young men emerged who seemed angrier and more determined to extract revenge for Mike Brown's death."[78] Under the cover of the nighttime protests, some vandals started looting a corner QuikTrip gas station, eventually setting it on fire. A riot was underway. *Washington Post* journalist Wesley Lowery notes that it was not the death of another unarmed Black man that drew national attention; rather, it was the destruction of property that brought the national media, including reporters like him, to Ferguson. "Yet another police shooting in a working-class black neighborhood, even the breaking of a young black body left on public display, didn't catch the gaze of the national media. It was the community's enraged response—broken windows and shattered storefronts—that drew the eyes of the nation."[79]

When the Michael Brown case did hit the headlines, the Black Lives Matter founders took action through social media. Darnell Moore, a Brooklyn-based writer, activist, and acquaintance of Patrisse Cullors, coordinated twenty-first-century "freedom rides" to Ferguson, bringing hundreds of people—multiracial groups from cities across the nation— to the St. Louis suburb to protest in solidarity with the local residents.[80] The response of the Ferguson Police Department to the protests was marked by its militarization, equipped with tanks and machine guns as well as tear gas and rubber bullets. Repeatedly the police used the tear gas and rubber bullets to disperse the crowd; repeatedly the protesters returned, determined to exercise their constitutional right to protest.[81] One of those protesters, Kayla Reed, a Ferguson resident turned activist, said, "What kept bringing me out was that the police were just not letting people hold space—gather in the street and on the sidewalks— for a young man who had just lost his life. . . . People were being tear-gassed, and people were running. There was that fear, and then also the determination not to back down. To show back up the next night. That was really inspiring for me."[82] The police arrested many, including journalists. Of the 172 people arrested over the period of twelve days following Brown's death, most (132) were arrested only because they refused to disperse.[83]

The oppressive relationship between the Ferguson police and the Black residents became increasingly visible on the nightly news. And indeed it had a long history, as was documented by the investigation done by the Civil Rights Division of the Department of Justice (DOJ) following the Michael Brown shooting. The DOJ investigation opened on September 4, 2014, and on March 4, 2015, the 102-page report of its findings, *Investigation of the Ferguson Police Department,* was issued. Known as "the Ferguson Report," it is comprehensive in its scope, grounded in objective data analysis of police records, and damning in its conclusions. The report "illuminates a municipality that is dependent on practices and policies that criminalize its majority Black populations through traffic violations, municipal ordinances, false arrests, charging practices, and impositions of penalties for petty violations and charges that lead to debt and imprisonment."[84] The Department of Justice concluded that "this investigation has revealed a pattern or practice of unlawful conduct within the Ferguson Police Department that violates the First, Fourth and Fourteenth Amendments to the United States Constitution, and federal statutory law. . . . Ferguson's police and municipal court practices both reflect and exacerbate existing racial bias, including racial stereotypes. Ferguson's own data establish clear racial disparities that adversely impact African Americans. The evidence shows that discriminatory intent is part of the reason for these disparities."[85]

A community of only twenty-one thousand residents, Ferguson's population had shifted dramatically in the last quarter of the twentieth century. It was 99 percent White in 1970; by 1990 the population was 25 percent Black, and by 2000 it had become a majority (52 percent) Black suburb.[86] By 2014, when the Department of Justice launched its investigation, the population was 67 percent Black, but the Ferguson Police Department (FPD) was still almost entirely White, as was the city council. As a matter of policy, the FPD was instructed to raise revenue for the city by generating fines and fees, mostly for traffic violations, so many that fines and fees became the second largest source of town revenue. Most of that money was being collected from Black residents, who were much more likely than White residents to be given several citations at one time. According to the DOJ report, "It is common for a single traffic stop or other encounter with FPD to give rise to fines in amounts that a person living in poverty is unable to immediately pay. This fact is attributable to FPD's practice of issuing multiple citations—frequently three or more—on a single stop."[87] While 67 percent of the town's population, African Americans represented 85 percent of the traffic stops and 92 percent of the arrests associated with traffic stops, whereas Whites were 29 percent of the population but only 15 percent of the stops. Once stopped, more than 50 percent of all African Americans received multiple citations while only 26 percent of the non–African American drivers did.[88]

The investigators found many instances of excessive fees, well above average compared to other municipalities. For example, a single "Manner of Walking" violation could result in a $302 fine; a single "Peace

Disturbance" violation, $427; a "High Grass and Weeds" violation could cost $531; $375 for "Failing to Provide Proof of Insurance," $777 for "Resisting Arrest," $792 for "Failure to Obey," and $527 for "Failure to Comply."[89] It is easy to see that someone who received multiple citations at one time might find it difficult to pay these seemingly exorbitant fines. Unpaid fines led to arrest warrants, so rampant that "on the day Mike Brown was killed, Ferguson had almost as many active warrants as it did residents."[90]

Particularly striking in the Ferguson Report is the data regarding disproportionate use of force on Black residents of Ferguson. The DOJ concluded that "FPD engages in a pattern of excessive force in violation of the Fourth Amendment. . . . They have come to rely on ECWs [Electronic Control Weapons], specifically Tasers, where less force—or no force at all—would do. They also release canines on unarmed subjects unreasonably and before attempting to use force less likely to cause injury. Some incidents of excessive force result from stops or arrests that have no basis in law. Others are punitive or retaliatory. . . . The overwhelming majority of force—almost 90%—is used against African Americans."[91] In every canine bite incident, the person bitten was African American.[92]

Lest one think the differential pattern of enforcement is the result of different rates of criminal behavior, the DOJ report addresses that point directly. For example, in the two-year period from October 2012 to October 2014, only 5 percent of White drivers were searched after a traffic stop, while more than double that number (11 percent) of stopped Black drivers were searched. Yet FPD officers were more likely to find illegal substances when searching the vehicles of White drivers (30 percent of the time) than when searching African Americans (24 percent of the time).[93] The report concludes, "Our investigation indicates that this disproportionate burden on African Americans cannot be explained by any difference in the rate at which people of different races violate the law. Rather, our investigation has revealed that these disparities occur, at least in part, because of unlawful biases against and stereotypes about African Americans."[94]

The pattern of policing that was spotlighted in Ferguson has been documented in many other municipalities around the country. "When it comes to racially lopsided arrests, the most remarkable thing about Ferguson, Missouri, might be just how ordinary it is."[95] An investigation by *USA Today* found that 1,581 other police departments, including those of major cities like Baltimore, Chicago, and San Francisco, arrested Black people at rates even higher than in Ferguson. Each of the three cities mentioned has also been investigated by the Department of Justice for racially discriminatory policing.[96]

The Ferguson Report makes clear that the seeds of the Ferguson rebellion had been sown years before the 2014 shooting of Michael Brown, but its eruption highlighted something new—the leadership of Black millennials, a new generation of activists who were prepared to stand their ground in the face of police power. One of those activists, Johnetta Elzie, described her own changing attitude:

> This was the first time I had ever seen police dogs ready for attack in real life. I felt as if time was rewinding back and showing me scenes from Selma, Alabama in the 1960's instead of Ferguson, Missouri in 2014. I never imagined that this would be my reality as a young adult in America in the 21st century. I tried to remain as calm as possible in such a volatile situation but seeing those police dogs snarling at young Black children filled me with anger and rage. I became less of a peaceful protestor and more of an active one. Using my voice to chant loudly along with other protestors seemed to be enough but it wasn't. Instead, I decided to yell directly at the police. I decided to dare the police to look at the faces of the babies and children their dogs were so ready to chase down. As more people began to look directly at the police and yell their grievances, the more aggravated they became.[97]

As the nightly news showed the escalating conflict between the police and the protesters in Ferguson, members of Congress, federal agents, and older civil rights leaders such as Reverend Al Sharpton and

Reverend Jesse Jackson Sr. made their way there, presumably to help bring calm to an increasingly explosive situation. But the young people in the streets—the multiracial coalition of both local and out-of-town protesters—were not eager to cede their leadership to these elders. In her book *From #BlackLivesMatter to Black Liberation*, Keeanga-Yamahtta Taylor chronicles what happened next:

> By the time Sharpton arrived in Ferguson, it was too late. Young Black people had already endured two standoffs with police that had ended with tear gas and rubber bullets. People were furious. These bullying tactics had transformed the marches into much more than a struggle for Mike Brown. The battle in the Ferguson streets was also fueled by the deep grievances of the young people, whose future was being stolen by the never-ending cycle of fines, fees, warrants, and arrests. They were fighting for their right to be on the street and to be freed from the vice grip of the Ferguson police. They had experienced their own collective power and were drawing strength from outlasting the police. They were losing their fear. And they were not about to stand down or move aside to accommodate Sharpton's arrival as the spokesperson for a local movement already in place. The conflict was almost immediate.[98]

In his first public statements, Sharpton's rhetoric was critical of some of the protesters, urging them to contain their anger and using terms like *gangster* and *thug* to describe them. In Ferguson, Sharpton, Jackson, and other established civil rights leaders were rejected as part of a generation out of touch with the young people's struggles.[99] Dontey Carter, a young Ferguson activist, said of these older leaders, "I feel in my heart that they failed us. They're the reason things are like this now. They don't represent us. That's why we're here for a new movement. And we have some warriors out here."[100]

The rift between the old guard and the new generation of activists continued to grow as the community waited to hear whether Officer Darren Wilson would be indicted by a grand jury to stand trial for the shooting of Michael Brown. The youth wanted to increase the pressure on public officials while their elders pushed for patience and allowing the justice system to run its course. On November 24, 2014, the process played out in favor of Darren Wilson. There was no indictment. President Obama urged restraint in the face of the grand jury's decision, reminding his television audience that "we are a nation built on the rule of law," but Ferguson youth weren't listening. That night there was a firestorm in Ferguson.[101]

By then, however, the issues of concern had moved beyond the individual case of Michael Brown. Many of the young activists had begun to link police shootings to a broader analysis of racism and inequality in the United States. Millennial Activists United activist Ashley Yates observed that "the youth knew something very early in that the older generation didn't. We knew that the system had already failed even before they began to show their hand publicly. We knew that not only was the murder of Mike Brown unjustified, it was another example of how the systems in place made it acceptable to gun us down. We are the generation that was ignited by Trayvon Martin's murder and placed our faith in a justice system that failed us in a very public and intentional manner."[102]

Just ten days later, the system failed them again. On December 3, 2014, the decision not to indict Officer Pantaleo for the choking death of Eric Garner generated nationwide protests, again large and multiracial in composition. Where there had been conflicting narratives about the shooting death of Mike Brown, in the case of Eric Garner the video was clear. "Hundreds of thousands of people had watched the video of him pleading for his life and repeating, eleven times, 'I can't breathe,' while Pantaleo squeezed the life out of his body."[103] Yet, inexplicably to many, the grand jury found no grounds on which to bring the officer to trial.

Whether it was professional athletes wearing "I Can't Breathe" T-shirts, medical students in "White Coats for Black Lives" staging die-ins, Bay Area public defenders organizing demonstrations, Stanford students blocking the San Mateo bridge, or the thousands of college students mobilizing protests on their own campuses, their rallying cry of "Black Lives Matter" had the nation's attention.[104] Twitter and other social media platforms were the strategic glue that linked the demonstrations and helped them spread without the benefit of more traditional structures of the kind the previous civil rights generation had used. DeRay McKesson, one of the most visible activists during the Ferguson uprising, explains:

> It is not that we're anti-organization. There are structures that have formed as a result of protest, that are really powerful. It is just that you did not need those structures to begin protest. *You* are enough to start a movement. Individual people can come together around things they know are unjust. And they can spark change. Your body can be part of the protest; you don't need a VIP pass to protest. And Twitter allowed that to happen. . . . I think that what we are doing is building a radical new community in struggle that did not exist before. Twitter has enabled us to create community.[105]

In the months that followed Michael Brown's and Eric Garner's deaths (and the failures to indict the officers that killed them), the names (and videos) of unarmed Black youth killed by police just kept coming. There was twelve-year-old Tamir Rice, playing in a park near his home with a toy gun. Perceiving him to be an "active shooter," a police car pulled up, and within two seconds of their arrival, they shot him dead.[106] On April 4, 2015, in North Charleston, South Carolina, Walter Scott, a fifty-year-old Marine Corps veteran, initially pulled over for a missing taillight on his car, tried to escape while the officer, Michael Slager, was busy checking his registration and license. Slager caught up with Scott, but after a brief struggle, Scott broke free and started running away again. That was when Slager pulled out his gun and shot the unarmed Scott several times in the back, and then placed his own stun gun next to the dying man's body in an apparent attempt to make it look like Scott had threatened him with it. Indeed, Slager told his supervisors that he shot Scott because he feared for his life. Unbeknownst to Slager, there was a witness, Feidin Santana, who captured cell phone video of the fatal shooting and Slager's planting of the weapon. When Santana realized that the version of the shooting being reported in the local news was contradicted by what he had recorded, he reached out to the attorney representing the Scott family and turned over his video. Millions of viewers were able to see what Mr. Santana saw—the execution of an unarmed man as he ran away. This time, in light of the video evidence, the officer was fired immediately and charged with murder, yet the jury could not reach a unanimous decision, and the case ended in a mistrial.

In Baltimore, just eight days after the shooting of Walter Scott, on April 12, 2015, a young African American named Freddie Gray spotted police officers on patrol and began running away from them. They pursued him, and when he was caught, they arrested him, though it is not clear why. He was not engaged in any criminal behavior.[107] Two bystander videos captured the forceful arrest, with Gray screaming in pain as he was dragged in handcuffs and placed facedown in the back of a police van without a seat belt, counter to standard police procedure. By the time the van arrived at the police station, four stops later, Gray was losing consciousness. He went into a coma and died a week later, the result of a fatal spinal cord injury. Exactly when or how the injury occurred is unknown (perhaps during the rough arrest or while sliding around the back of the van without a seat belt). Though each of the six officers was to be tried individually for their role in his death, after four trials and no convictions, the state's attorney, Marilyn Mosby, dropped the remaining charges.[108]

In the spring of 2015, the Twitter-enabled activist community chanting "Black Lives Matter!" had more and more to protest. A number of organizations formed since the murder of Trayvon Martin are engaged in this activism. Keeanga-Yamahtta Taylor writes, "From the BYP [Black Youth Project] 100, Dream Defenders, Hands Up United, Ferguson Action, and Millennials United to perhaps the most well known of the new organizations, #BlackLivesMatter (#BLM), this new era has produced an important cohort of activist organizations. Thus far, #BLM has become the largest and most visible group, with at least twenty-six chapters. #BLM describes itself as a 'decentralized network aiming to build the leadership and power of black people.'"[109]

That "Black Lives Matter" can be understood in multiple ways—as an online hashtag, a slogan, a "movement," and/or its own organizational network (#BLM)—leads to confusion in the media. Local protests of police shootings might be described as part of the Black Lives Matter movement writ large, but might be the work of an organization completely unaffiliated with the #BLM network.

It is worth noting here, as Keeanga-Yamahtta Taylor does, that unlike in previous generations, women's leadership has been *visibly* central to the development of this new era of protest. While Black women have always been integral to the struggle for civil and human rights, more often it was the male leaders who were on center stage.

> Today, though, the face of the Black Lives Matter movement is largely queer and female. How has this come to be? Female leadership may actually have been an outcome of the deeply racist policing Black men have experienced in Ferguson. According to the US Census Bureau, while there are 1,182 African American women between the ages of twenty-five and thirty-four living in Ferguson, there are only 577 African American men in this age group. More than 40 percent of Black men in both the 20–24 and 35–54 age groups in Ferguson are missing. It's not just Ferguson. Across the United States, 1.5 million Black men are "missing"—snatched from society by imprisonment or premature death.[110]

Taylor concludes that whether the result of male absence or the reality of the devastating impact of police violence in women's lives, families, and communities, the leadership of women has brought an intersectional perspective, highlighting the ways that the social categories of race, gender, class, sexual orientation, gender expression, immigrant status, and ability converge. This convergence results in the further societal devaluing of the people who embody those multiple identities, often making their struggles invisible.[111] The emphasis of these women leaders on inclusivity is notably different from the civil rights activism of the past. Charlene Carruthers of Black Youth Project 100 explains, "It's important because we are really serious about creating freedom and justice for all Black people, but all too often Black women and girls, Black LGBTQ folks, are left on the sidelines. And if we are going to be serious about liberation we have to include all Black people. It's really that simple."[112]

To that end, legal scholar Kimberlé Crenshaw, whose work on intersectionality has been an important influence in the thinking of these young activists,[113] has coauthored, with lawyer Andrea Ritchie, a report called *Say Her Name: Resisting Police Brutality Against Black Women* as a project of the African American Policy Forum and the Center for Intersectionality and Social Policy Studies at Columbia Law School. Among the many cases they highlight are those of Tanisha Anderson, killed just days before the Tamir Rice shooting by Cleveland police, who used excessive force as they restrained her; Michelle Cusseaux, shot by police in her Phoenix home as she held a hammer in her hand, just days after Michael Brown's death; and Yvette Smith, killed almost instantly, shot in the head, when she opened the door for police investigating a domestic disturbance between two men. Though there is no readily available national database on police violence, in New York City—one of the jurisdictions with the most extensive data collection on police stops—the rates of racial disparities in stops, frisks, and arrests are identical for Black men and Black women, clearly demonstrating the need to keep Black women's stories as well as those of Black transgender people visibly part of the justice-seeking narrative in the Black Lives Matter movement.[114]

One Black woman's story that captured national attention began with a traffic stop in Waller County, Texas, on July 10, 2015. Sandra Bland was pulled over for a minor traffic violation—failing to signal a lane change. That stop turned into an arrest, captured on video, with Bland pinned to the ground and surrounded by police officers. Charged with assault, she was taken to the Waller County Jail, where, three days later, she was found dead in her cell. Her jailers claimed that she committed suicide. Her family rejects that explanation and believes there was police wrongdoing involved.

When she was pulled over, Bland was on her way to start a new job at her alma mater, Prairie View A&M University.[115] Though she never made it back to her campus, her death in the summer of 2015, coinciding closely with the one-year anniversary of the Ferguson unrest, set the stage for college campus protests all over the nation.

## The Movement Goes to College

If Ferguson was the epicenter of the new civil rights movement known as the Black Lives Matter movement, the University of Missouri in Columbia (known as "Mizzou") became the most visible symbol of campus-based student activism in the fall of 2015. Less than two hours away from Ferguson, the University of Missouri is a campus of thirty-five thousand students, approximately 7 percent of whom are Black. The campus unrest that erupted in 2015 had begun the year before when three young Black women at Mizzou started a "@MU4MikeBrown" account on social media, which quickly attracted the interest of other students.[116] Throughout the 2014–2015 school year, the women and their followers hosted campus vigils, rallies, demonstrations, and weekly planning meetings, making connections between the discrimination they experienced on the Columbia campus and the way the Black residents of Ferguson were treated. Coming together was empowering for many. A demonstration and die-in they staged drew hundreds of people. One of the first-time protesters there described his reaction: "It touched me to the core. . . . It was the first time I saw that many students committed to the cause."[117] Yet not all student responses were positive. Postings on Yik Yak, an anonymous social media app commonly used by students, revealed the tension between those who saw the need to speak up for racial justice and those whose actions reminded others that racism was alive and well in their campus community. "They were calling us monkeys and niggers," said Ashley Bland, one of the @MU4MikeBrown founders. "It was blatant, it wasn't even hidden racism."[118]

Despite this climate of racial tension, Payton Head, a Black student from Chicago, was elected the 2015–2016 Missouri Students Association president. Earlier in his career at Mizzou, he had been involved in campus government work focused on diversity, social justice, and equity, and now, as a senior and MSA president, he was focused on creating an inclusive community. But on September 12, 2015, Head was painfully reminded of his own outsider status as a Black man on his campus. He and a friend were walking toward downtown Columbia at night when White men in a pickup truck drove up and began screaming racial slurs at them. Just two years before, Payton had experienced a very similar incident when walking by a stretch of fraternity and sorority houses near campus; a group of White students sitting in the back of a pickup truck had begun screaming racial slurs at him. The sense of déjà vu infuriated him. "What made me the most angry about the situation was the fact that I had been working on inclusion initiatives this entire year. . . . I'm getting to the end of my time in office and I'm still seeing the same things."[119] And he knew he was not alone, that nearly every Black student on campus had had similar experiences. Head wrote about the incident on Facebook, passionately calling for change on campus. His Facebook post went viral, yet there was no immediate response from the university leadership. Six days later, the chancellor, R. Bowen Loftin, issued a statement that left the students unsatisfied, vague in its language and with no specific mention of the MSA president's experience, stating simply that the university opposed bias and discrimination and was working "to address the issues brought forward."[120]

Just as the young activists of Ferguson felt betrayed by President Obama's inability to stop police violence, Black students on campus were angry that senior campus leaders were unable to prevent bias incidents on campus—but perhaps of more concern was that leaders' responses to those incidents too often lacked the sense of urgency that the students themselves felt. Jonathan Butler, a Black graduate student who would eventually play a key role in campus protests, said, "We have this dangerous culture of apathy where things aren't being addressed. If leadership wasn't going to do something, we had to do something."[121]

To further highlight the concerns of Black students, Jonathan Butler and ten other student activists formed Concerned Student 1950, named for the year when the first Black student enrolled. In October 2015, just a month after Payton Head's Facebook post, Concerned Student 1950 decided to stage a protest at homecoming by blocking the car in which University of Missouri System president Tim Wolfe was riding, determined to get the attention of the senior administration. During the homecoming parade, they blocked the path of the car, linking arms and speaking passionately about the issue of racial discrimination on campus, but Wolfe remained in his car and never acknowledged them.

The students were flabbergasted by Wolfe's refusal to speak to them. Eventually police dispersed the crowd. Though led by Black students, the protest attracted White students as well. Said one, "I joined in the line because white silence is compliance. . . . I feel like I can't just sit by and watch. It's not my fight, but I support it."[122]

On October 21, ten days after the homecoming incident, Concerned Student 1950 issued a statement of eight demands, including enforcement of mandatory campus-wide racial awareness training, increased hiring of Black faculty and staff, an increase in mental health support with counselors of color, and more staff for social-justice centers on campus. Among the demands was a call for a formal apology from President Wolfe for his lack of responsiveness to the students and a call for his removal from office. Just a few days later, a swastika made from human feces was found on a bathroom wall in a residence hall. The vandalism, recognized on campus as an "act of hate," added to the sense of urgency for campus leadership to respond. On October 27, representatives of Concerned Student 1950 met with Wolfe, but without resolution. On November 2, Jonathan Butler, one of the founders of Concerned Student 1950 and a graduate student at Mizzou, announced that he would go on a hunger strike until President Wolfe was removed. That evening student activists set up an encampment on the campus quadrangle in support of Butler's hunger strike, announcing their intention to stay until the end of the semester, if necessary. More students and faculty began to rally around the protesters and their call for Wolfe's removal.[123] A Mizzou sociology professor, Scott Brooks, said, "It's been a long boil. Students felt like they weren't being heard and the university wasn't taking them seriously. And in a post-Ferguson world, increasingly the students felt the mantra of 'all deliberate speed.'"[124]

In an unprecedented turn of events, the Mizzou football team asked to meet with Jonathan Butler to better understand why he was on his hunger strike. He shared with them his undergrad experiences with racial harassment going back to 2008, and his frustration that years later "nothing has changed." By the time the meeting ended, the football players were on board with the protest. Though only 60 of the 124 players were Black, the entire team took action as a collective. With the support of their coach, on Sunday, November 8, they announced, "We will no longer participate in any football related activities until President Tim Wolfe resigns or is removed due to his negligence toward marginalized students' experiences." On Monday morning, in an emergency meeting of the University of Missouri System Board of Curators, Tim Wolfe resigned as president of the University of Missouri System. Later the same day, Chancellor R. Bowen Loftin also resigned, and Jonathan Butler ended his hunger strike.[125]

To observers of higher education, the speed with which the events at Mizzou, culminating in the resignation of the two top campus leaders, unfolded was breathtaking, as was the wave of activism that swept across other campuses in solidarity with Concerned Student 1950 and in protest of their own campus concerns about racism and other social-justice issues. Again, social media played a critical role. "A protest on a single college campus can go viral within minutes. Shared photos of a particularly powerful demonstration might embolden others to take similar stands."[126] Indeed, a new website, TheDemands.org, was created to compile the growing list of institutions where student demands had been made, along with links to the demands on each campus, providing templates for student leaders at other institutions as they drafted their own demands. The website creators declared on the home page of the website, "Across the nation, students have risen up to demand an end to systemic and structural racism on campus."[127] As of December 8, 2015, student demands had been posted for eighty colleges and universities (including three in Canada)—ranging from small private liberal arts colleges like Amherst, Ithaca, Grinnell, and Wesleyan, to Ivy League universities like Harvard, Yale, and Dartmouth, to large flagship public universities like the University of California, Berkeley, Wisconsin, Michigan, and Alabama.

In an analysis of what students were demanding, researchers from the American Council on Education (ACE) found considerable commonality, identifying seven major themes. Most of the lists (91 percent) called for changes in institutional policies and practices affecting campus climate and diversity; 89 percent called on campus presidents to take specific actions, such as acknowledging institutional histories of racism, and demonstrate their leadership on behalf of marginalized students; 88 percent emphasized the need for greater allocation of resources (e.g., staff, programming, facilities) for the support of marginalized students; 86 percent demanded increases in diversity among faculty, staff, and students; 71 percent called for new or improved diversity training for all campus constituents (faculty, staff, students, administrators, campus police); 68 percent called for revising the curriculum to include more diverse perspectives and requiring students to take such courses; and 61 percent petitioned for increasing support services, including mental health support, for marginalized students. The researchers conclude, "These students are petitioning institutions to consider expansive shifts to institutional culture rather than merely stand-alone programs or add-on policies. The demands are calling for a change in how marginalized student groups access, experience, and are represented in higher education."[128]

Just days before his resignation, Tim Wolfe issued this statement: "I regret my reaction at the MU homecoming parade when the Concerned Student 1950 group approached my car. I am sorry and my apology is long overdue. My behavior seemed like I did not care. That was not my intention. I was caught off guard in that moment. Nonetheless, had I gotten out of the car to acknowledge the students and talk with them perhaps we wouldn't be where we are today."[129] His words are a cautionary tale for current campus leaders. Indeed, in a January 2016 anonymous online survey of college presidents conducted by the ACE Center for Policy Research and Strategy, of the 567 presidents who responded, nearly half said that students on their campuses had organized around concerns about racial diversity, the vast majority (86 percent of those leading four-year campuses) had met with student organizers more than once, and the majority (55 percent) indicated that addressing racial climate on campus had become a higher priority for them compared to three years ago.[130]

Not everyone is sympathetic to the cause of the student protesters at Mizzou and elsewhere. The pushback has come from all corners—from fellow students, from faculty, from administrators, from alumni, from trustees, from state legislators—people who say the students are "overreacting," "whining," "need to get over it," are "making things up," that "being the only Black person in the room is no big deal."[131] Often, though not always, those critics are White. Failure to empathize with the outrage of Ferguson protesters in the streets or the sense of isolation or threat students of color report around the country may be due in large part to the racially insulated lives many White people lead, the result of persistent school and residential segregation. According to a 2013 American Values Survey conducted by the Public Religion Research Institute (PRRI), the social networks of White people in the United States are very homogeneous. Indeed, the PRRI researchers found that 75 percent of Whites have entirely White social networks, without any minority presence. This degree of social-network racial homogeneity is significantly higher than among Black Americans (65 percent) or Hispanic Americans (46 percent). Robert P. Jones, the CEO of PRRI, writes, "The chief obstacle to having an intelligent, or even intelligible, conversation across the racial divide is that on average white Americans . . . talk mostly to other white people." The result is that most Whites are not "socially positioned" to understand the experiences of people of color—with the police or on predominantly White campuses—because they are not part of their social networks.[132]

Marcia Chatelain, class of 2001 alumna of Mizzou and now tenured professor at Georgetown University, tried to explain to those who might not know firsthand what the visceral experience of being marginalized at a school like Mizzou was like in her *Chronicle of Higher Education* essay "What Mizzou Taught Me." She writes, "I adored my time at Mizzou—my instructors, my friends, my experiences, all treasures that I find any excuse to talk about. But there was a lot of fear during those years." On entering as a first-year student in the fall of 1997, she says,

> The fear set in later, when I became a part of a student movement that focused on holding the administration accountable for a rash of hate crimes on campus, the lack of resources for LGBTQ students, and a chilling climate for students who often existed at the margins of campus culture. This was before Twitter, GroupMe, Instagram. We printed T-shirts with the logo INCLUSION NOW! We passed out

leaflets. We wore armbands. We disrupted a Board of Curators meeting. We wrote editorials in the school newspaper. We published a report on all the insulting graffiti on campus and first-hand accounts of bias. We felt we were slowly changing the campus climate.

Conjuring up those memories makes my stomach churn. We student activists received threatening letters in our mailboxes and, in the days of landlines, strange phone calls to our apartments. E-mail, still a novelty, delivered messages about who needed to shut up and die.

Pranks or promises? You never knew. Will someone follow me into a parking garage? Will I meet the authors of the strange letter I found at my doorstep in a dark corner of the library or an unattended bathroom? Will the man in the truck yelling "nigger" at us drive off—or will he hit the brakes, pull over, and teach us a lesson?

You sink into a hypervigilance that some read as paranoia. But the humiliation and fear become part of you. Every cell of your 19-year-old body holds the anxiety of the moments when you are put in your place because you dared to come into someone else's home and thought you could make it yours, too. . . .

When critics mock students for wanting safe spaces, they often argue that political correctness is undermining education and that students today are "too sensitive." Rarely do I ever hear any curiosity about what students are seeking shelter from; when my friends and I peered around the corners of our sprawling campus, dissenting opinions were the least of our worries.[133]

## Not Just a Black Matter

Perhaps because so much of the national media attention has been on the lethal encounters between Black people and police, especially since Ferguson, the national conversation about race, to the extent that it has occurred, has been focused on anti-Black racism, and the same has been true of many campus protests, where Black students, inspired by Ferguson, have been taking the lead. However, it is important to recognize that lethal police violence is not just a problem for Black communities. In fact, a special investigative report by Stephanie Woodward for *In These Times* highlights two aspects of the problem for Native Americans in the US. The first is the high rate of police shootings per capita in Native communities. The second is the invisibility of the problem in the mainstream media.

Citing a Center on Juvenile and Criminal Justice analysis of data collected by the Centers for Disease Control and Prevention (CDC), Woodward reports that "when compared to their percentage of the U.S. population, Natives were more likely to be killed by police than any other group, including African Americans. . . . Analysis of CDC data from 1999 to 2014 shows that Native Americans are 3.1 times more likely to be killed by police than white Americans."[134] Yet there is very little news coverage when the victim is an Indian. In a study by Claremont Graduate University researchers Roger Chin, Jean Schroedel, and Lily Rowen in which they reviewed articles about lethal police shootings published between May 1, 2014, and October 31, 2015, in the top ten US newspapers, they found that while there were hundreds of articles about 413 African Americans killed by police during that period, there was virtually no coverage of the 29 Native men and women killed during that same period. Of the twenty-nine, only one, Paul Castaway, a Rosebud Sioux man shot dead in Denver while threatening suicide, received sustained coverage (six articles) in the *Denver Post*. Though they were not critical of the news coverage regarding Black lives, the Claremont researchers concluded that the disparity in media coverage highlights the fact that issues of racial discrimination in the United States are typically framed in terms of Black-White race relations, while the experiences of other groups of color are overlooked. Yet there are particular parallels between the contemporary experiences of Native peoples and African Americans, as is discussed in the *In These Times* report:

> Federal investigations have found that on the borders of reservations, Native Americans are treated as second-class citizens by police and public agencies in ways that echo the experience of black Americans in towns like Ferguson. . . . Over the past 40 years, the U.S. Commission on Civil Rights (USCCR), an independent government agency, has held numerous hearings on discrimination in border towns surrounding reservations. . . . In South Dakota, the commission heard

testimony about a police department that found reasons to fine Natives hundreds of dollars, then "allowed" them to work off the debt on a ranch. USCCR Rocky Mountain director Malee Craft described the situation as "slave labor." [135]

Inspired by the Black Lives Matter (BLM) protests, a grassroots Native Lives Matter (NLM) movement was started in late 2014 by Lakota People's Law Project attorney Chase Iron Eyes to bring attention not only to the deaths but to other issues affecting Native Americans, such as child welfare and incarceration disparities.[136] Just as BLM spread through social media, so too is the use of the Native Lives Matter slogan expanding across indigenous communities, becoming an umbrella term for advocacy for environmental and social causes.[137]

In the same way that the problem of police violence extends beyond African Americans to other marginalized populations of color, so too does the problem of isolation and marginalization on historically White campuses extend beyond Black students to other underrepresented students. Indeed, while 13 percent of the student-demand statements found on TheDemands.org focus specifically on the concerns of Black students, over half have a more general focus on campus diversity, broadly defined.[138] For example, the Amherst College student demands begin in this wide-ranging way:

> President Martin must issue a statement of apology to students, alumni and former students, faculty, administration and staff who have been victims of several injustices including but not limited to our institutional legacy of white supremacy, colonialism, anti-black racism, anti-Latin@ racism, anti-Native American racism, anti-Native/ indigenous racism, anti-Asian racism, anti-Middle Eastern racism, heterosexism, cis-sexism, xenophobia, anti-Semitism, ableism, mental health stigma, and classism. Also include that marginalized communities and their allies should feel safe at Amherst College.[139]

The submission of the Amherst demands was the spontaneous outcome of a sit-in at the campus library that drew a diverse crowd—hundreds of students as well as faculty, staff, and administrators—on the afternoon of November 12, 2015. Originally conceived to show support for student protesters at Mizzou and elsewhere, the focus of the sit-in shifted when someone said, "Let's not pretend that the things that happen here at Amherst College aren't similar to the things that are happening in other places," opening the door for conversation about how people at Amherst treat each other, about things that happen in classrooms, in residence halls, and in lots of other places on campus.[140]

Reflecting on what happened in the library that day, the chair of the Amherst College Board of Trustees and member of the class of 1974, Cullen Murphy, writes:

> Students talked about their lives at Amherst but also their lives before and outside of Amherst. They said out loud what they had perhaps never said before, or had said individually to one another or to trusted advisers but not in such a large setting. They talked about the relatively small number of faces like theirs among the ranks of faculty and staff. About feeling excluded at social events. About distinctions of class that are all too visible when seen from one side but may be given little thought by those on the other. About casual remarks and behaviors that cause anger and pain, and whose residue inexorably accumulates. About the widespread ignorance of the path that many students of color travel as they make their way to Amherst. About legacies of personal history that other students can scarcely imagine and could never infer. About the exhaustion sometimes involved in juggling college life and family needs at home. About the utter disorientation that may occur when arriving at an idyllic spot with alien folkways that others take for granted. About having few people to talk with about any of this, and classmates who may be unaware that these issues loom as large as they do.[141]

That afternoon, after several hours of both speaking intensely and listening intensely, a group of student representatives from fifty-four different affinity groups, clubs, and other student organizations gathered to create their list of immediate demands in anticipation of presenting them to the president later that evening, giving themselves the name Amherst Uprising.[142] When the sit-in began, President Biddy Martin was away on college business, about to embark on an international flight. Learning of the campus protest, she canceled her trip and returned to campus to meet with the students in the library that night. She listened as the students read their demands and promised a timely response, which she provided that Sunday afternoon, sending an e-mail to the campus community as well as speaking directly to the students still engaged in the library sit-in.[143]

President Martin's response provides a useful counterpoint to what happened at Mizzou. She began by acknowledging the students' pain, letting them know that they had been heard. She wrote, "Over the course of several days, a significant number of students have spoken eloquently and movingly about their experiences of racism and prejudice on and off campus. The depth and intensity of their pain and exhaustion are evident. That pain is real. Their expressions of loneliness and sense of invisibility is heartrending. No attempt to minimize or trivialize those feelings will be convincing to those of us who have listened. . . . What we have heard requires a concerted, rigorous, and sustained response."

She also used the teachable moment to set parameters around students' expectations for immediate or unrealistic actions on the part of the institution.

> I explained that I did not intend to respond to the demands by item, or to meet each demand as specified, but instead to write a statement that would be responsive to the spirit of what they were trying to achieve—systemic changes that we know we need to make. I also talked about why apologies of the sort that were demanded would be misleading, if not downright dishonest, suggesting, as they implicitly would, that I or the College could make guarantees about things that are much larger than a single institution or group of people. Reacting immediately to strict timetables and ultimatums and speaking in the names of other people and for all times would be a failure to take our students seriously.

President Martin also reaffirmed core principles of the institution's commitment to a diverse learning environment where all felt welcome and supported as well as a commitment to freedom of inquiry and expression. "The commitments to freedom of inquiry and expression and to inclusivity are not mutually exclusive, in principle, but they can and do come into conflict with one another. Honoring both is the challenge we have to meet together, as a community."[144]

With her commitment to establish a committee, inclusive of all key campus constituents, "charged with studying issues of race and racial injury" and to make recommendations to her and the board of trustees, as well as other next steps, the protesters ended the sit-in. They felt that President Martin's statement had offered "clarification and hope." In response, they began to rethink their statement of demands, acknowledging the need for "revision and thoughtfulness."[145]

The sharing of experiences that was at the heart of the Amherst College sit-in in 2015 reflected a student population very different from that of 1974, when Cullen Murphy graduated from Amherst. In his 2016 essay he wrote, "Four decades ago, when I graduated, fewer than 10 percent of the incoming students were African-American, Latino, Asian-American, Native American, or of mixed heritage. Last year the corresponding figure was 40 percent." He observed accurately that the protest was fueled in part by "the challenge of fostering community in an environment of diversity," unfamiliar territory in a society still so deeply marked by segregation.[146] In that context, it is not surprising that so much of what was painfully discussed in the library was the discomfort that comes when interacting across lines of difference.

What cuts across the experiences of all marginalized groups on college campuses is the phenomenon known as *microaggressions.* The term *racial microaggressions* was first coined by Chester Pierce in the 1970s to describe the daily slights and insults experienced by Black people in the United States. However, the use of the term *microaggressions* has broadened to include all marginalized groups. Psychologist Derald Wing Sue defines the term as "the brief and commonplace daily verbal, behavioral, and environmental indignities, whether intentional or unintentional, that communicate hostile, derogatory, or negative racial, gender, sexual-orientation, and religious slights and insults to the target person or group."[147] Often involving the projection of stereotypes, they can occur at any moment of the day, a constant potential source of stress.

When Michael Luo, a Chinese American journalist, experienced one of those moments walking with his family after church on a Sunday morning in October 2016, he posted this message on Twitter: "Well dressed woman on Upper East Side, annoyed by our stroller, yells: 'Go back to China . . . go back to your f—ing country.' #thisis2016." In another tweet, he wrote, "Now my 7 year old, distressed by what happened, keeps asking, "Why did she say 'Go back to China?' We're not from China." Later Luo wrote "An Open Letter to the Woman Who Told My Family to Go Back to China" and, to his surprise, the *New York Times* published it on the front page.

> "Dear Madam," it begins, "Maybe I should have let it go."
>
> Turned the other cheek. . . . But I was, honestly, stunned when you yelled at us from down the block, "Go back to China!"
>
> I hesitated for a second and then sprinted to confront you. You pulled out your iPhone . . . and threatened to call the cops. It was comical, in retrospect. You might have been charged instead, especially after I walked away and you screamed, "Go back to your fucking country."
>
> "I was born in this country!" I yelled back.
>
> It felt silly. But how else to prove I belonged? . . .
>
> Maybe you don't know this, but the insults you hurled at my family get to the heart of the Asian-American experience. It's this persistent sense of otherness that a lot of us struggle with every day. That no matter what we do, how successful we are, what friends we make, we don't belong. We're foreign. We're not American.[148]

In response to his initial tweets and then to his open letter, Luo received a torrent of responses from other Asian Americans who shared similar experiences online. Here is just a sample of those he shared:[149]

"This has also happened to me . . . outside my own apartment building. A woman walked right up to me and told me to go back to my own country—a country I've lived in my entire life. I couldn't even believe it and for people who say, 'they're just words,' guess what: Words hurt and I went home and cried that day even though I didn't deserve to feel sad for being American."

"Introduced myself to a neighbor and she asked, 'what's your real name?' elizabeth is my real name."

"As an Asian-American physician, sad to say, I still get this in California: 'No, really, where are you FROM?' But at least no one asks me what I routinely got asked on the East Coast: 'Where did you learn to speak such beautiful English?' In the NY public schools, just like you. It is a continual reminder that despite being American, in many ways, we will always be 'other.'"

"Being Asian means putting up with 'acceptable racism' in America. I experience an incident a week."

Luo captured in his open letter the challenge that microaggressions pose to the recipients. The "persistent sense of otherness" that he describes takes a psychological and physiological toll. Social science research has demonstrated that the cumulative effect of microaggressions "assail the self-esteem of recipients, produce anger and frustration, deplete psychic energy, lower feelings of subjective well-being and worthiness, produce physical health problems, shorten life expectancy, and deny minority populations equal access and opportunity in education, employment and health care."[150]

As Marcia Chatelain's essay on Mizzou suggests, the experience of microaggressions is sometimes upsetting not just because it is unpleasant to be called names or yelled at on the street or receive hate mail or threatening phone calls but because it is impossible to know if there is a real threat of harm underlying those words. The fear of physical harm has deep roots in the African American community, with its not-so-distant history of lynching and current concerns about lethal police encounters. In an unexpected way, the presidential election of 2016 has heightened concerns for physical safety in other communities of color as well.

## The Election of 2016

When Donald J. Trump announced his intention to seek election as the Republican candidate for president of the United States on June 16, 2015, he launched his campaign with a speech remembered for its anti-Mexican sentiment. "When Mexico sends its people, they're not sending their best. . . . They're sending people that have lots of problems. . . . They're bringing drugs. They're bringing crime. They're rapists," he declared, then adding parenthetically, "And some, I assume, are good people."[151] This was the first of many such speeches in which he linked his campaign theme, "Make America Great Again," to the issue of illegal immigration, promising to deport anyone who is in the US without proper authorization and pledging to stop the flow of undocumented immigrants across the US-Mexico border by building a giant wall, for which Mexico, he said, would foot the bill.

Prior to this presidential announcement, Trump was known primarily as a billionaire real-estate developer and star of a popular reality TV show, *The Apprentice*. Because he had no previous experience as an elected official or politician, many political pundits believed he would not fare well against the crowded Republican field of candidates. In addition to Trump, sixteen people had announced they were seeking the Republican nomination, among them very experienced politicians—past and present governors, senators, and congressmen. By comparison, Trump seemed quite unqualified. Yet his initial rise to prominence as a political figure was aided not only by his celebrity status but also by his highly visible support of the "birther" idea that President Obama was not really born in the United States and that perhaps he was really a Muslim. Though neither statement is true—President Obama was born in Hawaii and is a practicing Christian—Trump's advocacy of those falsehoods attracted the interest of the Tea Party faction of the electorate that held those beliefs and helped create momentum for his campaign.[152] Disenchanted with the political status quo, they embraced Trump's promises to improve their lives by renegotiating international trade agreements, bringing manufacturing jobs back to the US, reducing taxes, improving infrastructure, and increasing homeland security—in short, to "Make America Great Again"—but these promises seemed to rest on the prerequisite of keeping some people out of America.[153]

His anti-Mexican statements, in particular, drew the attention of White nationalists. Two weeks after he made his campaign announcement, he received the endorsement of *The Daily Stormer*. Founded in 2013 by Andrew Anglin, a neo-Nazi of the millennial generation, *The Daily Stormer* is described as "among the most prominent online gathering places for white nationalists and anti-Semites, with sections devoted to 'The Jewish Problem' and 'Race War.'" Anglin liked that Trump was the only candidate "willing to speak the truth about Mexicans."[154] David Duke, former Grand Wizard of the Ku Klux Klan and Louisiana lawmaker turned radio host, encouraged listeners to vote for Donald Trump. Other known White nationalists added their support and began to actively engage in the campaign on his behalf. "For the first time in decades, overt white nationalism re-entered national politics. In Iowa, a new 'super PAC' paid for pro-Trump robocalls featuring Jared Taylor, a self-described race realist, and William Johnson, a white nationalist and the chairman of the American Freedom Party. ('We don't need Muslims,' Mr. Taylor urged recipients of the calls. 'We need smart, well-educated white people who will assimilate to our culture. Vote Trump.')"[155]

In the post–civil rights era of twenty-first-century politics, such endorsements would lead mainstream politicians to rebuke them immediately, but that is not what Donald Trump did. When asked about the robocalls in media interviews, his response might be seen as relatively nonchalant. "Nothing in this country shocks me; I would disavow it, but nothing in this country shocks me. . . . People are angry." When pressed harder by a CNN reporter on the support of White nationalists, Trump, irritated by the continued line of questioning, replied: "How many times you want me to say it? I said, 'I disavow.'"[156]

The phrase "I disavow" is a nonspecific one. Exactly what is being disavowed? The vagueness of this response was seen as covert encouragement to the White nationalists. American Freedom Party leader William Johnson said in a "pro-White" radio show, "He disavowed us, but he explained why there is so much anger in America that I couldn't have asked for a better approach from him." Donald Trump endeared himself further with White supremacists through his use of Twitter, often retweeting messages that have been posted from nationalist Twitter accounts with racist or anti-Semitic content. "When Little Bird, a social media data mining company, analyzed a week of Mr. Trump's Twitter activity, it found that almost 30 percent of the accounts Mr. Trump retweeted in turn followed one or more of 50 popular self-identified white nationalist accounts."[157]

It became clear that Donald Trump's campaign was giving new mainstream visibility to a movement that for many years had been in the shadows of American life. What is sometimes referred to as the "alternative right" (shortened to "alt-right") is defined by the Southern Poverty Law Center as "a set of far-right ideologies, groups and individuals whose core belief is that 'white identity' is under attack by multicultural forces using 'political correctness' and 'social justice' to undermine white people and 'their' civilization."[158] Those who identify with the alt-right are characterized by their heavy use of social media and online memes, their rejection of traditional conservatives as weak, and their embrace of White supremacist nationalism as a fundamental value. Much of their rhetoric is "explicitly racist, anti-immigrant, anti-Semitic and anti-feminist."[159] Richard Spencer, who coined the term "alt-right" and has been its most visible spokesperson, has said that Donald Trump should not be considered alt-right but that "white identity" is at the core of both the so-called alt-right White nationalist movement and the Trump movement, even if most Trump voters don't articulate it in that way.[160] Jonathan Greenblatt, the national director of the Anti-Defamation League, a prominent civil rights organization working against anti-Semitism and all forms of bigotry, speaks for many when he says he is troubled by the "mainstreaming of these really offensive ideas. . . . It's allowed some of the worst ideas into the public conversation in ways we haven't seen anything like in recent memory."[161]

Not only was Trump's promise to build a wall between the US and Mexico a prominent feature of every campaign speech, on December 7, 2015, in response to Islamic State–linked mass shootings in Paris that killed 130 people on November 13 and a domestic terror attack that took place in San Bernardino, California, three weeks later, Trump announced that he was "calling for a total and complete shutdown of Muslims entering the United States until our country's representatives can figure out what is going on."[162] Many of Trump's fellow Republicans, including House Speaker Paul Ryan, criticized him for this proposed ban, so contrary to the principle of religious freedom in the US and so unfairly stereotyping the millions of Muslims around the globe (and in the US) as potentially dangerous terrorists. His rhetoric represented a distinct ideological shift within American politics.

Candidates from both parties have courted Muslim voters for years. President Obama and President George W. Bush frequently described Islam as a peaceful religion marred by extremists. Republican governor Chris Christie gained the respect of New Jersey Muslims after standing up for his appointment of a Muslim lawyer to the Superior Court in Passaic County and dismissing concerns expressed by some conservatives that the jurist would enact sharia law as "crap."[163] Nevertheless, polls indicated that a majority of Republican voters supported the idea of a ban on Muslim immigration, and they began to rally in even greater numbers behind Trump's candidacy.[164]

Trump's list of controversial statements continued to grow, not limited to Mexicans and Muslims. During the campaign, he was captured on videotape making a speech in which he imitated a journalist with a physical disability in a mocking way. He made insulting comments about the physical appearance of women, including one of his Republican rivals, Carly Fiorina. He encouraged African Americans to support him by describing them as a group stereotypically (and inaccurately) confined to a hellish existence in inner cities: "You're living in poverty, your schools are no good. You have no jobs, 58 percent of your youth is unemployed. . . . What do you have to lose?"[165]

Particularly disturbing to many was the way he seemed to sanction violence among his supporters (most of whom were White) when anti-Trump protesters (often people of color) appeared at his rallies. Speaking to an enthusiastic crowd in Iowa, he said, "If you see someone getting ready to throw a tomato, knock the crap out of 'em, would you? Seriously. Okay? Just knock the hell—I promise you, I will pay for the legal fees, I promise. I promise." At a rally in Michigan a month later, when a protester caused an interruption, he said, "Get him out. Try not to hurt him. If you do, I'll defend you in court." At a North Carolina rally, he said, "See, in the good old days this didn't use to happen, because they used to treat them very rough. We've become weak." It was at that rally that a White male Trump supporter sucker punched a Black male protester in the face as a security guard was leading him out of the arena. Later, when Trump was asked by the moderator during a Republican debate if he was condoning violence at his rallies, Trump's first response was to express admiration for the passion of his followers. "When they see what's going on in this country, they have anger that's unbelievable. They love this country. . . . There is some anger, there's also great love for the country. It's a beautiful thing in many respects. But I certainly do not condone that at all."[166]

Even in the face of his controversial statements and bellicose style, or perhaps because of them, his popularity continued to grow. One by one, the other Republican candidates dropped out of the race. By May 4, 2016, Donald Trump was the presumptive nominee of the Republican Party.[167]

On the Democratic side, Senator Bernie Sanders of Vermont and former secretary of state Hillary Clinton had been locked for months in a fierce contest for the Democratic nomination. By the summer of 2016, however, it was clear that Hillary Clinton would be the Democratic choice to run against Donald Trump in the November 2016 election. Donald Trump would accept his party's nomination at the Republican convention on July 21, and Hillary Clinton would accept the Democratic nomination on July 28. But before either convention took place, the nation's attention was once again turned to lethal violence involving Black men and the police.

Within the space of three days, eight people in three different cities died in high-profile incidents. Thanks to cell phone video and social media, we again became a nation of eyewitnesses.[168] The first two deaths, that of Alton Sterling in Baton Rouge, Louisiana, and that of Philando Castile near St. Paul, Minnesota, were all too familiar—Black men shot and killed by police under very disturbing circumstances. In the case of Alton Sterling, two officers had him subdued and pinned to the ground when one of them took out his weapon and shot him in the chest.[169] What we saw on video looked like an execution. The killing of Philando Castile began with a traffic stop for a broken taillight. When Castile responsibly informed the officer that he had a lawfully carried gun in the car, the officer responded by shooting him seven times, fatally wounding him. Castile had made no threatening moves, never reached for the weapon. Witness to the shooting was Castile's girlfriend, Diamond Reynolds, and her four-year-old daughter, who was seated in the back of the car. Reynolds streamed the heart-wrenching aftermath of the shooting on Facebook Live with her cell phone.[170] In response to these new incidents, a peaceful protest organized by a local minister, head of the Next Generation Action Network, was taking place in Dallas on July 7, 2016, when a sniper opened fire, killing five Dallas police officers: Lorne Ahrens, Michael Krol, Michael J. Smith, Brent Thompson, and Patrick Zamarripa. The shooter, a Black army veteran named Micah Johnson, was not affiliated with the protesters, but his stated motive was one of retaliation for the police killings of Black people. He too was killed. Johnson's attack on the police was described as the deadliest for law enforcement officers in the United States since September 11, 2001.[171]

The series of events rocked the nation. Worse yet, the events in Dallas came just weeks after a horrific attack by an American-born Muslim man on a gay nightclub in Orlando, Florida, that left fifty people dead and fifty-three people wounded, the worst mass shooting in US history and the deadliest attack on the LGBT community. As the shooting began, the attacker called 911 to proclaim his allegiance to the Islamic State terrorist group.[172] The Orlando massacre forced both Hillary Clinton and Donald Trump to address issues of bigotry, domestic terrorism, and gun violence as they campaigned.[173] The events in Dallas forced them to come to terms with both police safety and police accountability, what was being represented in the public discourse as a choice between "Blue Lives Matter" and "Black Lives Matter."[174]

Conservative critics had been quick to blame the deaths of the Dallas policemen on the Black Lives Matter movement, claiming it encouraged violence against police. Alicia Garza, the cofounder of the BLM organization, pushed back against that criticism in an interview. "Standing up for the rights of Black people as human beings and standing against police violence and police brutality makes you get characterized as being anti-police or it has you being characterized as cop killers, neither of which we are. . . . At the same time that we can grieve the senseless loss of life of five police officers, we are also grieving the senseless loss of life that occurred at the hands of police. Those things can coexist."[175] Mike Rawlings, the mayor of Dallas, agreed with that sentiment and spoke in defense of the Black Lives Matter movement and the organizers of what had been a peaceful march. "Our police officers died for the Black Lives Matter movement. We were protecting those individuals. That is not a racist organization."[176]

The coexistence of so many strong emotions was captured in the remarks of Attorney General Loretta Lynch on the day after the Dallas shootings: "This has been a week of profound grief and heartbreaking loss. After the events of this week, Americans across our country are feeling a sense of helplessness, of uncertainty and of fear."[177] With the heavy shadow of Dallas and Orlando hanging over the upcoming political conventions, the candidates prepared to respond.

Donald Trump's acceptance speech emphasized law and order. "Our Convention occurs at a moment of crisis for our nation. The attacks on our police, and the terrorism in our cities, threaten our very way of life. . . . Americans watching this address tonight have seen the recent images of violence in our streets and chaos in our communities. . . . I have a message for all of you: the crime and violence that today afflicts our nation will soon come to an end. Beginning on January 20th 2017, safety will be restored. . . . In this race for the White House, I am the Law and Order candidate."[178] During the campaign, Trump surrogate Rudy Giuliani had given speeches advocating for aggressive policing, including stop-and-frisk policies, and condemning Black Lives Matter activists as "inherently racist," interpreting their slogan as a statement meaning *only* Black lives matter rather than as a statement of affirmation that Black lives matter, *too.*[179] Trump avoided any specific reference to Black Lives Matter in his speech. Instead he made this promise:

"When I am President, I will work to ensure that all of our kids are treated equally and protected equally. Every action I take, I will ask myself: does this make life better for young Americans in Baltimore, Chicago, Detroit, Ferguson who have as much right to live out their dreams as any other child in America?"[180]

At the Democratic convention, both the "Mothers of the Movement," Black women whose children were killed by police, as well as family members of police who had been killed in the line of duty were featured on the convention stage. In Hillary Clinton's acceptance speech, she did not mention the phrase "law and order" but instead called for healing and emphasized unity.

Her vision, captured in her campaign slogan, "Stronger Together," was one of inclusivity. In her acceptance speech at the Democratic National Convention, she said,

> Our country's motto is "e pluribus unum"—out of many, we are one. Will we stay true to that motto? . . .
>
> Now we are clear-eyed about what our country is up against. But we are not afraid. We will rise to the challenge, just as we always have. We will not build a wall. Instead, we will build an economy where everyone who wants a good job can get one.
>
> And we'll build a path to citizenship for millions of immigrants who are already contributing to our economy!
>
> We, we will not ban a religion. We will work with all Americans and our allies to fight and defeat terrorism. . . .
>
> We have to heal the divides in our country. Not just on guns. But on race. Immigration. And more.
>
> And that starts with listening, listening to each other. Trying, as best we can, to walk in each other's shoes.
>
> So let's put ourselves in the shoes of young black and Latino men and women who face the effects of systemic racism, and are made to feel like their lives are disposable.
>
> Let's put ourselves in the shoes of police officers, kissing their kids and spouses goodbye every day, heading off to do a dangerous and necessary job.

We will reform our criminal justice system from end to end and rebuild trust between law enforcement and the communities they serve.

And we will defend, we will defend all our rights—civil rights, human rights and voting rights, women's rights and workers' rights, LGBT rights and the rights of people with disabilities!

And we will stand up against mean and divisive rhetoric wherever it comes from.[181]

The differences between the two candidates were wide, but the polls were close. The weeks of campaigning that followed the convention were characterized by bitter personal attacks between them. Donald Trump called his opponent "Crooked Hillary," referring to the FBI investigation into her use of a private e-mail server while she was secretary of state, which potentially placed confidential information at risk, as well as other misdeeds (real or imagined) he accused her of. His supporters chanted "Lock her up" at his rallies. In her speeches, she castigated him for his lack of qualifications, the unsuitability of his temperament for the role of president, and his divisive rhetoric, which she called racist, sexist, and xenophobic, claiming he was drawing out the worst in us.

In October, just a month before the presidential election, Trump's moral character became an especially hot topic in the campaign when a previously unreleased video, taped in 2005, was made public. In it Trump was recorded talking with Billy Bush, then with the entertainment news program *Access Hollywood,* about his sexual exploits with women. In very vulgar terms, Trump bragged about being able to do whatever he wanted to women because he was a celebrity, including kissing them uninvited and trying to "grab them by the pussy." Taken literally, it was clear that he was describing behavior that could be described as sexual assault. In response to the released video, Trump explained his words away as just "locker room talk."[182] However, in the wake of the release, at least three dozen prominent Republicans came forward to say that he should drop out of the race, and many others running for reelection moved to distance themselves from him.[183] Trump's standing in the polls dropped and Hillary Clinton was seen as the clear favorite to win the election.

But then Hillary Clinton suffered a setback. FBI Director James Comey announced on Friday, October 28, just eleven days before the election, that he was reopening the Clinton e-mail inquiry because some new, relevant e-mails had been unearthed during the investigation of an unrelated case. It was an unprecedented announcement, as there was a long-standing policy of the Justice Department not to comment on an ongoing investigation and not to release any information that might influence the outcome of an election.[184] On November 6, just two days before the election, Comey indicated that there was nothing in the new information to support any criminal charges against Clinton, but the damage had been done.[185] The momentum that had been building in her favor was gone. Still, many people expected her to win the election.

To the shock of many, she did not. Though she captured the popular vote by more than 2.5 million votes, she failed to get the majority of votes in key states like Wisconsin, Florida, Pennsylvania, Ohio, and Michigan, giving Donald Trump the electoral votes he needed to win the election. He had 306 electoral votes to her 232; 270 were needed to win.[186] Clinton supporters were horrified and heartbroken, but Trump supporters were jubilant. The majority of the people had voted against their candidate, but still he was the winner—President-Elect Donald J. Trump.

The postelection analysis of voting patterns revealed a nation divided along racial lines. Put simply, the majority of White voters chose Trump; the majority of voters of color did not. According to analyses done by the Pew Research Center, White non-Hispanic voters preferred Trump over Clinton, 58 percent to 37 percent. During the course of the campaign there was a lot of discussion among political pundits about the fact that Trump was appealing to a non-college-educated, working-class base that was feeling left behind by globalism and the loss of manufacturing jobs in the US. Indeed, college graduates backed Clinton over Trump (52 percent to 43 percent), while the majority of voters without a college degree voted for Trump (52 percent to 44 percent). But among White voters, race seemed to carry more sway than education. More White voters, irrespective of whether they had a college education, voted for Trump.[187]

Given Hillary Clinton's history-making candidacy as the first female presidential nominee of a major political party and Donald Trump's highly offensive remarks about women, many people thought she would do well with women voters. And she did do very well with women voters of color. Black women voters were the most supportive, only 4 percent voting for Trump. But 62 percent of White women without college degrees voted for Trump, as did 45 percent of White women with college degrees.

Donald Trump became the first person to win a presidential election without having served in the military or having held any previously elected position. Remarkably, almost 25 percent of Trump supporters said he was not qualified but voted for him anyway. Laura Morgan and Robin Ely, both of Harvard Business School, explained the voting behavior of White women as reflecting both economic anxiety and gender dynamics: "The Trump campaign tapped into fears and frustrations among white working-class women about diminished possibilities for their husbands and sons to provide for their families. . . . Women and men have been socialized . . . to associate leadership with a particular version of masculinity, an image Trump exemplified in his persona as the supremely successful businessman."[188]

Van Jones, an African American political commentator on CNN, articulated another theory on the night of the election: "This was a rebellion against the elites. True. It was a complete reinvention of politics and polls. It's true. But it was also something else. . . . This was a white-lash. White-lash against a changing country. It was a white-lash against a Black president."[189] While perhaps not everyone who voted for Donald Trump shared the bigoted views of his White supremacist supporters or agreed with the offensive statements he himself made about Mexicans, Muslims, inner-city Black and Latinx communities, or women, on Election Day those things did not prevent millions of people from saying yes to Trump. That is a painful reality for those who have been his target.

"Who voted for Trump?" is an important question. For the health of our democracy, "Who was prevented from voting?" is even more important. The 2016 presidential election was the first without the full protection of the Voting Rights Act.[190] As discussed earlier, Republicans have been focused on reducing voter turnout in areas likely to vote Democratic since the strong showing of Barack Obama in the 2008 election. There are four key ways to suppress voting: create barriers to registration, such as by creating bureaucratic roadblocks to grassroots voter-registration drives; curtail the availability of early voting; require government-issued photo IDs; and disenfranchise ex-felons.[191] In 2016 fourteen states had new voting restrictions in place for the first time—including crucial swing states like Wisconsin and Ohio. For example, Donald Trump won Wisconsin by twenty-seven thousand votes, but three hundred thousand registered Wisconsin voters, according to a federal court, lacked the required forms of voter ID. "Turnout in Wisconsin was at its lowest level in 20 years and fell by 52,000 in Milwaukee, where 70 percent of the state's African-American population lives."[192]

In three states with a long and documented history of voter discrimination, Arizona, Texas, and North Carolina, there were 868 fewer polling places available, creating long lines and discouraging voters. In North Carolina, Black turnout decreased 16 percent during the first week of early voting because in forty counties with large Black populations, there were 158 fewer early polling places than in previous years.[193] Legal analyst Jeffrey Toobin observed, "The North Carolina Republican Party actually sent out a press release boasting about how its efforts drove down African-American turnout in this election."[194]

It seems clear that voter suppression had an impact on the 2016 election. Was it significant enough to actually change the election outcome? We will never know. What we do know is that more than fifty years after the passage of the 1965 Voting Rights Act, the struggle for the right to vote continues.

## Living in the Age of Trump

Donald Trump's election emboldened White nationalists who celebrated his victory in public gatherings. Less than two weeks after the election, a White nationalist conference took place in Washington, DC, just a few blocks from the White House, embracing Donald Trump's election as validation of their ideas. Not only had their preferred candidate been victorious, but he had quickly selected as his senior adviser and chief strategist Stephen K. Bannon, the man who had previously run *Breitbart News,* the most prominent media platform of the so-called alt-right. With Bannon as part of Trump's inner circle, the opportunity for White nationalists to influence presidential politics seemed a dream come true.[195]

For others, the days after the November 8 election were something out of a nightmare. Immediately after the election, hostile graffiti appeared. For example, in Durham, North Carolina, walls at a busy intersection read, "Black lives don't matter and neither does your votes." In Wellsville, New York, a baseball dugout was spray-painted with a swastika and the words "MAKE AMERICA WHITE AGAIN." National and local newspapers were filled with stories about the dramatic rise in bias-based attacks after the election.[196]

The Southern Poverty Law Center, which tracks hate-motivated incidents, released a report called *Ten Days After* documenting almost nine hundred reports of harassment and intimidation, not including online harassment, that were reported within the first ten days of the election. In these documented accounts from across the nation—every state is represented—many of the harassers invoked Trump's name during assaults, making it clear that the outbreak of hate stemmed in large part from his electoral success. According to the SPLC report, people have been targets of harassment at school, at work, at home, on the street, on public transportation, in their cars, in grocery stores and other places of business, and in their houses of worship. The most common occurrences involved hateful graffiti and verbal harassment, although a small number of the events included violent physical interactions. Only 23 of the 867 incidents reported were directed at the Trump campaign or his supporters.[197]

The detailed accounts are upsetting to read. They include: multiple reports of Black children being told to ride in the back of school buses; the words "Trump Nation" and "Whites Only" being painted on a church with a large immigrant population; a seventy-five-year-old gay man being pulled from his car and beaten by an assailant who said the "president says we can kill all you faggots now." Though SPLC has been documenting similar hateful incidents for many years, the people targeted since the election said this experience was new for them.

"I have experienced discrimination in my life, but never in such a public and unashamed manner," an Asian-American woman reported after a man told her to "go home" as she left an Oakland train station. Likewise, a black resident whose apartment was vandalized with the phrase "911 nigger" reported that he had "never witnessed anything like this." A Los Angeles woman, who encountered a man who told her he was "Gonna beat [her] pussy," stated that she was in this neighborhood "all the time and never experienced this type of language before." Not far away in Sunnyvale, California, a transgender person reported being targeted with homophobic slurs at a bar where "I've been a regular customer for 3 years—never had any issues."[198]

The SPLC reports that schools—K–12 settings and colleges—have been the most common venues for hate incidents. For example, a Washington State teacher reported: "'Build a wall'" was chanted in our cafeteria Wed [after the election] at lunch. 'If you aren't born here, pack your bags' was shouted in my own classroom. 'Get out spic' was said in our halls." Another example was provided by a mother from Colorado: "My 12-year-old daughter is African American. A boy approached her and said, 'Now that Trump is president, I'm going to shoot you and all the blacks I can find.'"[199]

The hurtful words of children can be frightening. Even more so are the physical acts of violence committed by adults. The hijab, the traditional head scarf worn by Muslim women in public, makes them easily identifiable for those who would target them. Less than a week after the election, a Muslim student at the University of Michigan, Ann Arbor, was forced to remove her hijab by a man who threatened to set her on fire if she didn't.[200] Two Muslim women were attacked in New York City, just two days apart. In one case, a man pushed a transit worker down a staircase at Grand Central Terminal in Manhattan, yelling, "You're a terrorist and you shouldn't be working for the city." In another, a Brooklyn man threatened an off-duty police officer and her teenaged son, both American-born, with his pit bull, telling them to "go back to your country." The first man escaped, but the second was arrested and charged with a felony hate crime.[201]

In response to these and other incidents, New York governor Andrew Cuomo and mayor of New York Bill de Blasio both spoke forcefully about them. Said Governor Cuomo, "This is the great State of New York—we welcome people of all cultures, customs and creeds with open arms. We do not allow intolerance or fear to divide us because we know diversity is our strength and we are at our best when we stand united." Mayor de Blasio held a news conference with the Muslim police officer, Aml Elsokary, at his side, saying: "This is Officer Elsokary's country. She is an American. She is a New Yorker. She's already at home. We cannot allow this kind of hatred and bias to spread."[202]

Civil rights advocates called on Donald Trump to demonstrate his own leadership and speak out against the harassment and denounce extremist groups, but his response seemed slow in coming, particularly given his propensity to send messages quickly on Twitter, as demonstrated throughout his campaign. In his *60 Minutes* interview that aired on November 13, 2016, President-Elect Trump claimed that he was "surprised to hear" that some of his supporters had been using racial slurs and making threats against African Americans, Latinxs, and members of the LGBT community. He took the opportunity to look into the camera and send a message to his audience, saying, "Stop it!"[203] On November 21, Hope Hicks, a Trump spokesperson, said, "Mr. Trump has always denounced these groups and individuals associated with a message of hate. . . . Mr. Trump will be a president for all Americans. However, he totally disavows the support of this group, which he does not want or need."[204] Are those statements sufficient to undo the damage of his campaign rhetoric? Probably not. The authors of the SPLC report called for more demonstrable leadership from Donald Trump. They write, "Rather than simply saying 'Stop it!' and disavowing the radical right, he must speak out forcefully and repeatedly against all forms of bigotry and reach out to the communities his words have injured. And rather than merely saying that he 'wants to bring the country together,' his actions must consistently demonstrate he is doing everything in his power to do so."[205]

His early personnel selections left many wondering if that kind of consistent anti-bias action was likely to come from his administration. Following the controversial choice of Stephen Bannon, he nominated Senator Jeff Sessions of Alabama for the role of attorney general. In that role, Sessions would be responsible for enforcing civil rights laws, but his record in Alabama as a US attorney is one of wrongly prosecuting Black voting-rights activists and opposing the Voting Rights Act.[206] More recently, as a member of the Senate, Sessions was the first to endorse Donald Trump's candidacy and is described as "one of the most strident anti-immigrant, anti-Muslim, anti-L.G.B.T. voices in the Senate."[207]

Donald Trump campaigned on the promise to deport millions of undocumented immigrants right at the beginning of his administration, a promise that has left a whole generation of young people and their families worried about their future. Some children, born in the United States, are citizens but worry what will happen to their undocumented parents, and to them, if family members are deported. Others arrived in the US as young children and, though they grew up in the US, don't have the protection of citizenship. Through executive action, President Obama implemented the Deferred Action for Childhood Arrivals (DACA) policy in 2012. The policy allows young people who entered the country without authorization before the age of sixteen and have lived in the US continually since 2007 the opportunity to work and go to school without fear of deportation. Young people protected by DACA must seek renewal of that legal protection every two years. Because the policy was created by executive order, rather than through the legislative process, it can easily be reversed by a new president with a different executive order. During his campaign, Trump indicated his intent to do so. Those who registered for DACA status are now part of a government database and consequently will be easy to find if the new president moves forward with his threats to engage in mass deportations. Their fears for their future are real.[208]

Fear and anxiety on the part of some White people may have been a key driver of the election results. The election outcome has created considerable fear and anxiety among communities of color and their White allies. How will the new president of the United States address the concerns of all of the people? In December 2016, as I write these words, the answer to that question remains to be seen.

What we do know is that leadership matters. How the leader describes who is in and who is out matters on a college campus, and it matters in our nation. Living in a time of rapid social change, one might ask, well, how am I supposed to manage my anxiety and my fear—by lashing out? Earlier, in reference to the election of President Obama in 2008, I spoke of "birthing pains" because something new was emerging, and perhaps it still is. But let us be clear: the moment of birth can be a dangerous time. And I think we *are* living in a dangerous time and should take that danger seriously.

When I listened to the polarizing rhetoric of radio and TV commentators during the long 2016 election campaign season, full of "us-them" language, I was reminded of a book I read a few years ago, *Left to Tell* by Immaculée Ilibagiza, a survivor of the Rwandan genocide. She wrote about the hostile rhetoric that was on the radio airwaves before and during the genocide, demonizing the ethnic minority to which she belonged. That rhetoric was made especially powerful because it came from the country's leaders.[209]

I do not mean to suggest that what we are seeing in the US today is on par with what was happening in Rwanda. But I do want to make clear that *what we say* matters, and *leadership* matters. The expectations and values of leaders can change the tone of the community and the nature of our conversation. Fundamentally, we know that human beings are not that different from other social animals. Not unlike wolves, we follow the leader. Yes, we have an innate tendency to think in "us" and "them" categories, but we look to the leader to help us know who the "us" is and who the "them" is. The leader can define who is in and who is out. The leader can draw the circle narrowly or widely. When the leader draws the circle in an exclusionary way, with the rhetoric of hostility, the sense of threat among the followers is heightened. When the rhetoric is expansive and inclusionary, the threat is reduced. It sounds simple, but we know it is not.

The leader has to ask the question, how is the circle being drawn? Who is inside it? Who is outside it? What can I do to make the circle bigger? As Martin Luther King Jr. once said, we are caught in a "network of mutuality," and that means our collective fate is intertwined. We will thrive or fail together.

*And here's what we must also consider:* If a person is twenty years old in 2017, born in 1997, all the critical issues I have written about in these pages thus far are the coming-of-age hallmarks of their generation. Having been born in 1954 in segregated Florida and raised in Massachusetts as part of the Great Migration out of the Jim Crow South, I—and others of my generation—have a long personal history with social progress. I saw Reverend Dr. Martin Luther King Jr. on television in real time. I heard his and others' speeches and watched the March on Washington on the nightly news. I saw people who had been denied the right to vote exercise that right for the first time on television. I have seen the colleges and universities at which I was educated and at which I have worked grow more diverse over time. That sense of racial progress is part of my generation's lived experience. Yet for those born in 1997, all of that is something in their history books. Their perspective is shaped by a very different set of events.

If you were born in 1997, you were eleven when the economy collapsed, perhaps bringing new economic anxiety into your family life. You were still eleven when Barack Obama was elected. You heard that we were now in a postracial society and President Obama's election was the proof. Yet your neighborhoods and schools were likely still quite segregated. And in 2012, when you were fifteen, a young Black teenager named Trayvon Martin, walking home in his father's mostly White neighborhood with his bag of iced tea and Skittles, was murdered and his killer went free. When you were seventeen, Michael Brown was shot in Ferguson, Missouri, and his body was left uncovered in the streets for hours, like a piece of roadkill, and in the same year, unarmed Eric Garner was strangled to death by police, repeatedly gasping "I can't breathe" on a viral cell phone video, to name just two examples of why it seemed Black lives did not matter, even in the age of Obama. When you were nineteen, Donald J. Trump was elected president and White supremacists were celebrating in the streets. How would a twenty-year-old answer the question posed to me, "Is it better?" The answer to that question would probably depend a great deal on the social identities of that twenty-year-old.

We have lived through a political campaign season in which we heard the president-elect and his campaign surrogates saying things like, "We're taking America back." Back to what? Back from whom? What is their definition of "better"? What is yours? We have a lot of work to do if we are to truly move forward together as a nation.

I hope that, in the chapters that follow, readers will find tools that help them better understand themselves and other people and how we are all shaped by the inescapable racial milieu that still surrounds us and that, in some ways, has grown more opaque and seemingly more impenetrable. Twenty years after I first wrote these chapters, how we see ourselves and each other is still being shaped by racial categories and the stereotypes attached to them. The patterns of behavior I described then still ring true because our social context still reinforces racial hier-archies, and still limits our opportunities for genuinely mutual, equita-ble, and affirming relationships in neighborhoods, in classrooms, or in the workplace. For that reason, this twentieth-anniversary edition will be quite familiar to those who have read earlier editions. The opening chapters of the book (Chapters 1–3) have updated citations but remain essentially the same in content. Chapters 4–9 have been completely re-written, with new reference material and expanded discussion. Chapter 10 remains much the same as in the original edition and is followed by a new epilogue, "Signs of Hope, Sites of Progress." The epilogue is offered as a remedy for despair, my effort to highlight people and places that are making a positive difference and, in doing so, point us in a direction that might change our current trajectory, so twenty years from now, we can say without hesitation, "Yes, it is better." Shall we begin?

# A Psychologist's Perspective

As a clinical psychologist with a research interest in Black children's racial identity development, I began teaching about racism many years ago when I was asked by the chair of the Black studies department of the large public university where I was a lecturer to teach a course called Group Exploration of Racism. None of my colleagues, all of whom had been trained in the traditional lecture style of college teaching, wanted to teach the course, which emphasized group interaction and self-revelation. But as a clinical psychologist trained to facilitate emotionally difficult group discussions, I was intrigued by the experiential emphasis implied by the course title, and I took on the challenge.

Aided by a folder full of handouts and course descriptions left behind by the previous instructor, a copy of *White Awareness: Handbook for Anti-Racism Training,*[1] and my own clinical skills as a group facilitator, I constructed a course that seemed to meet the goals outlined in the course catalog. Designed "to provide students with an understanding of the psychological causes and emotional reality of racism as it appears in everyday life," the course incorporated lectures, readings, simulation exercises, group research projects, and extensive class discussion to help students explore the psychological impact of racism on both Whites and people of color.

Though my first efforts were tentative, the results were powerful. The students in my class, most of whom were White, repeatedly described the course in their evaluations as one of the most valuable educational experiences of their college careers. I was convinced that helping students understand the ways in which racism operates in their own lives and what they could do about it was a true calling that I should accept. The freedom to institute the course in the curriculum of the psychology departments in which I would eventually teach became a personal condition of employment. Beginning in 1980, for more than twenty years, I taught this course, eventually called The Psychology of Racism, to hundreds of students at three different predominantly White institutions—a large public university, a small coeducational state college, and an elite private college for women.[2] I also developed a similar course especially for elementary and secondary school teachers and administrators, which hundreds of educators have taken.[3] These experiences, along with the countless parent-education workshops I have led and my research about the experiences of Black adolescents in predominantly White settings, have taught me a lot about the significance of racial identity in the lives of children as well as adults. In fact, my deepening understanding of racial identity development theory greatly informed my thinking about how best to teach these courses and lead these workshops.

After about ten years of teaching, I decided to share some of what I had learned in an article, "Talking About Race, Learning About Racism: An Application of Racial Identity Development Theory in the Classroom."[4] Published in the Spring 1992 edition of the *Harvard Educational Review,* the article has been read widely by my academic colleagues in the field of education, many of whom tell me that reading about the theoretical framework of racial identity development triggered an "aha" moment for them. Suddenly the racial dynamics in their classrooms and within their own campus communities made sense in a way that they hadn't before. Those who were parents of adolescents of color suddenly had a new lens with which to see the sometimes sudden shifts in their children's behavior both at home and at school. Cross-racial interactions with colleagues took on new meaning. Just as it had for me, an understanding of racial identity development gave them new ways of thinking about old problems and offered them new strategies for facilitating productive dialogue about racial issues.

What concerns me is how little most people outside my particular specialty know about racial identity development. Even those who have studied child psychology are not always well informed about the role of racial or ethnic identity in young people's development. Perhaps given the historical emphasis on the experiences of White, middle-class children in psychological research, this fact should not be surprising. Most introductory psychology or developmental psychology textbooks include limited discussion of racial or ethnic identity development. Because racial identity is not seen as salient for White adolescents, it is usually not discussed in depth in the texts.

One consequence of this omission that should concern all of us is that educators all across the country, most of whom are White, are teaching in racially mixed classrooms, daily observing identity development in process, and are without an important interpretive framework to help them understand what is happening in their interactions with students, or even in their cross-racial interactions with colleagues. Although educators are hungry for this information, too often it has not been made accessible to them, instead confined to scholarly journals and academic volumes.

And if my colleagues in education have limited information about racial identity development theory, the general public knows even less. Yet whenever I talk about this concept in workshops and public lectures, the response is always the same: "This is so helpful. Now I have a better understanding of those interactions, now I see why talking about racism is so hard, now I know what I can do to make it easier."

Kurt Lewin, a famous social psychologist, once said, "There is nothing so practical as a good theory." A theoretical framework that helps us make sense of what we observe in our daily lives is a very valuable resource. What I hope to provide with this book is a helpful understanding of racial identity development from the perspective of a psychologist who has been applying the theory in her teaching, research, clinical, consulting, and administrative practice for more than thirty-five years.

It is a perspective we need now more than ever. Daily news reports tell us of the rising racial tensions in the United States. As our nation becomes more diverse, we need to be able to communicate across racial and ethnic lines, but we seem increasingly less able to do so. New tools are needed. While the insights of sociologists, economists, political scientists, historians, and other social commentators have much to offer, a psychological understanding of cross-racial interactions has been noticeably absent from the public discourse. In the absence of such an understanding, many questions important to our daily lives go unanswered.

I am often asked by parents and educators to address questions about children's understanding of race, racial identity in adolescence, and how to combat racism in daily life. White parents and teachers, in particular, often ask me questions about how to talk to children and other adults about racial issues. They struggle with embarrassment about the topic, the social awkwardness that can result if the "wrong" words are used, the discomfort that comes from breaking a social taboo, the painful possibility of being perceived as racist. Parents of color, too, have questions. They are sometimes unsure about how to talk to their own children about racism, torn between wanting to protect them from the pain of racial realities and wanting to prepare them effectively to cope with a potentially hostile world.

Adults, both White and of color, often hesitate to speak to children about racism for fear they will create problems where perhaps none exist, afraid that they will make "color-blind" children unnecessarily color-conscious. A psychological perspective—informed by developmental psychology in general, racial identity development theory in particular, and the insights of social psychological research—allows me to respond to these questions and others in ways that I hope will add useful clarity to the daily discourse about race.

My audiences often tell me that what they appreciate about my articles and my public presentations is that I make the idea of talking about race and racism less intimidating. I help them to see the importance of dialogue about this issue and give them the confidence they need to break the silence about race at home, at work, among their friends, and with their children.

I decided to write this book when I received a letter from a school principal in New Jersey. He had heard me speak at a conference the summer before and wrote to say that I had given the best explanation he had ever heard of why, in racially mixed schools all over the country, Black kids were still sitting together in school cafeterias. He invited me to come to his school and give the same explanation to his staff. The letter came at a particularly busy time in the school year. My desk was covered with student papers to read, there were project deadlines to meet, and I had just returned from a series of speaking engagements with a bad case of laryngitis. I was exhausted, and the idea of traveling to yet another school to give yet another talk on adolescent racial identity development was painful even to contemplate. Yet the request represented a genuine need for information. I thought of the hundreds of times I had been asked the question, "Why are all the Black kids sitting together in the cafeteria?" The tone of voice implied what usually remained unsaid: "And what can we do to solve this problem?" It became apparent to me that it was time to address this question in print and to bring an understanding of racial identity development to a wider audience.

As the idea for the book percolated in my head, other frequently asked questions came to mind. How do you talk to children about such a painful historical event as slavery? When do children start to notice racial differences? How should I respond to racial jokes? Isn't racism a thing of the past? I thought about the many public conversations I have had with educators, parents, and students, and the private conversations I have had with family and friends. It seemed to me that there was value in making some of these conversations available to others, as I do in my public presentations, as a way of both sharing information and modeling a process of engagement, a way of talking about the legacy of racism in our lives.

At the center of these conversations is an understanding of racial identity, the meaning each of us has constructed or is constructing about what it means to be a White person or a person of color in a race-conscious society. Present also is an understanding of racism. It is because we live in a racist society that racial identity has as much meaning as it does. We cannot talk meaningfully about racial identity without also talking about racism.

Unless otherwise noted, all of the conversations in this book are drawn from my own life experience and are in the context of my own teaching about racism and racial identity at predominantly White institutions, as well as from my research on Black children and families in predominantly White settings. This book is also informed by the years I spent as the president of Spelman College, where I had the opportunity to witness the transformational power of an affirming educational environment on the lives of generations of Black women.[5] Because I am a Black woman, these conversations are often framed in the context of Black-White relations. However, one of the lessons I have learned in the years that I have been teaching about racism is that racism is a live issue for other groups of color as well. My Latinx, Asian, Native American, Middle Eastern, and biracial students have taught me that they have a developing sense of racial/ethnic identity, too, and that all of us need to see our experiences reflected back to us. In that spirit, I have included discussions of the identity development of adolescents from all of these groups, in addition to the experiences of both Black and White adolescents.

In envisioning this book, it was not my intention to write for an academic audience. Instead I wanted to talk to the many parents, educators, and community leaders who would come to one of my presentations on "Talking to Children About Race" or "Interrupting the Cycle of Oppression" or "Understanding Racial Identity Development" if it were held at their children's school or in their town, and to respond to the kinds of questions I often hear these concerned adults ask. I wanted to make this psychological perspective as jargon-free as possible while still maintaining the integrity of the ideas. To the extent that readers find ideas they can use in their daily conversations with colleagues, friends, and family, I have been successful.

James Baldwin wrote, "Not everything that is faced can be changed. But nothing can be changed until it is faced." Talking about racism is an essential part of facing racism and changing it. But it is not the only part. I am painfully aware that people of color have been talking about racism for a long time. Many people of color are tired of talking, frustrated that talk has not led to enough constructive action or meaningful social change. But in my own work, I have seen the effectiveness of talking about racism and teaching others to do the same. I have seen the impact on individual students who years later have written to me about the changes they are making in their workplaces. I have seen the impact on educators I have worked with who are now transforming their curricula and interacting with students of color in ways that facilitate rather than hinder those children's academic success. I have witnessed the parents who begin to use their own spheres of influence within the community to address racism and other forms of oppression in their own environments. I remain hopeful. It is with this spirit of optimism that I invite my readers to join me in these conversations about race.

# PART I

## A Definition of Terms

# ONE

# Defining Racism

*"Can we talk?"*

Early in my teaching career, a White student I knew asked me what I would be teaching the following semester. I mentioned that I would be teaching a course on racism. She replied, with some surprise in her voice, "Oh, is there still racism?" I assured her that indeed there was and suggested that she sign up for my course. Years later, after exhaustive media coverage of events such as the Trayvon Martin shooting, the Ferguson unrest and the Department of Justice report on the Ferguson Police Department, the Charleston church massacre, the Walter Scott trial, the appeal to racial prejudices in electoral politics, and the bitter debates about affirmative action and immigration reform, it seems hard to imagine that anyone would still be unaware of the reality of racism in our society. But in fact, in almost every audience I address, there is someone who suggests that racism is a thing of the past. There is always someone who hasn't noticed the stereotypical images of people of color in the media, who hasn't observed the housing discrimination in their community, who hasn't read the newspaper articles about documented racial bias in lending practices among well-known banks, who isn't aware of the racial tracking pattern at the local school, who hasn't seen the reports of rising incidents of racially motivated hate crimes in America—in short, someone who hasn't been paying attention to issues of race. But if you are paying attention, the legacy of racism is not hard to see, and we are all affected by it.

The impact of racism begins early. Even in our preschool years, we are exposed to misinformation about people different from ourselves. Many of us grew up in neighborhoods where we had limited opportunities to interact with people different from our own families. When I ask my audiences, "How many of you grew up in neighborhoods where most of the people were from the same racial group as your own?" almost every hand goes up. There is still a great deal of social segregation in our communities. Consequently, most of the early information we receive about "others"—people racially, religiously, or socioeconomically different from ourselves—does not come as the result of firsthand experience. The secondhand information we do receive has often been distorted, shaped by cultural stereotypes, and left incomplete.

Some examples will highlight this process. When I was teaching at Mount Holyoke College, one of my students conducted a research project investigating preschoolers' conceptions of Native Americans.[1] Using children at a local day-care center as her participants, she asked these three- and four-year-olds to draw a picture of a Native American. Most children were stumped by her request. They didn't know what a Native American was. But when she rephrased the question and asked them to draw a picture of an Indian, they readily complied. Almost every picture included one central feature: feathers. In fact, many of them also included a weapon—a knife or tomahawk—and depicted the person in violent or aggressive terms. Though this group of children, almost all of whom were White, did not live near a large Native population and probably had had little if any personal interaction with American Indians, they all had internalized an image of what Indians were like. How did they know? Cartoon images, in particular the Disney movie *Peter Pan*, were cited by the children as their number-one source of information. At the age of three, these children already had a set of stereotypes in place. Though I would not describe three-year-olds as prejudiced, the stereotypes to which they have been exposed become the foundation for the adult prejudices so many of us have.

Sometimes the assumptions we make about others come not from what we have been told or what we have seen on television or in books but rather from what we have *not* been told. The distortion of historical information about people of color leads young people (and older people, too) to make assumptions that may go unchallenged for a long time.

Consider this conversation between two White students following a discussion about the cultural transmission of racism:

"Yeah, I just found out that Cleopatra was actually a Black woman."

"What?"

The first student went on to explain the source of her newly learned information. The second student exclaimed in disbelief, "That can't be true. Cleopatra was beautiful!"

While scholars still argue the question of Cleopatra's ancestry, what is most important in this example is what this young woman had learned about who in our society is considered beautiful and who is not. Had she conjured up images of Hollywood icon Elizabeth Taylor when she thought of Cleopatra? The new information her classmate had shared and her own deeply ingrained assumptions about who is beautiful and who is not were too incongruous to allow her to assimilate the information at that moment.

Omitted information can have similar effects. For example, another young woman, preparing to be a high school English teacher, expressed her dismay that she had never learned about any Black authors in any of her English courses. How was she to teach about them to her future students when she hadn't learned about them herself? A White male student in the class responded to this discussion with frustration in his response journal, writing, "It's not my fault that Blacks don't write books." Had one of his elementary, high school, or college teachers ever told him that there were no Black writers? Probably not. Yet because he had never been exposed to Black authors, he had drawn his own conclusion that there were none.

Stereotypes, omissions, and distortions all contribute to the development of prejudice. *Prejudice* is a preconceived judgment or opinion, usually based on limited information. I assume that we all have prejudices, not because we want them but simply because we are so continually exposed to misinformation about others. Though I have often heard students or workshop participants describe someone as not having "a prejudiced bone in his body," I usually suggest that they look again. Prejudice is one of the inescapable consequences of living in a racist society. Cultural racism—the cultural images and messages that affirm the assumed superiority of Whites and the assumed inferiority of people of color—is like smog in the air. Sometimes it is so thick it is visible, other times it is less apparent, but always, day in and day out, we are breathing it in. None of us would introduce ourselves as "smog breathers" (and most of us don't want to be described as prejudiced), but if we live in a smoggy place, how can we avoid breathing the air? If we live in an environment in which we are bombarded with stereotypical images in the media, are frequently exposed to the ethnic jokes of friends and family members, and are rarely informed of the accomplishments of oppressed groups, we will develop the negative categorizations of those groups that form the basis of prejudice.

People of color as well as Whites develop these categorizations. Even a member of the stereotyped group may internalize the stereotypical categories about his or her own group to some degree. In fact, this process happens so frequently that it has a name, *internalized oppression*. Some of the consequences of believing the distorted messages about one's own group will be discussed in subsequent chapters.

Certainly some people are more prejudiced than others, actively embracing and perpetuating negative and hateful images of those who are different from themselves. When we claim to be free of prejudice, perhaps what we are really saying is that we are not hatemongers. But none of us is completely innocent. Prejudice is an integral part of our socialization, and it is not our fault. Just as the preschoolers my student interviewed are not to blame for the negative messages they internalized, we are not at fault for the stereotypes, distortions, and omissions that shaped our thinking as we grew up.

To say that it is not our fault does not relieve us of responsibility, however. We may not have polluted the air, but we need to take responsibility, along with others, for cleaning it up. Each of us needs to look at our own behavior. Am I perpetuating and reinforcing the negative messages so pervasive in our culture, or am I seeking to challenge them? If I have not been exposed to positive images of marginalized groups, am

I seeking them out, expanding my own knowledge base for myself and my children? Am I acknowledging and examining my own prejudices, my own rigid categorizations of others, thereby minimizing the adverse impact they might have on my interactions with those I have categorized? Unless we engage in these and other conscious acts of reflection and reeducation, we easily repeat the process with our children. We teach what we were taught. The unexamined prejudices of the parents are passed on to the children. It is not our fault, but it is our responsibility to interrupt this cycle.

## Racism: A System of Advantage Based on Race

Many people use the terms *prejudice* and *racism* interchangeably. I do not, and I think it is important to make a distinction. In his book *Portraits of White Racism*, David Wellman argues convincingly that limiting our understanding of racism to prejudice does not offer a sufficient explanation for the persistence of racism. He defines racism as a "system of advantage based on race."[2] In illustrating this definition, he provides  example after example of how Whites defend their racial advantage— access to better schools, housing, jobs—even when they do not embrace overtly prejudicial thinking. Racism cannot be fully explained as an expression of prejudice alone.

This definition of racism is useful because it allows us to see that racism, like other forms of oppression, is not only a personal ideology based on racial prejudice but a *system* involving cultural messages and institutional policies and practices as well as the beliefs and actions of individuals. In the context of the United States, this system clearly operates to the advantage of Whites and to the disadvantage of people of color. Another related definition of racism, commonly used by antiracist educators and consultants, is "prejudice plus power." Racial prejudice combined with social power—access to social, cultural, and economic resources and decision-making—leads to the institutionalization of racist policies and practices. While I think this definition also captures the idea that racism is more than individual beliefs and attitudes, I prefer Wellman's definition because the idea of systematic advantage and disadvantage is critical to an understanding of how racism operates in American society.

In addition, I find that many of my White students and workshop participants do not feel powerful. Defining racism as prejudice plus power has little personal relevance. For some, their response to this definition is the following: "I'm not really prejudiced, and I have no power, so racism has nothing to do with me." However, most White people, if they are really being honest with themselves, can see that there are advantages to being White in the United States. Despite the current rhetoric about affirmative action and "reverse racism," every social indicator, from salary to life expectancy, reveals the advantages of being White.[3]

The systematic advantages of being White are often referred to as *White privilege*. In a now well-known article, "White Privilege: Unpacking the Invisible Knapsack," Peggy McIntosh, a White feminist scholar, identified a long list of societal privileges that she received simply because she was White.[4] She did not ask for them, and it is important to note that she hadn't always noticed that she was receiving them. They included major and minor advantages. Of course she enjoyed greater access to jobs and housing. But she also was able to shop in department stores without being followed by suspicious salespeople and could always find appropriate hair-care products and makeup in any drugstore. She could send her child to school confident that the teacher would not discriminate against him on the basis of race. She could also be late for meetings and talk with her mouth full, fairly confident that these behaviors would not be attributed to the fact that she was White. She could express an opinion in a meeting or in print and not have it labeled the "White" viewpoint. In other words, she was more often than not viewed as an individual, rather than as a member of a racial group.

This article rings true for most White readers, many of whom may have never considered the benefits of being White. It's one thing to have enough awareness of racism to describe the ways that people of color are disadvantaged by it. But this new understanding of racism is more elusive. In very concrete terms, it means that if a person of color is the victim of housing discrimination, the apartment that would otherwise have been rented to that person of color is still available for a White person. The White tenant is, knowingly or unknowingly, the beneficiary of racism, a system of advantage based on race. The unsuspecting tenant is not to blame for the prior discrimination, but she benefits from it anyway.

For many Whites, this new awareness of the benefits of a racist system elicits considerable pain, often accompanied by feelings of anger and guilt. These uncomfortable emotions can hinder further discussion. We all like to think that we deserve the good things we have received and that others, too, get what they deserve. Social psychologists call this tendency a "belief in a just world." Racism directly contradicts such notions of justice.

Understanding racism as a system of advantage based on race is antithetical to traditional notions of an American meritocracy. For those who have internalized this myth, this definition generates considerable discomfort. It is more comfortable simply to think of racism as a particular form of prejudice. Notions of power or privilege do not have to be addressed when our understanding of racism is constructed in that way.

The discomfort generated when a systemic definition of racism is introduced is usually quite visible in the workshops I lead. Someone in the group is usually quick to point out that this is not the definition you will find in most dictionaries. I reply, "Who wrote the dictionary?" I am not being facetious with this response. Whose interests are served by a "prejudice only" definition of racism? It is important to understand that the system of advantage is perpetuated when we do not acknowledge its existence.

## Racism: For Whites Only?

Frequently someone will say, "You keep talking about White people. People of color can be racist, too." I once asked a White teacher what it would mean to her if a student or parent of color accused her of being racist. She said she would feel as though she had been punched in the stomach or called a "low-life scum." She is not alone in this feeling. The word *racist* holds a lot of emotional power. For many White people, to be called racist is the ultimate insult. The idea that this term might only be applied to Whites becomes highly problematic, for after all, can't people of color be "low-life scum" too?

Of course, people of any racial group can hold hateful attitudes and behave in racially discriminatory and bigoted ways. We can all cite examples of horrible hate crimes that have been perpetrated by people of color as well as Whites. Hateful behavior is hateful behavior no matter who does it. But when I am asked, "Can people of color be racist?" I reply, "The answer depends on your definition of racism." If one defines racism as racial prejudice, the answer is yes. People of color can and do have racial prejudices. However, if one defines racism as a system of advantage based on race, the answer is no. People of color are not racist because they do not systematically benefit from racism. And, equally important, there is no systematic cultural and institutional support or sanction for the racial bigotry of people of color. In my view, reserving the term *racist* only for behaviors committed by Whites in the context of a White-dominated society is a way of acknowledging the ever-present power differential afforded Whites by the culture and institutions that make up the system of advantage and continue to reinforce notions of White superiority. (Using the same logic, I reserve the word *sexist* for men. Though women can and do have gender-based prejudices, only men systematically benefit from sexism.)

Despite my best efforts to explain my thinking on this point, there are some who will be troubled, perhaps even incensed, by my response. To call the racially motivated acts of a person of color "acts of racial bigotry" and to describe similar acts committed by Whites as "racist" will make no sense to some people, including some people of color. To them, I respectfully say, "We can agree to disagree." At moments like these, it is not agreement that is essential but clarity. Even if you don't like the definition of racism I am using, hopefully you are now clear about what it is. If I also understand how you are using the term, our conversation can continue—despite our disagreement.

Another provocative question I'm often asked is, "Are you saying all Whites are racist?" When asked this question, I again remember that White teacher's response, and I am conscious that perhaps the question I am really being asked is, "Are you saying all Whites are bad people?"

The answer to that question is of course not. However, all White people, intentionally or unintentionally, do benefit from racism. A more relevant question is, "What are White people as individuals doing to interrupt racism?" For many White people, the image of a racist is a hood-wearing Klan member or a name-calling Archie Bunker figure. These images represent what might be called *active racism,* blatant, intentional acts of racial bigotry and discrimination. *Passive racism* is more subtle and can be seen in the collusion of laughing when a racist joke is told, letting exclusionary hiring practices go unchallenged, accepting as appropriate the omissions of people of color from the curriculum, and avoiding difficult race-related issues. Because racism is so ingrained in the fabric of American institutions, it is easily self-perpetuating.[6] All that is required to maintain it is to go about business as usual.

I sometimes visualize the ongoing cycle of racism as a moving walkway at the airport. Active racist behavior is equivalent to walking fast on the conveyor belt. The person engaged in active racist behavior has identified with the ideology of White supremacy and is moving with it. Passive racist behavior is equivalent to standing still on the walkway. No overt effort is being made, but the conveyor belt moves the bystanders along to the same destination as those who are actively walking. Some of the bystanders may feel the motion of the conveyor belt, see the active racists ahead of them, and choose to turn around, unwilling to go to the same destination as the White supremacists. But unless they are walking actively in the opposite direction at a speed faster than the conveyor belt—unless they are actively antiracist—they will find themselves carried along with the others.

So, not all Whites are actively racist. Many are passively racist. Some, though not enough, are actively antiracist. The relevant question is not whether all Whites are racist but how we can move more White people from a position of active or passive racism to one of active antiracism. The task of interrupting racism is obviously not the task of Whites alone. But the fact of White privilege means that Whites have greater access to the societal institutions in need of transformation. To whom much is given, much is required.

It is important to acknowledge that while all Whites benefit from racism, they do not all benefit equally. Other factors, such as socio-economic status, gender, age, religious affiliation, sexual orientation, and mental and physical ability, also play a role in our access to so-cial influence and power. A White woman on welfare is not privileged to the same extent as a wealthy White heterosexual man. In her case, the systematic disadvantages of sexism and classism intersect with her White privilege, but the privilege is still there. This point was brought home to me in a study conducted by one of my Mount Holyoke grad-uate students, Phyllis Wentworth.[7] Wentworth interviewed a group of female college students who were both older than their peers and the first members of their families to attend college about the pathways that led them to college. All of the women interviewed were White, from working-class backgrounds, and from families where women were expected to graduate from high school and get married or get a job. Sev-eral had experienced abusive relationships and other personal difficul-ties prior to coming to college. Yet their experiences were punctuated by "good luck" stories of apartments obtained without a deposit, good jobs offered without experience or extensive reference checks, and encour-agement provided by willing mentors. While the women acknowledged their good fortune, none of them discussed their Whiteness. They had not considered the possibility that being White had worked in their favor and helped give them the benefit of the doubt at critical junc-tures. This study clearly showed that even under difficult circumstances, White privilege was still operating.

It is also true that not all people of color are equally targeted by racism. We all have multiple identities that shape our experience. I can describe myself as a light-skinned, well-educated, heterosexual, able-bodied, Christian African American woman raised in a two-parent middle-class family in a small, predominantly White, middle-class town. As an Af-rican American woman, I am systematically disadvantaged by race and by gender, but I systematically receive benefits in the other categories, which then mediate my experience of racism and sexism. When one is targeted by multiple isms—racism, sexism, classism, heterosexism, ableism, anti-Semitism, ageism—in whatever combination, the effect is intensified. The particular combination of racism and classism in many communities of color is life-threatening. Nonetheless, when I, the middle-class Black mother of two sons, read another story about a Black man's unlucky encounter with a White police officer's deadly force, I know that racism by itself can kill.

I was reminded of this fact once again by Ta-Nehisi Coates, author of *Between the World and Me,* when he captures the heart-wrenching pain of Dr. Jones, whose twenty-three-year-old son, Prince Jones, was killed by police during a traffic stop. Her socioeconomic success as a prominent physician and the cultural and educational advantages she was able to provide for her son throughout his life could not protect him. She said, "I spent years developing a career, acquiring assets, engaging responsibilities. And one racist act. It's all it takes."[8]

## The Cost of Racism

Early in my teaching career, a White male student in my Psychology of Racism course wrote in his journal at the end of the semester that he had learned a lot about racism and now understood in a way he never had before just how advantaged he was. He also commented that he didn't think he would do anything to try to change the situation. After all, the system was working in his favor. Fortunately, his response was not typical. Most of my students left my course with the desire (and an action plan) to interrupt the cycle of racism. However, this young man's response did raise an important question. Why should Whites who are advantaged by racism *want* to end that system of advantage? What are the *costs* of that system to them?

In the late 1980s, a *Money* magazine article called "Race and Money" chronicled the many ways the American economy was hindered by institutional racism.[9] Thirty years later, the analysis still rings true. Whether one looks at productivity lowered by racial tensions in the workplace, or real estate equity lost through housing discrimination, or the tax revenue lost in underemployed communities of color, or the high cost of warehousing human talent in prison, the economic costs of racism are real and measurable.[10]

As a psychologist, I often hear about the less easily measured costs. When I ask White men and women how racism hurts them, they frequently talk about their fears of people of color, the social incompetence they feel in racially mixed situations, the alienation they have experienced between parents and children when a child marries into a family of color, and the interracial friendships they had as children that were lost in adolescence or young adulthood without their ever understanding why. White people are paying a significant price for the system of advantage. The cost is not as high for Whites as it is for people of color, but a price is being paid.[11] Wendell Berry, a White writer raised in Kentucky, captures this psychic pain in the opening pages of his book *The Hidden Wound*:

> If white people have suffered less obviously from racism than black people, they have nevertheless suffered greatly; the cost has been greater perhaps than we can yet know. If the white man has inflicted the wound of racism upon black men, the cost has been that he would receive the mirror image of that wound into himself. As the master, or as a member of the dominant race, he has felt little compulsion to acknowledge it or speak of it; the more painful it has grown the more deeply he has hidden it within himself. But the wound is there, and it is a profound disorder, as great a damage in his mind as it is in his society.[12]

The dismantling of racism is in the best interests of everyone.

## A Word About Language

Throughout this book I have used the term *White* to refer to Americans of European descent. In another era, I might have used the term *Caucasian*. I have used the term *people of color* to refer to those groups in America that are and have been historically targeted by racism. This includes people of African descent, people of Asian descent, people of Latin American descent, and indigenous peoples (sometimes referred to as Native Americans or American Indians).[13] Many people refer to these groups collectively as *non-Whites*. This term is particularly offensive because it defines groups of people in terms of what they are not. (Do we call women "non-men"?) I also avoid using the term *minorities* because it represents another kind of distortion of information that we need to correct. So-called minorities represent the majority of the world's population. While the term *people of color* is inclusive, it is not perfect. As a workshop participant once said, White people have color, too. Perhaps it would be more accurate to say "people of more color," though I am not ready to make that change. Perhaps fellow psychologist Linda James Myers is on the right track. She refers to two groups of people, those of acknowledged African descent and those of unacknowledged African descent, reminding us that we can all trace the roots of our common humanity to Africa.

I refer to people of acknowledged African descent as *Black*. I know that *African American* is also a commonly used term, and I often refer to myself and other Black people born and raised in America in that way. Perhaps because I am a child of the 1960s "Black and beautiful" era, I still prefer *Black*. The term is more inclusive than *African American* because there are Black people in the United States who are not African American—Afro-Caribbeans, for example—yet are targeted by racism and are identified as Black. I capitalize both *Black* and *White* because I use them synonymously with other terms that are always capitalized, *African American* and *European American*.

When referring to other groups of color, I try to use the terms that the people themselves want to be called. In some cases, there is no clear consensus. For example, some people of Latin American ancestry prefer *Latino*, while others prefer *Hispanic* or, if of Mexican descent, *Chicano*.[14] In the past I have preferred to use *Latino or Latina* rather than *Hispanic*. In this edition I am choosing to use the more recent term, *Latinx*, because it is a gender-inclusive term that encompasses everyone—men, women, and those who identify as transgender or gender-fluid. I realize that the word *Latinx* may be unfamiliar to some readers, but I have learned that many young Latinx students favor this term, and I want to be as inclusive in my language as possible. Though used less often in this text, you will find that I have also replaced the terms *Chicano* or

*Chicana* with the gender-inclusive term *Chicanx,* for the same reasons. There are regional variations in the use of the terms *Native American, American Indian,* and *Indian. American Indian* and *Native people* are now more widely used than *Native American,* and the language I use in this edition reflects that shift. People of Asian descent include Pacific Islanders, and that is reflected in the terms *Asian/Pacific Islanders* and *Asian Pacific Americans.* However, when quoting others I use whichever terms, spellings, and capitalizations they use.

My dilemma about the language to use reflects the fact that race is a social construction.[15] Despite myths to the contrary, biologists tell us that the only meaningful racial categorization is that of human. Van den Berghe defines race as "a group that is socially defined but on the basis of *physical* criteria," including skin color and facial features.[16]

*Racial identity development*, a central focus of this book, usually refers to the process of defining for oneself the personal significance and social meaning of belonging to a particular racial group. The terms *racial identity* and *ethnic identity* are often used synonymously, though a distinction can be made between the two. An ethnic group is a socially defined group based on *cultural* criteria, such as language, customs, and shared history. An individual might identify as a member of an ethnic group (Irish or Italian, for example) but might not think of himself in racial terms (as White). On the other hand, one may recognize the personal significance of racial group membership (identifying as Black, for instance) but may not consider ethnic identity (such as West Indian) as particularly meaningful.

Both racial and ethnic categories are socially constructed, and social definitions of these categories have changed over time. For example, in his book *Ethnic Identity: The Transformation of White America*, Richard Alba points out that the high rates of intermarriage and the dissolution of other social boundaries among European ethnic groups in the United States have reduced the significance of ethnic identity for these groups. In their place, he argues, a new ethnic identity is emerging, that of European American.[17]

Throughout this book, I refer to racial identity. It is important, however, to acknowledge that ethnic identity and racial identity sometimes intersect. For example, dark-skinned Puerto Ricans may identify cultur-ally as Puerto Rican and yet be categorized racially by others as Black on the basis of physical appearance. Culture is also an important part of one's sense of group membership, suggesting that what is referred to as racial identity is really more fully described as racial-ethnic-cultural (REC) identity, as will be discussed in Chapter 4. Whether speaking of racial or ethnic identity specifically, these identities remain most salient to individuals of racial or ethnic groups that have been historically dis-advantaged or marginalized.

The language we use to categorize one another racially is imperfect. These categories are still evolving, as changing census classifications in-dicate.[18] The original creation of racial categories was in the service of oppression. Some may argue that to continue to use them is to continue that oppression. I respect that argument. Yet it is difficult to talk about what is essentially a flawed and problematic social construct without us-ing language that is itself problematic. We have to be able to talk about it in order to change it. So this is the language I choose.

# TWO

# The Complexity of Identity

## *"Who am I?"*

THE CONCEPT OF IDENTITY IS A COMPLEX ONE, SHAPED BY INDIVIDUAL characteristics, family dynamics, historical factors, and social and political contexts. Who am I? The answer depends in large part on who the world around me says I am. Who do my parents say I am? Who do my peers say I am? What message is reflected back to me in the faces and voices of my teachers, my neighbors, store clerks? What do I learn from the media about myself? How am I represented in the cultural images around me? Or am I missing from the picture altogether? As social scientist Charles Cooley pointed out long ago, other people are the mirror in which we see ourselves.[1]

This "looking-glass self" is not a flat, one-dimensional reflection but a multidimensional one. Because a central topic of this book is racial identity in the United States, race is highlighted in these pages. Yet how one's racial identity is experienced will be mediated by other dimensions of oneself: male, female, or transgender; young or old; wealthy, middle-class, or poor; gay, lesbian, bisexual, or heterosexual; able-bodied or with disabilities; Christian, Muslim, Jewish, Buddhist, Hindu, or atheist.

Abigail Stewart and Joseph Healy's research on the impact of historical periods on personality development raises the question, Who is my cohort group?[2] Am I a product of the segregation of the 1940s and 1950s, or a beneficiary of the civil rights era? Did I come of age as Barack Obama was entering the White House or after the election of Donald Trump? Did I ride the wave of the women's movement? Or cast my first vote for Hillary Clinton? Did I see the Twin Towers of the World Trade Center fall on 9/11? Am I the child of newly arrived immigrants from Africa, Asia, or the Middle East? Was I born before or after the Supreme Court ruled that same-sex marriage is a legal right? What historical events have shaped my thinking?

What has my social context been? Was I surrounded by people like myself, or was I part of a minority in my community? Did I grow up speaking standard English at home or another language or dialect? Did I live in a rural county, an urban neighborhood, a sprawling suburb, or on a reservation?

Who I am (or say I am) is a product of these and many other factors. Erik Erikson, the psychoanalytic theorist who coined the term *identity crisis,* introduced the notion that the social, cultural, and historical context is the ground in which individual identity is embedded. Acknowledging the complexity of identity as a concept, Erikson writes,

> We deal with a process "located" *in the core of the individual* and yet *also in the core of his communal culture.* . . . In psychological terms, identity formation employs a process of simultaneous reflection and observation, a process taking place on all levels of mental functioning, by which the individual judges himself in the light of what he perceives to be the way in which others judge him in comparison to themselves and to a typology significant to them; while he judges their way of judging him in the light of how he perceives himself in comparison to them and to types that have become relevant to him. This process is, luckily, and necessarily, for the most part unconscious except where inner conditions and outer circumstances combine to aggravate a painful, or elated, "identity-consciousness."[3]

Triggered by the biological changes associated with puberty, the maturation of cognitive abilities, and changing societal expectations, this process of simultaneous reflection and observation, the self-creation of one's identity, is commonly experienced in the United States and other

Western societies during the period of adolescence.[4] Though the foundation of identity is laid in the experiences of childhood, younger children lack the physical and cognitive development needed to reflect on the self in this abstract way. The adolescent capacity for self-reflection (and resulting self-consciousness) allows one to ask, "Who am I now?" "Who was I before?" "Who will I become?" The answers to these questions will influence choices about who one's romantic partners will be, what type of work one will do, where one will live, and what belief system one will embrace. Choices made in adolescence ripple throughout the lifespan.

## Who Am I? Multiple Identities

Integrating one's past, present, and future into a cohesive, unified sense of self is a complex task that begins in adolescence and continues for a lifetime. The complexity of identity is made clear in a collection of autobiographical essays about racial identity called *Names We Call Home*.[5] The multiracial, multiethnic group of contributors narrate life stories highlighting the intersections of gender, class, religion, sexuality, race, and historical circumstance, and illustrating that "people's multiple identifications defy neat racial divisions and unidimensional political alliances."[6] My students' autobiographical narratives point to a similar complexity, but the less-developed narratives of the late adolescents that I taught highlight the fact that our awareness of the complexity of our own identity develops over time. The salience of particular aspects of our identity varies at different moments in our lives. The process of integrating the component parts of our self-definition is indeed a lifelong journey. *Autobiographical Author - Starts Young Adulthood.*

Which parts of our identity capture our attention first? While there are surely idiosyncratic responses to this question, a classroom exercise I regularly use with students and other adult audiences reveals a telling pattern. I ask them to complete the sentence, "I am _____," using as many descriptors as they can think of in sixty seconds. All kinds of trait descriptions are used—friendly, shy, assertive, intelligent, honest, and so on—but over the years I have noticed something else. Students of color usually mention their racial or ethnic group: for instance, I am Black, Puerto Rican, Korean American. White students who have grown up in strong ethnic enclaves occasionally mention being Irish or Italian. But in general, White students rarely mention being White. When I use this exercise in coeducational settings, I notice a similar pattern in terms of gender, religion, and sexuality. Women usually mention being female, while men don't usually mention their maleness. Jewish students often say they are Jewish, while mainline Protestants rarely mention their religious identification. A student who is comfortable revealing it publicly may mention being gay, lesbian, or bisexual. Though I know usually most of my participants are heterosexual, it is very unusual for anyone to include their heterosexuality on their list.

Common across these examples is that in the areas where a person is a member of the dominant or advantaged social group, the category is usually not mentioned. That element of the person's identity is so taken for granted that it goes without comment. It is taken for granted by them because it is taken for granted by the dominant culture. In Eriksonian terms, the person's inner experience and outer circumstance are in harmony with one another, and the image reflected by others is similar to the image within. In the absence of dissonance, this dimension of identity escapes conscious attention.

The parts of our identity that *do* capture our attention are those that other people notice, and that reflect back to us. The aspect of identity that is the target of others' attention, and subsequently of our own, often is that which sets us apart as exceptional or "other" in their eyes. In my life I have been perceived as both. A precocious child who began to read at age three, I stood out among my peers because of my reading ability. This "gifted" dimension of my identity was regularly commented upon by teachers and classmates alike and quickly became part of my self-definition. But I was also distinguished by being the only Black student in the class, an "other," a fact I grew increasingly aware of as I got older.

While there may be countless ways one might be defined as exceptional, there are at least seven categories of "otherness" commonly experienced in US society. People are commonly defined as other on the basis of race or ethnicity, gender (including gender expression), religion, sexual orientation, socioeconomic status, age, and physical or mental ability. Each of these categories has a form of oppression associated with it: racism, sexism, religious oppression / anti-Semitism,[7] heterosexism, classism, ageism, and ableism, respectively. In each case, there is a group considered dominant (systematically advantaged by the society because of group membership) and a group considered subordinate or targeted (systematically disadvantaged). When we think about our multiple identities, most of us will find that we are both dominant and targeted at the same time. But it is the targeted identities that hold our attention and the dominant identities that often go unexamined.

In her essay "Age, Race, Class, and Sex: Women Redefining Difference," Audre Lorde captured the tensions between dominant and targeted identities coexisting in one individual. This self-described "forty-nine-year-old Black lesbian feminist socialist mother of two" wrote,

> Somewhere, on the edge of consciousness, there is what I call a *mythical norm,* which each one of us within our hearts knows "that is not me." In america, this norm is usually defined as white, thin, male, young, heterosexual, christian, and financially secure. It is with this mythical norm that the trappings of power reside within society. Those of us who stand outside that power often identify one way in which we are different, and we assume that to be the primary cause of all oppression, forgetting other distortions around difference, some of which we ourselves may be practicing.[8]

Even as I focus on race and racism in my own writing and teaching, it is helpful to remind myself and my students of the other distortions around difference that I (and they) may be practicing. It is an especially useful way of generating empathy for our mutual learning process. If I am impatient with a White woman for not recognizing her White privilege, it may be useful for me to remember how much of my life I spent oblivious to the fact of the daily advantages I receive simply because I am heterosexual, or the ways in which I may take my class privilege for granted.

## Domination and Subordination

It is also helpful to consider the commonality found in the experience of being dominant or subordinate even when the sources of dominance or subordination are different. The pathbreaking psychiatrist Jean Baker Miller, author of *Toward a New Psychology of Women*, identified some of these areas of commonality.[9]

Dominant groups, by definition, set the parameters within which the subordinates operate. The dominant group holds the power and authority in society relative to the subordinates and determines how that power and authority may be acceptably used. Whether it is reflected in determining who gets the best jobs, whose history will be taught in school, or whose relationships will be validated by society, the dominant group has the greatest influence in determining the structure of the society.

The relationship of the dominants to the subordinates is often one in which the targeted group is labeled as defective or substandard in significant ways. For example, Blacks have historically been characterized as less intelligent than Whites, and women have been viewed as less emotionally stable than men. The dominant group assigns roles to the subordinates that reflect the latter's devalued status, reserving the most highly valued roles in the society for themselves. Subordinates are usually said to be innately incapable of being able to perform the preferred roles. To the extent that the targeted group internalizes the images that the dominant group reflects back to them, they may find it difficult to believe in their own ability.

When a subordinate demonstrates positive qualities believed to be more characteristic of dominants, the individual is defined by dominants as an anomaly. Consider this illustrative example: Following a presentation I gave to some educators, a White man approached me and told me how much he liked my ideas and how articulate I was. "You know," he concluded, "if I had had my eyes closed, I wouldn't have known it was a Black woman speaking." (I replied pleasantly, "This is what a Black woman sounds like.")

The dominant group is seen as the norm for humanity. Jean Baker Miller also asserts that inequitable social relations are seen as the model for "normal human relationships." Consequently, it remains perfectly acceptable in many circles to tell jokes that denigrate a particular group, to exclude subordinates from one's neighborhood or work setting, or to oppose initiatives that might change the power balance.

Miller points out that dominant groups generally do not like to be reminded of the existence of inequality. Because rationalizations have been created to justify the social arrangements, it is easy to believe everything is as it should be. Dominants "can avoid awareness because their explanation of the relationship becomes so well integrated *in other terms;* they can even believe that both they and the subordinate group share the same interests and, to some extent, a common experience."[10]

The truth is that the dominants do not really know what the experience of the subordinates is. In contrast, the subordinates are very well informed about the dominants. Even when firsthand experience is limited by social segregation, the number and variety of images of the dominant group available through television, magazines, books, and newspapers provide subordinates with plenty of information about the dominants. The dominant worldview has saturated the culture for all to learn. Even the Black or Latinx child living in a segregated community can enter White homes of many kinds daily via the media. However, dominant access to information about the subordinates is often limited to stereotypical depictions of the "other." For example, there are many images of White men and women in all forms of media, and while the presence of people of color on prime-time TV and in the movies has steadily increased, stereotypical portrayals persist, limiting the diversity in range of life experiences that are depicted.[11]

Not only is there greater opportunity for the subordinates to learn about the dominants, but there is also greater need. Social psychologist Susan Fiske writes, "It is a simple principle: People pay attention to those who control their outcomes. In an effort to predict and possibly influence what is going to happen to them, people gather information about those with power."[12]

In a situation of unequal power, a subordinate group has to focus on survival. It becomes very important for the subordinates to become highly attuned to the dominants as a way of protecting themselves from them. For example, women who have been battered by men often talk about the heightened sensitivity they developed to their partners' moods. Being able to anticipate and avoid the men's rage was important to survival.

Survival sometimes means not responding to oppressive behavior directly. To do so could result in physical harm to oneself, even death. In his essay "The Ethics of Living Jim Crow," Richard Wright describes eloquently the various strategies he learned to use to avoid the violence of Whites who would brutalize a Black person who did not "stay in his place."[13] Though it is tempting to think that the need for such strategies disappeared with Jim Crow laws, their legacy lives on in the frequent and sometimes fatal harassment Black men and women experience at the hands of White police officers.[14]

Because of the risks inherent in unequal relationships, the subordinates often develop covert ways of resisting or undermining the power of the dominant group. As Miller points out, popular culture is full of folktales, jokes, and stories about how the subordinate—whether the woman, the peasant, or the sharecropper—outwitted the "boss."[15] In his now-classic essay "I Won't Learn from You," Herbert Kohl identifies one form of resistance, "not-learning," demonstrated by targeted students who are too often seen by their dominant teachers as "others":

> Not-learning tends to take place when someone has to deal with unavoidable challenges to her or his personal and family loyalties, integrity, and identity. In such situations, there are forced choices and no apparent middle ground. To agree to learn from a stranger who does not respect your integrity causes a major loss of self. The only alternative is to not-learn and reject the stranger's world.[16]

The use of either strategy, attending very closely to the dominants or not attending at all, is costly to members of the targeted group. Not-learning may mean there are needed skills that are not acquired.

Attending closely to the dominant group may leave little time or energy to attend to one's self. Worse yet, the negative messages of the dominant group about the subordinates may be internalized, leading to self-doubt or, in its extreme form, self-hate. There are many examples of subordinates attempting to make themselves over in the image of the dominant group—Jewish people who want to change the Semitic look of their noses, Asians who have cosmetic surgery to alter the shape of their eyes, Blacks who seek to lighten their skin with bleaching creams. Whether one succumbs to the devaluing pressures of the dominant culture or successfully resists them, the fact is that dealing with oppressive systems from the underside, regardless of the strategy, is physically and psychologically taxing.

Breaking beyond the structural and psychological limitations imposed on one's group is possible, but not easily achieved. To the extent that members of targeted groups do push societal limits—achieving unexpected success, protesting injustice, being "uppity"—by their actions they call the whole system into question. Miller writes that they "expose the inequality, and throw into question the basis for its existence. And they will make the inherent conflict an open conflict. They will then have to bear the burden and take the risks that go with being defined as 'troublemakers.'"[17]

The history of subordinate groups is filled with so-called troublemakers, yet their names are often unknown. Preserving the record of those subordinates and their dominant allies who have challenged the status quo is usually of little interest to the dominant culture, but it is of great interest to subordinates who search for an empowering reflection in the societal mirror.

Many of us are both dominant and subordinate. Clearly racism and racial identity are at the center of discussion in this book, but as Audre Lorde said, from her vantage point as a Black lesbian, "There is no hierarchy of oppression."[18] The thread and threat of violence runs through all of the isms. There is a need to acknowledge each other's pain, even as we attend to our own.

For those readers who are in the dominant racial category, it may sometimes be difficult to take in what is being said by and about those who are targeted by racism. When the perspective of the subordinate is shared directly, an image is reflected to members of the dominant group that is disconcerting. To the extent that one can draw on one's own experience of subordination—as a young person, as a person with a disability, as someone who grew up poor, as a woman—it may be easier to make meaning of another targeted group's experience. For those readers who are targeted by racism and are angered by the obliviousness of Whites sometimes described in these pages, it may be useful to attend to your experience of dominance where you may find it—as a heterosexual, as an able-bodied person, as a Christian, as a man—and consider what systems of privilege you may be overlooking. The task of resisting our own oppression does not relieve us of the responsibility of acknowledging our complicity in the oppression of others.

Our ongoing examination of who we are in our full humanity, embracing all of our identities, creates the possibility of building alliances that may ultimately free us all. It is with that vision in mind that I move forward with an examination of racial identity in the chapters to follow. My goal is not to flatten the multidimensional self-reflection we see of ourselves but to focus on a dimension often neglected and discounted in the public discourse on race.

# PART II

# Understanding Blackness in a White Context

# THREE

# The Early Years

*"Is my skin brown because
I drink chocolate milk?"*

THINK OF YOUR EARLIEST RACE-RELATED MEMORY. HOW OLD WERE you? When I ask adults in my workshops this question, they call out a range of ages: "Three," "Five," "Eight," "Thirteen," "Twenty." Sometimes they talk in small groups about what they remember. At first they hesitate to speak, but then the stories come flooding forward, each person's memory triggering another's.

Some are stories of curiosity, as when a light-skinned child wonders why a dark-skinned person's palms are so much lighter than the backs of his hands. Some are stories of fear and avoidance, communicated verbally or nonverbally by parents, as when one White woman describes her mother nervously telling her to roll up the windows and lock the doors as they drove through a Black community. Some are stories of active bigotry, transmitted casually from one generation to the next through the use of racial slurs and ethnic jokes. Some are stories of confusing mixed messages, as when a White man remembers the Black maid who was "just like family" but was not allowed to eat from the family dishes or use the upstairs bathroom. Some are stories of terror, as when a Black woman remembers being chased home from school by a German shepherd, deliberately set loose by its White owner as she passed by. I often ask audience members, "What do you remember? Something someone said or did? A name-calling incident? An act of

nination? The casual observation of skin color differences? Were
he observer or the object of observation?"

In large groups, I hesitate to ask the participants to reveal their
memories to a crowd of strangers, but I ask instead what emotions are
attached to the memories. The participants use such words as *anger,
confusion, surprise, sadness, embarrassment.* Notice that this list does not
include such words as *joy, excitement, delight.* Too often the stories are
painful ones. Then I ask, "Did you talk to anyone about what happened? Did you tell anyone how you felt?" It is always surprising to me
to see how many people will say that they never discussed these clearly
emotional experiences with anyone. Why not? Had they already learned
that race was not a topic to be discussed?

If they didn't talk to anyone else about it, how did these three- or
five- or eight- or thirteen-year-old children make sense of their experience? Has the confusion continued into adulthood? Are we as adults
prepared to help the children we care about make sense of their own
race-related observations?

## Preschool Conversations

Like many African Americans, I have many race-related memories, beginning when I was quite small. I remember being about three years
old when I had an argument with an African American playmate. He
said I was "black." "No I'm not," I said, "I'm tan." I now see that we
were both right. I am Black, a person of African descent, but tan is
surely a more accurate description of my light-brown skin than black is.
As a three-year-old child who knew her colors, I was prepared to stand
my ground. As an adult looking back on this incident, I wonder if I
had also begun to recognize, even at three, that in some circles it was
better to be tan than to be black. Had I already started internalizing
racist messages?

Questions and confusion about racial issues begin early. Though
adults often talk about the "color blindness" of children, the fact is
that children as young as three do notice physical differences such as
skin color, hair texture, and the shape of facial features.[1] Certainly

*You have to discuss pictures to work through and understand them* preschoolers talk about what they see, and often they do it in ways that make parents uncomfortable. How should we respond when they do?

My own children have given me many opportunities to think about this question. For example, one winter day, my youngest son, David, observed a White mother helping her brown-skinned biracial daughter put on her boots in the hallway of his preschool. "Why don't they match, Mommy?" he asked loudly. Absentmindedly collecting his things, I didn't quite understand what he was talking about—mismatched socks, perhaps? When I asked, he explained indignantly, "You and I match. They don't match. Mommies and kids are supposed to match."

David, like many three-year-olds (and perhaps some adults), had overgeneralized from his routine observations of White parents with White children, and Black parents, like his own, with Black children. As a psychologist, I recognized this preschool tendency to overgeneralize as a part of his cognitive development, but as a mother standing with her child in the hallway, I was embarrassed, afraid that his comment might have somehow injured the mother-daughter pair standing in the hallway with us. I responded matter-of-factly, "David, they don't have to match. Sometimes parents and kids match, and sometimes they don't."

More often, my children and I have been on the receiving end of a preschooler's questions. The first conversation of this type I remember occurred when my oldest son, Jonathan, was enrolled in a day-care center where he was one of few children of color, and the only Black child in his class. One day, as we drove home from the day-care center, Jonathan said, "Eddie says my skin is brown because I drink too much chocolate milk. Is that true?"* Eddie was a White three-year-old in Jonathan's class who, like David, had observed a physical difference and was now searching for an explanation.

"No," I replied, "your skin is brown because you have something in your skin called melanin. Melanin is very important because it helps protect your skin from the sun. Eddie has melanin in his skin, too. Remember when Eddie went to Florida on vacation and came back

*With the exception of my own children's names, all names used in these examples are pseudonyms.

showing everybody his tan? It was the melanin in his skin that made it get darker. Everybody has melanin, you know. But some people have more than others. At your school, you are the kid with the most!"

Jonathan seemed to understand the idea and smiled at the thought that he was the child with the most of something. I talked more about how much I liked the color of his pecan-colored skin, how it was a perfect blend of my light-brown skin and his father's dark-brown complexion. I wanted to affirm who Jonathan was, a handsome brown-skinned child. I wanted to counter the implication of Eddie's question—that there was perhaps something wrong with brown skin, the result of "too much" chocolate milk.

This process of affirmation was not new. Since infancy I had talked about how much I liked his smooth brown skin and those little curls whenever I bathed him or brushed his hair. I searched for children's books depicting brown-skinned children. When Jonathan was one year old, we gave him a large brown rag doll, complete with curly black hair made of yarn, a Marcus Garvey T-shirt, and an African name. Olay-inka, or Olay for short, was his constant companion at home and at the day-care center during nap time. Especially because we had lived in predominantly White communities since his birth, I felt it was important to make sure he saw himself reflected positively in as many ways as possible. As many Black families do, I think we provided an important buffer against the negative messages about Blackness offered by the larger society.[2]

But Jonathan continued to think about the color of his skin, and sometimes he would bring it up. One Saturday morning I was cooking pancakes for breakfast, and Jonathan was at my side, eagerly watching the pancakes cook on the griddle. When I flipped the pancakes over, he was excited to see that the cream-colored batter had been transformed into a golden brown. Jonathan remarked, "I love pancakes. They are brown, just like me." On another occasion when we were cooking together, he noticed that I had set some eggs out on the kitchen counter. Some of the eggs were brown, and some of them were white. He commented on the fact that the eggs were not all the same color. "Yes," I said, "they do have different shells. But look at this!" I cracked open a brown egg and emptied its contents into a bowl. Then I cracked open a white egg. "See, they are different on the outside, but the same on the inside. People are the same way. They look different on the outside, but they are the same on the inside."

Jonathan's questions and comments, like David's and Eddie's, were not unusual for a child of his age. Preschool children are very focused on outward appearances, and skin color is the racial feature they are most likely to comment on.[3] I felt good about my ability as a parent to respond to Jonathan's questions. (I was, after all, teaching courses on the psychology of racism and child development. I was not caught completely off guard!) But I wondered about Jonathan's classmates. What about Eddie, the boy with the chocolate-milk theory? Had anyone set him straight?

In fact, Eddie's question, "Is your skin brown because you drink too much chocolate milk?" represented a good attempt to make sense of a curious phenomenon that he was observing. All the kids in the class had light skin except for Jonathan. Why was Jonathan's skin different? It didn't seem to be dirt—Jonathan washed his hands before lunch like all the other children did, and there was no change. He did often have chocolate milk in his lunch box—maybe that was it. Eddie's reasoning was first-rate for a three-year-old. The fact that he was asking about Jonathan's skin, rather than speculating about his own, reflected that he had already internalized "Whiteness" as the norm, which it was in that school. His question did not reflect prejudice in an adult sense, but it did reveal confusion. His theory was flawed, and he needed some help.

I decided to ask a staff member how she and the other preschool teachers were handling children's questions about racial differences. She smiled and said, "It really hasn't come up." I was amazed. I knew it had come up; after all, Jonathan had reported the conversations to me. How was it that she had not noticed?

Maybe it was easy not to notice. Maybe these conversations among three-year-olds had taken place at the lunch table or in the sand box, away from the hearing of adults. I suspect, too, that there may have been some selective inattention on the part of the staff. When children make comments to which we don't know how to respond, it may be easier simply not to hear what has just been said or to let it slip from our consciousness and memory. Then we don't have to respond, because it "hasn't come up."

Many adults do not know how to respond when children make race-related observations. Imagine this scenario. A White mother and preschool child are shopping in the grocery store. They pass a Black woman and child, and the White child says loudly, "Mommy, look at that girl! Why is she so dirty?" (Confusing dark skin with dirt is a common misconception among White preschool children.) The White mother, embarrassed by her child's comment, responds quickly with a "Ssh!"

An appropriate response might have been: "Honey, that little girl is not dirty. Her skin is as clean as yours. It's just a different color. Just like we have different hair colors, people have different skin colors." If the child still seemed interested, the explanation of melanin could be added.[4] Perhaps afraid of saying the wrong thing, however, many parents don't offer an explanation. They stop at "Ssh," silencing the child but not responding to the question or the reasoning underlying it. Children who have been silenced often enough learn not to talk about race publicly. Their questions don't go away, they just go unasked.

I saw the legacy of this silencing in my Psychology of Racism classes. My students had learned that there is a taboo against talking about race, especially in racially mixed settings, and creating enough safety in the class to overcome that taboo was the first challenge for me as an instructor. But the evidence of the internalized taboo is apparent long before children reach college.

When addressing parent groups, I often hear from White parents who tell me with pride that their children are "color-blind." Usually the parent offers as evidence a story of a friendship with a child of color whose race or ethnicity has never been mentioned to the parent. For example, a father reported that his eight-year-old daughter had been talking very enthusiastically about a friend she had made at school. One day when he picked his daughter up from school, he asked her to point out her new friend. Trying to point her out of a large group of children on the playground, his daughter elaborately described what the child was wearing. She never said she was the only Black girl in the group.

Her father was pleased that she had not, a sign of her color blindness. I wondered if, rather than a sign of color blindness, it was a sign that she had learned not to be so impolite as to mention someone's race.

My White college students would sometimes refer to someone as Black in hushed tones, sometimes whispering the word as though it were a secret or a potentially scandalous identification. When I detected this behavior, I liked to point it out, saying it is not an insult to identify a Black person as Black. Of course, sometimes one's racial group membership is irrelevant to the conversation, and then there is no need to mention it, but when it is relevant, as when pointing out the only Black girl in a crowd, we should not be afraid to say so.

## Blackness, Whiteness, and Painful History

Of course, when we talk to children about racial issues, or anything else, we have to keep in mind each child's developmental stage and cognitive ability to make sense of what we are saying. Preschool children are quite literal in their use of language and concrete in their thinking. They talk about physical differences and other commonly observed cultural differences such as language and style of dress because they are tangible and easy to recognize. They may be confused by the symbolic constructs that adults use.[5]

This point was brought home to me in another conversation with my son Jonathan. As a working mother, I often found trips to the grocery store to be a good opportunity for "quality" time with my then four-year-old. We would stroll the grocery aisles, chatting, as he sat in the top part of the grocery cart and I filled the bottom. On such an outing, Jonathan told me that someone at school had said he was Black. "Am I Black?" he asked me. "Yes, you are," I replied. "But my skin is brown," he said. I was instantly reminded of my own preschool "I'm not black, I'm tan" argument on this point. "Yes," I said, "your skin is brown, but *Black* is a term that people use to describe African Americans, just like *White* is used to describe people who came from Europe. It is a little confusing," I conceded, "because Black people aren't really the color black, but different shades of brown." I mentioned different members of our family and the different shades we represented, but I said that we were all African Americans and in that sense could all be called Black.

Then I said, "It's the same with White people. They come in lots of different shades—pink, beige, even light brown. None of them are white like this piece of paper." I held up the white notepaper on which my grocery list was written as proof. Jonathan nodded his agreement with my description of Black people as really being varying shades of brown but hesitated when I said that White people were not really white in color. "Yes they are," he said. I held up the paper again and said, "White people don't really look like this." "Yes, they do," he insisted. "Okay," I said, remembering that children learn from actual experiences. "Let's go find one and see." We were alone in the grocery aisle, but sure enough, when we turned the corner, there was a White woman pushing her cart down the aisle. I leaned over and whispered in Jonathan's ear, "Now, see, she doesn't look like this paper." Satisfied with this evidence, he conceded the point, and we moved on in our conversation. As I discovered, we were just getting started.

Jonathan's confusion about society's "color" language was not surprising or unusual. At the same time that preschoolers are identifying the colors in the crayon box, they are also beginning to figure out racial categorizations. The color-coded language of social categories obviously does not match the colors we use to label objects. People of Asian descent are not really "yellow" like lemons; Native Americans don't really look "red" like apples. I understood the problem and was prepared for this kind of confusion.

What was of most concern to me at that moment was the tone of my son's question. In his tone of voice was the hint that maybe he was not comfortable being identified as Black, and I wondered what messages he was taking in about being African American. I said that if he wanted to, he could tell his classmate that he was African American. I said that he should feel very proud to have ancestors who were from Africa. I was just beginning to talk about ancient African civilizations when he interrupted me. "If Africa is so great, what are we doing here?" he asked.

I had not planned to have a conversation about slavery with my four-year-old in the grocery store that day. But I didn't see how I could answer his question otherwise. Slavery is a topic that makes many of us uncomfortable. Yet the nature of Black-White race relations in the United States has been forever shaped by slavery and its social, psychological, and economic legacies. It requires discussion. But how does one talk to a four-year-old about this legacy of cruelty and injustice?

I began at the beginning. I knew his preschool had discussed the colonial days when Europeans first came to these shores. I reminded him of this and said:

A long, long time ago, before there were grocery stores and roads and houses here, the Europeans came. And they wanted to build roads and houses and grocery stores here, but it was going to be a lot of work. They needed a lot of really good, strong, smart workers to cut down trees, and build roads, and work on farms, and they didn't have enough. So they went to Africa to get the strongest, smartest workers they could find. Unfortunately they didn't want to pay them. So they kidnapped them and brought them here as slaves. They made them work and didn't pay them. And that was really unfair.

Even as I told this story I was aware of three things: (1) I didn't want to frighten this four-year-old, who might worry that these things would happen to him (another characteristic of four-year-old thinking); (2) I wanted him to know that his African ancestors were not just passive victims but had found ways to resist their victimization; and (3) I did not want him to think that all White people were bad. It *is* possible to have White allies.

So I continued:

Now, this was a long, long time ago. You were never a slave. I was never a slave. Grandmommy and Granddaddy were never slaves. This was a really long time ago, and the Africans who were kidnapped did whatever they could to escape. But sometimes the Europeans had guns and the Africans didn't, so it was hard to get away. But some even jumped off the boats into the ocean to try to escape. There were slave rebellions, and many of the Africans were able to escape to freedom after they got here, and worked to help other slaves get free. Now, even though some White people were kidnapping Africans and making them work without pay, other White people thought that this was very unfair, which it was. And those White people worked along with the Black people to bring an end to slavery. So now it is against the law to have slaves.

Jonathan was paying very close attention to my story, and when I declared that slavery had ended a long time ago, he asked, "Well, when they weren't slaves anymore, why didn't they go back to Africa?" Thanks to the African American history classes I took in college, I knew enough to say, "Well, some did. But others might not have been able to because they didn't have enough money, and besides that, by then they had families and friends who were living here and they might have wanted to stay."

"And this is a nice place, too," he declared.

"Yes it is."

Over the next few weeks, an occasional question would come up about my story, and I knew that Jonathan was still digesting what I had said. Though I did not anticipate talking about slavery with my four-year-old, I was glad in retrospect that it was I who had introduced him to the subject, because I was able to put my own spin on this historical legacy, emphasizing both Black resistance to victimization and White resistance to the role of victimizer.

Too often I hear from young African American students the embarrassment they have felt in school when the topic of slavery is discussed, ironically one of the few ways that the Black experience is included in their school curriculum. Uncomfortable with the portrayal of their group as helpless victims—the rebellions and resistance offered by the enslaved Africans are rarely discussed—they squirm uncomfortably as they feel the eyes of White children looking to see their reaction to this subject.

In my professional development work with White teachers, they sometimes remark how uncomfortable they, too, are with this and other examples of the painful history of race relations in the United States. As one elementary school teacher said,

> It is hard to tell small children about slavery, hard to explain that Black young men were lynched, and that police turned firehoses on children while other men bombed churches, killing Black children at their prayers. This history is a terrible legacy for all of us. The other day a teacher told me that she could not look into the faces of her students when she taught about these things. It was too painful, and too embarrassing. . . . If we are all uncomfortable, something is wrong in our approach.[6]

Something *is* wrong. While I think it is necessary to be honest about the racism of our past and present, it is also necessary to empower children (and adults) with the vision that change is possible. Concrete examples are critical. For young children these examples can sometimes be found in children's picture books. One of my favorites is Faith Ringgold's *Aunt Harriet's Underground Railroad in the Sky*.[7] Drawing on historical accounts of the Underground Railroad and the facts of Harriet Tubman's life, this story is told from the point of view of a young Black girl who travels back in time and experiences both the chilling realities of slavery and the power of her own resistance and eventual escape.

White people are present in the story both as enemies (slave owners) and as allies (abolitionists). This dual representation is important for children of color, as well as for White children. I remember a conversation I had a few years ago with a White friend who often talked to her then-preschool son about issues of social justice. He had been told over and over the story of Rosa Parks and the Montgomery bus boycott, and it was one of his favorites as a four-year-old. But as he got a little older she began to notice a certain discomfort in him when she talked about these issues. "Are all White people bad?" he asked her. At the age of five, he seemed to be feeling badly about being White. She asked me for some advice. I recommended she begin talking more about what White people had done to oppose injustice. Finding examples of this in children's literature can be a challenge, but one example is Jeanette Winter's book *Follow the Drinking Gourd*.[8] This too is a story about the Underground Railroad, but it highlights the role of a White man named Peg Leg Joe and other White allies who offer assistance along the escape route, again providing a tangible example of White resistance to injustice.

## A Question of Color

All of these preschool questions reflect the beginning of a developing racial identity. The particular questions my child asked me reflected his early experience as one of few Black children in a predominantly White community. Even in the context of all-Black communities, the color variations in the community, even within families, can lead to a series of skin-color-related conversations. For example, it is common to hear a preschool child describe a light-skinned Black person as White, often to the chagrin of the individual so identified. The child's misclassification does not represent a denial of Blackness, only the child's incomplete understanding of the adult world's racial classifications. As preschoolers, my own children occasionally asked me if I was White. When I am misidentified by children as White, I usually reply matter-of-factly, "I am an African American person. We come in all shades of brown, dark brown, medium brown, and sometimes light brown—like me."

The concept of *race constancy*, that one's racial group membership is fixed and will not change, is not achieved until children are six or seven years old. (The same is true of gender constancy.)[9] Just as preschool boys sometimes express a desire to have a baby like Mom when they grow up (and are dismayed when they learn they cannot), young Black children may express a desire to be White. Though such statements are certainly distressing to parents, they do not necessarily mean that the child has internalized a negative self-image. It may, however, reflect a child's growing awareness of White privilege, conveyed through the media. For example, in a study of children's race-related conversations, one five-year-old Black boy reportedly asked, "Do I have to be Black?" To the question of why he asked, he responded, "I want to be chief of

paramedics." His favorite TV show at the time featured paramed[ic]
firefighters, all of whom were White.[10]

Though such comments by young children are not necessarily rooted
in self-rejection, it is important to consider what messages children are
receiving about the relative worth of light or dark skin. The societal
preference for light skin and the relative advantage bestowed on light-
skinned Blacks historically, often referred to as *colorism,* manifests itself
not only in the marketplace but even within Black families.[11]

A particular form of internalized oppression, the skin-color prejudice found within Black communities is toxic to children and adults.
A by-product of the plantation hierarchy, which privileged the light-
skinned children of enslaved African women and White slave owners,
a postslavery class system was created based on color. Historically the
Black middle class has been a light-skinned group. But the racially mixed
ancestry of many Black people can lead to a great deal of color variation
among siblings and extended family members. The internalization of
White-supremacist standards of beauty and the desire to maintain what
little advantage can be gained in a racist system leads some families
to reject darker-skinned members. Conversely, in some families, anger
at White oppression and the pain of colorism can lead to resentment
toward and rejection of lighter-skinned members. According to family therapist Nancy Boyd-Franklin, family attitudes about skin color
are rarely discussed openly, but the messages are often clearly conveyed
when some children are favored over others, or when a relative teasingly
says, "Whose child are you?" to the child whose skin color varies from
other family members. Boyd-Franklin writes,

> All Black people, irrespective of their color, shade, darkness, or light-
> ness, are aware from a very early age that their blackness makes them
> different from mainstream White America. It sets them apart from
> White immigrant groups who were not brought here as slaves and
> who have thus had a different experience in becoming assimilated
> into mainstream American culture. The struggle for a strong posi-
> tive racial identity for young Black Afro-American children is clearly
> made more difficult by the realities of color prejudice.[12]

We need to examine not only our behavior toward our children but also the language we use around them. Is *black* ever used as a derogatory term to describe others, as in "that black so-and-so?" Is darkness seen as an obstacle to be overcome, as in "She's dark, but she's still pretty," or avoided, as in "Stay out of the sun, you're dark enough already?" Is lightness described as defective, as in "You need some sun, girl?" Do we sing hymns in church on Sunday proclaiming our wish to be washed "white as snow"? Even when our clear desire is to reflect positive images of Blackness to young Black children, our habits of speech may undermine our efforts unless we are intentional about examining the color-coded nature of our language.

Related to questions of color are issues of hair texture, an especially sensitive issue for Black women, young and old. I grew up with the expression "good hair." Though no one in my household used that phrase often, I knew what it meant when I heard it. "Good hair" was straight hair, the straighter the better. I still remember the oohs and aahs of my White elementary school classmates when I arrived at school for "picture day" with my long mane of dark hair resting on my shoulders. With the miracle of a hot comb, my mother had transformed my ordinary braids into what I thought was a glamorous cascade of curls. I received many compliments that day. "How pretty you look," the White teacher said. The truth is I looked pretty every day, but a clear message was being sent both at home and at school about what real beauty was.

I now wear my hair in its natural state of tiny curls. It has been that way since 1971. My sons are unfamiliar with Saturday afternoon trips to the beauty parlor, the smell of hot combs and chemical straighteners. Instead they grew up going with me or their father to the Black-owned barber shop where Black men and some women waited their turn for a seat in the barber's chair. I admire their neatly trimmed heads, and they admire mine. I genuinely like the way my short hair looks and feels, and that sends an important message to my sons about how I feel about myself as a Black woman and, by extension, how I feel about them.

Though a woman's choice to straighten her hair is not necessarily a sign of internalized oppression, it does reinforce the notion to an observant child that straight is better. In her book *Sisters of the Yam:*

*Black Women and Self-Recovery*, bell hooks relates a conversation she had with a Black woman frustrated by her daughter's desire for long blond hair, despite the family's effort to affirm their Blackness. Observing the woman's dark skin and straightened hair, she encouraged the mother to examine her own attitudes about skin color and hair texture to see what messages she might be communicating to her child by the way she constructed her own body image.[13]

Countering the images of the dominant culture is a challenge, but it can be done. Finding images that reflect the range of skin tones and hair textures in Black families is an important way to affirm a positive sense of Black identity. A wonderfully illustrated book for children that opposes the prevailing Eurocentric images of beauty is John Steptoe's *Mufaro's Beautiful Daughters: An African Tale*.[14] As the story states on the opening page, "Everyone agreed that Manyara and Nyasha are beautiful." These lovely brown-skinned sisters have broad noses and full lips, with hair braided in short cornrows.

Though it is easier than it used to be to find children's picture books depicting Black children authentically rather than as White children painted a darker shade, it may still be hard to find children's books depicting Black children with very dark or very light skin. A medium brown seems to be the color of choice. Decorating one's home with photographs of family and friends who represent a range of skin tones and hair textures is one way to begin to fill this representational gap.

## "It's That Stuff Again": Developing a Critical Consciousness

From the time my children were infants, reading has been a shared activity in our family. I have always loved to read, and that love of books has been imparted to my children, who rarely leave home without a book to read on the way. I worked hard to find good children's literature featuring African Americans and other children of color, but I also introduced my children to some of the books I liked when I was a child, most of which included only White children.

When Jonathan was just learning to read on his own and had advanced to "chapter books," I introduced him to the *Boxcar Children* series of easy-reading mysteries, which I'd loved as a child.[15] Written in the 1940s, these books feature four White children, two boys and two girls, orphaned and homeless, who lived in an abandoned railway car until they were found by their wealthy grandfather. From then on, they traveled with Grandfather and solved mysteries wherever they went.

Reading these volumes again with Jonathan, I had a new perception of them: how sexist they seemed to be. The two girls seemed to spend most of their time on these adventures cooking and cleaning and setting up house while the boys fished, paddled the canoe, and made the important discoveries. After reading several pages of this together, I decided to say something about it to my then-seven-year-old son. I asked if he knew what sexism was. He did not, so I explained that it was when girls were treated differently than boys just because they were girls. I said that the girls in this story were being treated differently than the boys, and I pointed out some examples and discussed the unfairness of it. Jonathan wanted to continue the story, and I agreed that we could finish it, despite my new perception. What pleased and surprised me as we continued to read was that Jonathan began to spot the gender bias himself. "Hey Mom," he interrupted me as I read on, "there's that stuff again!"

Learning to spot "that stuff"—whether it is racist, or sexist, or classist—is an important skill for children to develop. It is as important for my Black male children to recognize sexism and other forms of oppression as it is for them to spot racism. We are better able to resist the negative impact of oppressive messages when we see them coming than when they are invisible to us. While some may think it is a burden to children to encourage this critical consciousness, I consider it a gift. Educator Janie Ward calls this child-rearing process "raising resisters."[16] And there are infinite opportunities to do so.

One such opportunity came in the form of a children's book of Bible stories, a gift from a friend. My son and I sat down to read the story of Moses together. We hadn't gotten very far when I said, "You know, something is bothering me about this book." "What is it?" he replied. "You know, this story took place in Egypt, and the people in these pictures do not look much like Egyptians." "Well, what do Egyptians look like?" he asked. We turned to a children's world atlas and found that the photographs of the Egyptians in the atlas had noticeably darker skin and hair than the drawings in the book. Though we did not discard the book, we did discuss the discrepancy.

I did not point out every omission or distortion I noticed (and I am sure that a lot got by me unnoticed), and sometimes my children didn't agree with my observations. For example, when discussing with them my plans to talk about media stereotyping in this book, I offered the example of the Disney film *The Lion King*. A very popular family film, I was dismayed at the use of ethnically identifiable voices to characterize the hyenas, clearly the undesirables in the film. The Spanish-accented voice of Cheech Marin and the Black slang of Whoopi Goldberg clearly marked the hyenas racially. The little Lion King is warned never to go to the place where the hyenas live. When the evil lion (darker in shade than the good lions) takes over and the hyenas have access to power, it is not long before they have ruined the kingdom. "There goes the neighborhood!"

My sons, then ten and fourteen, countered that the distinguished Black actor James Earl Jones as the voice of the good lion offset the racial characterizations of the hyenas. I argued that to the target audience of young children, the voice of James Earl Jones would not be identified as a voice of color, while the voices of the hyenas surely would. The racial subtext of the film would be absorbed uncritically by many young children, and perhaps their parents. Whether we agreed or not, the process of engaging my children in a critical examination of the books they read, the television they watched, the films they saw, and the computer and video games they played was essential.

And despite my best efforts, the stereotypes still crept in. One Saturday afternoon, after attending choir rehearsal at our church, located in a Black section of a nearby city, my oldest son and I drove past a Black teenager running down the street. "Why is that boy running?" my son asked. "I don't know," I said absentmindedly. "Maybe he stole something," he suggested. I nearly slammed on the brakes. "Why would you say something like that?" I said. "Well, you know, in the city, there's a lot of crime, and people steal things," he said. He did not say "Black people," but I knew the cultural images to which he was responding. Now, this neighborhood was very familiar to us. We had spent many Saturdays at choir rehearsal and sat in church next to Black kids who looked a lot like that boy on the street. We had never personally experienced any crime in that location. In fact the one time my car was broken into was when it was parked in a "good neighborhood" in our own small town. I pointed out this contradiction and asked my son to imagine why he, also a Black boy, might be running down the street—in a hurry to get home, late for a bus, on his way to a job at the McDonald's up the street? Then we talked about stereotyping and the images of urban Black boys we see on television and elsewhere. Too often they are portrayed as muggers, drug dealers, or other criminals. My sons knew that such images were not an accurate representation of themselves, and I had to help them see that they are also a distorted image of their urban peers.

Children can learn to question whether demeaning or derogatory depictions of other people are stereotypes. When reading books or watching television, they can learn to ask who is doing what in the story line and why, who is in the role of leader and who is taking the orders, who or what is the problem and who is solving it, and who has been left out of the story altogether.[17]

But not only do children need to be able to recognize distorted representations, they also need to know what can be done about them. Learning to recognize cultural and institutional racism and other forms of inequity without also learning strategies to respond to them is a prescription for despair. Yet even preschool children are not too young to begin to think about what can be done about unfairness. The resource book *Anti-Bias Education for Young Children and Ourselves* includes many examples of young children learning to recognize and speak up against unfairness.[18] The book suggests increasing levels of activism for developing children. Two- and three-year-olds are encouraged to use words to express their feelings and to empathize with one another. With adult guidance, four- and five-year-olds are capable of group activism.

When I was living in Massachusetts, I read about a group of seven-year-olds in a second-grade class in Amherst, Massachusetts, who wrote letters to the state Department of Transportation protesting the signs on the Massachusetts Turnpike depicting a Pilgrim hat with an arrow through it. This sign was certainly a misrepresentation of history and offensive to American Indians. The children received national recognition for their efforts, and more important, the signs were changed.[19] I am sure the lesson that collective effort can make a difference will be remembered by those children for a long time. As early childhood educator Louise Derman-Sparks and her colleagues write:

> For children to feel good and confident about themselves, they need to be able to say, "That's not fair," or "I don't like that," if they are the target of prejudice or discrimination. For children to develop empathy and respect for diversity, they need to be able to say, "I don't like what you are doing" to a child who is abusing another child. If we teach children to recognize injustice, then we must also teach them that people can create positive change by working together. . . . Through activism activities children build the confidence and skills for becoming adults who assert, in the face of injustice, "I have the responsibility to deal with it, I know how to deal with it, I will deal with it."[20]

When we adults reflect on our own race-related memories, we may recall times when we did not get the help we needed to sift through the confusing messages we received. The task of talking to our children about racism and other isms may seem formidable. Our children's questions may make us uncomfortable, and we may not have a ready response. But even a missed opportunity can be revisited at another time. It is never too late to say, "I've been thinking about that question you asked me the other day . . . " We have the responsibility, and the resources available, to educate ourselves if necessary so that we will not repeat the cycle of oppression with our children.

# FOUR

# Identity Development
# in Adolescence

*"Why are all the Black kids
sitting together in the cafeteria?"*

WALK INTO ANY RACIALLY MIXED HIGH SCHOOL CAFETERIA AT LUNCH-time and you will instantly notice that in the sea of adolescent faces, there is an identifiable group of Black students sitting together. Conversely, it could be pointed out that there are many groups of White students sitting together as well, though people rarely comment about that. The question on the tip of everyone's tongue is, "Why are the Black kids sitting together?" Principals want to know, teachers want to know, White students want to know, the Black students who aren't sitting at the table want to know.

How does it happen that so many Black teenagers end up at the same cafeteria table? They don't start out there. If you walk into racially mixed elementary schools, you will often see young children of diverse racial backgrounds playing with one another, sitting at the snack table together, crossing racial boundaries with an ease uncommon in adolescence. Moving from elementary school to middle school (often at sixth or seventh grade) means interacting with new children from different neighborhoods than before, and a certain degree of clustering by race might therefore be expected, presuming that children who are familiar one another would form groups. But even in schools where the same children stay together from kindergarten through eighth grade, racial grouping begins by the sixth or seventh grade. What happens?

One thing that happens is puberty. As children enter adolescence, they begin to explore the question of identity, asking "Who am I? Who can I be?" in ways they have not done before. For Black youth, asking "Who am I?" usually includes thinking about "Who am I ethnically and/or racially? What does it mean to be Black?"

As I write this, I can hear the voice of a White woman who asked me, "Well, all adolescents struggle with questions of identity. They all become more self-conscious about their appearance and more concerned about what their peers think. So what is so different for Black kids?" Of course, she is right that all adolescents look at themselves in new ways, but not all adolescents think about themselves in racial terms.

The search for personal identity that intensifies in adolescence can involve several dimensions of an adolescent's life: vocational plans, religious beliefs, values and preferences, political affiliations and beliefs, gender roles, and ethnic identities. The process of exploration may vary across these identity domains. James Marcia described four identity "statuses" to characterize the variation in the identity search process: (1) *diffuse,* a state in which there has been little exploration or active consideration of a particular domain, and no psychological commitment; (2) *foreclosed,* a state in which a commitment has been made to particular roles or belief systems, often those selected by parents, without actively considering alternatives; (3) *moratorium,* a state of active exploration of roles and beliefs in which no commitment has yet been made; and (4) *achieved,* a state of strong personal commitment to a particular dimension of identity following a period of high exploration.[1]

An individual is not likely to explore all identity domains at once, therefore it is not unusual for an adolescent to be actively exploring one dimension while another remains relatively unexamined. Given the impact of dominant and subordinate status, it is not surprising that researchers have found that adolescents of color are more likely to be actively engaged in an exploration of their racial or ethnic identity than are White adolescents.[2]

Why do Black youths, in particular, think about themselves in terms of race? Because that is how the rest of the world thinks of them. Our self-perceptions are shaped by the messages that we receive from those around us, and when young Black men and women enter adolescence, the racial content of those messages intensifies. A case in point: When my son David was seven, if asked to describe himself, he would have told you many things: "I'm smart, I like to play computer games, I have an older brother." Near the top of his list, he would likely have mentioned, "I'm tall for my age." At seven, he probably would not have mentioned that he is Black or African American, though he certainly knew that about himself and his family. Why would he mention his height and not his racial group membership? As a child, when David met new adults, one of the first questions they asked was, "How old are you?" When David stated his age, the inevitable reply was, "Gee, you're tall for your age!" It happened so frequently that I once overheard seven-year-old David say to someone, "Don't say it, I know. I'm tall for my age." Height was salient for David because it was salient for others.

When David met new adults, they didn't say, "Gee, you're Black for your age!" If you are saying to yourself, of course they didn't, think again. Imagine David at fifteen, six foot two, wearing the adolescent attire of the day, passing adults he doesn't know on the sidewalk. Would the women hold their purses a little tighter, maybe even cross the street to avoid him? Would he hear the sound of the automatic door locks on cars as he passes by? Would he be followed around by the security guards at the local mall? As he stopped in town with his new bicycle, would a police officer hassle him, asking where he got it, implying that it might be stolen? Would strangers assume he plays basketball? Each of these experiences would convey a racial message. At seven, race was not yet salient for David because it was not yet salient for society. But later it would be.

## Understanding Racial-Ethnic-Cultural Identity Development

Psychologist William Cross, author of *Shades of Black: Diversity in African-American Identity*, offered a theory of racial identity development that I found to be a very useful framework for understanding what is happening not only with David but also with those Black students in the cafeteria.[3] Since the publication of that model in 1991, Cross and other researchers from the Ethnic and Racial Identity in the 21st Century Study Group have deepened our collective understanding of the central importance of the development of a group identity among youth of color. As William Cross and Binta Cross assert, it is clear that "racial, ethnic, and cultural identity overlap at the level of *lived experience*" to the point that there is little reason to discuss them separately.[4] What in the past (including in previous editions of this book) were referred to as models of racial identity development are now better understood as racial-cultural identity or racial-ethnic-cultural (REC) identity models.[5]

Most children of color, Cross and Cross point out, "are socialized to develop an identity that integrates competencies for transacting race, ethnicity and culture in everyday life."[6] But how does that identity development take place in the life of a young Black adolescent? From early childhood through the preadolescent years, Black children are exposed to and absorb many of the beliefs and values of the dominant White culture, including the idea that Whites are the preferred group in US society. The stereotypes, omissions, and distortions that reinforce notions of White superiority are breathed in by Black children as well as White. Simply as a function of being socialized in a Eurocentric culture, some Black children may begin to value the role models, lifestyles, and images of beauty represented by the dominant group more highly than those of their own cultural group. On the other hand, if Black parents are what I call race-conscious—that is, actively seeking to encourage positive racial identity by providing their children with positive cultural images and messages about what it means to be Black—the impact of the dominant society's messages are reduced.[7]

In either case, in the prepuberty stage, the personal and social significance of one's REC-group membership has not yet been realized, and REC identity is not yet under examination. Before puberty, David and other children like him could be described as being in a pre-awareness state relative to their REC identity. When the environmental cues change and the world begins to reflect their Blackness back to them more clearly, they begin to develop a new social understanding of their own REC-group membership and what that means for them and others. During adolescence their understanding evolves to include not just more about themselves but also more about their group, including an "understanding of a *common fate or shared destiny* based on ethnic or racial group membership and that these shared experiences differ from the experiences of individuals from other groups."[8]

Transition to this new understanding is typically precipitated by an event or series of events that force the young person to acknowledge the personal impact of racism. As the result of a new and heightened awareness of the significance of race, the individual begins to grapple with what it means to be a member of a group targeted by racism. Research suggests that this focused process of examination of one's racial or ethnic identity may begin as early as middle or junior high school.[9]

In a study of Black and White eighth graders from an integrated urban junior high school, Jean Phinney and Steve Tarver found clear evidence for the beginning of the search process in this dimension of identity. Among the forty-eight participants, more than a third had thought about the effects of ethnicity on their future, had discussed the issues with family and friends, and were attempting to learn more about their group. While White students in this integrated school were also beginning to think about ethnic identity, there was evidence to suggest a more active search among Black students, especially Black girls.[10] Phinney and Tarver's initial findings, and the findings of more than two decades of subsequent studies,[11] are consistent with my own study of Black youth in predominantly White communities, where the environmental cues that trigger an examination of REC identity often become evident in middle school or junior high school.[12]

Some of the environmental cues are institutionalized. Though many elementary schools have self-contained classrooms where children of varying performance levels learn together, many middle and secondary schools assign students to different subject levels based on their perceived ability, a practice known as tracking. Though school administrators often defend their tracking practices as fair and objective, there usually is a recognizable racial pattern to how children are assigned, which often represents the system of advantage operating in the schools.[13]

For example, in a study of the Charlotte-Mecklenburg School District in North Carolina, Roslyn Mickelson compared the placements of Black and White high school students who had similar scores on a national standardized achievement test they took in the sixth grade. More than half of the White students who scored in the ninetieth to ninety-ninth percentile on the test were enrolled in high school Advanced Placement (AP) or International Baccalaureate (IB) English, while only 20 percent of the Black students who also scored in the ninetieth to ninety-ninth percentile were enrolled in these more-rigorous courses. Meanwhile, 35 percent of White students whose test scores were below the seventieth percentile were taking AP or IB English. Only 9 percent of Black students who scored below the seventieth percentile had access to the more-advanced curriculum.[14]

This disproportionate access to the most rigorous college preparatory curriculum is so common that in 2014 the US Department of Education Office of Civil Rights issued a "Dear Colleague" letter to school districts across the country "to call your attention to disparities that persist in access to educational resources, and to help you address those disparities and comply with the legal obligation to provide students with equal access to these resources without regard to race, color, or national origin."[15]

Because Black children are much more likely to be in the lower track than in the honors track in racially mixed schools, such apparent sorting along racial lines sends a message about what it means to be Black. One young honors student I interviewed described the irony of this resegregation in what was an otherwise integrated environment, and hinted at the identity issues it raised for him. "It was really a very paradoxical existence, here I am in a school that's thirty-five percent Black, you know, and I'm the only Black in my classes. . . . That always struck me as odd. I guess I felt that I was different from the other Blacks because of that."

In addition to the changes taking place within school, there are changes in the social dynamics outside school. For many parents, puberty raises anxiety about interracial dating. In racially mixed communities, you often begin to see what I call the birthday party effect. Young children's birthday parties in multiracial communities are often a reflection of the community's diversity. The parties of elementary school children may be segregated by gender but not always by race. However, at puberty, when the parties become sleepovers or boy-girl events, they become less and less racially diverse.

Black girls, especially in predominantly White communities, may gradually become aware that something has changed. When their White friends start to date, often they do not. The issues of emerging sexuality and the societal messages about who is sexually desirable can leave young Black women feeling they are in a very devalued position. One young woman from a Philadelphia suburb described herself as "pursuing White guys throughout high school" to no avail. Since there were no Black boys in her class, she had little choice. She would feel "really pissed off" that those same White boys would date her White friends. For her, "that prom thing was like out of the question."[16]

Though Black girls living in the context of a larger Black community may have more social choices, they too have to contend with devaluing messages about who they are and who they will become, especially if they are poor or working-class. As social scientists Bonnie Ross Leadbeater and Niobe Way point out, "The school drop-out, the teenage welfare mother, the drug addict, and the victim of domestic violence or of AIDS are among the most prevalent public images of poor and working-class urban adolescent girls. . . . Yet, despite the risks inherent in economic disadvantage, the majority of poor urban adolescent girls do not fit the stereotypes that are made about them."[17]

Resisting the stereotypes and affirming other definitions of themselves is part of the task facing young Black women in both White and Black communities. That task has been made more complicated for Black adolescent girls because they are continually confronted with hypersexualized and other negative representations of Black women in the popular culture. Access to a broad range of cable stations, magazines, music videos, and web-based media catering to African Americans has given the hip-hop generation of young people wide exposure to Black people on the screen. Yet the familiar stereotypes of the past "have been transformed into contemporary distortions: the welfare queen, who is sexually promiscuous and schemes for money; the video vixen, a loose woman; and the gold digger who schemes and exploits the generosity of men."[18]

Black girls, who may experience puberty as young as nine or ten, are bombarded with these sexualized images of Black women "all of the time."[19] They have to struggle with coming to terms with their own changing bodies and how others, particularly male peers, are responding to those changes, even as they try to make sense of what the world expects them to be, a cognitively challenging task for an early adolescent. Again, proactive, race-conscious parenting can make a positive difference during this developmental period. "Black girls who receive protective and affirming racial/ethnic socialization and beauty messages at home may be less likely to accept negative stereotype images as reflective of all black women or themselves."[20]

As was illustrated in the example of David, Black boys also face a devalued status in the wider world. The all-too-familiar media image of a young Black man with his hands cuffed behind his back, arrested for presumed criminal activity, has primed many to view young Black men with suspicion and fear. In the context of predominantly White schools, however, Black boys may enjoy a degree of social success, particularly if they are athletically talented. The culture has embraced the Black athlete, and the young man who can fulfill that role is often pursued by Black girls and White girls alike. But even these young men will encounter experiences that may trigger an examination of their racial identity.

Sometimes the experience is quite dramatic. Lawrence Otis Graham, a prominent New York attorney and author, wrote an essay, published in the *Washington Post*, about an encounter his son had that left both of them shaken. Here's an excerpt:

It was a Tuesday afternoon when my 15-year-old son called from his academic summer program at a leafy New England boarding school and told me that as he was walking across campus, a gray Acura with a broken rear taillight pulled up beside him. Two men leaned out of the car and glared at him.

"Are you the only nigger at Mellon Academy*?" one shouted.

Certain that he had not heard them correctly, my son moved closer to the curb, and asked politely, "I'm sorry; I didn't hear you."

But he had heard correctly. And this time the man spoke more clearly. "Only . . . nigger," he said with added emphasis.

My son froze. He dropped his backpack in alarm and stepped back from the idling car. The men honked the horn loudly and drove off, their laughter echoing behind them.[21]

Even though the writer had imagined his privileged socioeconomic status would protect his son from such experiences, the incident forced the teen (and his dad) to think about his racial identity in a new way.

Malcolm Little, later to be known as Malcolm X, was just a little younger, thirteen perhaps, when he had his own identity-shifting encounter. *The Autobiography of Malcolm X* is a classic tale of racial identity development, and I assigned it to my Psychology of Racism students for just that reason. As a junior high school student, Malcolm was a star. Despite the fact that he was separated from his family and living in a foster home, he was an A student and was elected president of his class. One day he had a conversation with his English teacher, whom he liked and respected, about his future career goals. Malcolm said he wanted to be a lawyer. His teacher responded, "That's no realistic goal for a nigger," and advised him to consider carpentry instead.[22] The message was clear: you are a Black male, your racial group membership matters, plan accordingly. Malcolm's emotional response was typical—anger, confusion, and alienation. He withdrew from his White classmates, stopped participating in class, and eventually left his predominantly White Michigan town to live with his sister in Roxbury, a Black community in Boston.

No teacher would say such a thing now, you may be thinking, but don't be so sure. It is certainly less likely that a teacher would use the

*The name of the boarding school was fictionalized by the author.

n-word, but consider these contemporary examples shared by high school students. A young ninth-grade student was sitting in his home-room. A substitute teacher was in charge of the class. Because the ma-jority of students from this school go on to college, she used the free time to ask the students about their college plans. As a substitute she had very limited information about their academic performance, but she offered some suggestions. When she turned to this young man, one of few Black males in the class, she suggested that he consider a com-munity college. She had recommended four-year colleges to the other students. Like Malcolm, this student got the message.

In another example, a young Black woman attending a desegregated school to which she was bused was encouraged by a teacher to attend the upcoming school dance. Most of the Black students did not live in the neighborhood and seldom attended the extracurricular activities. The young woman indicated that she wasn't planning to come. The well-intentioned teacher was persistent. Finally the teacher said, "Oh come on, I know you people love to dance." This young woman got the message, too.

Though I have described single episodes in these examples, the grow-ing racial awareness characteristic of this adolescent stage can be triggered by the cumulative effect of many small incidents—microaggressions—that the young person begins to experience.[23] Sometimes the awakening comes vicariously through a highly publicized racial incident involv-ing someone with whom the adolescent identifies, like the shooting of Trayvon Martin or Jordan Davis.[24] Sometimes it comes through online experiences of racial discrimination.

Increasingly, online racial discrimination is impacting adolescents of color. According to a Pew Research Center study of teens and technol-ogy, at least 95 percent of American youth have access to the internet, and adolescents of color spend a lot of time using it—four and a half more hours per day on average than their White peers.[25] In a large comprehensive study of a diverse group of adolescents over a three-year period (2010–2013), more than half of the adolescents of color had experienced an act of online racial discrimination directed at them, de-fined as "denigrating or excluding individuals or groups on the basis of race through the use of symbols, voice, video, images, text and graphic representations. . . . These experiences include racial epithets and unfair treatment by others due to a person's racial or ethnic background, such as being excluded from an online space."[26] More than two-thirds had witnessed an act of online racial discrimination directed at someone else.

Though the adolescents of color in the study included a mix of African American, Latinx, Asian, and biracial teens, researchers found that African American youth experienced "a particularly virulent form of online racial discrimination" on such popular online platforms as Facebook, Twitter, and Instagram. For example, one student shared, "The worst thing that happened to me on the internet is that someone threatened to kill me because of my race." Another reported, "Almost every day on Call of Duty: Black Ops [a video game involving other online players] I see Confederate flags, swastikas and black people hanging from trees in emblems and they say racist things about me and my teammates." Another game-related incident was this one: "Me and my friends were playing Xbox and some kid joined the Xbox Live party we were in and made a lot of racist jokes I found offensive."[27]

Another well-publicized example is the targeting of Black freshmen at the University of Pennsylvania in the days immediately following the 2016 presidential election. Online hackers in Oklahoma added the Penn students to a social media account that included racial slurs and a "daily lynching" calendar. Among the messages the students received was a photo of people hanging from a tree. The response of those who were targeted by the messages (and their friends who experienced the incident vicariously) was visceral. Wrote one, "Quite honestly I just can't stop crying. I feel sick to my stomach. I don't feel safe."[28]

In these examples, the intrusion of racism into young people's lives comes uninvited and across all physical boundaries into their own homes through an Xbox or computer, or into the palms of their hands through their smartphones, often from unknown sources. The online expression of overt racial prejudice of the kind too often seen in real life during the pre–civil rights era is disturbing, and it has an adverse impact on its recipients. Tynes reports that online racial discrimination is linked to depressive symptoms, anxiety, lower academic motivation, and increased problem behavior.[29] These are all characteristics one might see in young people struggling with core questions of REC identity in a world that devalues their group identity.

## Coping with Encounters: Developing an Oppositional Identity

What do these encounters have to do with the cafeteria? Do experiences with racism inevitably result in so-called self-segregation? While certainly a desire to protect oneself from further offense is understandable, it is not the only factor at work. Imagine the young eighth-grade girl who experienced the teacher's use of "you people" and the dancing stereotype as a racial affront. Upset and struggling with adolescent embarrassment, she bumps into a White friend who can see that something is wrong. She explains. Her White friend responds, in an effort to make her feel better perhaps, and says, "Oh, Mr. Smith is such a nice guy, I'm sure he didn't mean it like that. Don't be so sensitive." Perhaps the White friend is right and Mr. Smith didn't mean it, but imagine your own response when you are upset, perhaps with a spouse or partner. Your partner asks what's wrong and you explain why you are offended. In response, your partner brushes off your complaint, attributing it to your being oversensitive. What happens to your emotional thermostat? It escalates. When feelings, rational or irrational, are invalidated, most people disengage. They not only choose to discontinue the conversation but are more likely to turn to someone who will understand their perspective.

In much the same way, the eighth-grade girl's White friend doesn't get it. She doesn't see the significance of this racial message, but the girls at the "Black table" do. When she tells her story there, one of them is likely to say, "You know what, Mr. Smith said the same thing to me yesterday!" Not only are Black adolescents encountering racism and reflecting on their identity, but their White peers, even when they are not the perpetrators (and sometimes they are), are unprepared to respond in supportive ways. The Black students turn to each other for the much-needed support they are not likely to find anywhere else.

In adolescence, as race becomes personally salient for Black youth, finding the answer to questions such as, "What does it mean to be a young Black person? How should I act? What should I do?" is particularly important. And although Black fathers, mothers, aunts, and uncles may hold the answers by offering themselves as role models, they hold little appeal for most adolescents. The last thing many fourteen-year-olds want to do is to grow up to be like their parents. In their view, it is the peer group, the kids in the cafeteria, that holds the answers to these questions. They know how to be Black. They have absorbed the stereotypical images of Black youth in the popular culture and are reflecting those images in their self-presentation.

Based on their fieldwork in US high schools, Signithia Fordham and John Ogbu described a psychological pattern they observed among African American high school students at this stage of identity development.[30] They theorized that the anger and resentment that adolescents feel in response to their growing awareness of the systematic exclusion of Black people from full participation in US society leads to the development of an oppositional social identity. This oppositional stance both protects one's identity from the psychological assault of racism and keeps the dominant group at a distance. Fordham and Ogbu wrote:

> Subordinate minorities regard certain forms of behavior and certain activities or events, symbols, and meanings as not appropriate for them because those behaviors, events, symbols, and meanings are characteristic of white Americans. At the same time they emphasize other forms of behavior as more appropriate for them because these are not a part of white Americans' way of life. To behave in the manner defined as falling within a white cultural frame of reference is to "act white" and is negatively sanctioned.[31]

Certain styles of speech, dress, and music, for example, may be embraced as "authentically Black" and become highly valued, while attitudes and behaviors associated with Whites are viewed with disdain. The peer group's evaluation of what is Black and what is not can have a powerful impact on adolescent behavior.

Reflecting on her high school years, one Black woman from a White neighborhood described both the pain of being rejected by her Black classmates and her attempts to conform to her peers' definition of Blackness:

> "Oh you sound White, you think you're White," they said. And the idea of sounding White was just so absurd to me. . . . So ninth grade was sort of traumatic in that I started listening to rap music, which I really just don't like. [I said] I'm gonna be Black, and it was just that stupid. But it's more than just how one acts, you know. [The other Black women there] were not into me for the longest time. My first year there was hell.

Sometimes the emergence of an oppositional identity can be quite dramatic as the young person tries on a new persona almost overnight. At the end of one school year, race may not have appeared to be significant, but often some encounter takes place over the summer and the young person returns to school much more aware of his or her Blackness and ready to make sure that the rest of the world is aware of it, too. There is a certain in-your-face quality that these adolescents can take on, which their teachers often experience as threatening. When a group of Black teens are sitting together in the cafeteria, collectively embodying an oppositional stance, school administrators often want to know not only why they are sitting together but what can be done to prevent it. We need to understand that in racially mixed settings, racial grouping is a developmental process in response to an environmental stressor, racism. Joining with one's peers for support in the face of stress is a positive coping strategy. What *is* problematic is that the young people are operating with a very limited definition of what it means to be Black, based largely on cultural stereotypes.

## Oppositional Identity Development and Academic Achievement

Unfortunately for Black teenagers, those cultural stereotypes do not usually include academic achievement. Despite that fact, the majority of Black students (more than 85 percent) express a desire to go on to college or other postsecondary education.[32] Certainly their families want that for them, with almost 90 percent of low- and moderate-income African American parents indicating a desire for their children to earn a college degree, according to a recent UNCF study.[33] In fact, according to a Pew Research Center survey, African American and Hispanic parents are significantly more likely than White parents to say that it is essential that their children earn a college degree.[34] As has been the case historically, these parents of color see college education as the ticket to their children's life chances, yet too often their children's academic performance lags behind that of their White counterparts. Does the fear of being accused of "acting White" by one's peers play a role in the academic behavior of Black adolescents in the process of defining their REC-group identity?

Researchers have explored this question with mixed results. It seems that the variability in their findings might be explained by the variability in the school settings in which the research was conducted.[35] In studies investigating the link between academic performance and concerns about "acting White," researchers have found that school context matters. In the hypersegregated schools that many Black students now attend, Black students represent the top of the class as well as the bottom. In that context, adolescents may be labeled pejoratively as "acting White" because of speech patterns, style of dress, or musical tastes, but not likely because of their academic performance. Yet in the context of racially mixed high schools where the AP and IB classes are overwhelmingly, if not exclusively, White and the regular and special education classes are disproportionately Black and Hispanic, in the minds of the students who attend those schools, academic success can become part of the "acting White" label some Black students seek to avoid. In those schools, academic opportunity is too often correlated with being White.[36] This point is underscored by the research of Karolyn Tyson.

> Black students in my studies rarely equated whiteness with academic ability and/or high achievement unless patterns of achievement by race (and usually social class) in their own school settings were

stark. . . . A burden of acting white . . . was most relevant to black students in school settings where only Whites (usually wealthy Whites) or disproportionately few Blacks had opportunities to participate in higher-level programs and courses. . . . Students who had not experienced such explicit linking of race and achievement—those who attended all-black schools or schools that had more racially balanced classrooms—rarely recalled ever being accused of acting white specifically because of their achievement or achievement-related behaviors.[37]

Particularly in the context of schools where racial status has been linked to achievement, during the active exploration phase of REC identity development, when the search for identity leads toward cultural stereotypes and away from anything that might be associated with Whiteness, academic performance may decline. The response to the charge of "acting White" in this context can be a shift in attitude. Edward L., a seventeen-year-old student in Mickelson and Velasco's study, says, "I've seen this happen to a couple of people, like, to fit in, they'll just change their whole . . . their whole attitude . . . the way they dress, the way they think, they'll stop doing work, you know. They won't do any type of work, homework."[38] Most of the academically successful students they interviewed, however, described themselves as being able to brush off that kind of peer pressure, even though it made them uncomfortable.

What's going on with those Black students who are not academically successful? Of course, their REC identity is developing, too. But lack of school success may lead to defining identity through other means—being a good athlete, being cool or tough, becoming the class clown—and seeking affirmation in other ways. Everyone wants and needs affirmation. "Excelling in one or more of these areas provides an identity that elicits respect, fear, and/or admiration from other students and simultaneously diverts attention from low academic performance."[39] Tyson adds, "Ridiculing the high achievers is a way of regaining a sense of dignity and power in the face of their own disappointment and resentment. . . . When black students disproportionately experience low achievement in the context of disproportionate white high achievement, some emphasize their black authenticity, seeking dignity in racial solidarity."[40]

The Black college students I have interviewed, almost all of whom were raised in predominantly White communities, commonly described some conflict or alienation from other African American teens because of their academic success in high school. For example, a twenty-year-old woman from a Washington, DC, suburb explained: "It was weird, even in high school a lot of the Black students were, like, 'Well, you're not really Black.' Whether it was because I became president of the sixth-grade class or whatever it was, it started pretty much back then. Junior high, it got worse. I was then labeled certain things, whether it was 'the Oreo' or I wasn't really Black." Others described avoiding situations that would set them apart from their Black peers. For example, one young woman declined to participate in a gifted program in her school because she knew it would separate her from the other Black students in the school.

Academically successful Black students in racially mixed schools typically want to maintain acceptance among their Black peers, but they also need a strategy to find acceptance among their White classmates, particularly since they may be one of very few Blacks in their advanced classes. Fordham described one such strategy as *racelessness,* wherein individuals assimilate into the dominant group by de-emphasizing  characteristics that might identify them as members of the subordinate group.[41] Lawrence Otis Graham's son seemed to be using this strategy when he told his father why he did not want to report his racial encounter to the school authorities. "His chief concern was not wanting the white students and administrators to think of him as being special, different, or 'racial.' That was his word. 'If the other kids around here find out that I was called a nigger, and that I complained about it,' my son pleaded, 'then they will call me "racial," and will be thinking about race every time they see me. I can't have that.'"[42]

Jon, a young man I interviewed, offered a classic example of this strategy as he described his approach to dealing with his discomfort at being the only Black person in his advanced classes. He said, "At no

point did I ever think I was White or did I ever want to be White. . . .
I guess it was one of those things where I tried to de-emphasize the
fact that I was Black." This strategy led him to avoid activities that
were associated with Blackness. He recalled, "I didn't want to do anything that was traditionally Black, like I never played basketball. I ran
cross-country. . . . I went for distance running instead of sprints." He
felt he had to show his White classmates that there were "exceptions to
all these stereotypes." However, this strategy was of limited usefulness.
When he traveled outside his home community with his White teammates, he sometimes encountered overt racism. "I quickly realized that
I'm Black, and that's the thing that they're going to see first, no matter
how much I try to de-emphasize my Blackness."

A Black student can play down his or her Black identity in order
to succeed in school and mainstream institutions without rejecting his
or her Black identity and culture.[43] Instead of becoming raceless, an
achieving Black student can become an *emissary,* someone who sees his
 or her own achievements as advancing the cause of the racial group. For
example, social scientists Richard Zweigenhaft and G. William Domhoff describe how a successful Black student, in response to the accu-
sation of acting White, connected his achievement to those of other
Black men by saying, "Martin Luther King must not have been Black,
then, since he had a doctoral degree, and Malcolm X must not have
been Black since he educated himself while in prison." In addition, he
demonstrated his loyalty to the Black community by taking an openly
political stance against the racial discrimination he observed in his
school.[44]

Similarly, Mickelson and Velasco found that some of their interviewees were motivated by the challenge of "representing the race" in the
face of other people's projection of stereotypes.

They considered the acting-white label to be part of the insidious
legacy that impugned black people's intelligence. . . . They deliberately embraced the challenge to do well, to work hard, and to succeed to prove the doubters wrong. They knew they were intelligent,
they knew they could handle high-level classes, and they consciously

wanted to disprove any notion that black students were not as intellectually competent as white students. And they wanted to reclaim academic achievement as entirely consistent with acting black.[45]

These examples make clear that an oppositional identity can *potentially* interfere with academic achievement, but that is not always the case. There are alternative responses that can lead to academic success. It may be tempting for educators to blame the adolescents themselves for their academic disinterest, in instances where that occurs. However, the questions that educators and other concerned adults must ask are these: What is it about the curriculum and the culture of academic opportunity within the school that reinforces the notion that academic excellence is a largely White domain? What curricular interventions might we use to encourage the development of an empowered emissary identity?

## The Search for Alternative Images

An oppositional identity discouraging academic achievement is not inevitable even in a racist society. If young people are exposed to images of African American academic achievement in their early years, as they look ahead to see what older students are achieving or as they read about the accomplishments and contributions of a diverse group of women and men in their textbooks, they will be less likely to define school success as something for Whites only. They will know that there is a long history of Black intellectual achievement. In this context, some have speculated about the potentially positive impact of the Obama presidency on the aspirations and academic achievement of young Black youth who, during Obama's eight years in office, embraced President Obama and his wife, Michelle Obama, as role models and highly visible examples of Black academic achievement. During the 2008 campaign, teachers and students from a predominantly Black middle school in Washington, DC, were interviewed about this "Obama effect." One of the teachers, noticing an increase in homework completion, teared up as she described the positive changes she saw in her students during the

Obama campaign. "She said, 'It was really moving for me to hear students who don't typically do well in school speak of, you know, different things that they know they can do because of what Barack Obama has shown them.'"[46]

Though he came of age before the election of Barack Obama, the point about the importance of visible role models was made quite eloquently by Jon, the young man I quoted earlier. Though he made the choice to excel in school, he labored under the false assumption that he was "inventing the wheel." It wasn't until he reached college and had the opportunity to take African American studies courses that he learned about other African Americans besides Martin Luther King, Malcolm X, and Frederick Douglass—the same three men he had heard about year after year, from kindergarten to high school graduation. As he reflected on his identity struggle in high school, he said:

It's like I went through three phases. . . . My first phase was being cool, doing whatever was particularly cool for Black people at the time, and that was like in junior high. Then in high school, you know, I thought being Black was basically all stereotypes, so I tried to avoid all of those things. Now in college, you know, I realize that being Black means a variety of things.

Learning his history in college was of great psychological importance to Jon, providing him with role models he had been missing in high school. He was particularly inspired by learning of the intellectual legacy of Black men at his own college:

When you look at those guys who were here in the Twenties, they couldn't live on campus. They couldn't eat on campus. They couldn't get their hair cut in town. And yet they were all Phi Beta Kappa. . . . That's what being Black really is, you know, knowing who you are, your history, your accomplishments. . . . When I was in junior high, I had White role models. And then when I got into high school, you know, I wasn't sure but I just didn't think having White role models was a good thing. So I got rid of those. And I basically just, you know, only had my parents for role models. I kind of grew up thinking that we were on the cutting edge. We were doing something radically different than everybody else. And not realizing that there are all kinds of Black people doing the very things that I thought we were the only ones doing. . . . You've got to do the very best you can so that you can continue the great traditions that have already been established.

This young man was not alone in his frustration over having learned little about his own cultural history in grade school. Time and again in the research interviews I conducted, Black students lamented the absence of courses in African American history or literature at the high school level and indicated how significant this new learning was to them in college, how excited and affirmed they felt by this newfound knowledge. The comments they made to me are now echoed in the student demands for curricular inclusion that spread across college campuses so rapidly in 2015.[47] Sadly, many Black students never get to college, alienated from the process of education long before high school graduation. They may never get access to the information that might have helped them expand their definition of what it means to be Black and, in the process, might have helped them stay in school. Young people are developmentally ready for this information in adolescence. We ought to provide it. *representation in history in school matters*

## Not at the Table

As we have seen, Jon felt he had to distance himself from his Black peers in order to be successful in high school. He was one of the kids *not* sitting at the Black table. Continued encounters with racism and access to new, culturally relevant information empowered him to give up his racelessness and become an emissary. In college, not only did he sit at the Black table, but he emerged as a campus leader, confident in the support of his Black peers. His example illustrates that one's presence at the Black table is often an expression of one's identity development, which evolves over time.

Some Black students may not be developmentally ready for the Black table in middle school or high school. They may not yet have had their own encounters with racism, and race may not be very salient for them. Just as we don't all reach puberty and begin developing sexual interest at the same time, REC-group identity development unfolds in idiosyncratic ways. Though my research suggests that early adolescence is a common time for Black students to begin actively identifying with their REC group, one's own life experiences are also important determinants of the timing. Young people whose racial identity development is out of sync with their peers' often feel in an awkward position. Adolescents are notoriously egocentric and assume that their experience is the same as everyone else's. Just as girls who have become interested in boys become disdainful of their friends still interested in dolls, the Black teens who are at the table can be quite judgmental toward those who are not. "If I think it is a sign of authentic Blackness to sit at this table, then you should too."

The young Black men and women who still hang around with the White classmates they may have known since early childhood may be snubbed by their Black peers. This dynamic is particularly apparent in regional schools where children from a variety of neighborhoods are brought together. When Black children from predominantly White neighborhoods go to school with Black children from predominantly Black neighborhoods, the former group are often viewed as trying to be White by the latter. We all speak the language of the streets we live on. Black children living in White neighborhoods often sound White to their Black peers from across town and may be teased because of it. This can be a very painful experience, particularly when the young person is not fully accepted as part of the White peer group either.

One young Black woman from a predominantly White community described exactly this situation in an interview. In a school with a lot of racial tension, Terri felt that "the worst thing that happened" was the rejection she experienced from the other Black children who were being bused to her school. Though she wanted to be friends with them, they teased her, calling her an "Oreo cookie" and sometimes beating her up. The only close Black friend Terri had was a biracial girl from her neighborhood.

Racial tensions also affected her relationships with White students. One White friend's parents commented, "I can't believe you're Black. You don't seem like all the Black children. You're nice." Though other parents made similar comments, Terri reported that her White friends didn't start making them until junior high school, when Terri's Blackness became something to be explained. One friend introduced Terri to another White girl by saying, "She's not really Black, she just went to Florida and got a really dark tan." A White sixth-grade "boyfriend" became embarrassed when his friends discovered he had a crush on a Black girl. He stopped telling Terri how pretty she was and instead called her "nigger" and said, "Your lips are too big. I don't want to see you. I won't be your friend anymore."

Despite supportive parents who expressed concern about her situation, Terri said she was a "very depressed child." Her father would have conversations with her "about being Black and beautiful" and about "the union of people of color that had always existed that I needed to find. And the pride." However, her parents did not have a network of Black friends to help support her.

It was the intervention of a Black junior high school teacher that Terri feels helped her the most. Mrs. Campbell "really exposed me to the good Black community because I was so down on it" by getting Terri involved in singing gospel music and introducing her to other Black students who would accept her. "That's when I started having other Black friends. And I thank her a lot for that."

The significant role that Mrs. Campbell played in helping Terri open up illustrates the constructive potential that informed adults can have in the identity development process. She recognized Terri's need for a same-race peer group and helped her find one. Talking to groups of Black students about the variety of living situations Black people come from and the unique situation facing Black adolescents in White communities helps to expand the definition of what it means to be Black and increases intragroup acceptance at a time when that is quite important.

For children in Terri's situation, it is also helpful for Black parents to provide ongoing opportunities for their children to connect with other Black peers, even if that means traveling outside the community they live in. Race-conscious parents often do this by seeking out a historically Black church to attend or by maintaining ties to Black social organizations such as Jack and Jill. Parents who make this effort often find that their children become bicultural, able to move comfortably between Black and White communities and able to sit at the Black table when they are ready.

Implied in this discussion is the assumption that connecting with one's Black peers in the process of identity development is important and should be encouraged. For young Black people living in predominantly Black communities, such connections occur spontaneously with neighbors and classmates and usually do not require special encouragement. However, for young people in predominantly White communities, they may only occur with active parental intervention. One might wonder if this social connection is really necessary. If a young person has found a niche within a circle of White friends, is it really *necessary* to establish a Black peer group as a reference point? Maybe not, but it certainly helps.

As one's awareness of the daily challenges of living in a racist society increases, it is immensely beneficial to be able to share one's experiences with others who have lived them. Even when White friends are willing and able to listen and bear witness to one's struggles, they cannot really share the experience. One young woman came to this realization in her senior year of high school:

> [The isolation] never really bothered me until about senior year when I was the only one in the class. . . . That little burden, that constant burden of you always having to strive to do your best and show that you can do just as much as everybody else. Your White friends can't understand that, and it's really hard to communicate to them. Only someone else of the same racial, same ethnic background would understand something like that.

When one is faced with what Chester Pierce calls the "mundane extreme environmental stress" of racism, in adolescence or in adulthood, the ability to see oneself as part of a larger group from which one can draw support is an important coping strategy.[48] Individuals who do not have such a strategy available to them because they do not experience a shared identity with at least some subset of their racial group are at risk for considerable social isolation and depression.[49]

Of course, who we perceive as sharing our identity may be influenced by other dimensions of identity, such as gender, sexual orientation, social class, geographical location, skin color, or ethnicity. For example, research indicates that first-generation Black immigrants from the Caribbean tend to emphasize their national origins and ethnic identities, distancing themselves from US Blacks, due in part to their belief that West Indians are viewed more positively by Whites than those American Blacks whose family roots include the experience of US slavery. To relinquish one's ethnic identity as West Indian and take on an African American identity may be understood as downward social mobility.[50]

Also, immigrants from the Caribbean, as well as those from African countries, are from social contexts in which they were in the numerical majority and Blacks occupied positions of power, a legacy of European colonialism notwithstanding. Thus the racial socialization for African and Afro-Caribbean immigrants may be significantly different from that of American-born Blacks.[51] Second-generation Black immigrants, however, without an identifiable accent to mark them as foreigners, may lose the relative ethnic privilege their parents experienced. In that context, they may be more likely to seek racial solidarity with Black American peers in the face of encounters with racism.[52] Whether it is the experience of being followed in stores because they are suspected of shoplifting, seeing people respond to them with fear on the street, or feeling overlooked in school, Black youth can benefit from seeking support from those who have had similar experiences.

## An Alternative to the Cafeteria Table

The developmental need to explore the meaning of one's identity with others who are engaged in a similar process manifests itself informally in school corridors and cafeterias across the country. Some educational institutions have sought to meet this need programmatically with the creation of school-sponsored affinity groups.

Twenty years ago several colleagues and I evaluated one such effort, initiated at a Massachusetts middle school participating in a voluntary desegregation program known as the Metropolitan Council for Educational Opportunity (METCO) program.[53] The historical context for our evaluation was the fact that the small number of African American students who were being bused from Boston to this suburban school had achieved disappointing levels of academic success. In an effort to improve academic achievement, the school introduced a program, known as Student Efficacy Training (SET), that allowed Boston students to meet each day as a group with two staff members. Instead of being in physical education or home economics or study hall, they were meeting, talking about homework difficulties, social issues, and encounters with racism. The meeting was mandatory, and at first the students were resentful of missing some of their classes. But the impact was dramatic. Said one young woman,

> In the beginning of the year, I didn't want to do SET at all. It took away my study and it was only METCO students doing it. In the beginning all we did was argue over certain problems, or it was more like a rap session, and I didn't think it was helping anyone. But then when we looked at records . . . I know that last year out of all the students, sixth through eighth grade, there was, like, six who were actually good students. Everyone else, it was just pathetic, I mean, like, they were getting like Ds and Fs. . . . The eighth grade is doing much better this year. I mean, they went from Ds and Fs to Bs and Cs and occasional As. . . . And those seventh graders are doing really good, they have a lot of honor roll students in seventh grade, both guys and girls. Yeah, it's been good. It's really good.

Her report was borne out by an examination of school records. The opportunity to come together in the company of supportive adults allowed these young Black students to talk about the issues that hindered their performance—racial encounters, feelings of isolation, test anxiety, homework dilemmas—in the psychological safety of their own group. In the process, the peer culture changed to one that supported academic performance rather than undermined it, as revealed in these two students' comments:

> Well, a lot of the Boston students, the boys and the girls, used to fight all the time. And now, they stopped yelling at each other so much and calling each other stupid.

> It's like we've all become like one big family, we share things more with each other. We tease each other like brother and sister. We look out for each other with homework and stuff. We always stay on top of each other 'cause we know it's hard with African American students to go to a predominantly White school and try to succeed with everybody else.

The faculty, too, were very enthusiastic about the outcomes of the intervention, as seen in the comments of these two classroom teachers:

> This program has probably produced the most dramatic result of any single change that I've seen at this school. It has produced immediate results that affected behavior and academics and participation in school life.

> My students are more engaged. They aren't battling out a lot of the issues of their anger about being in a White community, coming in from Boston, where do I fit, I don't belong here. I feel that those issues that often came out in class aren't coming out in class anymore. I think they are being discussed in the SET room, the kids feel more confidence. The kids' grades are higher, the homework response is greater, they're not afraid to participate in class, and I don't see them isolating themselves within class. They are willing to sit with other students happily. . . . I think it's made a very positive impact on their place in the school and on their individual self-esteem. I see them enjoying themselves and able to enjoy all of us as individuals. I can't say enough, it's been the best thing that's happened to the METCO program as far as I'm concerned.[54]

Although this intervention is not a miracle cure for every school, it does highlight what can happen when we think about the developmental needs of Black adolescents who are coming to terms with their own sense of identity. It might seem counterintuitive that a school involved in a voluntary desegregation program could improve both academic performance and social relationships among students by *separating* the Black students for one period every day. But if we understand the unique challenges facing adolescents of color and the legitimate need they have to feel supported in their identity development, it makes perfect sense.

Though they may not use the language of racial identity development theory to describe it, most Black parents want their children to achieve an internalized sense of personal security, to be able to acknowledge the reality of racism and to respond effectively to it. Our educational institutions should do what they can to encourage this development rather than impede it. When I talk to educators about the need to provide adolescents with identity-affirming experiences and information about their own cultural groups, they sometimes flounder because this information has not been part of their own education. Their understanding of adolescent development has been limited to the White middle-class norms included in most textbooks; their knowledge of Black history limited to Martin Luther King Jr. and Rosa Parks. They sometimes say with frustration that parents should provide this kind of education for their children. Unfortunately Black parents often attended the same schools the teachers did and have the same informational gaps. We need to acknowledge that an important part of interrupting the cycle of oppression is constant reeducation, and then sharing what we learn with the next generation.

## Group Identity and Stereotype Threat

As we have seen, developing a strong and positive sense of group identity can be a source of psychological protection for members of stigmatized groups, particularly when the exploration of that identity has moved beyond the negative stereotypes to a more accurate and complete understanding of the strengths and assets of one's group. However, there is one context in which a strong identification with one's group can be a source of vulnerability, and that is in relationship to a condition known as stereotype threat. As defined by social psychologist Claude Steele, stereotype threat is "the threat of being viewed through the lens of a negative stereotype, or the fear of doing something that would inadvertently confirm that stereotype."[55] In essence, stereotype threat is a kind of performance anxiety that can impact academic performance because "[stigmatized students] must contend with the threatening possibility that should their performance falter, it could substantiate the racial stereotype's allegation of limited ability."[56]

Anyone can experience stereotype threat under the right circumstances. For example, researchers have shown that talented female math students perform less well on a "math ability" measure when they are told that their scores will be compared to those of men than they do when that information is not provided. White male golfers perform less well on a golf course when they are told their performance is part of a measure of "natural athletic ability" than they do when no such information is provided.[57] Two decades of research has demonstrated that when an individual identifies with a group (e.g., race or gender) as part of their social identity  and that group is stereotyped in negative ways, the person is at risk for lower performance relative to the stereotyped dimension of that identity.[58]

In the case of Black students, the more they identify with their group and the more invested they are in doing well academically, the more vulnerable they can become to stereotype threat.[59] They know that "intellectually inferior" is a stereotype about their group, and they want to disprove it. That added pressure can inhibit performance, especially in high-stakes testing situations.

How does stereotype threat impede test-taking performance for Black students? In some of the research Steele and his colleagues conducted, computers were used to administer standardized tests, which allowed the researchers to study the test-taking behavior of the students in some detail. They found that:

Black students taking the test under stereotype threat seemed to be trying too hard rather than not hard enough. They reread the questions, reread the multiple choices, rechecked their answers, more than when they were not under stereotype threat. The threat made them inefficient on a test that, like most standardized tests, is set up so that thinking long often means thinking wrong, especially on difficult items like the ones we used.[60]

This result was particularly noted when students were asked to check a box indicating their racial group membership before taking the test. The act of checking the box brought racial-group membership (and resulting performance anxiety) to mind. When they were administered the same test without being asked to designate their race at the beginning, stereotype threat was not triggered and their performance on the test was significantly better—in fact, it equaled the performance of White peers taking the same exam.[61]

 Any situation in which the stigmatized identity is made more salient for the individual is likely to induce stereotype threat—not just in test-taking situations but in daily life, like being the only Black student in an advanced math or science class, for example. The student in such a circumstance is likely to have a heightened awareness of being "the only one."[62] However, there are strategies that caring adults (family members as well as educators) can use to reduce the impact of stereotype threat to the benefit of young people. Providing role models from the stigmatized group whose achievement defies the stereotypes is one important strategy. Indeed, researchers found that having a strong racial identity was most helpful to young Black girls and their academic success only when that identification included a belief that being African American is associated with achievement.[63] In my former role as the president of Spelman College, the oldest historically Black college for women, I witnessed daily the inspirational power of an environment where Black women were surrounded by examples of African American academic achievement, past and present, leading to exceptionally high rates of success in STEM fields, where Black women have historically been most underrepresented.[64]

What is hopeful about our growing understanding of stereotype threat and related theories is that they can guide us to change how we teach and what we say. As Steele puts it: "Although stereotypes held by the larger society may be hard to change, it is possible to create educational niches in which negative stereotypes are not felt to apply—and which permit a sense of trust that would otherwise be difficult to sustain."[65] Receiving honest feedback you can trust as unbiased is critical to reducing stereotype threat and improving academic performance. How you establish that trust with the possibility of stereotype swirling around is the question. The key to doing this seems to be found in clearly communicating both high standards *and* assurance of belief in the student's capacity to reach those standards.

Again, Claude Steele, this time joined by Geoffrey Cohen, offers important insights. To investigate how a teacher might gain the trust of a student when giving feedback across racial lines, they created a scenario in which Black and White Stanford University students were asked to write essays about a favorite teacher. The students were told that the essays would be considered for publication in a journal about teaching and that they would receive feedback from a reviewer who they were led to believe was White. A Polaroid snapshot was taken of each student and attached to the essay as it was turned in, signaling to the students that the reviewer would be able to identify the race of the essay writer. Several days later the students returned to receive the reviewer's comments, with the opportunity to "revise and resubmit" the essay. What was varied in the experiment was how the feedback was delivered.

When the feedback was given in a constructive but critical manner, Black students were more suspicious than white students that the feedback was racially biased, and consequently, the Black students were less likely than the White students to rewrite the essay for further consideration. The same was true when the critical feedback was buffered by an opening statement praising the essay, such as "There were many good things about your essay." However, when the feedback was introduced by a statement that conveyed a high standard (reminding the writer that the essay had to be of publishable quality) and high expectations (assuring the student of the reviewer's belief that with effort and attention to the feedback, the standard could be met), the Black students not only responded positively by revising the essays and resubmitting them, but they did so at a higher rate than the White students in the study.[66]

The particular combination of the explicit communication of high standards and the demonstrated assurance of the teacher's belief in the student's ability to succeed (as evidenced by the effort to provide detailed, constructive feedback) was a powerful intervention for Black students. Describing this two-pronged approach as "wise criticism," Cohen and Steele demonstrated that it was an exceedingly effective way to generate the trust needed to motivate Black students to make their best effort. Even though the criticism indicated that a major revision of the essay would be required to achieve the publication standard, Black students who received "wise criticism" felt ready to take on the challenge, and did. Indeed, "they were more motivated than any other group of students in the study—as if this combination of high standards and assurance was like water on parched land, a much needed but seldom received balm."[67]

Another factor in how stereotype threat is experienced has to do with how students think about their own abilities. Many students, like many teachers, believe intelligence (or lack of it) is a fixed, unchanging characteristic. Years of family members, friends, and teachers remarking, "What a smart boy/girl you are!" certainly reinforces this personal "entity theory" of intelligence. The alternative view of intelligence as changeable—as something that can be developed over time—is less commonly fostered, but it can be. Educator Verna Ford has summed up this alternative theory for use with young children quite succinctly: "Think you can—work hard—get smart."[68]

Educational psychologist Carol Dweck's research suggests that young people who hold the "entity" belief in fixed intelligence see academic setbacks as an indicator of limited ability. They are highly invested in appearing smart and consequently avoid tasks on which their performance might suggest otherwise. Rather than exerting more effort to improve their performance, they are likely to conclude "I'm not good at that subject" and move on to something else. Students who view intelligence as malleable—an "incremental theory"—are more likely to see academic setbacks as a sign that more effort is needed and then exert that effort. They are more likely to face challenges head-on rather than avoid them in an effort to preserve a fixed definition of oneself as "smart."[69] The incremental theory of intelligence as malleable—something that expands as the result of effective effort—fosters an academic resilience that serves its believers well.

Researchers Aronson, Fried, and Good wondered if a personal theory of intelligence as malleable might foster a beneficial academic resilience for students of color vulnerable to stereotype threat. Specifically, they speculated that if Black students believed that their intellectual capacity was not fixed but expandable through their own effort, the negative stereotypes that others hold about their intellectual ability might be less damaging to their academic performance. To introduce this alternative view of intelligence, they designed a study in which Black and White college students were recruited to serve as pen-pal mentors to disadvantaged elementary school students. The task of the college students was to write letters of encouragement to their young mentees, urging them to do their best in school. However, one group of college students was instructed to tell their mentees to think of intelligence as something that was expandable through effort, and in preparation for writing the letters, they were given compelling information, drawn from contemporary research in psychology and neuroscience, about how the brain itself can be modified and expanded by new learning. The real subjects of the study, however, were the college students, not their pen pals. Although the letter writing was done in a single session, the college students exposed to the malleable theory of intelligence seemed to benefit from exposure to the new paradigm. Both Black and White students who learned about the malleability of intelligence improved their grades more than did students who did not receive this information. The benefit was even more striking for Black students, who reported enjoying academics more, saw academics as more important, and had significantly higher grades at the end of the academic quarter than those Black students who had not been exposed to this brief but powerful intervention.[70]

What worked with college students also worked with seventh graders. Lisa Sorich Blackwell, Kali Trzesniewski, and Carol Dweck created an opportunity for some seventh-grade students in New York City to read and discuss a scientific article about how intelligence develops and its malleability. A comparable group of seventh-grade students did not learn this information but read about memory and mnemonic strategies instead. Those students who learned about the malleability of intelligence subsequently demonstrated higher academic motivation, better academic behavior, and higher grades in mathematics than those who learned about memory. Interestingly, girls, who have been shown to be vulnerable to gender stereotypes about math performance, did as well as or better than boys in math following the intelligence-is-malleable intervention, while girls in the other group performed well below the boys in math. As was the case with the Aronson, Fried, and Good study, the intervention with the seventh graders was quite brief—in this case only three hours—yet the impact was significant.[71]

The outcomes of numerous studies lead to this conclusion: "By encouraging students to adopt a malleable view of intelligence—either through directly teaching students about this perspective or by creating learning environments that embrace the incremental view rather than entity view of intelligence—we can help students overcome stereotype threat."[72] We can shift a student's focus from the anxiety of *proving ability* in the face of negative stereotypes to the confidence of *improving with effort* despite the negative stereotypes. Embracing a theory of intelligence as something that can develop—that can be expanded through effective effort—is something all of us can do to reduce the impact of stereotype threat and increase the achievement of all of our students.

# FIVE

# Racial Identity in Adulthood

*"Still a work in progress . . . "*

When I was in high school, I did not sit at the Black table in the cafeteria because there were not enough Black kids in my high school to fill one. Though I was naive about many things, I knew enough about social isolation to know that I needed to get out of town. As the child of college-educated parents and an honor student myself, it was expected that I would go on to college. My mother suggested Howard University, my parents' alma mater, but although it was a good suggestion, I had my own ideas. I picked Wesleyan University in Middletown, Connecticut. It was two hours from home, an excellent school, and of particular interest to me was that it had a critical mass of Black and Latinx students, most of whom were male. Wesleyan had just gone coed, and the ratio of Black male students to Black female students was seven to one. I thought it would improve my social life, and it did.

I thrived socially and academically. Since I had decided in high school to be a psychologist, I was a psychology major, but I took a lot of African American studies courses—history, literature, religion, even Black child development. I studied Swahili in hopes of traveling to Tanzania, although I never went. I stopped straightening my hair and had a large Afro à la Angela Davis circa 1970. I happily sat at the Black table in the dining hall every day. I look back on my days at Wesleyan with great pleasure. I maintain many of the friendships I formed there, and I can't remember the name of one White classmate. I don't say that with pride or malice. It is just a fact.[1]

I was having what William Cross might call an "immersion experience." I had my racial encounters in high school, so when I got to college I was ready to explore my Black identity, and I did so wholeheartedly. Typically this process of active exploration of REC identity is characterized by a strong desire to surround oneself with symbols of one's racial-ethnic identity and actively seek out opportunities to learn about one's own history and culture with the support of same-REC peers. While anger toward Whites is often characteristic of the adolescent phase, particularly in response to encounters with racism, during the immersion phase of active exploration, the developing Black person is likely to see White people as simply irrelevant. This is not to say that anger is totally absent, but the focus of attention is on self-discovery rather than on White people. If I had spent a lot of time being angry with the White men and women I encountered at Wesleyan, I would remember them. The truth is, I wasn't paying much attention to them. My focus was almost exclusively on exploring my own cultural connections.

The Black person in this identity phase of active exploration is energized by the new information he or she is learning—angry perhaps that it wasn't available sooner, but excited to find out that there is more to Africa than Tarzan movies and that there is more to Black history than victimization. In many ways, the person is unlearning the internalized stereotypes about his or her own group and is redefining a positive sense of self based on an affirmation of one's racial group identity. Feeling good about one's group (sometimes referred to as positive "private regard" or "group esteem") is an important outcome of the REC-identity development process. "The positive affect that individuals feel toward their ethnic-racial group is a critical component of ethnic-racial identity (ERI) and has been demonstrated to be associated with positive adjustment across different developmental periods."[2]

Ideally, one emerges from this process of active exploration with an achieved sense of security about and commitment to one's REC identity. As positive group esteem rises, the individual finds ways to translate a personal sense of REC identity into ongoing action, the tangible result of understanding that sense of shared destiny or common fate with one's REC group.[3] The rallying of Black students behind the "Black Lives Matter" slogan on campuses across the country is a contemporary example of that sense of commitment in action. Though during the period of active exploration the young adult's focus may have been turned inward, away from members of the dominant group, the result of the process often includes a willingness to establish meaningful relationships across group boundaries with others, including Whites, who are respectful of this new self-definition.

In my own life, I see this growth process clearly. I left Wesleyan anchored in my empowered sense of Blackness. I went off to graduate school at the University of Michigan and quickly became part of an extensive network of Black graduate students, but I did have a few White friends, too. I even remember their names. But there were also White people that I chose not to associate with, people who weren't ready to deal with me in terms of my self-definition. Throughout my adult life I have had a racially mixed group of friends, and I am glad to model that inclusivity for my children. My choice of research topics throughout my career reflects my concerns about my racial group. I like to think that I both perceive and transcend race, but I am still a work in progress. I know that from time to time I have revisited this process of development in response to new racial incidents in my life or in the lives of my children.

Sometimes I find it helpful to compare this growth process to learning another language. The best way to learn a second language is to travel to a place where it is spoken and experience complete immersion. Once you have achieved the level of proficiency you need, you can leave. If you worked hard to become conversant, you will of course take pride in your accomplishment and will not want to spend time with people who disparage your commitment to this endeavor. You may choose not to speak this new language all the time, but if you want to maintain your skill, you will need to speak it often with others who understand it.

Though the cultural symbols for the current generation of young adults may not be the same as for mine, the process of REC-identity exploration is quite similar. Black students practice their "language" in

Black student unions and cultural centers and at college dining halls on predominantly White campuses all over the United States. And they should not be discouraged from doing so. Like the Black middle school students from Boston, they need safe spaces to retreat to and regroup in the process of dealing with the daily stress of campus racism.

That life is stressful for Black students and other students of color on predominantly White campuses should not come as a surprise, but it often does. White students and faculty frequently underestimate the power and presence of the overt and covert manifestations of racism on campus, and students of color often come to predominantly White campuses expecting more civility than they find. Whether it is the loneliness of being routinely overlooked as a lab partner in science courses, the irritation of being continually asked by curious classmates about Black hairstyles, the discomfort of being singled out by a professor to give the "Black perspective" in class discussion, the pain of racist graffiti scrawled on dormitory room doors, the insult of racist jokes circulated through campus e-mail, or the injury inflicted by racial epithets (and sometimes beer bottles) hurled from a passing car, Black students on predominantly White college campuses must cope with ongoing affronts to their racial identity. The desire to retreat to safe space is understandable. Sometimes that means leaving the campus altogether.

For example, one young woman I interviewed at Howard University explained why she had transferred from a predominantly White college to a historically Black one. Assigned to share a dormitory room with two White girls, both of whom were from rural White communities, she was insulted by the assumptions her White roommates made about her. Conflict erupted between them when she was visited by her boyfriend, a young Black man. "They put padlocks on their doors and their dressers. And they accused me of drinking all their beers. And I was like, 'We don't drink. This doesn't make any sense.' So what really brought me to move out of that room was when he left, I came back, they were scrubbing things down with Pine Sol. I was like, 'I couldn't live here with you. You think we have germs or something?'"

She moved into a room with another Black woman, the first Black roommate pair in the dormitory. The administration had discouraged

Black pairings because they didn't want Black students to separate themselves. She and her new roommate got along well, but they became targets of racial harassment.

> All of a sudden we started getting racial slurs like "South Africa will strike. Africans go home." And all this other stuff. I knew the girls who were doing it. They lived all the way down the hall. And I don't understand why they were doing it. We didn't do anything to them. But when we confronted them they acted like they didn't know anything. And my friends, their rooms were getting trashed. . . . One day I was asleep and somebody was trying to jiggle the lock trying to get in. And I opened the door and chased this girl down the hallway.

Though she said the college administration handled the situation and the harassers were eventually asked to leave, the stress of these events had taken its toll. At the end of her first year, she transferred to Howard.

While stressful experiences can happen at any college, and social conflicts can and do erupt among Black students at Black colleges as well, there is considerable evidence that Black students at historically Black colleges and universities achieve higher academic performance, enjoy greater social involvement, and aspire to higher occupational goals than their peers do at predominantly White institutions.[4] For example, according to data from the National Science Foundation, Spelman College, a historically Black college for women, sends more Black women on to earn PhDs in the sciences than any other undergraduate institution.[5]

In 1992, drawing on his analysis of data from the National Study on Black College Students, Walter Allen offered this explanation of the difference in student outcomes.

> On predominantly White campuses, Black students emphasize feelings of alienation, sensed hostility, racial discrimination, and lack of integration. On historically Black campuses, Black students emphasize feelings of engagement, connection, acceptance, and extensive support and encouragement. Consistent with accumulated evidence

on human development, these students, like most human beings, develop best in environments where they feel valued, protected, accepted, and socially connected. The supportive environments of historically Black colleges communicate to Black students that it is safe to take the risks associated with intellectual growth and development. Such environments also have more people who provide Black students with positive feedback, support, and understanding, and who communicate that they care about the students' welfare.[6]

Nearly twenty-five years later, a national study of fifty thousand Black college alumni reported very similar findings. Black graduates of historically Black colleges were much more likely to have felt supported by a faculty member or mentor while in college and were more likely to be thriving financially and in terms of overall well-being than their Black peers who graduated from predominantly White institutions, according to a Gallup / Purdue University study. The researchers wrote, "The profoundly different experiences that black graduates of HBCUs and black graduates of non-HBCUs are having in college leave the HBCU graduates feeling better prepared for life after graduation, potentially leading them to live vastly different lives outside of college."[7]

While these and Allen's earlier findings make a compelling case for Black student enrollment at historically Black colleges, the proportion of Black students entering predominantly White institutions (PWI) continues to increase.[8] It is certainly possible to have a great learning experience at a PWI, as I did. Yet as negative campus interactions increase, as they did dramatically after the 2016 presidential election, predominantly White colleges concerned about attracting and retaining Black students must take seriously the psychological toll extracted from students of color in inhospitable environments and the critical role that cultural space can play. Having a place to be rejuvenated and to feel anchored in one's cultural community increases the possibility that one will have the energy to achieve academically as well as participate in the cross-group dialogue and interaction many colleges want to encourage. If White students or faculty do not understand why Black or

Latinx or Asian cultural centers are necessary, then they can be helped to understand.[9]

## Not for College Students Only

Once when I described the process of racial identity development at a workshop session, a young Black man stood up and said, "You make it sound like if you don't go to college you have to stay stuck [in your development]." It was a good observation. Though the college years are likely to provide consciousness-raising experiences in classrooms or through cocurricular interactions with a new set of peers,[10] identity development does not have to happen in college. *The Autobiography of Malcolm X* provides a classic example of consciousness-raising that occurred while he was in prison. As he began to read books about Black history and was encouraged by older Black inmates, Malcolm X began to redefine for himself what it meant to be a Black man. As he said in his autobiography,

> The teachings of Mr. Muhammad stressed how history had been "whitened"— when white men had written history books, the black man had simply been left out. Mr. Muhammad couldn't have said anything that would have struck me much harder. I had never forgotten how when my class, me and all of those whites, had studied seventh-grade United States history back in Mason, the history of the Negro had been covered in one paragraph. . . .
>
> This is one reason why Mr. Muhammad's teachings spread so swiftly all over the United States, among *all* Negroes, whether or not they became followers of Mr. Muhammad. The teachings ring true. . . . You can hardly show me a black adult in America—or a white one, for that matter—who knows from the history books anything like the truth about the black man's role. In my own case, once I heard of the "glorious history of the black man," I took special pains to hunt in the library for books that would inform me on details about black history.[11]

Malcolm's period of immersion included embracing the teachings of the Nation of Islam. Though Malcolm X later rejected the Nation's teachings in favor of the more racially inclusive message of orthodox Islam, his initial response to the Nation's message of Black empowerment and self-reliance was very enthusiastic.

One reason the Nation of Islam continues to appeal to some urban Black youth, many of whom are not in college, is that it offers another expanded, positive definition of what it means to be Black. In particular, the clean-shaven, well-groomed representatives of the Nation who can be seen on city streets in Black neighborhoods emphasizing personal responsibility and Black community development offer a compelling contrast to the pervasive stereotypes of Black men.

The hunger for positive expressions of identity can be seen in the response of many Black men to the Nation of Islam's organization of the Million Man March in October of 1995. The march can be understood as a major immersion event for every Black man who was there, and vicariously for those who were not. Author Michael Eric Dyson expressed this significance quite clearly: "As I stood at the Million Man March, I felt the powerful waves of history wash over me. There's no denying that this march connected many of the men—more than a million, I believe—to a sense of racial solidarity that has largely been absent since the '60s. I took my son to Washington so that he could feel and see, drown in, even, an ocean of beautiful black brothers."[12] It was an affirming and definition-expanding event for Black men. And despite the White commentators who offered their opinions about the march on television, it seemed to me that, for the participants, White people were that day irrelevant.

Twenty years later, in October of 2015, thousands of people, most of whom were Black men, gathered on the National Mall in Washington, DC, again in hopes of recapturing that empowering sense of solidarity. Among them was Reverend Ronald Bell Jr., a thirty-four-year-old pastor from Wilmington, Delaware, who at fourteen had attended the 1995 march with his father, Reverend Ronald Bell Sr. It made a significant impression on him then. "Just to see all those strong black men in one spot does something to you," said Bell, who heads Wilmington's

Arise congregation. Holding his four-year-old son's hand, he said, "I hope he gets the experience I did 20 years ago with just the visual that we are strong. That we may not be where we thought we'd be 20 years later but we're still strong."[13]

The need for space in which those who are subject to societal stigmatization—"low public regard"—can come together to construct a positive self-definition is, of course, also important for Black women. In her book *Black Feminist Thought*, Patricia Hill Collins identifies various ways that Black women have found to create such space in or out of the academy. "One location," she writes, "involves Black women's relationships with one another. In some cases, such as friendships and family interactions, these relationships are informal, private dealings among individuals. In others, . . . more formal organizational ties have nurtured powerful Black women's communities."[14] Whether in the context of mother-daughter relationships, small social networks, Black churches, or Black women's clubs and sororities, space is created for resisting stereotypes and creating positive identities.

Though Black churches can sometimes be criticized as purveyors of the dominant ideology, as evidenced in Eurocentric depictions of Jesus and sexist assumptions about the appropriate role of women, it is also true that historically Black churches have been the site for organized resistance against oppression and a place of affirmation for African American adults as well as for children. The National Survey of Black Americans, the largest collection of survey data on Black Americans to date, found very high rates of religious participation among Blacks in general and among women in particular.[15] The survey respondents clearly indicated the positive role that the churches had played in both community development and psychological and social support.[16] Many Black churches with an Afrocentric perspective are providing the culturally relevant information for which Black adults hunger. For example, in some congregations an informational African American history moment is part of the worship service and Bible study includes a discussion of the Black presence in the Bible. As these examples suggest, there are sources of information within Black communities that speak to the identity development needs of both young and older adults, but there is still a need for more.

## Cycles of Racial-Ethnic-Cultural Identity Development

The process of REC-identity development, often emerging in adolescence and continuing into adulthood, is not so much linear as circular. It's like moving up a spiral staircase: as you proceed up each level, you have a sense that you have passed this way before, but you are not in exactly the same spot. Moving through the immersion phase of intense and focused exploration to the internalization of an affirmed and secure sense of group identity does not mean there won't be new and unsettling encounters with racism or the recurring desire to retreat to the safety of one's same-race peer group, or that identity questions that supposedly were resolved won't need to be revisited as life circumstances change.

It is also important to note that not every Black person experiences every aspect of the REC-identity process described here. Some people may find that other dimensions of their identity are simply more salient for them, and their REC-group membership may remain relatively unexplored.[17] People of any educational background can get "stuck" without engaging in the active exploration that leads to more growth. In the language of James Marcia (discussed in Chapter 4), some may enter adulthood with a diffuse REC identity (little active exploration and no real psychological commitment to one's REC group) or a foreclosed REC identity (accepting what others, such as parents, have defined without any active exploration of one's own). For some, perhaps other dimensions of identity have been more salient (e.g., gender, religion, sexual orientation), becoming the focus of their psychological energy. In a longitudinal study of a diverse group of college students, researchers at the University of California, Santa Cruz, found that the ability to make connections across multiple domains of personal and social identity grew over time. "Typically during their first year, participants discussed the domains of personal and social identity . . . in relative isolation even when prompted by interview questions to discuss the connections between them. Such was not the case in senior interviews, when most spontaneously made these connections."[18]

In his classic article "Cycles of Psychological Nigrescence," counseling psychologist Thomas Parham expanded on Cross' original model of racial identity development to explore the kind of changes in REC identity that a Black person might experience throughout the life cycle, not just in adolescence or early adulthood.[19] For example, during middle adulthood, that broad span of time between the midthirties and the midfifties, individuals regardless of race come to terms with new physical, psychological, and social challenges. This period in the life span is characterized by changing bodies (gaining weight, thinning or graying hair, waning energy), increasing responsibilities (including rearing children and grandchildren and caring for aging parents), continuing employment concerns, and, often, increasing community involvement. In addition, Levinson argues that adults at midlife fluctuate between periods of stability and transition as they reexamine previous life decisions and commitments and choose to make minor or major changes in their lives.[20] What role does REC identity play for Black adults at midlife?

Parham argues that "the middle-adulthood period of life may be the most difficult time to struggle with racial identity because of one's increased responsibilities and increased potential for opportunities."[21] Those whose work or lifestyle places them in frequent contact with Whites are aware that their ability to "make it" depends in large part on their ability and willingness to conform to those values and behaviors that have been legitimated by White culture. While it is unlikely that the lack of racial awareness that characterizes a young adolescent who has yet to have identity-triggering experiences would be found in a Black adult at midlife, some Black adults may have consciously chosen to retreat from actively identifying with other Blacks. These adults may have adopted a "raceless" persona as a way of winning the approval of White friends and coworkers.

In terms of child-rearing, adults who have distanced themselves from their REC group are likely to de-emphasize their children's racial group membership as well. This attitude is captured in the comment of one father I interviewed who said that his children's peer group was "basically non-Black." Unlike other parents, who told me that they felt it was important that their children have Black friends and were regretful when they did not, this father said, "I think it's more important that they have a socioeconomic group than a racial peer group."[22] In this case, class identification seemed more salient than racial identification.

Those adults who have adopted a strategy of racelessness may experience racial encounters in middle adulthood with particular emotional intensity. Because of the increased family responsibilities and financial obligations associated with this stage of life, the stakes are higher and the frustration particularly intense when a promotion is denied, a dream house is unattainable, or a child is racially harassed at school. Parham distinguishes between these "achievement-oriented" stresses of the upwardly mobile middle class and the "survival-related" stresses experienced by poor and working-class Blacks. However, he concludes that, regardless of a person's social status, "if an individual's sense of affirmation is sought through contact with and validation from Whites, then the struggle with one's racial identity is eminent."[23]

Survival stress is described by another father I interviewed who was worried not about promotions but about simply holding on to what he had already achieved:

> Just being Black makes it hard, because people look at you like you're not as good as they are, like you're a second-class citizen, something like that. You got to always look over your shoulder like somebody's always watching you. At my job, I'm the only Black in my department and it seems like they're always watching me, the pressure's always on to perform. You feel like if you miss a day, you might not have a job. So there's that constant awareness on my part, they can snatch what little you have, so that's a constant fear, you know, especially when you have a family to support. . . . So I'm always aware of what can happen.[24]

The chronically high rates of Black unemployment form the backdrop for this man's fear. Under such circumstances, he is unlikely to speak up against the discrimination or racial hostility he feels.

While some adults struggle (perhaps in vain) to hold on to a "raceless" persona, other midlife adults express their racial identity through race-conscious, REC-group-affirming attitudes. On the job, they may be open advocates of institutional change, or because of survival concerns, they may feel constrained in how they express their anger. One male interviewee, working in a human service agency, fluctuated between being silent and speaking up:

> It's very difficult, and dealing with all the negative problems, and then going back and fighting the administration of the department that you're working in, and fighting the racism, and squabbling of White males as well as White females, it's really difficult, and one becomes programmed to be a little bit hard, but then in order to survive, you've got to control it, and generally I stay pretty much out of trouble. It's just like playing a game in order to survive.[25]

This man's experience was echoed in a study of Black professional workers in a variety of different occupations conducted by sociologist Adia Harvey Wingfield. She found that these adults had to manage their emotions carefully in order to be successful in the workplace. "In particular, black professionals had to be very careful to show conviviality and pleasantness, even—especially—in response to racial issues."[26] Though they may work in predominantly White settings, not unlike Black college students sitting together in the cafeteria, African American adults who are again actively exploring what it means to be Black in the context of a stressful work environment, for example, are likely to choose to spend most of their nonwork time in the company of other Black people.

Adults who have achieved a positive sense of REC identity are likely to be proactively race-conscious about their children's socialization experiences, often choosing to live in a Black community. If the demographics of their geographic area do not permit such a choice, they will, in contrast to "raceless" parents, actively seek out Black playmates for their children wherever they can find them. One mother explained, "I'm not opposed to my child interacting with White children or kids of any other race, but I want them to have a Black peer group just for the sense of commonality, and sharing some of the same experiences, and just not losing that identity of themselves."[27]

Individuals who have achieved resolution and have internalized their REC-group identity may also take a race-conscious perspective on child-rearing, but they may also have a multiracial social network. Yet, anchored in an empowered sense of racial identity, they make clear to others that their racial identity is important to them and that they expect it to be acknowledged. The White person who makes the mistake of saying, "Gee, I don't think of you as Black" will undoubtedly be corrected. However, the inner security experienced by adults at this stage often translates into a style of interaction that allows them to bridge racial differences more easily than those adults still struggling with the REC-identity-related challenge.

Summarizing Parham's concept of "identity recycling," Cross and Cross write, "With age and experience it is inevitable for a new challenge to arise that exposes the limits of one's foundational identity. . . . One must effectively process the challenge to resolution."[28] Some of the recycling that occurs in midlife is precipitated by observing the REC-identity processes of one's children. Parham suggests that "parents may begin to interpret the consequences of their lifestyle choices (i.e., sending their children to predominantly White schools, living in predominantly White neighborhoods) through their children's attitudes and behaviors and become distressed at what they see and hear from [them]."[29] For example, a Black professor struggling with guilt over his choice to live in a predominantly White community suggested to his daughter that she should have more Black friends. She replied, "Why do I have to have Black friends? Just because I'm Black?" He admitted to himself that he was more concerned about her peer group than she was. When he told her that she could "pay a price" for having a White social life, she replied, "Well, Daddy, as you always like to say, nothing is free."[30]

The process of reexamining racial identity can continue even into late adulthood. According to Erikson, the challenge of one's later years is to be able to reflect on one's life with a sense of integrity rather than despair.[31] Although racism continues to impact the lives of the elderly—affecting access to quality health care and adequate pension funds, for example—Black retirees have fairly high levels of morale.[32] Those who approach the end of their lives with a positive, well-internalized sense of REC identity are likely to reflect on life with that sense of integrity intact.

Just as group identity for people of color unfolds over the life span, so do gender, sexual, and religious identities, to name a few. Cross reminds us that "the work of internalization does not stop with the resolution of conflicts surrounding racial/cultural identity." Referring to the work of his colleague Bailey Jackson, he adds that racial identity development should be viewed as "a process during which a single dimension of a person's complex, layered identity is first isolated, for purposes of revitalization and transformation, and then, at Internalization, reintegrated into the person's total identity matrix."[33] Unraveling and reweaving the identity strands of our experience is a never-ending task in a society where important dimensions of our lives are shaped by the simultaneous forces of subordination and domination. We continue to be works in progress for a lifetime.

## The Corporate Cafeteria

When I told my sister I was writing a book called *Why Are All the Black Kids Sitting Together in the Cafeteria?* she said, "Good, then maybe people will stop asking me about it." My sister spends her time not at a high school or college campus but in a corporate office. Even in corporate cafeterias, Black men and women are sitting together, and for the same reason. As we have seen, even mature adults sometimes need to connect with someone who looks like them and who shares the same experiences.

It might be worth considering here why the question is asked at all. In *A Tale of "O,"* psychologist Rosabeth Moss Kanter offers some insight. She highlights what happens to the O, the token, in a world of Xs.[34] In corporate America, Black people are still in the O position. One consequence of being an O, Kanter points out, is heightened visibility. When an O walks in the room, the Xs notice. Whatever the O does, positive or negative, stands out because of this increased visibility. It is hard for an O to blend in. When several Os are together, the attention of the Xs is really captured. Without the tokens present in the room, the Xs go about their business, perhaps not even noticing that they are all Xs. But when the O walks in, the Xs are suddenly self-conscious about their X-ness. In the context of race relations, when the Black people are sitting together, the White people notice and become self-conscious about being White in a way that they were not before. In part, the question reflects that self-consciousness. What does it say about the White people if the Black people are all sitting together? A White person may wonder, "Am *I* being excluded? Are they talking about me? Are my own racial stereotypes and perhaps racial fears being stimulated?"

Particularly in work settings, where people of color are isolated and often in the extreme minority, the opportunities to connect with peers of color are few and far between. White people are often unaware of how stressful such a situation can be. There are many situations where White people may say and do things that are upsetting to people of color. For example, a Black woman working in a school district where she was one of few Black teachers—and the only one in her building—was often distressed by the comments she heard her White colleagues making about Black students. As a novice, untenured teacher, she needed support and mentoring from her colleagues but felt alienated from them because of their casually expressed prejudices. When participating in a workshop for educators, she had the chance to talk in a small group made up entirely of Black educators and was able to vent her feelings and ask for help from her more-experienced colleagues about how to cope with this situation. Though such opportunities may not occur daily, as in a cafeteria, they are important for psychological survival in such situations.

In fact, more and more organizations are creating opportunities for these meetings to take place, providing time, space, and refreshments for people of color and other underrepresented groups (e.g., women, people with disabilities, those who identify as LGBTQ) to get together for networking and support. Some corporate leaders have found that such interventions (sometimes called "affinity groups" or "employee resource groups"), particularly when championed by a senior executive, support the recruitment, retention, and heightened productivity of their employees.[35] Like the SET program described in Chapter 4, a company-sponsored resource group can be an institutional affirmation of the unique challenges facing historically marginalized employees of color.

I was invited once to give a speech at the annual meeting of a national organization committed to social justice. All the managers from around the country were there. Just before I was introduced, a Black man made an announcement that there would be a breakfast meeting the next day for all interested people of color in the organization. Though this national organization had a long history, this was the first time that the people of color were going to have a "caucus" meeting. Following the announcement, I was introduced and I gave my talk, entitled "Interrupting the Cycle of Oppression." After a warm round of applause, I asked if there were any questions. Immediately a visibly agitated White woman stood up and asked, "How would you feel if just before you began speaking a White person had stood up and said there would be a breakfast meeting of all the White people tomorrow?" I replied, "I would say it was a good idea." What I meant by my response is the subject of the next chapter.

# PART III

## Understanding Whiteness in a White Context

# SIX

# The Development of White Identity

*"I'm not ethnic, I'm just normal."*\*

I often begin the classes and workshops I lead by asking participants to reflect on their own social class and ethnic background in small discussion groups. The first question I pose is one that most people of color answer without hesitation: "What is your class and ethnic background?" White participants, however, often pause before responding. On one such occasion a young White woman quickly described herself as middle-class but seemed stumped as to how to describe herself ethnically. Finally, she said, "I'm just normal!" What did she mean? She explained that she did not identify with any particular ethnic heritage and that she was a lot like the other people who lived in her very homogeneous, White, middle-class community. But her choice of words was telling. If she is "just normal," are those who are different from her "just abnormal"?

Like many White people, this young woman had never really considered her own racial and ethnic group membership. For her, Whiteness was simply the unexamined norm. Because they represent the societal

---

\*Portions of this chapter are taken from two previously published articles: Beverly Daniel Tatum, "Teaching White Students About Racism: The Search for White Allies and the Restoration of Hope," *Teachers College Record* 95, no. 4 (1994): 462–76; and Beverly Daniel Tatum, "Talking About Race, Learning About Racism: The Application of Racial Identity Development Theory in the Classroom," *Harvard Educational Review* 62, no. 1 (1992): 1–24.

norm, Whites can easily reach adulthood without thinking much about their racial group. For example, one White teacher who was taking a professional development course on racism with me wrote in one of her papers: "I am thirty-five years old and I never really started thinking about race too much until now, and that makes me feel uncomfortable. . . . I just think for some reason I didn't know. No one taught us."[1] There is a lot of silence about race in White communities, and as a consequence Whites tend to think of racial identity as something that other people have, not something that is salient for them.

That is just how Debby Irving understood racial identity until, at age forty-eight, she "woke up White." In her memoir, *Waking Up White*, she recalls, "The way I understood it, race was for other people, brown and black-skinned people. Don't get me wrong—if you put a census form in my hand, I would know to check 'white' or 'Caucasian.' It's more that I thought all those other categories, like Asian, African American, American Indian, and Latino, were the real races. I thought white was the raceless race—just plain, normal, the one against which all others were measured."[2] Like my students, Irving's awakening came in the context of an academic course she was taking.

Whether the silence about race is broken in a college classroom, in a cross-racial friendship or intimate relationship, in a corporate office, or in some other life circumstance, once it is meaningfully broken, a process of identity development—specifically linked to an understanding of what it means to be White in a race-conscious society—begins to unfold. Counseling psychologist Janet Helms has described this unfolding for Whites in her book *Black and White Racial Identity: Theory, Research, and Practice*.[3] She assumes, as do I, that in a race-conscious society, racial group membership has psychological implications. The messages we receive about assumed superiority or inferiority shape our perceptions of reality and influence our interactions with others. While the task for people of color is to resist negative societal messages and develop an empowered sense of self in the face of a racist society, Helms says the task for Whites is to develop a positive White identity based in reality, not on assumed superiority. In order to do that, each person must become aware of his or her Whiteness, recognize that it is personally and socially significant, and learn to feel good about it, not in the sense of a Klan member's "White pride" but in the context of a commitment to a just society.

It comes as a surprise to some White people to think about their race in this way. "Of course White people feel good about being White," they say. But that is not my experience with my students or with the people who come to my workshops. Many of the White people in my audiences either have not given much thought to the meaning of their racial group membership and so don't feel anything, or they have thought about it and feel uncomfortable. The nature of the discomfort can vary and is often linked to their socioeconomic position. Social justice educator Paul Kivel, author of *Uprooting Racism: How White People Can Work for Racial Justice*, notes:

> Those of us who are middle-class are more likely to take it for granted that we are white without having to emphasize the point, and to feel guilty when it is noticed or brought up. Those of us who are poor or working-class are more likely to have had to assert our whiteness against the effects of economic discrimination and the presence of other racial groups. Although we share the benefits of being white, we don't share the economic privileges of being middle-class, and so we are more likely to feel angry and less likely to feel guilty than our middle-class counterparts. Whatever our economic status, many white people become paralyzed with some measure of fear, guilt or defensiveness when racism is addressed.[4]

This psychological discomfort is part of the hidden cost of racism for Whites.

How can White people achieve a healthy sense of White identity? Helms' model is instructive.[5] There are two major developmental tasks in this process, the abandonment of individual racism and the recognition of and opposition to institutional and cultural racism. These tasks are represented by what Helms calls six statuses (or states of mind): *contact, disintegration, reintegration, pseudo-independent, immersion/emersion,* and *autonomy.*[6]

## Abandoning Racism

In the contact frame of mind, like the women quoted in the opening of this chapter, Whites are paying very little attention, if any, to the significance of their racial identity. As exemplified by the "I'm just normal" comment, individuals operating from this perspective rarely describe themselves as White. If they have lived, worked, or gone to school in predominantly White settings, they may simply think of themselves as being part of the racial norm and take this for granted without conscious consideration of their White privilege, the systematically conferred advantages they receive simply because they are White.

While they have been breathing the "smog" and internalizing many of the prevailing societal stereotypes of people of color, they typically are unaware of this socialization process. They often perceive themselves as color-blind, completely free of prejudice, unaware of their own assumptions about other racial groups. In addition, they usually think of racism as the prejudiced behaviors of individuals rather than as an institutionalized system of advantage benefiting Whites in subtle as well as blatant ways. Peggy McIntosh speaks for many Whites with a contact frame when she writes, "I was taught to recognize racism only in individual acts of meanness by members of my group, never in invisible systems conferring unsought racial dominance on my group from birth."[7]

Some White people may grow up in families where they are actively encouraged to embrace the ideology of White superiority (children of Klan members or members of other White nationalist groups, for example), and as a result, they may have an elevated sense of White identity from an early age. In such cases, socialization of attitudes about Whiteness and the assumed inferiority of others has been overt and intentional.[8] However, for most Whites, the contact frame of mind in Helms' model of racial identity development represents the passive absorption of subtly communicated messages.

Robert Carter, another racial identity researcher, illustrates this point when he quotes a forty-four-year-old White male who grew up in upstate New York, where he had limited direct exposure to Black people or other communities of color.

There was no one to compare ourselves to. As you would drive through other neighborhoods, I think there was a clear message of difference or even superiority. The neighborhoods were poorer, and it was probably subtle, I don't remember my parents being bigoted, although by today's standards they clearly were. I think there was probably a message of superiority. The underlying messages were subtle. No one ever came out and said, White people are this and Black people are like this. I think the underlying message is that White people are generally good and they're like us, us and them.[9]

These messages may go unchallenged and unexamined for a long time, perhaps a lifetime.

While active exploration of what it means to be Black is an almost universal experience for African American adolescents due to the encounters with racism they commonly have, the same is not true for White youth. For White people living in largely White environments, it is possible to live one's entire life without giving focused attention to what it means to be White. Ethnic identity (being of Irish, Italian, Polish ancestry, for example) may be celebrated as part of a family's cultural traditions, but being White may go unexplored because it just seems "normal." But if one's social context changes, in college for instance, there may be new experiences that trigger active exploration of this dimension of identity. If that happens, the disintegration state is likely to occur next.

Disintegration is marked by a growing awareness of racism and White privilege as a result of personal encounters in which the social significance of race is made visible. For some White people, disintegration occurs when they develop a close friendship or a romantic relationship with a person of color. The White person then sees firsthand how racism can operate. For example, one female college student described her experiences shopping with a Puerto Rican roommate. She couldn't help noticing how her Latinx friend was followed around in stores by suspicious store clerks. She also saw how her friend's Black boyfriend was frequently asked to show his college ID when he visited their residence hall, while young White men came and went without being questioned.

For other White people, disintegration may result from seeing racial incidents captured on video, as was the case for Jill Robbins, a White female blogger. She titled her essay describing her reaction to the on-line video of the shooting of Philando Castile "How I Finally 'Got' the Meaning of White Privilege." Here's an excerpt:

> If I look into my rearview mirror and see flashing red lights, I'm not afraid. I probably have an "oh shit" moment but I have zero fear that I'll be harmed or even harassed by a police officer. I'm a nice white lady in a minivan . . . in suburbia USA. I might walk away with a ticket or maybe just a warning. No police officer is going to perceive me as a threat or a problem. I don't know what it's like to be hunted or profiled.
>
> And that right there is white privilege. It's the knowledge that being a victim of police brutality is probably never going to happen to me. . . . I know that if my white husband had been the one pulled over for a busted tail light that odds of him getting shot are almost nonexistent . . .
>
> A man I don't know who died two days before his 33rd birthday has had such a profound impact on me. It means more than something ugly on the news. I don't know if walking away less tunnel-visioned here in my white, suburban bubble means anything to anyone else but it means something to me.[10]

When that bubble starts to pop, the cycle of racism becomes increasingly visible. The visual image of Philando Castile slumped and bleeding in his car while his girlfriend tries to make sense of what just happened and her four-year-old daughter sits in the backseat is hard to explain away. But there are other, more commonly encountered visual images that also illuminate the cycle of racism in operation. For example, in my Psychology of Racism class, I often showed a very powerful video, *Ethnic Notions*,[11] on the dehumanizing images of African Americans in popular culture from before the Civil War through the late twentieth century. The video links the nineteenth-century caricatures of Black physical features, commonly published racial epithets, and the early cinematic portrayals of stupid but happy "darkies," menacing Black "savages," and heavyset, caretaking "mammies," to their updated forms in today's media. After seeing this film, students reported that they couldn't help but notice the pervasiveness of contemporary forms of racial stereotyping on television each night. The same programs they used to find entertaining now offended them.

They also started to notice the racism in the everyday language of family and friends. For example, one White student reported that when she asked her roommate to get her a glass of water, the White roommate jokingly replied, "Do I look Black to you?" Although I had never heard of this expression, it was very familiar to the student. Yet, before then, she had never recognized the association of Blackness with servitude and the assumed superiority of Whiteness being conveyed in her room-mate's casual remark.

This new awareness is usually characterized by discomfort. The un-comfortable emotions of guilt, shame, and anger are often related to a new awareness of one's personal prejudices or the prejudices within one's family. The following excerpts from the journals of two White students illustrate this point:

> Today was the first class on racism. . . . Before today I didn't think I was exposed to any form of racism. Well, except for my father. He is about as prejudiced as they come.

> It really bothers me that stereotypes exist because it is from them that I originally became uninformed. My grandmother makes all kinds of decisions based on stereotypes—who to hire, who to help out. When I was growing up, the only Black people that I knew were adults [household help], but I admired them just as much as any other adult. When I expressed these feelings to my parents, I was always told that the Black people that I knew were the exceptions and that the rest . . . were different. I, too, was taught to be afraid.

Others' parents were silent on the subject of racism, simply accepting the status quo.

Those whose parents were actively antiracist might have felt less guilt but often still felt unprepared for addressing racism outside the family, a point highlighted by the comments of this young woman:

> Talking with other class members, I realized how exceptional my parents were. Not only were they not overtly racist but they also tried to keep society's subtle racism from reaching me. Basically I grew up believing that racism was no longer an issue and all people should be treated as equals. Unfortunately, my parents were not being very realistic as society's racism did begin to reach me. They did not teach me how to support and defend their views once I was interacting in a society without them as a buffer.

When the disintegration frame of mind emerges, White individuals begin to see the degree to which their lives, and the lives of people of color, have been affected by racism in our society. The societal inequities they now notice directly contradict the idea of an American meritocracy, a concept that has typically been an integral part of their belief system. The cognitive dissonance that results is part of the discomfort that is experienced at this point in the process of development. Responses to this discomfort may include denying the validity of the information that is being presented or psychologically or physically withdrawing from it. The logic is, "If I don't read about racism, talk about racism, watch those documentaries or special news programs, or spend time with those people of color, I won't have to feel uncomfortable." (In the case of my students, this was usually not an option. By the time they were feeling these emotional responses deeply, it was too late to drop the course.)

The desire to withdraw physically or psychologically to avoid the discomfort is a symptom of what Robin DiAngelo has called "white fragility": in essence, a low tolerance for the cognitive and emotional stress that comes from exposure to new information that disrupts one's sense of racial equilibrium.[12]

If, despite the strong impulse to withdraw, the individual remains engaged, he or she can turn the discomfort into action. Once they have an awareness of the cycle of racism, many people are angered by it and want to interrupt it. Often action comes in the form of educating others—pointing out the stereotypes as they watch television, interrupting racial jokes, writing letters to the editor, sharing articles with friends and family. Like new converts, people experiencing disintegration can be quite zealous in their efforts. A White woman in her forties who participated in an antiracist professional development course for educators described herself at this stage:

> What it was like for me when I was taking the course [one year ago] and just afterwards, hell, because this dissonance stuff doesn't feel all that great. And, trying to put it in a perspective and figure out what to do with it is very hard. . . . I was on the band wagon so I'm not going to be quiet about it. So there was dissonance everywhere. Personally, I remember going home for Thanksgiving, the first Thanksgiving [while taking the course], back to our families . . . and turning to my brother-in-law and saying, "I really don't want you to say that in front of me—I don't want to hear that joke—I am not interested." . . . At every turn it seemed like there, I was *responsible* for saying something. . . . My husband, who I think is a very good, a very liberal person, but who really hasn't been through [this], saying, "You know I think you're taking yourself too seriously here and where is your sense of humor? You have lost your sense of humor." And my saying, "It isn't funny; you don't understand, it just isn't funny to me." Not that he would ever tell a racial joke, but there were these things that would come up and he would just sort of look back and say, "I don't understand where you're coming from now." So there was a lot of dissonance. . . . I don't think anybody was too comfortable with me for a while.[13]

My college students had similar experiences with family members and friends. Though they wanted to step off the cycle of racism, the message from the surrounding White community seemed to be, "Get back on!" A very poignant example of this was shared with me by a young White man from a very privileged background. He wrote:

I realized that it was possible to simply go through life totally oblivious to the entire situation or, even if one realizes it, one can totally repress it. It is easy to fade into the woodwork, run with the rest of society, and never have to deal with these problems. So many people I know from home are like this. They have simply accepted what society has taught them with little, if any, question. My father is a prime example of this. . . . It has caused much friction in our relationship, and he often tells me as a father he has failed in raising me correctly. Most of my high school friends will never deal with these issues and propagate them on to their own children. It's easy to see how the cycle continues. I don't think I could ever justify within myself simply turning my back on the problem. I finally realized that my position in all of these dominant groups gives me power to make change occur. . . . It is an unfortunate result often though that I feel alienated from friends and family. It's often played off as a mere stage that I'm going through. I obviously can't tell if it's merely a stage, but I know that they say this to take the attention off of the truth of what I'm saying. By belittling me, they take the power out of my argument. It's very depressing that being compassionate and considerate are seen as only phases that people go through. I don't want it to be a phase for me, but as obvious as this may sound, I look at my environment and often wonder how it will not be.

The social pressure from friends and acquaintances to collude, to not notice racism, can be quite powerful.

But it is very difficult to stop noticing something once it has been pointed out. The conflict between noticing and not noticing generates internal tension, and there is a great desire to relieve it. Relief often comes through what Helms calls reintegration. In the reintegration frame of mind, the previous feelings of guilt or denial may be transformed into fear and anger directed toward people of color. The logic is, "If there is a problem with racism, then you people of color must have done something to cause it. And if you would just change your behavior, the problem would go away." The elegance of this argument is that it relieves the White person of all responsibility for social change.

I am sometimes asked if it is absolutely necessary to experience this kind of reintegration thinking. Must one resort to blaming the victim to restore a sense of emotional equilibrium? Although it is not inevitable, most White people who speak up against racism will attest to the temptation they sometimes feel to slip back into collusion and silence. Because the pressure to ignore racism and to accept the socially sanctioned stereotypes is so strong, and the system of advantage so seductive, many White people get stuck in reintegration thinking. The psychological tension experienced at this stage is clearly expressed by Connie, a White woman of Italian ancestry who took my course on the psychology of racism. After reading about the process of White identity development, she wrote:

> There was a time when I never considered myself a color. I never described myself as a "White, Italian female" until I got to college and noticed that people of color always described themselves by their color/race. While taking this class, I have begun to understand that being White makes a difference. I never thought about it before, but there are many privileges to being White. In my personal life, I cannot say that I have ever felt that I have had the advantage over a Black person, but I am aware that my race has the advantage.
>
> I am feeling really guilty lately about that. I find myself thinking: "I didn't mean to be White, I really didn't mean it." I am starting to feel angry toward my race for ever using this advantage toward personal gains. But at the same time I resent the minority groups. I mean, it's not my fault that society has deemed us "superior." I don't feel any better than a Black person. But it really doesn't matter because I am a member of the dominant race. . . . I can't help it . . . and I sometimes get angry and feel like I'm being attacked.
>
> I guess my anger toward a minority group would enter me into the next stage of Reintegration where I am once again starting to blame the victim. This is all very trying for me and it has been on my mind a lot. I really would like to be able to reach the last stage . . . where I can accept being White without hostility and anger. That is really hard to do.

## "But I'm an Individual!"

Another source of the discomfort and anger that Whites often experience in this phase stems from the frustration of being seen as a group member, rather than as an individual. People of color learn early in life that they are seen by others as members of a group. For Whites, thinking of oneself only as an individual is a legacy of White privilege. As McIntosh writes, "I can swear, or dress in secondhand clothes, or not answer letters, without having people attribute these choices to the bad morals, the poverty, or the illiteracy of my race. . . . I can do well in a challenging situation without being called a credit to my race. . . . I am never asked to speak for all the people of my racial group."[14] In short, she and other Whites are perceived as individuals most of the time.

The view of oneself as an individual is very compatible with the dominant ideology of rugged individualism and the American myth of meritocracy. Understanding racism as a system of advantage that structurally benefits Whites and disadvantages people of color on the basis of group membership threatens not only beliefs about society but also beliefs about one's own life accomplishments. For example, organizational consultant Nancie Zane writes that senior White male managers "were clearly invested in the notion that their hard work, ingenuity and skills had won them their senior-level positions." As others talked about the systemic racist and sexist barriers to their own achievement, "white men heard it as a condemnation that they somehow didn't 'deserve' their position."[15] If viewing oneself as a group member threatens one's self-definition, making the paradigm shift from individual to group member will be painful.

In the case of White men, both maleness and Whiteness are normative, so acknowledging group status may be particularly difficult. Those White women who have explored their subordinate gender identity have made at least some movement away from the notion of a strictly individual self-definition and may find it easier to grasp the significance of their racial group membership. However, as McIntosh and others have pointed out, understanding one form of oppression does not guarantee recognition of another.

Those Whites who are highly identified with a particular subordinate identity may also struggle with claiming Whiteness as a meaningful group category because they feel far from the White male middle-class norm. For example, Whites who grew up in impoverished circumstances often struggle with the idea that they had anything described as "privilege." Jewish people of European ancestry sometimes do not think of themselves as White because for them the term means "White Christian." Also, in Nazi Germany, Jews were defined as a distinct, non-Aryan racial group. In the context of an anti-Jewish culture, the salient identity may be the targeted Jewish identity. However, in terms of US racial ideology, Jews of European ancestry are also the beneficiaries of White racial privilege.[16] My White Jewish students often struggled with the tension between being targeted and receiving privilege. In this case, as in others, the reality of multiple identities complicates the process of coming to terms with one particular dimension of identity. For example, one student wrote: "I am constantly afraid that people will see my assertion of my Jewish identity as a denial of whiteness, as a way of escaping the acknowledgment of white privilege. I feel I am both part of and not part of whiteness. I am struggling to be more aware of my white privilege . . . but I will not do so at the cost of having my Jewishness erased."

Similarly, White people whose central group identification is with the LGBTQ community sometimes find it hard to claim privileged status as Whites when they are so targeted by homophobia and heterosexism, often at the hands of other Whites. Heather Hackman, a social-justice educator who identifies as a lesbian, describes her own journey as a college student, initially resisting any new understanding of race.

I just wanted people to stop calling me a racist. [I] took in just enough information to make it seem like I was on board with racial issues. But if one were to scratch beneath the surface, one would see that I had no real *knowledge* of racial issues, and worse, I had no real *desire* to know. . . . I could not see *why* I should care about it because I could not see myself in this country's story of race. . . . But something was percolating in me that made this ignorance untenable for much longer. My identity as a feminist, coming out as a lesbian, and learning how the systems of oppression associated with those identities worked were beginning to make it impossible for me to persist in my racial delusions. My last two years of college were filled with moment after moment, lesson after lesson, and conversation after conversation that helped me to see that learning about racial issues in earnest and then speaking out about racial oppression was deeply connected to my speaking out about gender and queer oppression and that I could not advocate for the latter without addressing the former.[17]

Even when White men and women don't see or think of themselves as White, other people still do. As White people begin to understand that they are viewed as members of a dominant racial group not only by other Whites but also by people of color, they are sometimes troubled, even angered, to learn that simply because of their group status they may be viewed with suspicion by many people of color. "I'm an individual, view me as an individual!" For example, in a racially mixed group of educators participating in an antiracist professional development course, a Black man commented about using his "radar" to determine if the group would be a safe place for him. Many of the White people in the room, who believed that their very presence in the course was proof of their trustworthiness, were upset by the comment, initially unprepared to acknowledge the invisible legacy of racism that accompanied any and every interaction they had with people of color.[18] The White people in the course found some comfort in reading Lois Stalvey's classic memoir, *The Education of a WASP*, in which she describes her own responses to the ways Black people tested her trustworthiness. She writes,

> I could never resent the tests as some white people have told me they do. . . . But to me, the longest tests have always indicated the deepest hurts. We whites would have to be naive to expect that hundreds of years of humiliation can be forgotten the moment we wish it to be. At times, the most poignant part of the test is that black people have enough trust left to give it. Testing implies we might pass the test. It is safer and easier for a black person to turn his back on us. If he does

not gamble on our sincerity, he cannot be hurt if we prove false. Testing shows an optimism I doubt I could duplicate if I were black.[19]

Sometimes poorly organized antiracism workshops or other educational experiences can create a scenario that places participants at risk for getting stuck in their anger. Effective consciousness-raising about racism must also point the way toward constructive action. When people don't have the tools for moving forward, they tend to return to what is familiar, often becoming more vigorous in their defense of the racial status quo than they were initially.

As we have seen, many White people experience themselves as powerless, even in the face of privilege. But the fact is that we all have a sphere of influence, some domain in which we exercise some level of power and control. The task for each of us, White and of color, is to identify what our own sphere of influence is (however large or small) and to consider how it might be used to interrupt the cycle of racism.

## Defining a Positive White Identity

As a White person's understanding of the complexity of institutional racism in our society deepens, resorting to explanations that blame the victim becomes less likely. Instead, deepening awareness usually leads to a commitment to unlearn one's racism and marks the emergence of the pseudo-independent status.

Sometimes epitomized by the "guilty White liberal" persona, the individual whose thinking is dominated by a pseudo-independent mindset has achieved an intellectual understanding of racism as a system of advantage but doesn't quite know what to do about it. Self-conscious and feeling guilty about one's own Whiteness, the individual often desires to escape it by associating with people of color. Ruth Frankenberg, author of *White Women, Race Matters: The Social Construction of Whiteness*,[20] describes the confusing emotions of this process in an autobiographical essay. "I viewed my racial privilege as total. I remember months when I was terrified to speak in gatherings that were primarily of color, since I feared that anything I did say would be marked by my whiteness, my racial privilege (which in my mind meant the same)."[21] When her friends of color were making casual conversation—chatting about their mothers, for example—she would worry that anything she might say about her own mother would somehow reveal her race privilege, and by the time she had sorted it out mentally, the topic of conversation would have changed. She writes, "In that silence, I tried to 'pass' (as what? as racially unmarked? as exceptional? as the one white girl who could 'hang'?)."[22]

Similarly, a student of mine wrote:

One of the major and probably most difficult steps in identity development is obtaining or finding the consciousness of what it means to be White. I definitely remember many a time that I wished I was not White, ashamed of what I and others have done to the other racial groups in the world. . . . I wanted to pretend I was Black, live with them, celebrate their culture, and deny my Whiteness completely. Basically, I wanted to escape the responsibility that came with identifying myself as "White."

How successful these efforts to escape Whiteness via people of color will be depends in part on the REC-identity development of the people of color involved. Remember the Black students at the cafeteria table? If they are having racial encounters and are in the immersion mode of active exploration of their Black identity, they are not likely to be interested in cultivating White friendships. If a White person reaches out to a Black person and is rebuffed, it may cause the White person to retreat into "blame the victim" thinking. However, even if those efforts to build interracial relationships are successful, the reality of one's own Whiteness must eventually be confronted.

We all must be able to embrace who we are in terms of our racial and cultural heritage, not in terms of assumed superiority or inferiority but as an integral part of our daily experience in which we can take pride. But, as we see in these examples, for many White people who have come to understand the everyday reality of racism, Whiteness is still experienced as a source of shame rather than as a source of pride.

Recognizing the need to find a more positive self-definition is a hall-mark of the immersion/emersion status, as described by Helms. Bob, a White male student in one of my racism classes, clearly articulated this need.

I'm finding that this idea of White identity is more important than I thought. Yet White identity seems very hard to pin hole. I seem to have an idea and feel myself understanding what I need to do and why and then something presents itself that throws me into mass confusion. I feel that I need some resources that will help me through the process of finding White identity.

The resource Bob needs most at this point are not people of color but other Whites who are further along in the process and can help show him the way.

It is at just this point that White individuals intensify their efforts to see their Whiteness in a positive light. Just as Cross describes the period of Black redefinition as a time for Black people to seek new ways of thinking about Blackness, ways that take them beyond the role of victim, White people must seek new ways of thinking about Whiteness, ways that take them beyond the role of victimizer.

## The Search for White Allies and the Restoration of Hope

In fact, another role does exist. There is a history of White protest against racism, a history of Whites who have resisted the role of op-pressor and who have been allies to people of color. Unfortunately these Whites are often invisible to us. While the names of active racists are easily recalled—past and present Klan leaders and Southern segrega-tionists, for example—the names of White allies are often unknown. I have had the experience of addressing roomfuls of classroom teachers who have been unable to name even one White person who has worked against racism without some prompting from me. If they can't do it, it is likely that their students can't either.

Those who have studied or lived through the civil rights era (many of today's students have not) may know the names of Viola Liuzzo, James Reeb, or Michael Schwerner, White civil rights workers who were killed for their antiracist efforts. But most people don't want to be martyrs. There is a need to know about White allies who spoke up, who worked for social change, who resisted racism and lived to tell about it. How did these White allies break free from the confines of the racist socialization they surely experienced to claim this identity for themselves? These are the voices that many White people at this point in their learning process are hungry to hear.

Biographies of and autobiographies by White individuals who have been engaged in antiracist activities can be very helpful. For example, there is *A Season of Justice*, the autobiography of Morris Dees, the founder of the Southern Poverty Law Center and a vigorous anti-Klan litigator,[23] as well as *Memoir of a Race Traitor*, by Mab Segrest, a powerful account of her experiences as a White lesbian with deep Southern roots organizing against neo-Nazi and Klan activity in North Carolina.[24] There is *Outside the Magic Circle*, the oral history of Virginia Foster Durr, a Southern belle turned civil rights activist.[25] And, already quoted in this chapter, there is *The Education of a WASP*, the story of Lois Stalvey, a mother struggling to create an antiracist environment for her children during the civil rights era.[26] Each of these books is anchored in events of the twentieth century and explores family histories that go back to the nineteenth century or before. Becky Thompson's book *A Promise and Way of Life: White Antiracist Activism* is based on the life histories of thirty-nine people who collectively represent a social history of White antiracist activism from the 1950s to the end of the twentieth century.[27] Examples of contemporary narratives that extend into the twenty-first century include Bernestine Singley's edited volume *When Race Becomes Real: Black and White Writers Confront Their Personal Histories*,[28] *White Like Me: Reflections on Race from a Privileged Son—The Remix* by Tim Wise,[29] *Waking Up White and Finding Myself in the Story of Race* by Debby Irving,[30] *Witnessing Whiteness: The Need to Talk About Race and How to Do It* by Shelly Tochluk,[31] *Fire in the Heart: How White Activists Embrace Racial Justice* by Mark Warren,[32] and *Everyday White People Confront Racial and Social Justice: 15 Stories*, edited by Eddie Moore, Marguerite W. Penick-Parks, and Ali Michael.[33]

These narratives can provide an antidote to the feelings of isolation and loneliness that White people often feel at this point. There is comfort in knowing that others have traveled this terrain. One of the consequences of racism in our society is that those who oppose racism are often marginalized, and as a result, their stories are not widely known. To quote Mark Warren, "While studies of white racism might fill a small library, the studies of white antiracism, if you will, could fit in a small bookcase."[34] Having access to these narratives makes a difference to Whites who are looking for ways to be agents of change. White people who are doing this work need to continue to make their stories known to serve as guides for others.

In my classes I tried to address the lack of knowledge of White role models by providing concrete examples of such people. In addition to assigning reading material, my strategy was to invite a local White antiracist activist, Andrea Ayvazian, to my class to speak about her own personal journey toward an awareness of racism and her development as a White ally. Students typically asked her questions that reflected their fears about social isolation at this phase of development. "Did you lose friends when you started to speak up?" "My boyfriend makes a lot of racist comments. What can I do?" "What do you say to your father at Thanksgiving when he tells those jokes?" These are not just the questions of late adolescents. The mature White teachers I worked with asked the same things.

My White students often found the topic of racism depressing— especially as they deepened their understanding of how deeply ingrained it is in the structures of our society. Yet they found the opportunity to talk with this ally gave them renewed hope. Through her example, they could see that the role of the ally is not to "help" those targeted by racism but to stand in solidarity with them, speaking up against systems of oppression, and to challenge other Whites to do the same. One point that Andrea Ayvazian emphasizes in her speaking and writing is the idea that "allies need allies," others who will support their efforts to swim against the tide of cultural and institutional racism.[35] This point was especially helpful for one young woman who had been struggling with feelings of isolation. She wrote:

> About being an ally, a positive role model: . . . it enhanced my pos-
> itive feelings about the difference each individual (me!) can make. I
> don't need to feel helpless when there is so much I can do. I still can
> see how easily things can back-up and start getting depressing, but
> I can also see how it is possible to keep going strong and powerful.
> One of the most important points she made was the necessity of a
> support group/system; people to remind me of what I have done,
> why I should keep going, of why I'm making a difference, why I
> shouldn't feel helpless. I think our class started to help me with those
> issues, as soon as I started to let it, and now I've found similar sup-
> ports in friends and family. They're out there, it's just finding and
> establishing them—it really is a necessity. Without support, it would
> be too easy to give up, burn-out, become helpless again. In any en-
> deavor support is important, but when the forces against you are so
> prevalent and deep-rooted as racism is in this society, it is the only
> way to keep moving forward.

Participation in White consciousness-raising groups organized specifically for the purpose of examining one's own racism is a powerful
way to "keep moving forward." During my tenure as a professor at
Mount Holyoke College, such a group, White Women Against Racism,
was formed by White students eager to engage each other in this work.
There are similar groups with different names operating formally and
informally in local communities around the country.[36] Support groups
of this nature help to combat the social isolation that antiracist Whites
often experience and provide places to forge new identities.

For example, Showing Up for Racial Justice (SURJ) is a national
network founded in 2009 specifically to educate and organize White
people to work for racial justice, not alone but in collaboration with
local and national multiracial racial-justice organizing efforts. However,
SURJ recognizes the need to provide spaces where White people can be
"called in, not called out," supported in their learning by other White

people, knowing that mistakes are inevitable. As stated on the website, the SURJ goal is "to learn from those mistakes and keep showing up again and again for what is right and for racial justice." As an organization, SURJ has a particular commitment to engaging with low-income and working-class Whites in order to counteract the way that race has been used to pit disenfranchised Whites against people of color: "While people of color bear the brunt of racism, large numbers of white people have also been failed by the system—facing job loss, inadequate housing and cutbacks in core services. Instead of addressing real fears and insecurity, racist elites actively target working class white people into blaming people of color for the problems their families and vulnerable communities face."[37]

In this age of rising racial tensions *and* economic anxiety, making space for these intragroup conversations among White people is very useful.

I am sometimes asked why such groups need to be made up of Whites only. To many Whites it seems inconceivable that there would be any value in participating in all-White discussions of racism. While of course there is value in cross-racial dialogue, all-White support groups serve a unique function. Particularly when Whites are trying to work through their feelings of guilt and shame, separate groups give White people the "space to speak with honesty and candor rarely possible in racially-mixed groups."[38] Even when Whites feel comfortable sharing these feelings with people of color, frankly, people of color don't necessarily want to hear about it. The following comment, written by a Black woman in my class, illustrates this dilemma:

Many times in class I feel uncomfortable when White students use the term Black because even if they aren't aware of it they say it with all or at least a lot of the negative connotations they've been taught goes along with Black. Sometimes it just causes a stinging feeling inside of me. Sometimes I get real tired of hearing White people talk about the conditions of Black people. I think it's an important thing for them to talk about, but still I don't always like being around when they do it. I also get tired of hearing them talk about how hard it is for them, though I understand it, and most times I am very willing to listen and be open, but sometimes I can't. Right now I can't.

Though a White person may need to describe the racist things a parent or spouse has said or done, to tell the story to a person of color may reopen that person's wounds. Listening to those stories and problem-solving about them is a job that White people can do for each other.

It is at this stage of redefining Whiteness, immersion/emersion, that the feelings of guilt and shame start to fade. Reflecting on her own White identity development, sociologist Becky Thompson chronicles this process: "[I understood] that I didn't have to recreate the wheel in my own life. I began to actively seek writing by white women who have historically stood up against racism—Elly Bulkin, Lillian Smith, Sara Evans, Angelina Grimke, Ruth Frankenberg, Helen Joseph, Melanie Kaye/Kantrowitz, Tillie Olsen, Minnie Bruce Pratt, Ruth Seid, Mab Segrest, and others."

She also realized that she needed antiracist White people in her daily life with whom she could share stories and whom she could trust to give her honest feedback. Her experience in a White antiracism group helped her to stop feeling bad because she was White. She writes, "I started seeing ways to channel my energies without trying to leave a piece of my identity behind."[39]

The last status, autonomy, represents the most developed of the racial identity frames. With this mind-set, a person has incorporated the newly defined view of Whiteness as part of a personal identity. The positive feelings associated with this redefinition energize the person's efforts to confront racism and oppression in daily life. Clayton Alderfer, a White man with many years of personal and professional experience as an organizational psychologist, described the thinking that characterizes this stage. "We have a more complete awareness of ourselves and of others to the degree that we neither negate the uniqueness of each person, regardless of that person's group memberships, nor deny the ever-present effects of group memberships for each individual."[40]

While autonomy might be described as racial self-actualization, racial identity development never really ends. The person who has experienced the deeper understanding of autonomy is characteristically open to new information and new ways of thinking about racial and cultural variables.[41] Yet Helms describes each of the six statuses as representing a pattern of thinking that *predominates* at particular points of development. Even when active antiracist thinking predominates, there may still be particular situations that trigger old modes of responding. It is in those moments that being part of a White support group can be especially helpful.

In her book *Witnessing Whiteness*, Shelly Tochluk adds to the thinking about this autonomy phase by proposing that rather than striving to "become an ally," which suggests a completed process, it might be better to speak of "doing effective ally work," which implies a continuing process of growth and learning.[42] Tochluk is part of Alliance of White Anti-Racists Everywhere—Los Angeles (AWARE-LA),[43] a grassroots organization that is pushing the "ally" concept further, to what they call a "Radical White Identity." She explains,

> The exploration the Radical White Identity requires and the way it locates white people as meaningful stakeholders in efforts toward social justice offer a sense of hope and inspiration. Within this approach, our antiracism efforts are not *in service of* people of color, they are part of our own effort to shed the socialization that has led to us behaving in ways that support and maintain the oppression of others. In this way, our sense of ourselves as being fully human is realized when we work toward educational, economic, social, and environmental justice. . . .
>
> Within this community are people who can help me see privilege and racism more clearly, motivate me to continue constructing a healthy and effective antiracism practice, and support me to keeping moving forward in times when I fail.[44]

Tochluk also notes that moving from an unconscious or guilty phase to becoming an effective ally is a "massive leap" that requires scaffolding, all the more reason why becoming part of a community of support is so helpful.

A major benefit of the racial identity development process described in this chapter is increased effectiveness in multiracial settings. The White person who has made a significant effort to work through his or her own racial identity process will have a deepened understanding of racism and an appreciation and respect for the identity struggles of people of color. When we see strong, mutually respectful relationships between people of color and Whites, we are usually looking at the tangible results of both people's identity processes. If we want to promote positive cross-group relations, we need to help young White people engage in the kind of dialogue that precipitates this kind of identity development, just as we need to help youth of color achieve an empowered sense of group identity.

Though the process of examining their racial identity can be uncomfortable and even frightening for Whites, those who persist in the struggle are rewarded with an increasingly multiracial and multicultural existence. In our still quite segregated society, this "borderland" is unfamiliar to many Whites and may be hard to envision. Becky Thompson has experienced it, and she writes: "We need to talk about what living in this borderland feels like, how we get there, what sustains us, and how we benefit from it. For me, this place of existence is tremendously exciting, invigorating, and life-affirming."[45] Though it can also be "complicated and lonely," it is also liberating, opening doors to new communities, creating possibilities for more authentic connections with people of color, and, in the process, strengthening the coalitions necessary for genuine social change.

# SEVEN

# White Identity, Affirmative Action, and Color-Blind Racial Ideology

*"Affirmative action was nice. It had its time.*
*Its time is over."*

THE WORDS ABOVE COME FROM A PARTICIPANT IN WHITENESS PROJECT, an interactive investigation into how Americans who identify as White understand and experience their race.[1] He was not the only project participant to express the sentiment that affirmative action should be a policy of the past. Are they right? In 1996, when I was working on the first edition of this book, I knew that one of the topics I would need to write about was affirmative action. My students always wanted to talk about it. Even White students who supported the concept of expanding opportunity for historically disadvantaged groups worried that it would limit their opportunities, that they might become victims of what some called "reverse discrimination." Many did not have a clear understanding of what affirmative action actually was, what was allowed by law, what was not. And so I included a brief overview in this chapter. Twenty years later, that overview is still needed, but the conversation about affirmative action has changed.

What is different today is the widespread belief among Whites (and some people of color) that racial discrimination has declined in the post–civil rights era and affirmative action programs are no longer needed. For some, the election of President Barack Obama (not once but twice), the phenomenal success of Black celebrities like Oprah Winfrey, and the increased visibility of Black executives in corporate America are all evidence that the doors of opportunity are now wide open for those with talent and tenacity. We are now, they argue, well on our way to becoming a truly egalitarian society.

Findings from the 2015 American Values Survey conducted by the Public Religion Research Institute (PRRI) seem to reflect that thinking.[2] On the one hand, a majority of survey participants agree that Blacks (61 percent) and Hispanics (56 percent) face a lot of discrimination in the United States. On the other hand, they think enough has been done to address it. More than half (59 percent) of White Americans believe that the United States has made the changes necessary to give Blacks equal rights with Whites. Combining several questionnaire items together to form a "Racial Inequity Index," the PRRI researchers found that a majority (54 percent) of White Americans perceive low levels of racial inequality, "believing that racial minorities today have equal opportunities as whites" do. White working-class Americans, in particular, hold that point of view (61 percent), compared to less than half (45 percent) of White college-educated Americans. By comparison, 66 percent of Black Americans perceive high levels of inequality, "believing generally that systemic discrimination against blacks and other minorities impacts racial inequality today," while 17 percent perceive moderate levels of inequality and another 17 percent perceive low levels of inequality. Hispanic Americans were more evenly divided in their outlook: 45 percent believe that there are still high levels of racial inequality, 22 percent hold attitudes in the moderate range, and 34 percent perceive low levels of inequality, as measured by the survey.

Of particular relevance to a discussion of affirmative action are the results regarding White beliefs about discrimination against White people. "Although only one-quarter (25 percent) of the public believe that whites face a lot of discrimination in America today, a significantly larger number express concern about the existence of so-called 'reverse discrimination' against whites. More than four in ten (43 percent) Americans say that discrimination against whites has become as big a problem as discrimination against blacks and other minorities."[3]

Not surprisingly, when those results are broken down by race, there are significant differences between groups. Half (50 percent) of White Americans agree that discrimination against Whites has become a problem equivalent to that against people of color. That percentage is even higher among working-class Whites (60 percent), with 39 percent of working-class Whites disagreeing. Among White college-educated Whites, the percentages are almost exactly reversed. Only 36 percent of that group agrees that discrimination against Whites is equal to discrimination against people of color, while 63 percent of college-educated Whites disagree. Among Blacks and Hispanics, there is widespread disagreement (74 percent and 70 percent, respectively) with the idea that discrimination against Whites is as big a problem as discrimination against people of color, yet there are some who do agree with that statement (25 percent of Blacks and 29 percent of Hispanics).

Of course, the survey doesn't tell us why the participants hold the views that they hold, only that they do. It is puzzling to look at the survey results against factual data about racial gaps on measures of social or economic well-being. Whether we consider measures of housing, education, the labor market, the criminal justice system, the media, politics, or health care, Whites as a group fare better than just about every other racial/ethnic group in the United States on measures of access, participation, and success.[4] I reviewed some of the information about disparities in housing, education, the criminal justice system, and politics (voting) in the prologue of this book. Drawing on data from the US Bureau of Labor Statistics, Bell and her colleagues highlight labor market patterns:

> For example, the highest-paying occupational categories in management, professional, and related occupations are dominated by whites (39%) and Asians (50%) compared with Blacks (29%) and Hispanics (20%). At the lower end of the occupational ladder, we see the reverse: Latinos are overrepresented in lower-paying fields of agriculture (50%), grounds maintenance (45%), and maids and housekeeping (44%), while Blacks are slotted into jobs as aides in nursing, psychiatric, and home health care (36%), bus drivers (27%),

and security guards and gaming surveillance officers (27%). Asians make up a majority of manicurists, pedicurists, skin care specialists, barbers, and cosmetologists (57%), as well as 29% of software developers, and 22% of physicians and surgeons. Whites are at the top of the occupational pyramid, accounting for 96% of farmers, ranchers, and agricultural managers; 93% of construction managers; and 91% of chief executives.[5]

Only 3 percent of executives, senior-level officials, and managers in the US are Black. Only 4 percent of doctors and 5 percent of attorneys are Black.[6] Additionally, a 2016 analysis of federal government data by the Pew Research Center finds that Blacks are, on average, at least twice as likely as Whites to be poor or to be unemployed; in 2014 the median White household income was $71,300 while the median Black household income was $43,300. Little has changed in twenty years. Back then the median Black household income was about $37,800, compared to $63,600 for the median white household. In terms of median net worth, white households are about thirteen times as wealthy as Black households—a gap that has grown wider since the Great Recession.[7]

Though these data leave me wondering why so many White people are worried about discrimination against them, I am reminded of the tendency that Americans of all backgrounds have to overestimate how many people of color there are in the United States. Though demographics are changing, they are not changing as fast as the average person thinks they are. In 2013, the Center for American Progress (CAP), an independent, nonpartisan policy institute, joined with other nonprofit organizations (Policy Link, Latino Decisions, and the Rockefeller Foundation) to "assess how Americans view issues of rising diversity and policy proposals to better integrate these communities into the mainstream of American society and its economy." The resulting study is one of the largest of its kind, based on nearly three thousand interviews with a very diverse group of Americans. Researchers found that "when asked to estimate the current percentage of the U.S. population that is composed of racial and ethnic minorities, Americans are considerably off the mark. The median response—49 percent—indicates that the typical American thinks we are nearly a majority-minority nation already; the actual percent of the nation that is a minority is about 37 percent." Respondents were wrong about the future as well, estimating that the population of color in 2050 will be 62 percent, considerably more than the Census Bureau projection of 53 percent.[8]

Though the researchers concluded that there was general openness about the increasing diversity, particularly among younger and college-educated respondents, they also found that one of the greatest concerns respondents had about rising diversity was job availability. Fifty-four percent agreed with the survey statement, "There will not be enough jobs for everybody." Consistent with the 2015 American Values Survey, a significant percentage (42 percent) expressed fear that discrimination against Whites will increase as the diversity of the population increases. This anxiety was particularly prevalent among White conservatives (61 percent) and White respondents ages sixty-five or older (56 percent).[9]

The concern expressed by White respondents about discrimination being directed against them also reminded me that our tendency as human beings is to focus on the "micro" rather than the "macro" when it comes to our own lives. Even if only 3 percent of executives nationwide are Black, if you are White and one of them happens to get the job you thought was yours, you may feel your worry about discrimination against White people has been validated. Such an explanation might ease the pain of your disappointment, even as it might fuel your racial resentment.

Sociologist Arlie Russell Hochschild offers further insight into the mind-set of White working-class Americans, who were the most likely (60 percent) to say that discrimination against Whites has become as much of a concern as discrimination against people of color. In her book *Strangers in Their Own Land: Anger and Mourning on the American Right,* she describes White working-class men and women who feel as if they have been waiting in line for the promise of the American Dream of intergenerational progress to be fulfilled for a long time. Instead of moving forward, they feel as if they are moving backward, with stagnant wages, the loss of jobs in manufacturing and other areas, and the growing threat of globalization. And yet, they see others getting ahead. It feels like something has gone painfully wrong in the world. Hochschild calls this the "deep story," and it sounds like this:

> Look! You see people *cutting in line ahead of you!* You're following the rules. They aren't. . . . How can they just do that? Who are they? Some are black. Through affirmative action plans, pushed by the federal government, they are being given preference for places in colleges and universities, apprenticeships, jobs, welfare payments, and free lunches. . . . And President Obama: how did *he* rise so high? The biracial son of a low-income single mother becomes president of the most powerful country in the world; you didn't see that coming. And if he's there, what kind of a slouch does his rise make you feel like, you who are supposed to be so much more privileged? Or did Obama get there *fairly?* How did he get into an expensive place like *Columbia University?* How did Michelle Obama get enough money to go to *Princeton?* And then *Harvard* Law School, with a father who was a city water plant employee? You've never seen anything like it, not up close.[10]

In this narrative, it is not just Black people who are cutting in line, it is other groups too—like women, immigrants, and refugees—and it is the line-cutter-in-chief who has been helping them. Psychologically speaking, the deeply internalized racial hierarchy that has White men at the head of the line has been set askew, and that by itself is unsettling for some. This "deep story" helps explain why, despite the actual data about opportunity in America, the perception of discrimination against Whites is so widely expressed in the survey responses.

What is clear is that, whether the result of collective anxiety driven by demographic overestimates, individualized and specific job concerns, or the election of a Black president, in the context of the survey results, the debate about affirmative action is destined to continue for some time. For a moment, let's step back from these survey results and take a brief overview of affirmative action.

## What Is Affirmative Action?

The term *affirmative action* was introduced into our language and legal system by Executive Order 11246, signed by President Lyndon Johnson in 1965 and later amended by Presidents Nixon and Clinton. This order, as amended by subsequent presidents, obligates all contractors who employ more than fifty people and who conduct more than $50,000 of business with the federal government to "take affirmative action to ensure that applicants are employed, and that employees are treated during employment without regard to their race, color, religion, sex, or national origin." As set forth by this order, contractors were to commit themselves to "apply every good faith effort" to develop procedures that would result in equal employment opportunity for historically disadvantaged groups. The groups targeted for this "affirmative action" were White women and men and women of color (specifically defined by the federal government as American Indians / Alaska Natives, Asian or Pacific Islanders, Blacks, and Hispanics). Later legislation broadened the protected groups to include persons with disabilities and veterans.[11]

There has been much public debate about affirmative action since its inception, with little attempt to clarify concepts. The interchangeable use of the terms *affirmative action* and *quotas* by politicians and in the media has contributed to the confusion. The term *quota* has a repugnant history of discrimination and exclusion. For example, in the early part of the twentieth century, quotas were used to limit how many Jews were admitted to prestigious institutions of higher learning.[12] But despite common public perceptions, affirmative action programs do not involve quotas.

Quotas, defined here as fixed numerical allocations, are *illegal*, except in those rare situations when a court has ordered them as a temporary remedy for a well-documented, proven pattern of racially motivated discrimination.

Public-sector employers may use quotas or preferences when a sufficiently compelling government interest has been established—that is, to remedy discrimination by the government entity itself. Even in these cases, preferences are acceptable only if no reasonable demographically neutral alternative exists. And the preferences must be flexible, focused, limited in duration, and not overly burdensome to nonbeneficiaries. Federal government regulations explicitly prohibit private employers from utilizing quotas or preferences.[13]

*Goals*, on the other hand, are *essential*. Goals are not a fixed allocation meant to limit (as quotas did in the past). Instead, goals provide a necessary target for which to aim. As any long-range planner knows, goals are necessary in order to chart one's course of action and to evaluate one's progress. Goals are a fundamental component of effective affirmative action programs.

In practice, federal contractors are expected to monitor their own records to make sure they are employing qualified people from specified targeted classes—such as women or African Americans—in proportion to their availability in the workforce. If they find that there is a significant pattern of underrepresentation, they are expected to make a plan to address the discrepancy. Organizations that don't have federal contracts are not required to have affirmative action programs, but over the years many companies have adopted them voluntarily.[14]

Though much of what we have seen in the news about affirmative action is in reference to Supreme Court cases focused on admissions at public universities, in fact, most of the laws related to affirmative action are in reference to employment. Social psychologist and expert on affirmative action Faye Crosby points out that "affirmative action in employment affects many more citizens than does affirmative action in education. . . . Educators estimate that no more than half of the four-year institutions are selective. The rest admit everyone who applies. Thus, issues concerning college admissions relate, at most, to about 6 million Americans. In contrast, about six times as many people are affected by affirmative action programs in employment."[15] Employment-based affirmative action will be the focus of our discussion here.

Though Executive Order 11246 required affirmative action, it did not specify exactly what the action should look like. Given this lack of specificity, it is not surprising that there is great variety in the way affirmative action programs have been developed and implemented around the country.[16] The emphasis on action is apparent in this widely accepted nontechnical definition: "Affirmative action is the expenditure of energy or resources by an organization in the quest for equality among individuals from different, discernible groups."[17] These attempts can be categorized as either *process-oriented* or *goal-oriented*.

Process-oriented programs focus on creating a fair application process, assuming that a fair process will result in a fair outcome. If a job opening has been advertised widely, and anyone who is interested has a chance to apply, and all applicants receive similar treatment (e.g., standard interview questions, same evaluation criteria and procedures), the process is presumed to be fair. The search committee can freely choose the best candidate knowing that no discrimination has taken place. Under such circumstances, the "best" candidate will sometimes be a person of color, "too good to ignore."[18] In theory, such would seem to be the case, and because process-oriented programs seem consistent with the American ideal of the meritocracy, most people support this approach.[19] At the very least, it is an improvement over the "old boy network" that filled positions before outsiders even had a chance to apply.

Unfortunately, research suggests that bias can enter into the selection process at the very start of the search process. For example, economists Marianne Bertrand and Sendhil Mullainathan conducted a study on hiring behavior in which they sent out close to 5,000 fictitious résumés in response to over 1,300 help-wanted ads in Chicago and Boston newspapers, for jobs in the sales, administrative support, clerical, and customer service categories. The résumés were similar except that half of them were assigned an African American–sounding name (Lakisha Washington or Jamal Jones, for example) and the other half had names more commonly associated with Whites (such as Emily Walsh or Greg Baker). Then they waited to see what the callback response would be. The results showed significant discrimination against the Black-identified résumés: White names received 50 percent more callbacks for interviews. The degree of discrimination was similar across job categories. Even federal contractors and employers with "Equal Opportunity Employer" listed in their ads showed the same level of discrimination as other employers. The authors concluded, "A White applicant should expect on average one callback for every 10 ads she or he applies to; on the other hand, an African American applicant would need to apply to about 15 different ads to achieve the same result."[20]

In another study of hiring behavior, conducted in Milwaukee, sociologist Devah Pager sent paired testers to apply in person for jobs that required no experience, just a high school degree. White applicants were twice as likely to be called back for an interview as the matched Black applicants. Surprisingly, even White applicants who indicated that they had a criminal record received more callbacks (17 percent) than Black applicants *without* a criminal record (14 percent).[21]

In a subsequent study, this time in New York City, Pager and her colleagues fielded teams of White, Black, and Latinx testers to apply for real entry-level jobs. The testers were articulate, clean-cut, college-educated young men between the ages of twenty-two and twenty-six, similar in height, physical attractiveness, verbal skill, and interactional style and demeanor. The Latinx testers were US citizens of Puerto Rican descent and spoke without a Spanish accent. The testers were trained to present themselves in similar ways to potential employers as high school graduates with steady work experience in entry-level jobs. They applied for jobs in restaurants and retail sales, as warehouse workers, couriers, telemarketers, stockers, movers, customer service representatives, and other similar jobs available to someone with a high school degree and little previous experience. In applications to 171 employers, the White testers received a positive response (interview or job offer) 31 percent of the time, the Latinx testers received a positive response 25.2 percent of the time, and the Black testers, 15.2 percent of the time. Stated differently, the Black applicant had to search twice as long as the equally qualified White applicant before receiving a callback or a job offer.[22]

In another version of the same experiment, the White testers presented themselves as ex-felons (having served eighteen months for possessing cocaine with intent to sell) and were teamed up with Latinx and Black applicants with no criminal records. Whites with criminal records still had more callbacks or job offers (17.2 percent) than did Latinx testers (15.4 percent) and Black testers (13 percent) with no criminal records. Though the discriminatory outcomes were clear, "few interactions between our testers and employers revealed signs of racial animus or hostility toward minority applicants."[23] In the absence of prejudiced remarks, would rejected Black applicants even be aware that discrimination was operating without being able to compare their results to those of their White and Latinx teammates? Maybe not. But as these studies demonstrate, getting to the point of an interview is a higher hurdle for Black applicants than White ones, and in the case of the last study, a higher hurdle than for Latinx applicants as well.

Goal-oriented affirmative action can help address this problem. At each step of the process, the question is asked: is our pool of qualified candidates diverse, and if not, have we cast our net wide enough? In this approach, more of those résumés of Black candidates would likely have been at least considered for the next step in the evaluation process. In a goal-oriented process, once the qualified pool of applicants has been identified, those in the pool who move the organization closer to its diversity hiring goals are likely to be favored. This doesn't mean that underrepresented candidates would always be the ones selected (the consistently lower rates of White unemployment let us know that White people are still being hired), but some of the time candidates of color would prevail. The White candidates who are not selected are likely to feel disappointed and might even believe that they were better candidates than the ones selected, but such perceptions are by definition subjective.

I am reminded of a dialogue I had with one of my White female students about affirmative action. In an essay on the topic she wrote, "I am in favor of affirmative action except when it comes to my jobs." I wrote in response, "Which jobs have your name on them?" Of course she wanted to get the jobs she applied for and did not want to lose out to anyone, especially on the basis of race, a factor over which she had no control. Yet she seemed to assume that because she wanted them, they belonged to her. She assumed that she would, of course, be qualified for the job and would therefore be entitled to it. What was she assuming about the candidates of color? She did not seem to take into account the possibility that one of them might be as qualified, or more qualified, than she was. The idea that she as a White woman might herself be the beneficiary of affirmative action was apparently not part of her thinking.

We have all heard someone tell a story about a friend or relative who lost a coveted job opportunity because a "less-qualified" person took that spot, almost always reported to be a person of color, usually Black, not a White woman. I always wonder how the speaker knows so much about the selected candidate's résumé or what happened in the final interview. Can we really say with confidence any particular hiring decision was not the best choice for the organization and its goals?

Despite the attempts to ensure a fair process, without the clarity of a clear set of institutional diversity goals to guide their decision-making, too often well-intentioned search committees find the "best" person is yet another member of the dominant group. What goes wrong? Some answers may be found in the research of social psychologists.

## Aversive Racism, Uncomfortable Egalitarians, and Color-Blindness

Psychologists Samuel Gaertner and John Dovidio, along with numerous colleagues, have been studying race relations, and its relevance to our question, for more than forty years. They argue that White opposition to affirmative action programs is largely rooted in a subtle but pervasive form of racism they call "aversive racism." Aversive racism is defined as "an attitudinal adaptation resulting from an assimilation of an egalitarian value system with prejudice and with racist beliefs." In other words, most Americans have internalized the espoused cultural values of fairness and justice for all *at the same time* that they have been breathing the smog of racial biases and stereotypes pervading popular culture. "The existence, both of almost unavoidable racial biases and of the desire to be egalitarian and racially tolerant, forms the basis of the ambivalence that aversive racists experience."[24] The key to understanding this framework is to recognize that the internalization of the biases and stereotypes of popular culture and continued segregation from (and therefore lack of familiarity with) Blacks leave many Whites feeling uneasy, uncomfortable, even perhaps fearful in the presence of

Black people, often without their conscious awareness of these feelings. Consequently, interracial interactions may generate discomfort and lead White people to avoid or withdraw from such situations, finding them "aversive." The idea that they might be considered prejudiced by anyone (including themselves) is also an "aversive" idea, hence the name "aversive racism."[25]

Pointing to the findings of several impressive research studies, Dovidio and Gaertner argue that because so-called aversive racists see themselves as nonprejudiced and racially tolerant, they generally do not behave in overtly racist ways. When the norms for appropriate, nondiscriminatory behavior are clear and unambiguous, they "do the right thing," because to behave otherwise would threaten the nonprejudiced self-image they hold. However, in situations when it is not clear what the "right thing" is, or if an action can be justified on the basis of some factor other than race, racial bias will reveal itself. In these ambiguous situations, an aversive racist can discriminate against Blacks and still preserve the racially tolerant self-image.

For example, in a 1989 study of hiring decisions, Dovidio and Gaertner asked White college students to review application materials and evaluate candidates for a peer-counseling position on campus. The application materials were arranged in three categories—those of a highly qualified candidate, those of a moderately qualified candidate, and those of a weakly qualified candidate—with half of the materials in each category identified as those of a White applicant and half identified as those of a Black candidate. When the decision was unambiguous (as in "hire the strong candidate"), there was no selection bias. Both White and Black "strongly qualified" candidates received positive recommendations from the students. Similarly, when the candidates were "weakly qualified," there was no discrimination. The choice was unambiguous—"reject weakly qualified" applicants. However, when the candidates were "moderately qualified," the decision to recommend or reject was less clear. In that instance, "moderately qualified" White candidates were recommended significantly more often than the "moderately qualified" Black candidates, even though the credentials were the same. Seventy-five percent of the moderately qualified Whites were recommended, compared to only 50 percent of the moderately qualified Black candidates. In 1999, ten years later, Dovidio and Gaertner repeated the same experiment with a new group of White undergraduate students and found almost identical results. Seventy-seven percent of the moderately qualified Whites were recommended compared to 40 percent of the Black candidates in that same category. As part of these studies, they also measured the students' overt expressions of prejudice using a self-reported prejudice scale. The students in 1999 expressed less prejudice on the survey than the students from 1989, but the pro-White bias in their decision-making was virtually the same.[26]

In a subsequent study, participants were asked to help make admissions decisions for the university. Again, Black and White applicants were matched and described as either uniformly strong (high SAT scores and high grades), uniformly weak (low SAT scores and low grades), or unevenly strong (either grades were high or SAT scores were high, but not both). When applicants were clearly strong or clearly weak, there was no anti-Black bias. The right decision—to admit or reject—was unambiguous. However, when applicants were strong in one area but not both, differential treatment emerged. Black candidates were more likely to be rejected based on the weak area (either weak grades or weak SATs), minimizing the strength in the other area, but White candidates were more likely to be accepted based on the area of strength, minimizing the weakness in the other area. In other words, the participants systematically changed how they weighed the criteria to justify their decisions on the basis of race. Unevenly qualified White candidates were given the benefit of the doubt in a way that Black candidates were not. Summarizing the variety of studies they conducted, Dovidio and Gaertner concluded, "Aversive racism—racism among people who are good and well-intentioned—can produce disparate outcomes. . . . Although the bias of aversive racists may be subtle and unintentional, its consequences may ultimately be as severe as old-fashioned racism—threats to the well-being of blacks and the restriction of opportunities."[27]

The foundational work that Dovidio and Gaertner did in the twentieth century has been expanded upon by Mahzarin Banaji and Anthony Greenwald using twenty-first-century technology. With advances in our understanding of human cognition, psychologists now agree that much of human judgment and behavior is produced with little conscious thought. Our internalized stereotypes and biases are not always consciously known to us, but they can still influence our behavior. The implicit-association test (IAT) developed by Banaji and Greenwald was designed to measure the strength of associations between concepts (e.g., black people, gay people) and evaluations (e.g., good, bad) or stereotypes (e.g., athletic, clumsy) by tapping into thoughts and feelings outside of conscious awareness and control.[28]

As the researchers describe on the Project Implicit website, "The main idea is that making a response is easier when closely related items share the same response key. When doing an IAT you are asked to quickly sort words into categories" using computer keys. Since reaction times are recorded in milliseconds, responses are not subject to the kind of conscious control one might use when responding to a survey question. By timing their reactions, the researchers can see the pattern of associations that participants are making. (If you want to try out the Race IAT, you can do so by going to the website. It takes about ten minutes.) Most who take the Race IAT are faster at linking racial White images to pleasant words than at linking racial Black images to pleasant words. This pattern is described as showing "automatic preference for White relative to Black."[29] Does an "automatic White preference" on the Race IAT mean a person harbors deep-seated prejudices? Not necessarily. Banaji and Greenwald write that nothing about the IAT suggests that it taps into the kind of dislike, disrespect, or even hatred that we associate with strongly held prejudices. But now that millions of people have taken the test and many research studies have been done using the methodology, they have reached two important conclusions.

First, we now know that automatic White preference is pervasive in American society—almost 75 percent of those who take the Race IAT on the Internet or in laboratory studies reveal automatic White preference. This is a surprisingly high figure. . . .

Second, the automatic White preference expressed on the Race IAT is now established as signaling discriminatory behavior. It predicts discriminatory behavior even among research participants who earnestly (and, we believe, honestly) espouse egalitarian beliefs. That last statement may sound like a self-contradiction, but it's an empirical truth. Among research participants who describe themselves as racially egalitarian, the Race IAT has been shown, reliably and repeatedly, to predict discriminatory behavior that was observed in the research.[30]

For example, it predicts results like the ones Dovidio and Gaertner found—in a simulated hiring situation, White applicants were judged more favorably than equally qualified Black applicants. It also predicts doctors' differential treatment of Black and White patients—emergency room and resident physicians recommend the optimal treatment, thrombolytic (blood-clot-dissolving) therapy, less often for a Black patient than for a White one with the same acute cardiac symptoms.[31] (The Institute of Medicine has concluded that racial and ethnic minorities receive less-effective care even when income levels and insurance benefits are the same, pointing to implicit bias as the cause.)[32]

Of the more than 1.5 million White Americans who have taken the Race IAT on the internet, approximately 40 percent regard themselves as egalitarian and still show the automatic White preference in their response times. This combination of egalitarian attitudes and unconscious bias is similar to what Dovidio and Gaertner described in their definition of aversive racism. Banaji and Greenwald agree with their theoretical understanding of the issue but suggest what might be described as a "kinder, gentler" label—"uncomfortable egalitarians." They write,

We have some observations about these uncomfortable egalitarians. First, there are a lot of them. . . . Second, their differential behavior toward White and Black Americans can well be responsible for a substantial portion of the disadvantage experienced by Black Americans. . . . Third, and perhaps most needing explanation—is that uncomfortable egalitarians are extremely unlikely to notice that their differential behavior toward Whites and Blacks contributes in any way to the disadvantages experienced by Black Americans. . . . Uncomfortable egalitarians may be the prototypical "good people" who have hidden biases. They see themselves as helpful, but it turns out that their helpfulness is selective, caused in part by their discomfort in interracial interactions. Their discriminatory behavior consists of being selectively ready or able to help only or mostly those who are like them—in other words, those in the groups for which they have automatic preferences . . . unaware that their comfort and helpfulness in interactions with in-group members is not matched by similar levels of comfort and helpfulness toward out-group members.[33]

There is no malice in helping people like yourself—what Banaji and Greenwald call "in-group favoritism"—but as we saw in the Dovidio and Gaertner hiring simulations, it does mean that a lot more White people will get jobs ahead of equally qualified Blacks. At the conclusion of their book, *Blindspot: Hidden Biases of Good People,* Banaji and Greenwald review decades of social science research and come to this conclusion: "Black disadvantage exists. . . . The further conclusion— one demanded by the great weight of evidence—is indisputable. Some portion of Black disadvantage is attributable to the way people respond to Blacks just because they are Black."[34] Social science research is also conclusive that, while explicit bias is infrequent, implicit bias (automatic race preference) is pervasive and contributes to the racial discrimination against Black Americans.[35]

The next question many people ask is, "What can I do about an implicit preference that I don't want?" Banaji, Greenwald, and their colleagues offer this advice on their Project Implicit website:

It is well-established that implicit preferences can predict behavior. But, there is not yet enough research to say for sure that implicit biases can be reduced, let alone eliminated. . . . Therefore, we encourage people not to focus on strategies for reducing bias, but to focus instead on strategies that deny implicit biases the chance to operate. One such strategy is ensuring that implicit biases don't leak out in the first place. To do that, you can "blind" yourself from learning a person's gender, race, etc. when you're making a decision about them (e.g., having their name removed from the top of a resume). If you only evaluate a person on the things that matter for a decision, then you can't be swayed by demographic factors. Another strategy is to try to compensate for your implicit preferences. For example, if you have an implicit preference for young people you can try to be friendlier toward elderly people. Although it has not been well-studied, based on what we know about how biases form we also recommend that people consider what gets into their minds in the first place. This might mean, for example, going out of our way to watch television programs and movies that portray women and minority group members in positive or counter-stereotypical ways.[36]

There is some evidence that repeated exposure to positive counter-stereotypic images can be useful, but it is truly difficult to disrupt the stereotypes we learn early and often in our lives.

## Color-Blind Racial Ideology

Despite so much evidence that people are not color-blind even when they want to be, color-blind racial ideology has become commonplace among Whites in the United States, particularly in the twenty-first century. In fact, what psychologists Dovidio and Gaertner called "aversive racism," Eduardo Bonilla-Silva, looking through a sociologist's structural lens, has called "color-blind racism." He describes color-blind racism as the dominant racial ideology of contemporary America, in which White people deny or minimize the degree of racial inequality or explain contemporary racial inequality as the result of factors unrelated to racial dynamics (such as Black cultural values or economic forces unrelated to race.)[37]

Color-blind racial ideology can be expressed in multiple ways. One is what Ruth Frankenberg calls "color evasion"—as when someone says, "I don't see color; we are all the same," for example. This emphasis on sameness is a way of denying or rejecting the idea of White racial superiority. In theory, this sounds good, but it overlooks the fact that people of color are not having the same experiences as White people. As the research discussed earlier demonstrates, their racial group membership is impacting their daily lives. Another expression of color blindness is what Frankenberg calls "power evasion," as when someone minimizes the impact of racism, claiming that everyone has the same opportunities to succeed and those who don't have only themselves to blame.[38] In *The Myth of Racial Color Blindness*, the editors, Helen Neville, Miguel Gallardo, and Derald Wing Sue, explain, "To deny race and ignore the existence of racism actually causes harm to people of color because it a) falsely perpetuates the myth of equal access and opportunity, b) blames people of color for their lot in life, and c) allows Whites to live their lives in ignorance, naiveté, and innocence."[39]

Another feature of color-blind racial ideology is the belief that talking about race makes things worse—that it promotes racism and/or is racist in and of itself.[40] Those who bring up race are "playing the race card" and creating problems where otherwise there would be none, or so the logic goes. This last feature of color-blind racial ideology serves to silence those who seek to challenge institutional racism within organizations and the larger society and is another way that color blindness perpetuates the status quo. When someone raises questions about racial practices or policies in an environment where White color blindness is the norm, the response is often one of hurt and defensiveness, as in "Are you calling me a racist?!" Remember Dovidio and Gaertner's description of aversive racism—called "aversive" because the person is *averse* to acknowledging any link to prejudice or racism. The conversation then often becomes about hurt feelings rather than the systemic issues that need addressing.

Ian Haney López, author of *Dog Whistle Politics,* succinctly describes this pattern:

> Claims to have been personally attacked take productive conversations about current racial patterns and collapse them into a stultifying ventilation of wounded feelings. It shifts attention from racial dynamics that hurt everyone, and focuses our eyes instead on the bruised egos of those whites who feel themselves personally targeted

whenever the conversation turns to race. The imagined charge is of small-minded bigotry. The actual charge, written across society . . . is that race in various forms continues to harm us all. Histrionic distress about supposedly having been called a racist impedes recognizing the truth about race's continued harmful power.[41]

Learning how to have these conversations is a necessary part of moving forward as a healthy society. You can't fix what you can't talk about. "Refusing to talk about powerful social realities does not make them go away but rather allows racial illiteracy, confusion, and misinformation to persist unchallenged."[42] Learning to have the conversation is of particular importance for White people who want to see social change.

Because one of the characteristics that White aversive racists or uncomfortable egalitarians exhibit is the tendency to avoid or withdraw from interracial interactions due to the unease they often feel in those situations, it may be more effective for a White peer to take the initiative in naming and addressing racial bias in organizational or group settings.[43] The White person who has engaged in the kind of exploration of racial identity and reeducation described in the previous chapter (Chapter 6) is often willing to demonstrate that kind of courage. It is not easy, but that is the way effective ally work gets done. Keep in mind that when the environmental cues are *clear* about what the right thing to do is, the aversive racist or uncomfortable egalitarian will do the right thing. The voices of white allies in the room can help to make the right thing clear.

## Affirmative Action Revisited

It is clear from the research evidence that interventions like affirmative action programs are still needed. It is not clear from the survey data discussed earlier that public support for these programs will be maintained. Eight states have already passed legislation eliminating any such programs in state educational or employment settings.[44]

Nevertheless, it is important to note the benefits of affirmative action programs in the workplace. To the extent that employee diversity is enhanced throughout an organization, employers find that they are better able to serve the needs of a diverse customer base. Diverse work teams lead to more effective problem-solving.[45] Removing artificial barriers to advancement broadens the talent pool. Affirmative action programs have also been shown to strengthen the bottom line. Companies that have increased their representation of women of all backgrounds and men of color have outperformed less-diverse companies in stock performance and reputational standing.[46]

Much of the research that has been discussed in this chapter has been framed in terms of Black-White relationships, a reflection of the way most of the studies were conducted. Of course, affirmative action programs may also involve other people of color as well as White women.[47] Yet the Black-White emphasis in the aversive racism framework seems well placed when we consider that researchers have found that negative attitudes toward affirmative action are expressed most strongly when Blacks are identified as the target beneficiaries. When asked in research studies to respond to affirmative action programs benefitting people with disabilities, Native Americans, or Blacks, the most negative responses were directed to policies benefitting Blacks. As Audrey Murrell and her colleagues discovered, "Whereas giving preference based on nonmerit factors is perceived as unfair, giving such preference to Blacks is perceived as more unfair."[48]

## Keeping Our Eyes on the Prize:
## Goal-Oriented Affirmative Action

Though the research on evaluator bias is dismaying, it also points us in the direction of an effective response. Again, recall that when expectations for appropriate behavior are clearly defined and a biased response can be recognized, most egalitarian Whites are consistently as positive in their behavior toward Blacks as toward other Whites. If administrators clearly articulate the organization's diversity goals and the reasons that such goals are in the organization's best interests, the appropriate behavior in the search process should be clear. If we keep our eyes on the prize, we can get past the bias.

Some might say, "Doesn't such an outcome-based focus lead to instances of 'reverse discrimination,' when well-qualified majority-group candidates are rejected in favor of a less-qualified candidate from an underrepresented group simply because that candidate meets the diversity goal?" Certainly that could happen, but only in a poorly administered program. When affirmative action programs are functioning appropriately, no one is ever hired who is not qualified for the job. Such an occurrence would undermine the program and would be patently unfair to the newly hired person, who has in effect been set up to fail.

In a well-conceived and well-implemented affirmative action program, the first thing that should be done is to establish clear and meaningful selection criteria. What skills does the person need to function effectively in this environment? How will we assess whether the candidates have these required skills? Will it be on the basis of demonstrated past performance, scores on an appropriate test, or the completion of certain educational requirements?[49] Once the criteria have been established, anyone who meets the criteria is considered qualified.

Now we can consider who among these qualified candidates will best help us achieve our organizational goals for diversifying our institution. If one candidate meets the criteria but also has some additional education or experience, it may be tempting to say this candidate is the "best," but this one may not be the one who moves us toward our diversity goal. Because of the systematic advantages that members of the dominant group receive, it is often the case that the person with the extra experience or educational attainment is a person from the majority group. If our eyes are on our organizational goal, we are not distracted by these unasked-for extras. If we need someone who has toured Europe or had a special internship, it should already be part of our criteria. If it is not part of the criteria, it shouldn't be considered.

And if making our organization a more-inclusive environment is a goal, then perhaps that goal should be reflected in our criteria so that whoever is selected can support the organization's goals. Fletcher Blanchard, author of "Effective Affirmative Action Programs," suggests what some of these new criteria might be: the extent and favorability of one's experience working in multicultural settings, the experience of being supervised by managers of color, experience of collaborating in multicultural workgroups or living in racially mixed communities, fluency in a second language, or substantial college coursework in the study of multicultural perspectives.[50]

In my own consultation with school systems interested in increasing their faculty of color, we have discussed the need for such new criteria. The number of young people of color entering the teaching profession is still too small to meet the demand. While effective recruiting strategies can increase a school system's likelihood of being able to attract new teachers of color, many White teachers will still be needed to replace retiring teachers in the coming years. Schools concerned about meeting the needs of an increasingly diverse student population should be looking specifically for teachers of all backgrounds with demonstrated experience in working with multiracial populations, with courses on their transcripts like Psychology of Racism; Race, Class, Culture, and Gender in the Classroom; and Foundations of Multicultural Education, to name a few.

Criteria like these are important for all candidates, but they are also criteria that are more likely to be met by candidates of color, because people of color often have more life experience in multiracial settings than many White people do. However, because such criteria are not explicitly race-based, they also should withstand the legal assaults that some affirmative action programs have experienced.[51] Should these legal challenges move us into a post–affirmative action age, such criteria will be increasingly important in the search and selection process. Under any circumstance, clarity about organizational goals and qualification criteria will lead to better and more equitable selection decisions.

Faye Crosby, a White female psychologist who has studied affirmative action for many years, explains why it is so important to her: "[M]y fervent support of affirmative action comes ultimately from being the mother of White boy-men. It is because I want a better world for my children that I bother to fight for affirmative action."[52] All of us want a better, more peaceful world for our children. If we want peace, we must work for justice. How do we achieve a more just society in the present context of institutional and cultural racism? Goal-oriented affirmative action is but one potentially effective strategy. Serious dialogue about other strategies is needed, and that dialogue needs to be expanded beyond the Black-White paradigm that has shaped discussions of affirmative action. The voices of other disenfranchised groups need to be acknowledged in the process, because, as my students taught me long ago, "racism is not just a Black-White thing."

# PART IV

# Beyond Black and White

# EIGHT

# Critical Issues in Latinx, Native, Asian and Pacific Islander, and Middle Eastern / North African Identity Development

*"There's more than just Black and White, you know."*

To get to know my culture, I would tell teachers to understand my language. Take a course or something. . . . The other way they can learn about our culture is by asking us about it. Ask us.[1]

　—Alicia, a Chicana high school student

There's a certain amount of anger that comes from the past, realizing that my family, because they had to assimilate through the generations, don't really know who they are.[2]

　—Don, an American Indian college student

Being an Asian person, a person of color growing up in this society, I was taught to hate myself. I did hate myself, and I'm trying to deal with it.[3]

　—Khanh, an Asian American college student

I'm not really sure I understood what was going on when 9/11 happened, but I was old enough to feel the world shift on its axis that day and change everything forever.[4]

　—Amani, a Muslim girl of Middle Eastern heritage

LIKE THE AFRICAN AMERICAN AND EUROPEAN AMERICAN STUDENTS I have described, each of the young people quoted above has experienced a process of racial or ethnic identity development, an internal process triggered by external events and interactions with others. Although conversations about race, racism, and racial identity tend to focus on Black-White relations, to do so ignores the experiences of other targeted racial or ethnic groups. When we look at the experiences of Latinxs, Native Americans, Asian and Pacific Islanders (APIs), and, more recently, Middle Easterners and North Africans (MENAs) in the United States, we can easily see that racial and cultural oppression has been a part of their lived experiences and that it plays a role in the identity development process for individuals in these groups as well.[5]

In this multiracial/multiethnic context, Jean Phinney's model of adolescent ethnic identity development is particularly useful. Grounded in both an Eriksonian understanding of adolescence and research studies of adolescents from various racial or ethnic groups, Phinney's model is made up of three unique phases: (1) unexamined ethnic identity, when race or ethnicity is not particularly salient for the individual; (2) ethnic identity search, when individuals are actively engaged in defining for themselves what it means to be a member of their own racial or ethnic group; and (3) achieved ethnic identity, when individuals are able to assert a clear, positive sense of their racial or ethnic identity.[6] Phinney's model shares with both Cross' and Helms' models the idea that an achieved identity develops over time and that race-related encounters often lead to the exploration, examination, and eventual internalization of a positive, self-defined sense of one's own racial or ethnic identity.

While Phinney's work describes the identity process for adolescents of color in general, it is important to continually keep in mind the cultural diversity and wide range of experience represented by the groups known as Latinxs, APIs, Native peoples, and MENAs. Because of this tremendous diversity, it is impossible in the space of one chapter to detail the complexities of the identity process for each group.[7] Therein lies my dilemma. How can I make the experiences of the Latinx, API, Native, and MENA students visible without tokenizing them? I am not sure that I can, but I have learned in teaching about racism that a sincere, if imperfect, attempt to interrupt the oppression of others is usually better than no attempt at all. In that spirit, this chapter is an attempt to interrupt the frequent silence about the impact of racism on these communities of color. It is not an attempt to provide an in-depth discussion of each group's identity development process, an attempt that would inevitably be incomplete. Rather, this chapter highlights a few critical issues pertinent to the identity development of each group, particularly in schools, and points the reader to more information.

## What Do We Mean When We Say "Latinx"?

Latinxs now represent the largest "minority" group in the United States, a position formerly held by African Americans. According to the US census, as of 2015, Hispanics (so labeled by the federal government) numbered approximately fifty-seven million, representing 17.6 percent of the total US population.[8] Though the largest community of color in size, the Latinx population is no longer the fastest-growing demographic segment in the US, a designation now held by Asian Americans. Since the onset of the Great Recession in December 2007, there has been both a drop-off in immigration from Latin America and a declining birth rate among Latinx women in the US, slowing the growth rate of the Latinx population. Still, Latinxs have accounted for 54 percent of the total US population growth thus far in the twenty-first century (2000–2014).[9] Over the last two decades of the twentieth century (1980–2000), the Latinx immigrant population jumped from 4.2 million to 14.1 million; however, between 2000 and 2014, it was the increase in babies born to Latinx families in the US that drove the population growth. In the first decade of the twenty-first century, there were 9.6 million Latinx births as compared to 6.5 million new immigrants.[10] Consequently, as of 2014, two-thirds of all Latinxs living in the US were born in the US, and nearly half of those US-born were under the age of eighteen. With a median age of twenty-eight, Latinxs are the youngest major racial or ethnic group in the US. (By comparison, the median age of Whites in 2014 was forty-three; for Blacks and Asians, the median age was thirty-three and thirty-six, respectively.)[11]

Approximately 67 percent of Latinxs are of Mexican ancestry, a population that includes US-born Mexican Americans (also known as Chicanxs), whose families may have been in the Southwest for many generations, as well as recent Mexican immigrants. Approximately 9.5 percent of Latinxs are Puerto Rican, 3.8 percent are Salvadoran, 3.7 percent are Cuban, 3.3 percent Dominican, and 2.4 percent Guatemalan. The remaining 10.3 percent are from other Central or South American countries.[12] Each of these groups is a distinct population with a particular historical relationship to the United States.

In the case of the Chicanx population, the US conquest and annexation of Mexican territory (a geographical area extending from Texas to California) following the Mexican-American War (1846–1848) created a situation in which people of Mexican ancestry became subject to White domination. Like African Americans and Native peoples, Mexican Americans were initially incorporated into US society against their will. It was the general feeling among White settlers that they were superior to Mexicans, who were descendants of Native peoples or mestizos, with a combination of Native and European ancestry. The question of how Mexicans should be classified racially was decided in 1897 by Texas courts, which ruled that Mexican Americans were not White. In California, they were classified as "Caucasian" until 1930, when the state attorney general decided they should be categorized as "Indians," though "not considered 'the original American Indians of the US.'"[13] In both Texas and California, Mexican Americans were confined to segregated schools, and in both states legislation was passed in the nineteenth century outlawing the use of Spanish for instruction in the public schools. During that time, Mexican families sought to preserve their culture and language by sending their children to Catholic schools or private Mexican schools where bilingual instruction was maintained.[14]

Though the Mexican population in the contested territory declined immediately after the conquest due to forced relocations, it increased again during the early twentieth century when US farmers actively encouraged an influx of Mexicans across the border as an inexpensive source of agricultural labor. Since then, political and economic conditions in Mexico have fueled a steady stream of immigrants to the United States.[15]

While people of Mexican descent are often stereotyped as undocumented immigrants, the fact is that most Mexican-origin Latinxs are legal residents. Most Mexican Americans continue to live in the West and Southwest, particularly California and Texas. According to the most recent census data, Mexican-origin Latinxs are the youngest of all Latinx subgroups. Among Latinxs younger than eighteen in 2014, 69 percent are Mexican.[16] Educational attainment and family income remain below the US average. Only 9 percent of Mexican Americans age twenty-five and older have earned at least a bachelor's degree (compared to 13 percent of all Latinx adults and more than 30 percent of all US adults over twenty-five).[17] In 2014 the median household income in the US was roughly $51,400, but it was only $38,000 for Mexican families. The median income for Puerto Ricans, the second largest Latinx group in the US, was even lower—$36,000.[18]

Like the conquered Mexicans in the Southwest, Puerto Ricans did not choose to become US citizens, it was imposed upon them. Puerto Rico became an unincorporated territory of the United States in 1898, ceded by Spain at the conclusion of the Spanish-American War. Puerto Rico, which had struggled to become independent of Spain, did not welcome subjugation by the United States. An active policy of Americanization of the island population was implemented, including attempts to replace Spanish with English as the language of instruction on the island. The attempts to displace Spanish were vigorously resisted by Puerto Rican teachers and students alike. In 1915, resistance to the imposition of English resulted in a student strike at Central High School in San Juan, part of a rising wave of nationalism and calls for independence. Rather than let the Puerto Rican people vote on whether they wanted citizenship, the US Congress passed the Jones Act of 1917, imposing citizenship and the obligation to serve in the US military but denying Puerto Ricans the right to vote in national elections. In 1951, Puerto Ricans were allowed to vote on whether to remain a territory or to become a commonwealth. Though there were those who urged a third option, Puerto Rican independence, commonwealth status was the choice. Commonwealth status allowed Puerto Ricans greater control of their school systems, and Spanish was restored in the schools.[19]

Economic conditions on the island have driven many Puerto Ricans to New York and other northeastern US cities. Many came in the 1940s and 1950s to work in the factories of the Northeast, but as industry left the region many Puerto Rican workers were displaced. Fluctuating employment conditions have contributed to a pattern of circular migration to and from Puerto Rico, which is made easier by US citizenship. However, since 2005, more Puerto Ricans live on the US mainland than on the island of Puerto Rico. By 2013, the number on the mainland had grown to 5.1 million, compared to 3.6 million on the island. Mainland Puerto Ricans (sometimes referred to as Nuyoricans or Diasporicans)[20] are concentrated in the Northeast (51 percent), primarily in New York, and in the South (31 percent), mainly in Florida.[21] A multiracial population descended from European colonizers, enslaved Africans, and the indigenous Taíno Indians, a significant number of Puerto Ricans are dark-skinned. Consequently, on the mainland they have experienced patterns of residential and school segregation similar to that of African Americans.[22]

Salvadorans and Cubans are the next largest populations of Latin American origin living in the United States. As of 2016, Salvadorans had surpassed the Cubans in population, representing 3.8 percent of the US population while Cubans are 3.7 percent.[23] Of the two groups, Cubans have a longer history in the US. Although Cuban communities have existed in Florida and New York since the 1870s, nearly 60 percent of Cubans in the US are foreign-born, most having been in the country for twenty years or more.[24] Cuban immigration to the United States increased dramatically following the 1959 revolution led by Fidel Castro. The first wave of immigrants were upper-class, light-skinned Cubans who left in the very first days of the revolution. They were able to bring their personal fortunes with them and established businesses in the United States. The second major group left after Castro had been in power for a few months and largely consisted of middle-class professionals and skilled workers. Though many were unable to bring possessions with them, they received support from the US government and charitable organizations.[25]

Cuba's close proximity to the US mainland and the tense political relationship between the two countries has led to unique immigration policies specifically for Cubans escaping its communist regime. In 1966, the Cuban Adjustment Act was passed by the US Congress to provide an accelerated pathway to permanent residence for Cuban refugees.[26] In 1980, another major group of Cuban immigrants arrived as part of the Mariel boatlift. These Cubans had lived most of their lives under a socialist government and were more impoverished, less educated, and darker-skinned than earlier refugees. Another surge of immigrants arriving by boat occurred in 1994, prompting an agreement between the United States and Cuba known as the "wet foot, dry foot policy," whereby those Cubans who were intercepted on the water ("wet foot") would be returned to Cuba but those who made it to the US shore ("dry foot") would be allowed to remain and given permanent resident status after one year, putting them on a faster path to citizenship than most immigrants experience. As of 2013, 59 percent of Cubans living in the US were naturalized US citizens. In December 2014, US president Barack Obama and his Cuban counterpart, Raúl Castro, agreed to normalize relations between the two countries, opening the door for potential changes to the pattern of Cuban migration to the US.[27] In fact, in January 2017, just a few days before the end of his term, with the encouragement of the Cuban government, President Obama announced an end to the wet foot, dry foot policy, stating, "Effective immediately, Cuban nationals who attempt to enter the United States illegally and do not qualify for humanitarian relief will be subject to removal, consistent with U.S. law and enforcement priorities. . . . By taking this step, we are treating Cuban migrants the same way we treat migrants from other countries."[28]

When compared to other Latinx communities in the US, Cubans are more concentrated geographically—77 percent live in Florida.[29] They also have the highest education levels—approximately 25 percent of Cubans over age twenty-five are college graduates. A majority (60 percent) of Cubans over the age of five speak English fluently, but despite the longevity in the United States, more Cubans speak Spanish at home: 79 percent, compared to 73 percent of Latinxs as a group.[30] Perhaps because the early Cuban immigrants viewed themselves as people in exile who might return to Cuba when the government changed, they have worked to keep Spanish an integral part of their lives in the United States.[31]

In the wake of civil war and natural disasters, hundreds of thousands of Salvadorans have fled El Salvador to come to the United States. The first wave came between 1980 and 1990, resulting in a fivefold increase in population—from 94,000 to 465,000.[32] In the two decades that followed, the number of Salvadoran immigrants continued to grow as families sought to reunite and to escape the aftermath of additional hurricanes and earthquakes. As of 2016, approximately two million Salvadorans were living in the US. More than half live in California and Texas, but they are also concentrated in New York and the metropolitan DC/Maryland/Virginia area. Nearly two-thirds of immigrants from El Salvador (64 percent) arrived in the US in 1990 or later. Only 29 percent of Salvadoran immigrants are US citizens. Almost half (48 percent) of Salvadorans ages five and older speak English proficiently, compared to 66 percent of Latinxs overall.[33]

Like the four groups described here, those Latinxs who do not trace their family background to Mexico, Puerto Rico, Cuba, or El Salvador are an extremely heterogeneous group. They include South Americans as well as other Central Americans, well-educated professionals as well as rural farmers, those who immigrated for increased economic opportunities as well as those escaping civil war and other violence. Venezuelans are the most likely to have a college degree (51 percent) while Guatemalans and Salvadorans are among the least likely (7 percent). Argentineans have the highest annual median household income ($55,000) while Hondurans have the lowest ($31,000).[34]

Just as the White settlers in the nineteenth century were initially uncertain how to classify the Mexicans racially, the US Census Bureau has also struggled. The term *Hispanic* was used by the Census Bureau as an ethnic label and not to denote a "race," because Hispanics are a racially mixed group, including combinations of European White, African Black, indigenous peoples, and, in some cases, Asian. It is possible for an individual to identify as ethnically Hispanic and racially Black, White, or Asian at the same time.[35] As in African American families, there can be wide color variations in the same family. *Racismo* within Latinx communities is akin to colorism in Black American communities, advantaging lighter-skinned individuals.[36] Although a majority of Latinxs share the Roman Catholic faith and speak Spanish, not all do. Researchers Gerardo Marín and Barbara VanOss Marín argue that cultural values—not demographic characteristics—help Hispanics self-identify as members of one panethnic group.

## All in the Family: Familism in Latinx Communities

In particular, the cultural value of *familism,* defined as "a set of normative beliefs . . . that emphasize the centrality of the family unit and stress the obligations and support that family members owe to both nuclear and extended kin,"[37] has been identified as a characteristic shared by most Latinx families independent of their national background, birthplace, dominant language, or any other sociodemographic characteristic.[38]

In a carefully designed comparative study of four groups of adolescents—Mexicans living in Mexico, immigrant Mexicans in the United States, US-born Mexican Americans, and White Americans—researchers Carola and Marcelo Suárez-Orozco investigated the nature of familism among the four groups. In particular, they examined perceptions of the degree of emotional and material support provided by the family, the sense of obligation to provide support to one's family, and the degree to which families served as one's reference group (as opposed to peers, for example). They predicted that the three Latinx groups would demonstrate more familism than White American adolescents and that Mexican immigrants would demonstrate the highest level of familism, because immigrants frequently turn to the family for support and comfort. They found that the Latinx groups were indeed more family oriented than the White American group but that there was no significant difference among the three Latinx groups. All the adolescents of Mexican ancestry had a strong family orientation that expressed itself in a variety of ways.

For example, achieving in school and at work was considered important by Latinx teens in the study because success would allow them to take care of family members. Conversely, White American teens considered education and work as a means of gaining independence from their families. The researchers concluded that "in Mexico the family seems to be a centripetal force; in the United States it is a centrifugal force."[39] Because both immigrant and nonimmigrant Latinx adolescents expressed this value, the researchers also concluded that familism is related to enduring psychocultural features of the Latinx population, not only the stresses of immigration. Similarly, Fabio Sabogal and his colleagues found that Mexican Americans, Central Americans, and Cuban Americans all reported similar attitudes toward the family, this familism standing in contrast to the rugged individualism so often identified with White Anglo American culture.[40] Researchers have found that the values of familism support positive academic outcomes for Latinx students and mitigate against the negative influence of peers engaged in delinquent behavior.[41]

Though familism is not caused by immigration, it is reinforced by it. The ongoing influx of new Latinx immigrants and the circular migration of some populations (Puerto Ricans, for example) help to keep cultural values alive in the US mainland communities. The Suárez-Orozcos write, "For many second- and third-generation Latinos the immigrant past may also *be* the present. . . . Among Latinos the past is not only kept alive through family narratives but unfolds in front of our very eyes as recent arrivals endure anew the cycle of deprivation, hardship, and discrimination that is characteristic of first-generation immigrant life."[42] In this context, perhaps the most critical task facing the children of immigrants is reconciling the culture of home with the dominant American culture.

Drawing on the work of social identity theorist Tajfel and others, Phinney describes four possible outcomes for coping with this cultural conflict: *assimilation, withdrawal, biculturalism,* and *marginalization.* Assimilation is the attempt to blend into the dominant culture as much as possible, distancing oneself from one's ethnic group. Individuals using this strategy may actively reject the use of Spanish. Withdrawal results in an emphasis on one's ethnic culture and an avoidance of contact with the dominant group. This strategy is seen in highly segregated communities where English is rarely spoken. Someone with a bicultural identity incorporates selected aspects of both the home culture and the dominant culture, often achieving bilingual fluency in the process. The bicultural strategy can be a very positive one, but it is not easily achieved. For some, the attempt to bridge two worlds may result in alienation from both. Having rejected the "old country" ways of the family yet unable to find full acceptance in the dominant culture, these adolescents often experience marginalization. These alienated young people, relying on their peers for a sense of community, may be at particular risk for gang membership. School programs that help bridge the gap between the culture of home and the culture of the dominant society can reduce the risks of alienation.[43]

## "Who Are You If You Don't Speak Spanish?" Language and Identity Among Latinx Youth

As is suggested above, language is inextricably bound to identity. Language is not only an instrumental tool for communication but also the carrier of cultural values and attitudes. It is through language that the affect of *mi familia*, the emotions of family life, are expressed. Richard Rodriguez, in his classic memoir, *Hunger of Memory*, describes what happened in his family when the nuns at his parochial school told his Mexican parents to stop using Spanish at home, so their children might learn English more quickly. Gradually, he and his parents stopped speaking to each other. His family was "no longer so close; no longer bound tight by the pleasing and troubling knowledge of our public separateness. . . . The family's quiet was partly due to the fact that as we children learned more and more English, we shared fewer and fewer words."[44] What did it mean to his understanding of familism and other aspects of ethnic identity when he relinquished his Spanish?

For Jose, a young Puerto Rican man, the answer to this question is clear.

I think that the only thing that Puerto Ricans preserve in this country that is Puerto Rican is the language. If we lose that, *we* are lost. I think that we need to preserve it because it is the primordial basis of our culture. It is the only thing we have to identify ourselves as Puerto Rican. If you don't know your language, who are you? . . . I believe that being Puerto Rican and speaking Spanish go hand in hand.[45]

This sentiment was echoed repeatedly by other young Puerto Rican adults who were interviewed by Maria Zavala as part of a study of language and ethnic identity among Puerto Ricans.[46]

However, these young people had also learned that their language was devalued by the dominant culture. Those who had spent their childhoods in the United States in particular recalled feeling ashamed to be bilingual. Said Margarita,

In school there were stereotypes about the bilingual students, big time. [Since] they don't speak "the" language, they don't belong here. That's number one. Number two, they were dumb, no matter what. . . . Everyone said "that bilingual person," but they didn't realize that bilingual means they speak *two* languages. To them bilingual was not a good thing. There was a horrible stigma attached to them and I think I fell in the trap sometimes of saying "those bilingual people" just because that was what I was hearing all around me.[47]

A common coping strategy in childhood was to avoid the use of Spanish in public, a strategy akin to the "racelessness" adopted by some African American students, particularly in a predominantly White environment. Said Cristina, a young woman raised in the United States, "I remember pretending I didn't know how to speak Spanish. You know, if you pretended that you were that American then maybe you would get accepted by the White kids. I remember trying not to speak Spanish or speaking it with an [English] accent."[48]

However, avoiding the use of Spanish does not guarantee acceptance by the dominant society. A growing awareness of this reality and the unfolding process of adolescent identity development led these students to reclaim their Spanish, a process integral to their exploration of Puerto Rican identity. Cristina was able to do that as a college student, explaining:

> I'm a lot more fluent with English. I struggle with Spanish and it's something that I've been trying to reclaim. I've been reading a lot of literature written by Latinos lately, . . . some Puerto Rican history. Before [college] I didn't even know it existed. Now I'm reading and writing more and more in Spanish and I'm using it more in conversations with other Puerto Ricans. Now I have confidence. I don't feel inferior any more. I used to in high school, I did. People don't want you to speak Spanish and before I was one of those that's very guilty of not speaking it because I didn't want to draw attention to me, but now you can't tell me not to speak Spanish because for me that's the biggest form of oppression. My kids are going to speak Spanish and they're going to speak it loud. They're not going to go with the whispering stuff. As a matter of fact, if a White person comes by, we're going to speak it even louder. I am going to ingrain that in them, that you need to be proud of that.[49]

Zavala effectively demonstrates that while these young people are still in the process of exploring identity, the resolution of their feelings about the Spanish language is a central dimension of the identity development process. The linguicism to which they all had been subjected had been internalized by some and had to be rejected in order for them to assert a positive sense of identity.

While Zavala's study focused only on Puerto Ricans, a similar pattern was described by Paul, a young Chicano, reflecting on his early adolescence:

When I was in middle school me and my sister we were the only Latinos in the whole school. You know, all my friends were White just because I assimilated myself with White folks because I had moved out of my neighborhood and into a White neighborhood. You know I wanted to be like them. I started to lose my Spanish. . . . I really wanted to change my name, I just didn't want to be Mexican. You know, so my middle school years I really had a hard time because I wanted to assimilate my whole life to like White culture. But then as soon as I hit high school that changed cause there were so many Latinos, and so then I wanted to be more Chicano than ever. I lost my self-identity during my middle school.[50]

Vasti Torres in her qualitative study of Latinx college students, extending over a two-year period, heard similar sentiments echoed by Elizabeth, a young Cuban American whose exploration of ethnic identity was integrally connected with reclaiming her Spanish. In her first year, she felt "like an outsider" among other Latinx students because she no longer spoke fluent Spanish. Yet by her second year, she had become eager to change that.

I was in a class this past semester with a professor. . . . And there are a lot, like tons, of Hispanic kids in that class. And my last name is [common Spanish surname], so everyone looks at me, even at [the food court on campus], the people that work there will speak Spanish to me, and I'm just like, I can understand them but I can't really speak back. . . . So, in that class, I just really felt Whiter than White, like more American than ever, and they would stay afterwards with the professor and speak Spanish and . . . oh, I just hurt. I really want to be able to do that and that's like a really big deal why I am studying [abroad] the entire year, because my Spanish is horrendous and . . . I want to be fluent by the time I get back. I want to be able to read in Spanish, write in Spanish, and be good at it. And it's been really hard because the Hispanic kids don't look at me as very Hispanic. But the White kids or the American kids, [with] their racism issue, they'll look at me and they'll hear me sing a Spanish song or listen to Spanish music . . . or I want to eat Spanish food and they look at me like, "oh God, she is so Spanish," you know, and I am not. . . . It's hard.[51]

The racism of the White students and the discomfort with Spanish-speaking Latinx students left her in a lonely spot. Affirming her identity through her reengagement with Spanish as well as taking courses on Latin America is consistent with the phase of active exploration Phinney describes. Elizabeth elaborated on her identity quest:

My quest or journey to learn Spanish is a really big deal but also the education I get and the different classes in Latin America . . . they all kind of deal with like the same things, like cultural identity, and that's why I am really, really interested in anthropology. But that's like a really big deal, how people see themselves, how people [self-identify] because it really has an effect on your whole outlook on life.[52]

Though these young people clearly connect the Spanish language to their ethnic identity, a 2016 poll by the Pew Research Center found that while 95 percent of Latinxs said it was important for future generations to speak Spanish, most Latinx adults (71 percent) said it is *not* necessary to speak Spanish to be considered Latinx. It may be that the adult poll respondents are at a level of maturity and comfort with their own ethnic identity—and define it more broadly—than the adolescents in the interview studies cited here. In the active exploration stage of ethnic identity, visible symbols of one's identity—in this case one's spoken language—are very important, but they may be less so later on. While it may not be considered essential by all, the Pew researchers conclude, "Spanish is still a characteristic that, for the most part, unites much of a group. About three-quarters of Latinos, no matter where they are from, speak Spanish at home."[53]

Given the strong connection between language and identity, it seems very important for educators to think carefully about how they respond to Latinx children's use of Spanish at school. As Sonia Nieto points out, schools often work hard to strip away the child's native language, asking parents to speak English to their children at home, punishing children with detention for using their native language at school, or even withholding education until children have mastered English. While of course fluency in English is a necessary educational goal, the child's fluency in Spanish need not be undermined in order to achieve it.[54]

The bilingual education programs of the late twentieth century have largely been eliminated. In 1998, California voters approved Proposition 227, replacing bilingual education with Structured English Immersion (SEI), an approach that involves separating English-language learners from their English-speaking classmates and teaching them not only the English language but some of their academic content in English, rather than using the foundation of the child's first language to build understanding of academic content. In 2002, with the introduction of the federal No Child Left Behind law, signed by President George W. Bush, the Bilingual Education Act of 1967 was effectively repealed. Regrettably, research indicates that the elimination of bilingual education programs has had a negative impact on student learning.[55]

All good teachers know that learning builds on prior knowledge and experiences. In the case of language-minority students, this means that their native language can be a strong foundation for future learning. If we think of language development as the concrete foundation of a building, it makes sense that it needs to be strong to sustain the stress of many tons of building materials that will be erected on top of it. This is analogous to what takes place when English-speaking students enter school: they use the language they know as a foundation for learning the content of the curriculum. Because they know the majority language, this is usually a seamless process. For English-language learners, however, not knowing English is a tremendous disadvantage, not because their native language is ineffectual for learning but because schools do not generally view languages other than English as a resource for learning. Extending the metaphor further, it would be as if the strong foundation that had been created were abandoned and the building materials were placed on top of a sandlot across the street. Needless to say, the building would crumble quickly.[56]

Nieto and others are quick to point out that bilingual education alone could not completely reverse the history of school failure that Latinx students have experienced. But it does challenge the alienating and emotionally disruptive idea that native language and culture need to be forgotten in order to be successful.

## Living in the Shadows: The Undocumented Immigrants

In the days following Donald Trump's victory in the 2016 presidential election, there were reports of schoolchildren teasing their Mexican American classmates that they could be deported.[57] The Los Angeles Unified School District launched a hotline to help immigrant students and their families deal with their fears about the incoming president's campaign promise to deport millions of undocumented immigrants.[58] Though the vast majority of Mexican Americans are US citizens, in some cases for many generations, Latinxs in general and Mexican Americans in particular are often stereotyped and suspiciously regarded as "illegals." For that reason alone, all are impacted, directly or indirectly, by the rhetoric and attitudes toward undocumented immigrants.

According to the Pew Research Center, as of 2014 there were 11.1 million unauthorized immigrants in the US, representing 3.5 percent of the total population, a number that has been relatively stable since 2009. At that time, Mexicans made up 52 percent of all unauthorized immigrants (5.8 million people).[59] Keep in mind that the total Latinx population in 2015 was 56.6 million and of that the Mexican American population was 63.4 percent, or approximately 36 million people. Since 2009 the number of unauthorized immigrants from Mexico has been declining while the number of immigrants without authorization has increased from Central America (i.e., Guatemala, El Salvador, and Honduras) and Asia (primarily China), as well as sub-Saharan Africa.[60] The population of unauthorized immigrants is concentrated in six states—59 percent live in California, Texas, Florida, New York, New Jersey, and Illinois.[61] Sixty-six percent of adult immigrants without legal status in 2014 had been living in the US for at least ten years. During that time, many had given birth to children, who, due to their birth in the US, are citizens.[62]

There are approximately 5.5 million children who have at least one undocumented parent. Of those children, 4.5 million (81 percent) are US-born citizens. So-called mixed status families, where some members are citizens or legal permanent residents and others are not, suffer tremendous anxiety about the possibility of a family member's deportation.[63] "The most damaging family event associated with parental unauthorized status is the removal of a parent from the United States. . . . Between July 2010 and September 2012, 205,000 noncitizens who were deported claimed to have at least one US-citizen child, representing an annual average of about 90,000 parental deportations."[64]

The impact of a parent's removal on children is significant both emotionally and in terms of their physical security. The loss of a parent's income is devastating to the remaining family members' economic well-being, and fears of additional government action may lead families to flee or to keep children out of school. Even if there has been no arrest or parental removal, the chronic fear and toxic stress experienced by parents can manifest as behavioral problems, anxiety, and depressive symptoms in children.[65]

For the population of children who are themselves unauthorized immigrants, brought to the US in early childhood by their parents, their awareness of their undocumented status becomes part of their identity development in adolescence and young adulthood in very painful ways. Sociologist Roberto G. Gonzales studied the transition to adulthood experienced by undocumented Latinx young adults, twenty to thirty-four years of age, who came to the US before the age of twelve and live in California, still the state where the largest population of undocumented immigrants live.[66] It is worth noting that undocumented children may grow up unaware of their immigration status. Out of a desire to protect them from worry or to prevent them from exposing the family's secret, parents may not tell their children that they are undocumented. The Supreme Court ruled in 1982 (*Plyler v. Doe*) that undocumented children have a right to a K–12 education, and schools are required by the Federal Educational Rights and Privacy Act (FERPA) to keep students' records confidential, so immigration authorities do not have access to them. Consequently, children's immigration status has little impact on life at school until adolescence; they are in what Gonzales calls a state of "suspended illegality."[67] They sit alongside US-born peers, learn to speak English, socialize with friends, participate in school activities, and make plans for their future as all young people do.

It is around age sixteen, when US-born peers start to drive, get part-time jobs, and fill out financial aid forms for college applications, that undocumented teens' awareness of their dilemma becomes acute. All of these activities require a Social Security number, which they can't get. When the realization hits, the emotional response is anger, frustration, confusion, and despair—a "period of paralyzing shock." Miguel describes his response: "During most of high school, I thought I had my next 10 years laid out. College and law school were definitely in my plans. But when my mom told me I wasn't legal, everything was turned upside down. I didn't know what to do. I couldn't see my future anymore."[68]

Cory, a young Latina, first felt shock, then anger toward her parents for not telling her the truth earlier.

They thought that by the time I graduated I would have my green card. But they didn't stop to think that this is my life. . . . Everything I believed in was a big lie. Santa Claus was not coming down the chimney, and I wasn't going to just become legal. I really resented them. . . . I feel as though I've experienced this weird psychological and legal-stunted growth. I'm stuck at 16, like a clock that has stopped ticking. My life has not changed at all since then. Although I'm 22, I feel like a kid. I can't do anything adults do.[69]

As Gonzales writes, "Illegal status places undocumented youth in a developmental limbo."[70]

It is a natural response to seek comfort from friends when one learns upsetting news, but in this case, undocumented adolescents may be afraid of revealing their newly discovered status because of the stigma and the legal risk. One study participant described hearing a teammate using derogatory terms to describe players on an opposing team, assuming that they were undocumented. What would this friend say about him if he knew his status? What would teachers say?

Feeling scared and alone, some of the adolescents Gonzales studied lost hope for the future and dropped out of school. Others confided in a trusted adult and were encouraged to stay in school, and in some cases, they were able to get to and through college with the assistance of mentors who helped them find financial assistance. Sadly, whether they successfully completed high school and college or not, eventually they hit an occupational dead end due to their legal limbo. Gonzales found that by their midtwenties, both college-goers and school dropouts held similar occupations—the same low-wage jobs that their parents held. They had few legal choices even if they had earned advanced degrees. Coming to that realization was like "waking up to a nightmare."[71]

Gonzales closes his study with these words: "We must ask ourselves if it is good for the health and wealth of this country to keep such a large number of U.S.-raised young adults in the shadows. We must ask what is lost when they learn to be illegal."[72] These questions are exactly the questions the nation is facing as of this writing in January 2017 as the transition of presidential power goes from Barack Obama to Donald Trump. The Deferred Action for Childhood Arrivals (DACA) program created by President Obama's executive order in 2012 has allowed more than 750,000 young unauthorized immigrants who arrived in the US before the age of sixteen and have no serious criminal convictions to go to school or get a work permit and receive protection from deportation for a two-year period. Not all who are eligible have come forward, some perhaps wary about reporting themselves to the federal authorities, but it is estimated that 78 percent of those eligible have applied to the program.[73] Once an individual is approved for the program, the benefits can be renewed after the first two-year period expires. Gonzales interviewed his study respondents before DACA was initiated—today the program offers a potential lifeline to young people like Margarita:

I graduated from high school and have taken some college credits. Neither of my parents made it past fourth grade, and they don't speak any English. But I'm right where they are. I mean, I work with my mom. I have the same job. I can't find anything else. It's kinda ridiculous, you know. Why did I even go to school? It should mean something. I mean, that should count, right? You would think. I thought. Well, here I am, cleaning houses.[74]

Will that lifeline be taken away from DACA beneficiaries by the new president? At this writing, we don't know.

It is easy to feel sympathy for the young people caught in this undocumented dilemma and to lament the potential loss of human capital for a nation in need of talent. Yet what is the role of racism in this narrative? Some readers may say, "This is not about race or racism; it is about illegal activity—crossing the border without permission has consequences for adults and, unfortunately, their children." Historian Natalia Molina has another perspective on that question that is worth considering. She writes:

What we are seeing is the reanimation of longstanding stereotypes— what I call racial scripts . . . that present Mexicans as unassimilable, criminal, even diseased. . . . The history of who gets to be "legal" in our country is complex. European immigrants who came to the US in the 19th and early 20th centuries faced few restrictions. And even when immigrants broke the rules, short statutes of limitation meant they were rarely deported. When laws changed in 1924, the federal government took steps to make European immigrants "legal" and pave the way for their eventual assimilation. Deportations were suspended, and immigrants could pay a small fee to register when they arrived in the United States. Mexican immigrants enjoyed no such opportunities. Instead, they faced increasing regulation through the Border Patrol, established in 1924. . . . In the 1920s, like now, employers opposed immigration quotas because they limited the availability of low-wage labor. But even this supposed openness to Mexicans nonetheless cast them as alien workers, not as immigrants arriving to the American melting pot. And during the Great Depression, when Mexican labor was no longer needed, the U.S. sent an estimated 1 million Mexicans back to Mexico, including some U.S. citizens of Mexican descent.[75]

Drawing the contrast between the way European immigrants were viewed and the way Mexican immigrants were regarded during the same historical periods, Molina revisits the history of Mexican segregation (akin to the Jim Crow treatment that Blacks experienced in the South—Mexican immigrants were barred from swimming pools and restaurants, separated in neighborhoods, movie theaters, and cemeteries). What becomes clear is that the "you don't belong here" message was undoubtedly part of the Latinx past, even for those who were US citizens, and for now it continues to be a part of their present.

## What Do We Mean When We Say "Native"?

It is impossible to know just how many millions of indigenous people there were in North America prior to 1492. What is certain is that contact with the Europeans was disastrous for them. The explorers brought with them the diseases of Europe, such as smallpox, to which the Native Americans had no immunity. It is estimated that more than 90 percent of the native population was wiped out by virulent epidemics. By the time European settlers began to arrive in large numbers, the indigenous population had already been reduced significantly. Military conflict, forced relocations, and other traumas added to the depopulation. By the early twentieth century, census figures reported the American Indian population above the Rio Grande to be just 490,000.[76]

Now, as of 2015, the number of people who self-identify as American Indians or Alaska Natives is 6.6 million, including those who choose more than one racial group on the census form. They represent 567 different cultural communities federally recognized as sovereign entities with which the United States has a government-to-government relationship.[77]

Each of these cultural communities has its own language, customs, religion, economy, historical circumstances, and environment. They range from the very traditional, whose members speak their indigenous language at home, to the mostly acculturated, who speak English as their first language. Most Native people identify with their particular ancestral community first and as American Indians second.[78]

The Native population grew slowly in the first half of the twentieth century but has grown rapidly in the second half due to a high birth rate and reduced infant mortality. Another source of the population increase, however, has been the fact that since 1970 a significant number of people have changed their census identification to American Indian from some other racial category on the census forms.[79] This shift in self-identification raises the questions, who is Native and how is that category defined?

The answers depend on whom you ask. Each Indian nation sets its own criteria for membership. Some specify a particular percentage of ancestry (varying from one-half to one-sixty-fourth), others do not. Some nations specify Native language fluency as a prerequisite for service in their government, others do not. The US government requires one-quarter blood quantum (as indicated on a federal "certificate of Indian blood") in order to qualify for Bureau of Indian Affairs college scholarships. Other federal agencies, such as the Census Bureau, rely on self-identification. Declining social discrimination, growing ethnic pride, a resurgence in Native activism, and the pursuit of sovereign rights may account for the growing numbers of racially mixed US citizens who are now choosing to identify themselves as American Indian.[80]

Despite the stereotypes to the contrary, there is great diversity among this population. K. Tsianina Lomawaima, a professor of American Indian studies, makes this point very clearly when she writes:

> A fluent member of a Cherokee Baptist congregation living in Tahlequah, Oklahoma, is different from an English-speaking, pow-wow-dancing Lakota born and raised in Oakland, California, who is different from a Hopi fluent in Hopi, English, Navajo, and Spanish who lives on the reservation and supports her family by selling "traditional" pottery in New York, Santa Fe, and Scottsdale galleries. The idea of being generically "Indian" really was a figment of Columbus's imagination.[81]

However, there are general demographic statements that can be made about the Native population. The majority live in one of ten states: California, Oklahoma, Arizona, New Mexico, Texas, North Carolina, Washington, Alaska, New York, or South Dakota. Over the last forty years, significant numbers have moved from rural areas to major cities. In 1970, 45 percent lived in a metropolitan area; by 2010, that number had grown to 70 percent.[82] The cities with the greatest number of indigenous people are New York, Los Angeles, Phoenix, Oklahoma City, and Anchorage, Alaska. Only 22 percent of all American Indians (including Alaska Natives) live on reservations and trust lands, with the remaining percentage living in nearby rural communities.[83] According to 2015 census data, the median income of single-race American Indian and Alaska Natives households was $38,530; the national median was $55,775. More Native people live in poverty than any other racial group. Approximately 27 percent of Native families are at or below the official poverty level, compared to a national poverty rate of approximately 15 percent. Among single-race American Indians and Alaska Native adults (twenty-five or older), 14.1 percent had earned a bachelor's, graduate, or professional degree. Overall, Natives have the lowest educational attainment rates of all ethnic and racial groups in the United States and face some of the lowest high school graduation rates nationwide.[84]

Beyond these demographic patterns, there are shared cultural values that are considered characteristic of American Indian families. For example, as with Latinxs (who often have indigenous ancestry), extended family and kinship obligations are considered very important. Consequently, group needs are more important than individual needs. Communal sharing with those less fortunate is expected. Traditional Indian culture sees an interdependent relationship among all living things. Just as one seeks harmony with one's human family, so should a person try to be in harmony with nature, rather than be dominant over it.[85]

## Surviving the Losses

From the beginning of their encounters with Europeans, these and other Indian values were at odds with the individualistic and capitalistic orientation of the White settlers. US government leaders were convinced that changing Indian cultural values were the key to "civilizing" Indians and acquiring Indian-controlled lands.[86]

Following the establishment of reservations, one of the major strategies used to facilitate this cultural conversion was the establishment of off-reservation boarding schools for Indian children. The first such school was the Carlisle Indian School in Carlisle, Pennsylvania, established in 1879. Over the fifty years that followed, thousands of Indian children as young as five were forcibly removed from their families and placed in boarding schools, too far away for their poverty-stricken families to visit. Parental nurturing was replaced with forced assimilation, hard physical labor, harsh discipline, and emotional, physical, and often sexual abuse. Though the US government's practice of removing children from their home environments was reversed in the 1930s, by then several generations of Indian children had lost their traditional cultural values and ways, and yet remained alienated from the dominant American culture.[87]

Further cultural disruptions occurred in the 1940s and 1950s when federal Indian policy shifted again, this time with the goal of terminating the official relationship between the Indian nations and the US government. Many Indians were taken from their homes and relocated in urban areas, in a manner reminiscent of the earlier forced removal to reservations.[88] The upheaval brought on by the relocation process was devastating. Alcoholism, suicide, and homicide increased to epidemic proportions and continue to be among the leading causes of death among American Indians.[89]

The intergenerational impact of these disruptions can be seen in this Native woman's narrative:

For 500 years, my people have been told in so many ways, "You're no good. You are a savage. Change your ways. You are not civilized. Your ways are heathen and witchery. Your ways are not Christian!" My grandfather gave up his tribal religion and customs. He adopted Christianity. He, my grandmother, and the other people on the reservation did their best to give up the old ways, become farmers, quit hunting, go to church and be "good Indians, civilized Indians." They wept when the federal agents rounded up their children to take them away to boarding school. Some of the children never came home. Some came home to be buried. My grandparents and the people wept again because their children grew up learning alien ways, forgetting their language and customs in schools too far away to visit.

My parents married soon after they came home from the boarding school. They came from different tribes. They left my father's reservation encouraged by the U.S. government and the boarding school system to find jobs in the "real world." . . . The promised jobs never materialized and, stuck between two worlds, the big city and the reservation, the Indian world and the White, my father drank and beat my mother. My mother worked at menial jobs to support us. My life was built on this foundation. I was never parented because my parents, raised in government boarding schools, had nothing to give me. They had lost their languages and retained only traces of their cultures. They had never been parented themselves. Boarding school nurturing was having their mouths washed out with soap for talking Indian and receiving beatings for failing to follow directions.

So this is my legacy and the legacy of many Indians, both reservation and urban. . . . We are survivors of multigenerational loss and only through acknowledging our losses will we ever be able to heal.[90]

The legacy of loss is accompanied by a legacy of resistance. As they had in the past, Native peoples resisted the termination policy, and the policy ended in the 1960s following the election of John F. Kennedy. The civil rights era included Native demands for greater self-determination and the development of a pan-Indian movement based on the assumption that indigenous peoples shared a common set of values and interests. In response to American Indian activism, the federal government condemned its own destructive policies of the past and increased support for Indian self-determination, passing legislation in the 1980s and 1990s designed to promote Indian-controlled schools, protect American Indian religious freedom, and preserve traditional Indian languages.[91] During the civil rights era, tribal colleges were established to improve postsecondary educational opportunities for Native communities on or near reservations. As of 2017, there are thirty-two fully accredited Tribal Colleges and Universities (TCUs) in the United States. Diné College, established in 1968 by the Navajo Nation, was the first and is the largest of these tribally controlled institutions, awarding "associate degrees and certificates in areas important to the economic and social development of the Navajo Nation."[92]

Given the poverty that has resulted from the long history of relocation, isolation, and cultural disruption, economic development is critical for Native communities. A significant development in the economic history of Native peoples in the United States was the passage of the Indian Gaming Regulatory Act (IGRA) in 1988, in which Congress "recognized the exclusive right of tribes to regulate gaming on their lands and sought to promote tribal economic development, self-sufficiency and strong self-government."[93] Specifically, Congress mandated that gaming revenues cannot be used for individual private gain but must be used primarily for public purposes, such as funding tribal government operations or programs, providing for the general welfare of the Indian tribe and its members, promoting tribal economic development, donating to charitable organizations, and funding operations of local government agencies. In addition, revenues can be paid on a per capita basis to individual tribal members with the approval of the secretary of the interior.[94]

The impact of this legislation has been quite dramatic. Revenues have grown from $225 million in 1987 (generated from tribal bingo operations) to $9.8 billion in casino gaming revenue in 1998 and $26.5 billion in 2009. Native American casinos now represent 40 percent of the gaming industry in the US. While not all American Indian nations have chosen to participate or are located near population centers that would make gaming success possible, by 2009 approximately 237 tribes were operating 442 gaming facilities in the US.[95] Two of the largest—Foxwoods, operated by the Mashantucket Pequots, and Mohegan Sun, operated by the Mohegans, both in Connecticut—have been generating billions of dollars annually, dramatically improving the economic well-being of the two nation's members. The gains for members of other tribal groups have been quite modest. American Indians on gaming reservations experience a 7.4 percent increase in per capita income and reductions in both family and child poverty rates as compared to those on non-gaming reservations.[96]

Those who have experienced gaming success have also experienced backlash from non-Native communities. "Local reactions to tribal sovereignty, often elicited in response to a tribe's decision to pursue gaming, may belie historically anti-tribal and anti-Native attitudes, that while pre-dating Indian gaming, find new vitality in a decade of increasingly plausible Native viability."[97] The stereotype of "rich Indians" who are not paying "their fair share" has been part of the political discourse in California, in particular, home to more people of Native American heritage than any other state in the nation.[98]

> Although we should recognize tribes' limited economic alternatives to gaming, we should be ready to acknowledge as well the role of gaming in politicizing Native identity. Indian gaming has added "rich Indians" and "real Indians" to the vocabulary of policymakers and their constituents. It has served as fodder for caricatures on television and in newspapers, such as a *Family Circus* comic strip depicting a cowboy-dressed child playing a modern "cowboys and Indians" opposite a tuxedo-clad casino operator. At first blush, the *Family Circus* image may seem harmless, but it works, which is to say it is "funny" because it points up the incongruity of cultural perceptions. The subtext of such an image is that the tuxedo-wearing "Indian" is not really authentic, or is at a minimum less authentic than other representations of "Indian-ness."[99]

## "Have You Ever Seen a Real Indian?"

In 2001, the American Indian College Fund (AICF) launched an advertising campaign featuring accomplished Native professionals and tribal college students in an attempt to portray a contemporary and accurate image of Native American people, shown with the caption, "Have you ever seen a real Indian?" Richard Williams, then the executive director of

AICF, said the organization's goal was "to challenge the American public's notions about who Indian people are and what they can become."[100] That 2001 challenge is still part of the Native American reality in 2017, due to both widespread invisibility in terms of contemporary images and continued and pervasive use of stereotypes rooted in the past.

Invisibility in classrooms is a common experience for Native students. In her article "Is There an 'Indian' in Your Classroom?," Lee Little Soldier makes the point that teachers might find it hard to determine whether there even are Native American students in their classrooms.[101] Natives often have European names, and because of the high proportion of mixed-heritage individuals, there are wide variations in physical appearance. While some are easily recognized as people of color, others have light skin, light eyes, and brown or blond hair and may be identified by others as White. Those who are products of Black-Native unions may simply be assumed to be African American. Particularly in those parts of the United States with small indigenous populations, many people may be surprised to discover that Natives still exist at all. For example, American Indian studies professor Donald Andrew Grinde Jr. described his own history professor's response when he expressed an interest in studying American Indian history: "My advisor told me I needed to focus on an area such as American economic history to secure employment. When I told him I was an American Indian and thus still wanted to do research in this area, he smiled and murmured, 'I thought that we had killed all of them.'"[102] This perception is not surprising given the missing information about Native peoples in most US history curricula.

Viena, a Native American teen living on a reservation in northwest Washington, recalls her experience in a predominantly White elementary school off the reservation.

There was a time, I was in third grade, there was a film about Native Americans, something in the movie I knew wasn't right and I came home really sad about the Paiute. The movie said the so-called pioneers came westward. They were in some fort and their fort was encircled by the Paiute and burnt to the ground. The whole class got to watch that film. The class was saying how horrible the Paiute were. My mom went in and talked to the teacher; she said to the teacher, "Did you know Viena is Paiute?" She could not deal with it. She could not deal with the fact—the European Americans did bring diseased blankets, how many people died. You cannot just say one side. . . . Our people did not just attack people for no reason. It is true that Indians did burn down forts, but it is the way in which the story has been told [that bothers me]. Why did they have to defend themselves in this way?[103]

Historical omissions and distortions don't just affect Native students, they also contribute to the miseducation of everyone else. The same can be said of the stereotypical images popularized by the use of American Indians as mascots. One consequence of the relative invisibility of Native peoples is that the knowledge most Americans have about them is "formed and fostered by *indirectly* acquired information (e.g., media representations of American Indians.)"[104]

The most highly visible example has been, and at this writing continues to be, the NFL football team in the nation's capital, the Washington Redskins. The term *redskin* was widely used in the nineteenth century to describe the scalped head of a Native American for which state governments paid bounties. The ugliness of its history continues in the present, as it is now used as a derogatory racial slur.[105] There is growing pressure on the Washington football team to change its name, and there are media outlets that now refuse to use it, referring to the NFL team as simply "the Washington football team." The NFL owner asserts that the name will "never change." As disturbing as that is, what is more problematic than the name of this national team is the use of similarly derogatory mascots in public K–12 schools.[106]

In 2001 the US Commission on Civil Rights issued a statement on the issue: "The stereotyping of any racial, ethnic, religious or other groups when promoted by our public educational institutions, teach all students that stereotyping of minority groups is acceptable, a dangerous lesson in a diverse society. Schools have a responsibility to educate their students; they should not use their influence to perpetuate misrepresentations of any culture or people."[107]

Since then, the American Psychological Association, the American Sociological Association, the American Counselors Association, and the National Collegiate Athletics Association have all called for the elimination of such usage of American Indian and Alaska Native names, mascots, symbols, and logos. Several state boards of education have taken action to ban the use of these mascots and symbols in the schools within their states. But not all have.[108]

Leaving these symbols in place can create a hostile learning environment for students. Consider this example shared by Dahkotah Kicking Bear Brown, Miwok student and football player at a California high school:

> One of our school's biggest rivals is the Calaveras Redskins. Calaveras has always had an obscene amount of school pride, but little do they know how damaging their game-time routines are. With so many around me, I feel ganged up on, but at the same time, all of these screaming fans don't know how offensive they are, or that they are even in the presence of a Native. Most of the time, they don't even know that Natives are still around. Worst of all, the most offensive stuff doesn't even come from the Redskins. It comes from their rival schools, mine included. I have heard my own friends yelling around me, "Kill the Redskins!" or "Send them on the Trail of Tears!"[109]

Some have argued that some of the mascot representations, such as a "chief," are positive, honoring American Indian heritage. However, Native students say they do not feel honored. Cierra Fields, a Cherokee member of the National Congress of American Indians Youth Cabinet, articulated this viewpoint:

> When I see people wearing headdresses and face paint or doing the tomahawk chop, it makes me feel demeaned. The current society does not bother to learn that our ways, customs, dress, symbols, and

images are sacred. They claim it's for honor but I don't see honor in non-Natives wearing face paint or headdresses as they are not warriors who have earned the right. My heritage and culture is not a joke. My heritage and culture is not a fashion statement. For me it ultimately boils down to respect. Respect our heritage by not using a caricature of a proud people but by learning our history.[110]

The research of social psychologist Stephanie Fryberg and others has demonstrated that whether the stereotypical image is "negative" or "positive" in its content, the impact on Native American youth is harmful in terms of lowering self-esteem, feelings of community worth, and achievement-related possible selves. In the absence of a broader range of societal images of American Indians, the stereotypes have a disproportionate impact.

The current American Indian mascot representations function as inordinately powerful communicators, to Natives and non-Natives alike, of how American Indians should look and behave. American Indian mascots thus remind American Indians of the limited ways in which others see them. Moreover, because identity construction is not solely an individual process (i.e., you cannot be a self by yourself), the views of American Indians held by others can also limit the ways in which American Indians see themselves.[111]

The antidote to these limited images is to "either eliminate them or to create, distribute, and institutionalize a broader array of social representations of American Indians."[112] Parents, educators, and students themselves can work to eliminate the stereotypical representations from schools. Sonia Nieto and Patty Bode share a case study in their book, *Affirming Diversity*, of a group of eighth-grade students who did just that, with the support of their teacher.[113]

Paul Ongtooguk, an Alaskan Native educator, has made it his mission to develop curricula that assumes Alaska Natives such as the Inupiaq are not just people with a past but also people with a future. As he said in a speech to fellow educators in Alaska,

We have a suicide rate for Alaska Native males that is about eight times the national average in the age category from 15 through 24. What does that say? Some people would look at that statistic and say, well, that's not about education—it's not an educational statistic. But I look at that, and I look at the lives of the people who are trapped in it. We are talking about young people who are going through life so ill-prepared for the future, whose opportunities are so narrow, whose sense of the future is so bleak, and whose circumstances are so overwhelming that death is preferable to the life that lies before them. Isn't that an educational issue? Something for us to consider.[114]

Throughout his career, Ongtooguk has pushed to create curricular materials that would inspire Native students to see themselves in the future. He worked to reconstruct the "Inupiaq Heritage Curriculum," which at the time he began consisted primarily of Native arts and crafts projects. While the traditional arts and crafts were worthy of study, the curriculum embodied a "museum" perspective whereby the traditional life of Alaska Natives was studied as "an interesting curiosity commemorating the past." Ongtooguk explained, "The most disturbing picture of Inupiaq culture, then, was of its static nature—something that had happened 'back then' rather than something that was happening now. Did this mean that the people living in the region now were like a cast of actors who had run out of lines?"

He set out to reconstruct the curriculum to reflect not only traditional life but also transitional life and the modern period. "If, as their teachers commonly implied, being Inupiaq only meant being traditional (or Ipani), then both assimilation and all of modern schooling were essentially cultural genocide in that they moved the students away from things traditional. . . . [Students] needed to know both what was and what is crucial for survival and for leading productive lives within the Inupiaq community."[115]

The inclusion of contemporary life as part of this revised Inupiaq studies curriculum was essential if Inupiaq students were to see themselves reflected in the schools and see the Inupiaq identity as having a future, not only a past. They needed a coherent picture of the continuity, conflict, and cultural transformation that had shaped and continued to shape the Inupiaq community. Ongtooguk's reconstructed curriculum was eventually adopted by the Northwest Arctic School District and became a model for Yup'ik studies in several school districts in southwest Alaska.[116]

Such curricular interventions stand in stark contrast to the deculturalization that has been the legacy of American Indian education, reminding us that education does not have to mean alienation. More such interventions are needed if faculty and students, both Native and White, are to realize that the Native community is not a relic of the past but a growing community with a future.

Another growing population, which, unlike American Indians, is usually assumed to have a very bright future, is the Asian and Pacific Islander (API) community. The collective image of Asians as the "model minority" in the United States is a pervasive one. Yet, as we will again see, even a "positive" stereotype can have negative consequences, and like the Latinx and Native communities, the API community is not a monolith.

## What Do We Mean When We Say "Asian"?

The terms *Asian* and *Asian American* encompass people of many different national origins, histories, cultures, languages, and religions. The federal government, for the purpose of the census, defines "Asian" as "a person having origins in any of the original peoples of the Far East, Southeast Asia, or the Indian subcontinent, including for example, Cambodia, China, India, Japan, Korea, Malaysia, Pakistan, the Philippine Islands, Thailand and Vietnam."[117]

Cultural traditions and religious beliefs vary greatly across this vast geographic region and include Buddhism, Islam, Christianity (both Protestant and Catholic), Hinduism, Shintoism, Confucianism, ancestor worship, and animism.[118]

Given the wide range of countries of origin and the cultural diversity represented, it is reasonable to ask whether the umbrella category of "Asian" is a useful one. Scholars Min Zhou and Jennifer Lee say it is, primarily because of the way race operates in American society.

In the United States, race often overrides many major socioeconomic and cultural factors—including education, occupation, language, and religion—to affect the everyday lives of all Americans. . . . Asian-origin Americans . . . adopt the pan-ethnic label because of convenience and because other Americans cannot and often do not even try to make ethnic distinctions, despite vast differences in national origin, religion, language, and culture.[119]

Collectively, Asian Americans have the highest median family incomes, highest levels of education, highest rates of intermarriage, and the lowest rates of residential segregation in the country.[120] They are also the fastest-growing racial group in the United States.[121] The Asian population in the US grew by 43 percent, from 10.2 million to 14.7 million, between 2000 and 2010, while the US population overall grew 9.7 percent.[122] In 2014, the estimated number of people of Asian descent was 20.3 million, approximately 6 percent of the total US population. At 4.5 million, the Chinese are the largest Asian group, followed by Asian Indians (3.8 million), Filipinos (3.8 million), Vietnamese (2.0 million), Koreans (1.8 million), and Japanese (1.4 million).[123] Together these top six groups account for approximately 85 percent of the total Asian population. Asians in the US are concentrated on the West Coast (47 percent), with 20 percent living in the Northeast, 21 percent in the South, and just 11 percent in the Midwest.[124]

In 1960, most Asian Americans were descendants of early Chinese and Japanese immigrants. Changes in immigration policy in 1965 dramatically increased Asian immigration, significantly altering the demographic makeup of the Asian American community. By 2010, 59 percent of Asians in the US were foreign-born, compared to 13 percent of the total US population. Among Asian adults over the age of twenty-five, the percentage of foreign-born is even higher—74 percent. As is the case among Latinxs, each national group has its own unique immigration history that has shaped its experience in the United States. While it is not possible to review the immigration history of all these groups, the immigration experience of the most populous groups will be briefly summarized here.[125]

The Chinese were the first Asians to immigrate to the United States in large numbers, arriving in California in 1850 as part of the rush for gold. These first arrivals were single men who paid their own way to the California gold fields, hoping to get rich and then return to China. As the gold rush waned, many Chinese did not have enough money to go home. Hired at wages one-third below what Whites would have been paid, Chinese men found employment as laborers working on the transcontinental railroad and on California farms.[126] When the US economy took a sharp downturn in the mid-1870s, White labor union leaders blamed Chinese workers for the depressed wage levels and the Chinese became a frequent target of racial bigotry and violence. In fact, in 1871 the largest mass lynching in US history took place in Los Angeles when a mob of White men attacked and lynched more than twenty Chinese men.[127]

The anti-Chinese sentiment culminated in the passage of the Chinese Exclusion Act of 1882.[128] Immigration was severely restricted by the Chinese Exclusion Act and completely forbidden by the 1924 Immigration Act. Like Blacks and Indians, the Chinese, referred to as the "yellow peril," were reviled and viewed as a threat to White racial purity. Laws prohibiting marriage between a White person and a "negro, mulatto, or Mongolian" were passed.[129] These laws, combined with immigration restrictions, special taxes directed against the Chinese, and discrimination in housing and employment, limited the growth of the Chinese population. Most of the men did not start families in the United States, and many returned to China.[130]

A second wave of Chinese immigration occurred after World War II. In an effort to promote an alliance with China against Japan, the US government repealed the Exclusion Act to allow a few thousand Chinese to enter the country. Chinese scientists and professionals and their families escaping communism were part of this second wave.[131]

A third wave of Chinese immigration occurred after the 1965 Immigration Act (and its 1990 extension). Because racial quotas on immigration were eliminated by this legislation, Chinese immigration dramatically increased, with entire families immigrating at once. The Chinese population grew from 237,000 in 1960 to over 4 million in

2010.[132] In the last fifty years, Chinese immigrants have come not only from China but also from Hong Kong, Taiwan, Vietnam, Laos, and Cambodia, as well as other parts of Asia, some arriving with little education and few resources while others have college and graduate degrees, family savings, and in-demand job skills. The latter group of new Chinese immigrants is not drawn to ethnic enclaves like the Chinatowns found in major cities; instead, they have the financial ability to settle in affluent suburbs or in "new suburban ethnic enclaves known as 'ethnoburbs.'"[133]

In contrast to the Chinese and other Asian immigrants, more than three-quarters of the people with Japanese ancestry in the United States are American-born, descendants of those who came to the US mainland or Hawaii before 1924. These early immigrants were attracted by higher US wages, and because the Japanese government encouraged women to emigrate as well, often as "picture brides" in arranged marriages, Japanese families quickly established themselves. While Japanese workers were welcomed on the plantations of Hawaii, there was considerable anti-Japanese feeling on the West Coast.[134] In 1906 the San Francisco Board of Education established a separate school for Chinese, Japanese, and Korean children, and the California Alien Land Law of 1913 prohibited Japanese immigrants and other foreign-born residents from purchasing agricultural land because they were ineligible for citizenship. (The Naturalization Act, passed in 1790, only allowed Whites to become naturalized citizens, so while children born in the United States automatically became citizens, until this law was repealed, their immigrant parents could never be eligible.) As with the Chinese, immigration of Japanese came to a halt with the Immigration Act of 1924.[135]

The Japanese bombing of Pearl Harbor in 1941 certainly intensified anti-Japanese sentiment. In March 1942, Executive Order 9102 established the War Relocation Authority, making it possible to remove 120,000 Japanese Americans from their West Coast homes without a trial or hearing and confine them in internment camps in places as far away as Idaho, Colorado, and Utah.[136] One response to this internment experience was for Japanese American families to encourage their children to become as "American" as possible in an effort to prevent further discrimination. For this reason, as well as their longevity in the United States, Japanese Americans as a group are the most acculturated of the Asian American communities, and the only Asian ethnic group not currently growing in population size. Japanese have high rates of intermarriage—more than half of Japanese American newlyweds in 2010 married a non-Asian—and 35 percent of Japanese Americans identified themselves as multiracial in the 2010 census.[137]

Like the Chinese, Koreans arrived in the US in distinct waves of immigration, beginning with seven thousand farmers who came to Hawaii to escape poverty and work on plantations there in the early 1900s, followed there by Korean "picture brides." Koreans were subject to the same antimiscegenation laws that affected the Chinese. Another small group of immigrants came to the United States after World War II and the Korean War. This group included Korean adoptees and Korean women who were married to US soldiers. As with the Chinese, the 1965 Immigration Act dramatically increased Korean immigration of entire families, with thirty thousand Koreans arriving annually between 1970 and 1990. Most Korean Americans currently living in the United States were part of this post-1965 immigration. Typically these families consist of immigrant parents and American-born or American-raised children, families in which differing rates of acculturation may contribute to generational conflicts.[138] Koreans in the US come from a wide range of socioeconomic and educational levels, but more than half (53 percent) of Korean adults over the age of twenty-five have a college degree, earned either in Korea or in the United States.[139]

Filipino Americans also experienced a pattern of male immigration to Hawaii, and then the mainland United States, in the early 1900s. Because these men could not establish families, there are few descendants from this wave of immigration. This pattern ended in 1930 when Congress set a Filipino immigration quota of fifty per year. As with Chinese and Koreans, tens of thousands of Filipinos have immigrated annually since 1965. As of the 2010 census, 69 percent of Filipinos were foreign-born. Forty-seven percent of Filipino adults have a college degree, and the poverty rate is only 6 percent, the lowest of all Asian groups in the US.[140] Reflecting the colonial history of the Philippines,

Filipinos have a multicultural heritage of Chinese, Spanish, Malayan, Indonesian, South Asian, American, and Muslim cultural influences and are similar to Pacific Islanders in many ways.[141]

Southeast Asian refugees are quite different from other Asian immigrant groups in their reasons for coming to the United States and their experiences in their homelands. After the end of the Vietnam War in 1975, a large number of mostly educated Vietnamese arrived. After 1978, a second group of immigrants, many of them uneducated rural farmers traumatized by the war and its aftermath, came to the United States to escape persecution. This group includes Vietnamese, Chinese Vietnamese, Cambodians, Lao, Hmong, and Mien.[142]

Among Vietnamese, another wave of immigration occurred after 1980 as the result of an agreement negotiated between Vietnam and the US. A subsequent wave of Vietnamese immigration in the 1990s was the result of the process of family unification, as new immigrants came to join family members that had already established a presence in the United States. Vietnamese now represent 10 percent of the adult Asian American population, 84 percent of whom are foreign-born. Less well educated than other Asians, 26 percent of Vietnamese adults have college degrees and 15 percent live in poverty, compared to 12 percent of Asians overall.[143]

Asian Indians have also experienced a dramatic population growth in the United States since 1965. The number of Asian Indians in the United States increased from eight hundred thousand in 1990 to almost four million in 2014. The first wave of immigrants from India—about six thousand—came to work as farmhands, arriving in the first decade of the twentieth century. Initially, Indians were classified in court cases of 1910 and 1913 as "Caucasians" and consequently were allowed to intermarry with US-born Whites.[144] Because previous Supreme Court rulings had established that being Caucasian was synonymous with being White, a group of Asian Indians, on the basis of their Caucasian classification, pursued their right to become citizens but were denied because of their brown skin. In 1923 the case went to the Supreme Court—*United States v. Bhagat Singh Thind*. The judges ruled that while Asian Indians were Caucasians (descended from the Caucasoid region of Eurasia), they could not be considered White and consequently were not eligible for US citizenship. This ruling made explicit the concept of skin color as a bar to becoming a citizen. As the court ruling stated, "It may be true that the blond Scandinavian and the brown Hindu have a common ancestor in the dim reaches of antiquity, but the average man knows perfectly well that there are unmistakable and profound differences between them today," adding that "the intention of the Founding Fathers was to 'confer the privilege of citizenship upon the class of persons they knew as white.'"[145] This racial barrier to citizenship was not removed until 1952 when the passage of the McCarran-Walter Act revoked the Naturalization Act of 1790.

The real turning point in Asian immigration occurred in 1965 during the civil rights movement when US leaders decided to abandon previous racist desires to maintain a primarily all-White republic. The Immigration Act of 1965 provided for annual admission of 170,000 immigrants from the Eastern Hemisphere and 120,000 from the Western, with 20,000 immigrants per country allowed from the Eastern Hemisphere.[146]

As we have seen, the legislative action of 1965 dramatically changed the flow of immigration from Asian countries. In the case of India, it allowed for an influx of well-educated, English-speaking adults to come to the US for skilled employment. As of 2010, 87 percent of Asian Indians in the US were foreign-born, and 70 percent of all Asian Indian adults over the age of twenty-five had earned at least a bachelor's degree, making them more highly educated as a group than other Asians and more than the US population as a whole. Because of their high level of education, median family incomes are also higher—in 2010, the median annual income for Indians was $88,000, much higher than for all Asians ($66,000) and all US households ($49,800). While the majority of Indians in India are Hindus, as of 2012 only about half (51 percent) of Indian immigrants to the US are Hindus; 18 percent identified as Christians and 10 percent are Muslim.[147] Pakistanis are also considered part of the Asian American population, linguistically and culturally similar to Indians, and there are also high levels of education among

Pakistani immigrants in the US. Because most Pakistanis are Muslim, they are sometimes mistakenly thought to be from the Middle East.[148]

Another population group often discussed in the context of Asian Americans is the Native Hawaiian and Pacific Islanders (NHPI). In the 1990s they were included in the census data with Asians but advocated for their own separate census category, which was granted in 2000. The NHPI population is much smaller than that of other Asian groups—approximately 1.5 million in 2014—and has a very different history relative to the United States. Theirs is not a story of migration but rather one of colonial conquest, particularly in Hawaii. Plantation economies and US military installations in the Pacific have played an important role in the NHPI experience. A highly diverse group, Native Hawaiians make up 41 percent of the NHPI population, followed by Samoans (13 percent), Guamanians or Chamorros (10 percent), Tongans (5 percent), Fijians (3 percent), and Marshallese (2 percent), and 26 percent are from other, much smaller Pacific island origins.[149] Relative to the Asian American population, NHPIs have lower levels of educational attainment (20.9 percent have a college degree) and a higher poverty rate (18.4 percent).[150]

The linguistic, religious, and other cultural diversity of these disparate groups, some of whom have long histories of conflict with one another in Asia—for example, Japan and Korea, Japan and China, China and Vietnam—gives validity to the question posed by Valerie Lee, director of the 1992 Asian American Renaissance Conference: "What do we have in common except for racism and rice?"[151] Social scientists Kenyon Chan and Shirley Hune argue that racism is quite enough. Because the treatment of early Asian immigrant communities was so similar and distinctions between them ignored by the dominant culture, the foundation of a group identity was laid.

> Racial ideologies defined Pacific immigrants as aliens ineligible for citizenship, unfair economic competitors, and socially unassimilable groups. For the first one hundred years of "Asian America"—the 1840s to the 1940s—the images of each community were racialized

and predominantly negative. The Chinese were called "Mongolians" and depicted in the popular press as heathens, gamblers, and opium addicts. The Japanese and Koreans were viewed as the "yellow peril." Filipinos were derogatorily referred to as "little brown monkeys," and Asian Indians, most of them Sikhs, were called "ragheads."[152]

In the late 1960s, as part of the social transformation of the civil rights era, the concept of a panethnic Asian American identity emerged among second- and third-generation Japanese, Chinese, and Filipino American college students. Chan and Hune write: "Racial identity and ethnic consciousness were fundamentally transformed along with the racial order. The polarization of civil rights protests required Asians in America to consider their identity, their self-definition, and their place in racialized America. They discovered that racial quotas and legal inequalities applied to them just as they did to other minorities. 'Colored' was clearly defined as anyone nonwhite."[153]

Consequently, the terms *Asian American* and *Asian Pacific American* emerged as a unifying political construct encompassing all US residents of Asian and Pacific Island ancestry, encouraging individuals to work across ethnic lines for increased economic, political, and social rights. Asian American groups have lobbied for bilingual education, curricular reform, Asian American studies, improved working conditions for garment and restaurant workers, and support for community-based development. They have also opposed media misrepresentations and sought more opportunities for Asian Pacific Americans in theater, film, and television. Racial politics have continued to foster this unifying panethnic identity, though the large influx of new immigrants has changed the character of the Asian American community from the stable third- and fourth-generation community of the 1960s to one now composed largely of newcomers.[154]

## Unpacking the Myth of the Model Minority

"What do you know about Asians?" a young Chinese American woman asks Mark, a young White man of Italian descent. His response: "I'm going to be honest with you. I completely believed the stereotype. Asian people are hard workers, they're really quiet, they get good grades because they have tons of pressure from their families to get good grades. . . . Asians are quiet so people can't have a problem with them."[155]

This exchange captures the essence of the current stereotypes about Asian Americans. The "model minority" characterization is a pervasive one. The first public presentation of this idea is generally credited to a 1966 article by William Petersen entitled "Success Story, Japanese-American Style." It reviewed the success of Japanese Americans despite the history of discrimination they had endured. A similar article describing the success of Chinese Americans appeared in *U.S. News and World Report* the same year.[156] Both articles used statistics on rising educational attainment and income levels, along with statistics on low rates of reported crime and mental illness, to demonstrate how Asian cultural values had allowed these groups to succeed against the odds.[157] Now, more than fifty years later, Asian American youth are routinely depicted in the media as star students (especially in math and science) supported by industrious, entrepreneurial, and upwardly mobile parents.

In their book *The Asian American Achievement Paradox*, sociologists Min Zhou and Jennifer Lee reflect on how, despite decades of institutional discrimination and racial prejudice, the stereotypes of Asian Americans changed from "undesirables" to "models of success."[158] The answer, they say, lies in the dramatic shift in the immigrant population itself. Unlike the low-skilled laborers who came to California in the nineteenth century, the Chinese immigrants who arrived after 1965 are a "hyperselected" group. They define *hyperselectivity* as a relative concept that uses two reference groups against which to compare a group of immigrants—the first comparison group being the peers they are leaving behind in their country of origin and the second being the native-born citizens of the host country. When the immigrants have above-average education as compared to their peers at home, they are a "highly selected" group, but when they have above-average education relative to the host country peers as well, they can be described as "hyperselected." By these criteria, there is no doubt that Chinese immigrants are a hyperselected group. While only 4 percent of adults in China have at least an undergraduate degree, half of Chinese adult immigrants to the US do, and nearly half of the college-educated Chinese immigrants have earned a master's or doctoral degree as well, mostly from US universities. Not only are they twelve times more likely than Chinese at home to have a college degree, with a college graduation rate of 50 percent, their education rate is far above the college-going rate among the general US population (28 percent). Because of their higher level of education, they are able to earn above-average incomes in the US.[159]

By contrast, Vietnamese immigrants are not hyperselected, because their educational attainment does not exceed the general US population's, but they are highly selected, because 23 percent of Vietnamese immigrant adults have at least a bachelor's degree, compared to only 5 percent of their peers in Vietnam. While not all Vietnamese are well educated—in fact, a significant portion did not finish high school—the positive perception of Asians as highly educated is cast over them as well.[160] "Although Vietnamese immigrants are not hyper-selected as are Chinese immigrants, they benefit from the hyper-selectivity of the Chinese because they are racialized as Asian American; the hyper-selectivity of Chinese immigrants (the largest Asian immigrant population in the United States) drives the general American perception that all Chinese immigrants and all Asian immigrants more generally are highly educated."[161]

Compare this perception to the situation of Mexican immigrants. As a group, they are "hyposelected" because on average their educational attainment is lower than their peers' back in Mexico, and it is also lower than the general population's in the United States. Though the overall education level of Mexicans in Mexico is relatively high, Americans tend to perceive all Mexicans as poorly educated because of the low selectivity of Mexican immigration. Conversely, Asian Indians are another hyperselected group, creating the perception that Indians as a whole are highly educated, but most Indians in India do not have formal schooling.[162] In general, Asian immigrants are likely to be more economically successful upon arrival in the US than Mexican immigrants, for example, because they are coming with more social capital in the form of their advanced education.

Zhou and Lee argue that the hyperselectivity of Asian immigration sets the foundation for Asian immigrant parents and their second-generation children "to create and adopt a specific cultural frame about achievement and success that is supported by public and ethnic resources, reinforced in institutional contexts and buttressed by social psychological processes. Together, these factors explain the Asian American achievement paradox, or the so-called exceptional academic outcomes of Asian Americans."[163] Because so many Asian immigrants have high levels of education, they have the resources to re-create institutions (e.g., businesses, cultural institutions, ethnic organizations) that help them and their fellow Asian immigrants adapt to their new country and help their children succeed in school. Those institutions, once created, benefit not only the hyperselected but also the less-educated of their ethnic community, who may find employment opportunities and supplemental educational resources for their children within the same ethnic community. "Chinese ethnic communities and ethnic newspapers are dotted with signs for Chinese language schools, after-school tutoring, academic enrichment programs, and cultural enrichment programs (such as music, dance, and sports) that arm Chinese immigrants with supplemental skills that help them excel academically."[164] They also bring with them a very specific definition of achievement and success, a "success frame" that includes earning straight As (an A- is described as an "Asian F"), graduating at the top of one's class, earning a degree at an elite university, and working in one of four high-status professions (medicine, law, engineering, or science).[165]

This "success frame" is rewarded by teachers and guidance counselors who assume that Asian children are smart, hardworking, and destined to be high-achievers and consequently are more likely to provide them access to the best resources in public schools (gifted and talented programs and honors or Advanced Placement courses) than non-Asian students.[166] Unlike the stereotype threat that tends to depress the performance of Black students, Asian students are likely to benefit from "stereotype promise," the performance-enhancing benefit of being expected to succeed. For example, a second-generation Chinese student offered this example from her junior high school: "Like in math, they [my teachers] would be like, 'Oh, Nancy, this should be easy for you.' Just like passing tests out, they would make little comments like, 'Oh, I expected you to do better.' Math isn't my thing, you know. Just because I'm Asian doesn't mean I'm smart in math."[167]

In Nancy's case, not wanting to disappoint her teacher or her parents, she put in extra effort, with the help of the tutors her parents provided, and eventually was placed in an AP math class in high school. Stereotype promise can become a self-fulfilling prophecy.

Zhou and Lee found that even Asian students who exhibited mediocre or below-average academic performance were given the benefit of the doubt by teachers and encouraged to improve, and sometimes placed in honors or AP courses without the academic profile usually required for such placement. By contrast, Mexican participants in their study were rarely placed in the honors or AP classes. Asian students in Zhou and Lee's study sample noticed that the expectations others held for them were not extended to other groups of color. Lily, a 1.5-generation Chinese woman, explained, "Like it's expected that every Asian goes to college, gets a college degree or more. It's just, like, they expect you to do well in school. I don't think it's expected much, like, say for Mexicans."[168]

The "ethnic capital" of the hyperselected Asian community also benefits working-class Chinese and Vietnamese children whose parents have just a grade-school education, because they are able to learn from more highly educated immigrant peers about the importance of being in honors and AP classes for college admissions and how to navigate the school system to get placed at that level. Children of Mexican immigrants noticed that they were not in the same classes as their Asian peers, but because of the lower educational attainment in their ethnic community, they did not have access to the same kind of shared knowledge about maximizing the school resources within their social networks.[169]

Zhou and Lee identify another factor important to the successful educational outcomes of Asian children: mind-set. "Asian immigrants have been raised in countries where the prevalent belief is that effort, rather than ability, is the most critical ingredient for achievement. . . . By contrast, native-born American parents believe that their children's out-comes are more heavily influenced by innate ability."[170] As was discussed in Chapter 4, if you have an "effort" mind-set, you are more likely to persist in the face of academic challenges. Families with an effort mind-set emphasize the value of practice and are more likely to invest in sup-plemental resources (like tutors) to achieve the desired outcomes.

The downside of high expectations and a belief in the power of effec-tive effort is that those who do not achieve the high standard of success set by their families and teachers describe feelings of failure and see themselves as "ethnoracial outliers" who have to distance themselves from their Asian peers and their ethnic community. One such young man was Adam, the son of highly educated Vietnamese immigrants, who was not able to maintain the high level of academic success that his family expected in high school or in college. By comparison, his brother achieved all aspects of the success frame. Because Adam does not feel successful according to Vietnamese standards, he has distanced himself from his ethnic group, avoiding contact with other Vietnamese. Adam said, "I'm not sure how people see me. If they ask what I am, I say Viet-namese, but I don't consider myself Vietnamese enough." His brother, he says, is more truly Vietnamese.[171] Similarly, Zhou and Lee report that many 1.5- and second-generation Koreans who have not achieved the key elements of the success frame—graduation from an elite university and a high-status career—are embarrassed by their "failure" and feel a need to disassociate themselves from the Korean American community because they do not feel "authentically Korean or Korean American."[172]

Though many children of Asian immigrants have internalized the cultural expectations and the stereotype of stellar academic achieve-ment, only a small percentage attain the culturally specific hallmarks of success, and many deviate widely from them.

Even based on the Immigration and Intergenerational Mobility in Metropolitan Los Angeles (IIMMLA) data, we find that nearly two-fifths of 1.5 and second generation Chinese do not graduate from college, and half of Vietnamese do not obtain a bachelor's degree. Yet Asians and non-Asians alike tend to overlook those Asian Americans who do not graduate from college, do not attain the success frame, and do not fit the model minority stereotype. These Asian Americans either go unnoticed or are dismissed as exceptions. The cultural lag keeps the association between ethnoracial status and achievement in place, despite the bevy of disconfirming evidence.[173]

Whether positive or negative in content, stereotypes are hard to erase once they have been etched in our collective memories.

Another dimension of the Zhou and Lee study using data from the IIMMLA survey was the comparison they were able to make between the outcomes of Chinese and Vietnamese immigrants and their 1.5- and second-generation children and the outcomes of Mexicans and their 1.5- and second-generation children. Perhaps not surprisingly, they found that the Chinese children of immigrants exhibited the highest levels of education—as with native-born families, the strongest predictor of a child's level of education is the parent's level of education. But they found that Mexican children of immigrants had made the greatest educational advances relative to their parents.

Though more than 55 percent of Mexican immigrant parents did not graduate from high school, this figure dropped to 14 percent within one generation. In essence, the 1.5 and second generation nearly doubled the high school graduation rates of their parents. Moreover the college graduation rate of 1.5 and second-generation Mexicans (18 percent) is far lower than the rate for the Chinese (63 percent), but it is more than double that of their Mexican immigrant fathers (7 percent) and triple that of their immigrant mothers (5 percent). Thus, when we measure attainment intergenerationally rather than cross-sectionally, the children of Mexican immigrants exhibit the greatest educational gains of the three second-generation groups. In this respect, the children of Mexican immigrants are successfully assimilating and doing so rapidly.[174]

In terms of intergroup relations, the myth of the model minority has served to pit Asian Americans against other groups targeted by racism.

The accusing message of the dominant society to Blacks, Latinxs, and Native Americans is, "They overcame discrimination—why can't you?" Of course, as the research of Zhou and Lee makes clear, any group comparisons that don't take into account differential starting points are inherently flawed.

In addition, uncritical acceptance of the stereotype has concealed the needs and problems of those Asian ethnic groups in America that have not experienced uniformly high levels of success. While the Asian high school dropout rate is very low overall (2 percent), there are some Asian subgroups that have much higher dropout rates: Bhutanese (37 percent), Burmese (21 percent), Nepalese (11 percent), and Cambodian (6 percent). In general, the high school dropout rate among Southeast Asians (5 percent) is more than double that of the total Asian rate.[175] Among eighteen- to twenty-four-year-olds, college-going rates also vary across Asian ethnic groups, ranging from 20 percent for Bhutanese young adults to 84 percent for other Southeast Asian (e.g., Indonesian and Malaysian) young adults. In 2013, the total college enrollment rate for Asian eighteen- to twenty-four-year-olds was 67 percent.[176]

Do teachers sometimes overlook the learning needs of Asian students because they assume they don't need help? For individual students, the stereotype of success may have negative consequences for the quality of instruction they receive. For example, educator Lisa Delpit reports her observation of a five-year-old Asian American girl in a Montessori kindergarten class dutifully engaged in the task the teacher had assigned, placing a number of objects next to the various numerals printed on a cloth. The child worked quietly without any help from the teacher, and when the time was up, she put her work away. Delpit writes, "The only problem was that at the end of the session no numeral had the correct number of objects next to it. The teacher later told me that Cathy, like Asian-American students she had taught previously, was one of the best students in the class." In this case, the stereotype of good Asian students meant Cathy had not received the instruction she needed.[177]

Vinh, a Vietnamese student, noted the feedback he gets from his teachers is not always as helpful as he would like, perhaps because it is too positive.

Sometimes, the English teachers, they don't understand about us. Because something we not do good . . . like my English is not good. And she say, "Oh, your English is great!" But that's the way American culture is. But my culture is not like that. If my English is not good, [the teacher] has to say, "Your English is not good. So you have to go home and study." And she tell me what to study and how to study to get better. But some Americans, you know, they don't understand about myself. So they just say, "Oh! You're doing a good job! You're doing great! Everything is great!" Teachers talk like that, but my culture is different. They say, "You have to do better." So, sometimes when I do something not good, and my teachers say, "Oh, you did great!" I don't like it. I want the truth better.[178]

Asian students in America know that their teachers expect them to excel in math and science, and they may be encouraged to pursue those fields at the expense of other academic interests. Educators Pang, Kiang, and Pak report that Asian Pacific American students often suffer from communication anxiety, feeling inadequate about their writing and speaking ability. This anxiety may contribute to a student's choice to pursue subject areas, such as math, that require less verbal fluency. In this case, the model-minority stereotype actually serves to restrict their academic options.[179]

## Finding a Voice

Another dimension of the model-minority stereotype is the notion that Asian Pacific Americans are quiet and content with the status quo. Mitsuye Yamada challenges that stereotype in her classic essay, "Invisibility Is an Unnatural Disaster: Reflections of an Asian American Woman."[180] She recounts her experiences teaching the Asian segment of an ethnic American literature course and discovering that her White students were offended by the angry tone of the Asian American writers. Yamada was puzzled by this response, since her students had not been offended by the Black, Chicanx, or Native American writings. When she pressed them for an explanation, they said they understood the anger of Blacks and Chicanxs and empathized with the frustrations and sorrows of the American Indians. But the anger of the Asian Americans took them by surprise. As one student said, "It made me angry. Their anger made me angry, because I didn't even know the Asian Americans felt oppressed. I didn't expect their anger."[181]

The myth of the model minority obscures the reality of racism in the lives of Asian Pacific Americans and encourages their silence about it. One of my Korean American students wrote about this silence: "When racial comments were said around me I would somehow ignore it and pretend that nothing was said. By ignoring comments such as these, I was protecting myself. It became sort of a defense mechanism." While denial is a common coping strategy for dealing with racism, when the experiences are too numerous or too painful to be ignored, the silence is broken. Unfortunately, the voices of Asian Pacific American students often fall on deaf ears.

In his essay "We Could Shape It: Organizing for Asian Pacific American Student Empowerment," Peter Nien-chu Kiang cites examples from urban and suburban schools in Massachusetts in which Asian Pacific American students were frequent victims of racial harassment.[182] For example, Thuy, a Vietnamese immigrant, recalled, "When we pass by them they give you some kind of like a dirty look. . . . They say, 'Look at that Chinese girl,' and they call like, 'Chinks, go back where you belong.'"[183]

Yet in each case cited by Kiang, school administrators seemed unresponsive. Responding to this indifference, one young Asian American woman said: "It made me realize even more that . . . no one listens to [Asians]. Like if the African Americans came out and said something, probably the people in the school would have done something, but when the Asians come out, no one really does anything."[184]

Out of this context grew a regional youth conference organized by an ad hoc group of adults and teens who initially gathered to discuss how community resources could support Asian Pacific American students confronting racial harassment at school. The result was the Conference for Asian Pacific American Youth, attended by seven hundred students from fifty area high schools. The conference brought together many Asian Pacific American students who had been isolated in their own schools and created a place for them to see themselves reflected in each other and to explore their identities as Asian Pacific Americans. The power of this process is reflected in Amy's comments. She recalls her first meeting:

> When I first walked in, I swear, I just wanted to turn around and walk right out, I was so intimidated. I've never really been in a room with so many Asian students in my age group. I was like, what am I doing here? And then I started coming to the meetings, and I got more involved in it, and I was like, oh my god, you know this is really cool! Asians are cool! [laughs][185]

Planning for the conference sessions and workshops introduced the student organizers to older generations of Asian Pacific American activists. The topics they discussed ranged from gangs and media stereotypes to interracial dating, civil rights strategies, and curriculum reform. The opportunity to work with Asian adults was very meaningful because there were no Asian Pacific American teachers in most of the schools they represented. For Amy and others, the conference planning process was a transformative experience not unlike Paul Ongtooguk's discovery of his Inupiaq history. Said Amy, "I've become really proud of who I am and where I come from, and I know that I've become stronger. I'm no longer that silent anymore. . . . I have really found myself."[186]

The process of finding oneself in the face of invisibility, silence, and stereotypes is not an easy one. In her analysis of thirty-nine autobiographical narratives written by Asian American adults, Lucy Tse uncovered their struggle to face and name their oppression, then to affirm a positive sense of their identity as Asian Americans.[187] Documentary filmmaker Eunice Lau has captured that struggle in a forthcoming (2017) film about Asian American gang members in Atlanta called *A-Town Boyz*. Lau describes confusion about identity as the common thread in the stories of the young people she encountered in the process of making the documentary.

> There's the big question of this myth of the model minority: we all go to school, we get our straight A's, and we take a certain path and end

up as law-abiding Ivy League college graduates who get white collar jobs. . . . But the truth is that the majority of our community did not take that path. What happened to those guys who didn't take the 'prescribed' route to success?[188]

Hoping that her film will broaden the conversation about Asian American identity, Lau is joined in the project by her producer Grace Jung. Jung recalls her own growing-up experience,

Being of a lower middle-class household, both of my parents worked full-time during the week and on Saturdays. . . . I was often lonely, and in my social circles, I never once felt completely accepted for who I was. I thought I was the only one but as it turns out, feelings of instability and insecurity are typical for many Asian-American kids growing up in the U.S., and the subjects of this film illustrate it for us, along with the choices they've made in reaction to that pain.[189]

## Racial Formation and Racial Identity

Asian Pacific Americans, Latinxs, and Native Americans are disparate groups, but they all share with people of African descent the struggle for identity where European heritage—or Whiteness—is defined as the American norm. As social scientists Chan and Hune remind us, the racialization of America has never been simply Black and White. Early European settlers used race-based policies toward Native Americans long before Africans were introduced to this continent. The US government applied race-based discriminatory and exclusionary policies to Mexican residents and Chinese settlers in the Western territories immediately upon contact. The social categories we now use are the legacy of those racial formations.[190] Cultural identities are not solely determined in response to racial ideologies, but racism increases the need for a positive self-defined identity in order to survive psychologically.

To find one's racial or ethnic identity, one must deal with negative stereotypes, resist internalizing negative self-perceptions, and affirm the meaning of ethnicity for oneself.[191] If educators and parents wish to foster these positive psychological outcomes for the children in our care, we must hear their voices and affirm their identities at school and at home. And we must interrupt the racism that places them at risk.

## Middle Eastern and North Africans (MENAs)

Coming to terms with the social meaning of one's racial-ethnic-cultural identity in the face of negative stereotyping is a challenging task for all members of marginalized groups, but it may be particularly complex for those who do not fit neatly into standard racial categories. The group of people whose families originate from the Middle East and North Africa (MENA) are among those who are not neatly categorized. In 2016, the federal government announced a proposal to add a new ethnic category to the US Census form specifically for people of MENA ancestry. Though the proposal must be approved by Congress and would not be in use until the 2020 census, the working MENA classification includes people with origins in Algeria, Bahrain, Egypt, Iraq, Iran, Israel, Jordan, Kuwait, Lebanon, Libya, Morocco, Oman, Palestine, Qatar, Saudi Arabia, Syria, Tunisia, the United Arab Emirates, or Yemen, as well as those who identify as Amazigh, Berber, Arab, Assyrian, Bedouin, Chaldean, Copt, Druze, Kurdish, or Syriac. Groups that could be added in the future include Turks, Sudanese, Somalis, Afghans, Armenians, Azerbaijanis, Cypriots, Djiboutians, Georgians, Mauritanians, South Sudanese, and Turkish Cypriots.[192]

As this long list suggests, those whose country of origin is in the MENA region are a very heterogeneous group that is multicultural, multiracial, and multiethnic. Some have historically been identified as "White" in the US, an important designation during the era when US citizenship was for Whites only. Other darker-skinned peoples might have been classified as "Black" or self-identified as "Other."[193] As with the Asian Pacific Americans, there is a tendency to lump those from the MENA region under one umbrella category—Arabs or Muslims—but neither term can be applied across the region with accuracy. Some are Arabs and some are not. Some are Muslims and some are not. Although

"Arab" and "Muslim" are often linked together in the popular culture, many Arabs are Christian, and many Muslims are not Arabs.

In fact, the first wave of MENA immigrants came to the United States between 1890 and 1940 from regions now known as Syria and Lebanon. Ninety percent were Christian, with limited education, seeking economic opportunity. These early immigrants seem to have assimilated in their new country with relative ease, recognized by others as White based on their physical appearance.[194]

The second wave of MENA immigrants began after World War II, following the 1948 Arab-Israeli War and revolutions in Egypt and Iraq in the 1950s. Dominated by Palestinians and Muslims with an "Arab identity" from Egypt, Iraq, and Syria, this group consisted of highly educated elites.[195] Following the Immigration and Nationality Act of 1965, the third wave of immigrants came to the US seeking family reunification, education, and employment opportunities and an escape from the war and violence in the MENA region. Many of this cohort of immigrants are Muslim. The growth of the MENA immigrant population has been steady, going from 223,000 in 1980 to slightly more than one million in 2013.[196] Approximately 70 percent of the MENA population is from the Middle East and 30 percent from North Africa, and it is concentrated in California, Michigan, and New York.[197] It is important to note that while the MENA population is only about one million people (not all of whom are Muslim), the Muslim population in the US is approximately 3.3 million, the majority of whom are US-born. Only a quarter of American Muslims are of Arab descent. Approximately one-third of the Muslim community is African American, one-third is of South Asian descent, and the rest are from all over the world, including a growing Latinx Muslim population.[198]

The MENA population, whether Arab or not, Muslim or not, has been increasingly impacted by anti-Arab sentiments and "terrorist" stereotyping in the US. For MENA youth, the terrorist attack of September 11, 2001, forever known as "9/11," marked a turning point in how others looked at them and how they looked at themselves in the United States. In his introduction to *Growing Up Muslim: Muslim College Students in America Tell Their Life Stories* (edited by Andrew

Garrod and Robert Kilkenny), Eboo Patel writes: "On the evening of September 10, 2001, these were sensitive, intelligent young people experiencing adolescent identity issues typical of the children of immigrants who practice a minority faith tradition. Twenty-four hours later, an important part of their identity had been marked as the source of absolute evil."[199]

The 9/11 attacks brought a heightened salience to the Muslim aspect of their identities that has been hard for young people to carry. For Zahra, who describes herself as a "black Muslim Somali girl," 9/11 brought her Muslim identity to the foreground. She was a sophomore in high school then. "We had never realized how vulnerable we were as minorities until 9/11. I always viewed myself as a racial minority, as my being black seemed most significant to others in American society. After the attacks, however, my being Muslim was the characteristic that was most openly challenged and discriminated against."[200]

Aly, a Muslim student of Pakistani descent, described his college experience before and after 9/11.

> I never felt particularly marginalized as a Muslim student. I had always been vocal on a range of political issues and prided myself on being a political liberal. . . . After 9/11, however, the comfort zone started to contract. Having an openly Muslim identity in an increasingly hostile public arena is a daunting experience. I have read virulent columns by tenured professors at elite universities attacking Islam as intrinsically violent and hateful. I have sat through lectures at Dartmouth at which my religion has been derided as a dangerous ideology. . . . I find myself being more and more on the defensive, having to explain why I can be both a part of North American society and a Muslim. It is draining to constantly feel that you have to be on the defensive and to justify who you are, which I am beginning to increasingly resent. These challenges seem relentless, and not always separate or impersonal.[201]

To avoid the relentless challenges, for some there is the temptation to "pass" by altering one's appearance—for women, choosing not to wear the hijab (traditional Muslim head scarf), or for men, remaining clean-shaven rather than wearing a beard, or changing one's name to something less ethnically identifiable. Commonly, people of Middle Eastern descent have dark hair, large facial features, and skin tones of varying shades of tan. In a study of Middle Eastern Americans, researchers Amir Marvasti and Karyn McKinney found that some Middle Eastern Americans "try to pass by trading their own ethnic identity with a less controversial one." Moving to an ethnically diverse region allows a chameleon-like experience of blending in with others around them. Some of their respondents found that by living in South Florida they avoided some of the negative encounters with Islamophobic or anti-Arab bigotry because they were assumed to be Hispanic.[202] Denying a core part of one's own identity comes with a psychological cost, increasing the risk of internalizing the negative attitudes one is seeking to avoid.

Claiming one's identity with pride, even in the face of hostility, is for some a much preferred stance, the outcome of a quest for identity of the kind Jean Phinney has described. This process is visible in the narrative of Amani Al-Khatahtbeh, author of *Muslim Girl: A Coming of Age*. She was in the fourth grade in 2001. She writes:

> I'm not really sure I understood what was going on when 9/11 happened, but I was old enough to feel the world shift on its axis that day and change everything forever. . . . That day has become crystallized in my memory not just for how harrowingly scary it was—how we didn't know what would come after that—but also because I deeply believe that my generation of millennial Muslims has, whether we like it or not, come to be defined by it.[203]

The child of Palestinian and Jordanian immigrant parents, she was bullied at school, and her parents were harassed at their workplace. Their New Jersey home was defaced with rotten eggs and water balloons. She was in the sixth grade when she first decided to deny her religion.

It happened one sunny afternoon on our yellow school bus, heading home from another exhausting day of middle school in which I

constantly tried to blend away my differences and fit in, only to inevitably capture the attention of bullies in my classes, and even ones
I didn't know in the halls. I would get taunted for being a "monster"
as I walked to class between periods, and all I ever wanted to do was
disappear.[204]

A schoolmate on the bus asked her what religion she was. Not wearing a head scarf, she was not immediately identifiable as a Muslim. The
question prompted a wave of panic, and after a long hesitation, she
replied, "Oh, I don't know. Something Mediterranean, I forget." Rather
than the relief she longed for, instead she experienced a deep sense of
shame for denying something so much a part of her sense of identity.
She writes, "I didn't realize it at the time, but that decision would become a pivotal moment in my journey."[205]

Amani captures the confusion she felt at that early adolescent period
in her life. "I was so fractured by my Muslim identity and Western
society that I was completely lost in this weird enigma of awkward girl
puberty and unbearable racism that emerged as a total disconnect."[206]
What she needed was the opportunity to immerse herself in an active
exploration of identity in the company of supportive peers. That opportunity came when her father decided to take his family back to Jordan.
Though the time spent in Jordan was relatively short, just nine months,
it was transformational for Amani. "The culmination of my experience
in Jordan, where I heard Muslim and Arab people's narratives and diverse stories in their own voices, reignited my pride in my heritage and
religion and prompted my desire to finally reclaim my identity."[207]

With new and deeper knowledge of her family's heritage, she began
to redefine her identity as a Muslim as not a source of harassment but
instead a source of pride.

I decided [then] that I wanted to wear a headscarf, as a public marker
that I belonged to this people. I wanted it to be so that before people
even knew my name, the first thing they would know about me is
that I am a Muslim. I told myself that upon my return to the States, I
would wear the headscarf with pride as my outward rebellion against

the Islamophobia that had seized me and suffocated me most of my life. With that decision, I inherited the entire history to which the hijab has been tied, and carried it on my head like an issue for public debate.[208]

Amani's assertion of her identity through the claiming of her head scarf, despite her earlier rejection of it, is reminiscent of the example of the Latina who reclaimed her Spanish and its importance to her identity in college after her childhood rejection of the language that had set her apart from the mainstream, again illustrating the similarity of the process of identity exploration among marginalized groups in the face of that marginalization.

When Amani's family returned to New Jersey, she stuck to her decision to wear the hijab, though other women in her family, including her mother, did not. It was not easy. "On my first day back to junior high school in New Jersey, I had a panic attack." Afraid of how her classmates would respond to her head scarf, she was awash in anxiety. Her father assured her that she could take it off but said, "Just know that if you are able to commit to this, then there's nothing else in your life that you wouldn't be strong enough to commit to." With that, she went forward with her hijab still on. For her, the wearing of the head scarf is a physical symbol of the intersection of both her gender identity and Muslim identity. "The headscarf is not only intertwined with our respective cultures, but it has also become the strongest emblem of our distinct identities as Muslim women. And how could it not? It is hyper-visible and unmistakable."[209]

Back in New Jersey, she yearned to be part of a community of young women like herself, and in 2009, still a teenager, she created a virtual "cafeteria table" for herself and other young Muslim women by launching the website MuslimGirl.[210] Reflecting on that time, Al-Khatahtbeh writes:

I acutely identified that I was leading a unique and trying experience as a millennial Muslim, the daughter of an immigrant and a refugee, born and raised in the United States—ostracized through bullying, heightened Islamophobia, and the difficult task of growing up as a young girl in a misogynistic and hypersexualized society. My life, and the lives of others like me, reflected a deeply entrenched double jeopardy to which Frances Beal first introduced us: the intersectional concept of being subjected to racism, and then further being subjected to sexism within that racist framework. While it refers to the unique and incomparable oppression of black women in the United States, Beal's concept of double jeopardy can unfortunately be applied in varying degrees to the exacerbation of many Muslim women's struggles in a post-9/11 era. Not only do we have to battle today's modern assault on our religion, but we also have to defy its sexist application to us both inside and outside of our own communities, all on top of the preexisting anti-black racism that black Muslim women suffer from Muslims and non-Muslims alike.

I knew that there *had* to be other girls who were going through these experiences, who also wanted to have conversations that were directly relevant to our Muslim lifestyles in today's society. I wanted to find them.[211]

Realizing that the opportunity for connection was missing, that there was a void, Amani realized she could do something about that. "I thought, *Why not?* I would make a new community entirely." MuslimGirl evolved from a teenager's refuge to a cultural phenomenon, garnering attention from mainstream media outlets and giving its founder a platform and eventually national visibility as a media commentator.

The empowerment that comes from connecting with others who have shared experiences and concerns is critical for those whose identities are challenged by stereotyping and the bigotry of others. Like Amani, Zahra, the Somali Muslim quoted earlier, found that the opportunity to connect deeply with Muslim friends in college reduced her sense of isolation. She said, "I had friends from all sorts of backgrounds, but my closest friends—the ones I spoke to about serious and personal topics . . . whom I related to as if they were family—were three Muslims."[212] They understood why she didn't want to go to alcohol-heavy campus parties and why she chose to wear her hijab. Her family members had feared that in college she would lose herself, feeling forced to conform in negative ways. Zahra found the opposite was true. "On the contrary, I believe that the more I discovered who I am and what my relationship is with the world around me, the stronger I became academically and professionally. I could be me—African, American, Muslim, a woman . . . it took all the life experiences I have had thus far to bring me to this point, where I am feeling most content."[213]

It is also critical for allies—those who are not the targets of anti-Arab racism and Islamophobia—to raise their voices in support of those who are. Though most mass shootings in the US have been committed by US-born White men, it is rare (if ever) that those shooters are identified by their religious affiliations. They are viewed and talked about as individuals, not as representatives of a racial, ethnic, or religious group. When an attack is carried out by someone who is a Muslim, the acts of the individual or extremist group are projected onto a global population of 1.6 billion Muslims (3.3 million in the US), the vast majority of whom live peacefully in their communities, just as most White men do. The repeated representation of Muslims as a dangerous presence in American society has served to legitimize anti-Muslim feelings and has fueled the rise in anti-Muslim hate crimes. According to the FBI, in 2015 there were 257 reports of assaults, attacks on mosques, and other hate crimes against Muslims, a sharp increase of about 67 percent over 2014. Not since 2001, when in the aftermath of the 9/11 attacks more than 480 attacks occurred, have there been so many anti-Muslim hate crimes.[214]

Muslim women are particularly vulnerable because of their identifiable religious attire. Sadly, male members of the Sikh religion, who are typically from India and also wear religious attire—turbans—have also become hate-crime targets, mistakenly identified as Muslims.[215] The anti-Muslim rhetoric that fuels such violence escalated during the presidential campaign of 2016 as Donald Trump proposed a ban on Muslim immigrants. In the first weeks of his presidency, Trump issued an executive order halting immigration from seven majority-Muslim countries, stranding travelers, young and old, with visas in hand, suddenly unable to enter the US.[216] At this writing, it is unclear whether this is just the beginning of presidential actions impacting the American Muslim community. As difficult as this situation is for the Muslim community, Al-Khatahtbeh has seen signs of goodwill.

> Amid all the chaos, I witnessed one interesting development for the first time in my entire life since 9/11. When Trump's words rang around the country, many Americans were roused to rise to the defense of their Muslim neighbors. Social and broadcast media highlighted heartwarming stories of extended hands between Muslims and non-Muslims, images popped up on my feed of non-Muslim Americans going the extra distance to make Muslims feel safe here in their own hometowns, and my Muslim friends from across the country recorded moments of increased acts of warmth and kindness towards them—seemingly as though our fellow countrymen were making an effort to remind us that this was our country, too. It was as if, through Trump's outrageously hateful rhetoric, America had awoken to the reality that now was time to defend and protect a minority community that needed it. Even though Trump represented the racist underbelly of a nation, light rose to the surface, even through the most negligible of cracks, to resist it.[217]

## Spreading the Light

What can concerned educators do to support Middle Eastern, North African, and/or Muslim students, recognizing that sometimes these identities intersect and sometimes they don't?

*Acknowledge their presence institutionally.* During the years I served as president of Spelman College, I made an effort to recognize the presence of Muslim students on our campus. The school was founded by two Christian missionaries in 1881, and its motto, "Our Whole School for Christ," is directly linked to that history. Yet my goal as president was to ensure that all of our students, regardless of religious affiliation, felt welcome and included in our campus community. One tangible way to do so was to host an *iftar* (a special meal commemorating the end of Ramadan, the month of fasting) at the president's residence on campus for Muslim students, faculty, and staff and their invited guests.

Another important act of affirmation of our Muslim students was to invite a Muslim student to participate in the baccalaureate service on commencement weekend. Just as we had a student read from the Hebrew scriptures (Old Testament) and a student read from the New Testament, we also asked a Muslim student to read a text from the Quran as an integral part of the service. When we had Baha'i students, a reading from that faith tradition was included as well. In these ways, we signaled to those who might otherwise feel excluded in the midst of a majority-Christian environment that they too were an important part of our community. Everyone wants to feel included. Though I have described here relatively small acts, the impact was meaningful for community members who too often were accustomed to being treated as either invisible or dangerous in the wider society.

*Educate yourself.* Though I identify as a Christian, I had the wonderful opportunity to learn something about Islam when I was a student at Hartford Seminary, an academic community that is committed to fostering interfaith dialogue. Not everyone will take a course on Islam, as I did at Hartford Seminary, but all of us can learn more about Islam and the MENA region from reliable sources like the American-Arab Anti-Discrimination Committee and Teaching Tolerance, both of which offer educational resources for teachers. Get beyond the stereotypes. Seek out ways to include the voices of MENA and Muslim students, but don't ask members of these marginalized communities to speak for their whole community.

*Speak up against Islamophobia.* Anyone can interrupt an offensive joke, challenge stereotypes, or offer assistance to someone who is being harassed or is fearful that they might be. If you don't know how best to be helpful, ask and then *listen.* Use your own privilege to question policies that are discriminatory. Be public in your support for those who are targeted, so they will know where to find help when it is needed. In a time of darkness, we all have to generate more light.

# NINE

# Identity Development in Multiracial Families

*"But don't the children suffer?"*

WHENEVER I GIVE A PRESENTATION ON THE RACIAL IDENTITY DEVELOP-
ment of young people of color or White youth, I am inevitably asked,
"What about the identity development process for biracial children?" It
is a hard question to answer quickly because there are so many factors to
consider. What racial combination are we talking about: Black-White,
White-Asian, Asian-Black, Black–Native American? What does the
young person look like: visibly identifiable as Black or Asian, apparently White, or racially ambiguous? What is the family situation? Are
both parents actively involved in the child's socialization? If not, what
is the racial membership of the primary caregiver? What racial identification have the parents encouraged, and is there agreement between
the parents about it? Are the extended families accepting of the parents'
union and of their biracial child? Where does the young person live: in a
community of color, a predominantly White neighborhood, or one that
is racially mixed? Are there other multiracial families in the vicinity, or
is being biracial an oddity in that context? Is the racial climate one of
harmony or hostility? The answer to each of these questions is relevant
to the identity development process for biracial children.

Constructing our identities is a complex and multidimensional process for all of us, but for some there are more dimensions to consider
than for others. The multiracial population has grown substantially since

2000, the year that the Census Bureau began allowing people to designate more than one racial category on the census form. Between the census of 2000 and the census of 2010, the number of biracial Americans describing themselves as White and Black more than doubled, and the number describing themselves as White and Asian increased by 87 percent. The percentage of multiracial babies born in the US has grown from 1 percent in 1970 to 10 percent in 2013. In 2013, the US Census Bureau found that nine million Americans chose two or more racial categories to describe their race.[1] Among this group of multiracial Americans is the forty-fourth president of the United States, Barack Obama, the son of a Black father from Kenya and a White mother from Kansas. Just as the population has expanded, models of multiracial identity development have evolved to capture the dynamic process of identity, that sense of self "that evolves and changes, based on the interaction and changing level of salience of numerous factors."[2] In order to understand the contemporary meaning of claiming a multiracial identity, it is useful to review briefly the history of racial categorization in the US.

## The One-Drop Rule: Racial Categorization in the United States

It was 1967 when the Supreme Court in the case of *Loving v. Virginia* overturned the last remaining laws prohibiting interracial marriage of all types.[3] The growing acceptance of interracial relationships in the United States since the civil rights era has created a new context in which children of those relationships can define themselves. Yet even as the context is changing, the history of racial classification in the United States is an enduring legacy that plays a large role in the identity development process.

As discussed in Chapter 1, race is a social construction that has little biological meaning. Though populations from particular geographic regions can be distinguished from each other by commonly occurring physical traits such as hair texture, skin tone, facial structure, or blood type, most biologists and physical anthropologists tell us that there is no such thing as a "pure" race. All human populations are "mixed" populations. However, in terms of social realities, boundaries have been clearly drawn in the United States between those who are considered White and those who are considered non-White.

Maria P. P. Root, psychologist and editor of the landmark publication *Racially Mixed People in America*, the first collection of studies on racially mixed persons since the repeal of antimiscegenation laws, points out that there has been little research attention given to mixing between communities of color (e.g., American Indians and Blacks, Filipinos and Native Americans, Latinxs and Blacks), since these cross-group relationships do not threaten the sanctity of Whiteness.[4] Historically, the racial mixes on which there was the most research focus were those between groups that were the most socially distant: Blacks and Whites, Japanese and Blacks, and Japanese and Whites.[5] However, in the context of the United States, the most vigilant attention to so-called racial purity has been given to the boundary between Whites and Blacks.[6]

Paul Spickard, a scholar who has studied the history of racial categories, writes:

> The most important thing about races was the boundaries between them. If races were pure (or had once been), and if one were a member of the race at the top, then it was essential to maintain the boundaries that defined one's superiority, to keep people from the lower categories from slipping surreptitiously upward. Hence U.S. law took pains to define just who was in which racial category. Most of the boundary drawing came on the border between White and Black.[7]

Physical appearance was an unreliable criterion for maintaining this boundary, because the light-skinned children of White slave masters and enslaved Black women sometimes resembled their fathers more than their mothers. Ancestry, rather than appearance, became the important criterion. In both legal and social practice, anyone with any known African ancestry (no matter how far back in the family lineage) was considered Black, while only those without any trace of known African ancestry were called Whites. Known as the "one-drop rule," this practice solidified the boundary between Black and White.

The use of the one-drop rule was institutionalized by the US Census Bureau in the early twentieth century. Prior to 1920, "pure Negroes" were distinguished from "mulattoes" in the census count, but in 1920 the mulatto category was dropped and "Black" was defined as any person with known Black ancestry. In 1960, the practice of self-definition began, with heads of household indicating the race of household members. However, the numbers of Black families remained essentially the same, suggesting that the heads of household were using the same one-drop criteria that the census takers had been using. Though it is estimated that 75–90 percent of Black Americans have White ancestors and about 25 percent have Native American ancestry, the widespread use of the one-drop rule meant that people with known Black ancestry, regardless of appearance, were classified by society and self-classified as Black.[8] During that time period, the choice of a biracial or multiracial identity was not a viable option. The one-drop rule essentially meant that a "multiracial identity was equivalent to black identity."[9]

For example, Carol Calhoun, a biracial woman born in the late 1930s, in an interview by journalist Lise Funderburg, explained why she identified herself as Black, even though others often assumed she was White based on her physical appearance. Raised by her White mother until she was eight, then adopted by a Black family, Carol stated, "This is the way I was brought up, and this is where I'm comfortable. Had I stayed with my biological mother I might not have, except that in those times, a bastard child, or an illegitimate child of a mixed union, wouldn't have stood a snowball's chance in hell of being white. Not at all."[10]

F. James Davis, author of *Who Is Black? One Nation's Definition*, highlights the fact that no other ethnic population in the United States is defined and counted according to the one-drop rule.

> For example, individuals whose ancestry is one-fourth or less American Indian are not generally defined as Indian unless they want to be. . . . The same implicit rule appears to apply to Japanese Americans, Filipinos, or other peoples from East Asian nations and also to Mexican Americans who have Central American Indian ancestry, as a large majority do. For instance, a person whose ancestry is

one-eighth Chinese is not defined as just Chinese, or East Asian, or a member of the mongoloid race. . . . Americans do not insist that an American with a small fraction of Polish ancestry be classified as a Pole, or that someone with a single remote Greek ancestor be designated Greek, or that someone with any trace of Jewish lineage is a Jew and nothing else.[11]

According to Davis, the one-drop rule applies only to Blacks in the United States, and to no other racial group in any other nation in the world.

In 1983 the one-drop rule was challenged in the Louisiana courts by Susie Guillory Phipps, a woman who had been denied a passport because she had given her race as White on the passport application although her birth certificate designated her race as "colored." The designation had been made by the midwife, presumably based on her knowledge of the family's status in the community; however, the information came as a shock to Phipps, who had always considered herself White. She asked the Louisiana courts to change the classification on her deceased parents' birth certificates to White so that she and her siblings could be legally designated as White. They all appeared to be White, and some were blue-eyed blonds. At the time, Louisiana law indicated that anyone whose ancestry was more than one-thirty-second Black was categorized as Black. In this case, the lawyers for the state claimed to have proof that Phipps was three-thirty-seconds Black, which was more than enough African ancestry to justify her parents' classification as "colored." Consequently, she and her siblings were legally Black. The case was decided in May 1983, and in June 1983 the state legislature gave parents the right to designate the race of newborns themselves rather than relying on the doctor or midwife's assessment. In the case of previous misclassification, parents were given the right to change their children's racial designation to White if they could prove the children's Whiteness by a "preponderance of the evidence." But the 1983 statute did not abolish the one-drop rule. In fact, when Phipps appealed her case, the state's Fourth Circuit Court of Appeals upheld the lower court's decision, concluding that the preponderance of the evidence was that her parents were indeed "colored." In 1986, when the case was appealed to the Louisiana Supreme Court and then to the US Supreme Court, both courts refused to review the decision, in effect leaving the one-drop rule untouched.[12]

It is this historical backdrop that provides the context for the contemporary question of multiracial identity. While it is clear that many people of color (and some Whites) have a multiracial heritage, the terms *mixed-race* and *biracial* are usually used to refer to the offspring of parents who are labeled as being from two differing racial groups. Though these terms can apply to racial combinations such as White-Asian or Black–Native American, they most often conjure up images of Black-White pairings. The history of racial categorization suggests that the Black-White combination has been the most controversial. Social scientists Rockquemore and Brunsma note that "in the United States, blacks and whites continue to be the two groups with the greatest social distance, the most spatial separation, and the strongest historically rooted taboos against interracial marriage."[13]

Though the number of interracial marriages across all groups has grown significantly since 1967, up from less than 1 percent of all marriages in 1970 to 6.3 percent in 2013, Black-White marriages are among the least common. Although they have increased from 167,000 in 1980 to 558,000 in 2010, Black-White unions still represent less than 1 percent of all married couples.[14]

Researchers report that biracial Asian-White and White-Latinx children appear to have more acceptance in White communities than biracial Black-White children do. For example, researchers report that multiracial adults with a Black background who are perceived by others as Black based on appearance are much more likely to experience various forms of discrimination (e.g., being subject to racial slurs or jokes, receiving unfair treatment in employment situations, being unfairly stopped by police) than multiracial adults who do not have a Black background (e.g., White and Asian, White and Native American).[15] Given the unique historical and contemporary context, it is the biracial identity development of children of Black and White parents that I will focus on here.

## "But Don't the Children Suffer?"

American attitudes toward interracial marriage have grown dramatically more favorable in the last half century. In 2013 87 percent of Americans polled said they approve of marriage between Blacks and Whites, compared to only 4 percent in 1958.[16] Yet it is still common to hear Black and White adults alike express ambivalence toward or, in some cases, disapproval of interracial relationships because of stated concerns about the hardship the children of these relationships are assumed to suffer.[17] The stereotype of the "tragic mulatto"—as portrayed in the classic film *Imitation of Life*, for example—is one of marginality and maladjustment.[18] This stereotype has been reinforced to some degree by clinical reports of biracial individuals receiving mental health services. For example, in a 1980s survey of social service, mental health, special education, and probation agencies located in the San Francisco area, 60 percent of the responding agencies reported that referrals of biracial adolescents had increased during the previous ten years and that this group was overrepresented among their adolescent client population.[19]

Such reports were countered in the 1990s by a carefully designed comparison study of the social adjustment of biracial adolescents conducted by Ana Mari Cauce and her colleagues at the University of Washington.[20] They compared a group of both Black-White and Asian-White adolescents with a control group of monoracial adolescents who were matched in terms of their gender, age, year in school, family income, family composition, and race of the parent of color. In other words, biracial adolescents with one White parent and one Black parent were matched with adolescents with two Black parents, and Asian-White teens were matched with monoracial Asian Americans. While the researchers could have matched the biracial participants with White adolescents (matching the White parents), they concluded that choosing a control group made up of adolescents of color would also control, in part, for the effects of racial discrimination related to growing up as a person of color in this society. Consequently, any differences found between the two groups would be more likely due to the unique circumstances associated with being biracial than to the more pervasive difficulties facing all people of color.

Forty-four adolescents (half biracial, half control group) participated in interviews of one to two hours and completed a series of standardized questionnaires designed to assess family relations, peer relations, self-esteem, life stress, and overall psychological adjustment. The results of the comparisons did not suggest significant differences on any of the measures examined. Cauce and her colleagues concluded that the biracial adolescents were indistinguishable from adolescents of color who were similar to themselves. They wrote:

> Biracial early adolescents appear to be remarkably similar to other children of color matched on basic demographic variables. This does not mean that the adolescents were not experiencing difficulties, either as individuals or as a group. It does imply that to the degree that such difficulties were experienced they were no greater in our sample of biracial adolescents than they were in similar adolescents of color.[21]

For both groups, all measures of psychological adjustment were in the normal range, suggesting that biracial adolescents can be as reasonably healthy and happy as other young people are. The findings of this study are supported by other studies of biracial teens, which have also found most of these adolescents to be well adjusted with high levels of self-esteem.[22]

While it is clear that biracial children can grow up happy and healthy, it is also clear that particular challenges associated with a biracial identity must be negotiated. One such challenge is embodied in the frequently asked question, "What are you?" While the question may be prompted by the individual's sometimes racially ambiguous appearance, the insistence with which the question is often asked represents society's need to classify its members racially. The existence of the biracial person challenges the rigid boundaries between Black and White, and the questioner may really be asking, "Which side are you on? Where do you stand?" Choosing a standpoint and an identity (or identities) is a lifelong process that can manifest itself in different ways at different times.

Since the US Census provided survey respondents the option to choose more than one racial category in the year 2000, social science research on the identity choices of mixed-race individuals has proliferated. In their book *Beyond Black: Biracial Identity in America*, Kerry Ann Rockquemore and David Brunsma describe one of the largest such studies exploring what it means to be mixed-race with one Black parent and one White parent in post–civil rights era America. Unlike previous studies of multiracial youth, all of which had small sample sizes (forty subjects or fewer), Rockquemore and Brunsma identified more than two hundred participants from the Midwest, South, and East to participate in surveys and, for a subset, semistructured, in-depth interviews as well. The researchers assembled a sample population that was 39 percent male and 61 percent female and had an average age of twenty-four, and that represented a range of socioeconomic backgrounds and a diversity of physical characteristics. Their core question was, "How do mixed-race people racially self-identify? In other words, what does it mean to be mixed-race according to members of this population? Is there just one way that people with one black and one white parent understand their racial identity or does being mixed-race lead to different racial self-understandings for different people?"[23]

The answer to their question was clear and significant. "What is historically unique and theoretically important is that among a group of 230 people who all have one white and one black parent, individuals understand who they are in dramatically different ways."[24] Rockquemore and Brunsma categorized these diverse understandings into four types of racial identification:

1. the *singular identity* (either exclusively Black or exclusively White),
2. the *border identity* (defining oneself as biracial),
3. the *protean identity* (shifting back and forth between Black, White, and biracial), and
4. the *transcendent identity* (rejecting all racial categories).

The "exclusively Black" singular identity has been the historical and cultural norm in the United States, consistent with the one-drop rule. If the mixed-race person has a combination of skin color, hair texture, and facial features associated with people of African descent, others will assume based on appearance that the individual is Black and treat him or her accordingly. Aisha, one of the young women in the study, grew up in a racially diverse neighborhood in New York City and self-identified as "mixed" throughout childhood and adolescence while living at home with her Black (of Haitian descent) father and White (German American) mother. When she went off to college, however, her self-definition changed to "Black."

> When asked to explain why she made this identity change, she said that in this mostly white environment, others assumed she was black (based on her physical appearance) and treated her as a black person. Nobody ever asked her "What are you?" Because she was both assumed black by others and had experienced repeated painful incidents of racism, she came to strongly identify exclusively as black. Aisha never denies the existence of her white parent if anyone asks, but the fact that nobody [at college] ever asks only reinforces her black identity. Aisha's parents support her evolving self-definition as black because it reflects her appearance and the way she experiences the social world.[25]

Aisha is an example of what psychologist Maria Root calls "accepting the identity that society assigns,"[26] and this is perhaps what would be expected most of the time given US history, but Rockquemore and Brunsma found that only 13 percent of their participants defined themselves as "exclusively Black."[27]

What might not be expected is that 3 percent of the participants defined themselves as "exclusively White." Michelle attends the same northeastern college as Aisha, but her experience is very different. She grew up in an affluent Boston suburb with her Black father and White mother, both of whom are doctors. With the exception of her own family, her neighborhood was entirely White and her schools were almost entirely White. Her friendship networks were almost entirely White, and all of her boyfriends have been White. On those few occasions where she was in majority-Black environments, she felt uncomfortable. Michelle looks more like her White mother than her Black father, and she is perceived by others as White. Hence, that is the identity she claims. "Her logic for determining her racial identification is that she *looks* white, she is *identified by others* as white, she was *raised* in a white community, she is *culturally* white, and therefore she *is* white. In her mind, and in her social world, having a black parent does not preclude her from claiming a white identity."[28] Her internal sense of being White is externally accepted and validated by others, suggesting that the one-drop rule may be losing its cultural authority.

Rockquemore and Brunsma make clear that Michelle is not "passing" for White in the way that some light-skinned people of African descent did during the Jim Crow era to escape its relentless oppression. Back then, those claiming a White identity had to hide their Black heritage and cut themselves off from anything and anyone that might give their secret away. These twenty-first-century respondents who have identified as "exclusively White" in the way Michelle has are not hiding their family history. Michelle openly acknowledges her Black father, but she doesn't believe the fact of a Black parent keeps her from a White identity. Michelle does make use of her mixed-race status when it is convenient, however.

> She claims blackness when she perceives it to be useful and provide her with financial, social, or educational opportunities (such as on her college admission forms), but in her everyday life and self-understanding she is white. Michelle so deeply and clearly self-identifies as white that she describes the act of claiming a black identity on her college admissions forms as "passing for black."[29]

As is apparent in these two examples, the development of a singular identity is heavily influenced by physical appearance and cultural context. Whether identifying as "exclusively Black" or "exclusively White," those who develop a singular identity understand their mixed-race status as a fact of their birth that's otherwise not meaningful in their daily lived experience. They acknowledge the existence of the parent whose identity is different from their own but generally don't mention that part of their heritage unless asked.

The self-understanding of those who claim a "border identity," a term coined by Gloria Anzaldúa, is quite different. The fact of their mixed-race birth is at the heart of their self-definition. "Mixed-race people who have a border identity don't consider themselves to be either black or white, but instead incorporate both 'blackness' and 'whiteness' into a separate hybrid category of self-reference."[30] Among the participants in the Rockquemore and Brunsma study, the border "biracial" identity was the most common self-identification (58 percent). However, among this group, there were those whose self-identification as biracial was externally validated through their interactions with others, and those whose biracial identity was not validated by other people. Whether or not others validate the chosen identity makes an important difference in one's daily life.

Among the study participants, Anthony is an example of someone whose biracial identity has been externally validated since childhood. Though he would not be perceived as White, he is not immediately identifiable as Black. His physical appearance is racially ambiguous. His Black father left the family when Anthony was young, leaving Anthony feeling resentful toward him, one reason among many perhaps that Black is not his self-identification. Raised by his White mother in a predominantly White community, he attended a school in which half of the children of color identified as biracial. In that context, it was easy for Anthony to also develop a strong sense of himself as biracial, an identity validated by others in his social environment.

Chris is an example of someone whose self-identification as biracial is unvalidated. Because of her physical appearance, most people assume she is Black, and like the earlier example of Aisha, nobody asks her about her family background. They simply assume they know what it is. However, unlike Aisha, whose family was cut off from their White relatives, Chris grew up in a close and loving extended family that included both her Black and Irish relatives and their cultural influences. For that reason perhaps, Chris says her identity is "biracial" yet she is painfully aware that other people do not see her that way. "I experience the world as a black woman."

> She felt that her family and close friends appreciated, understood and validated her as biracial, but when she had to interact with people outside of her immediate social network, they categorized her as black and attributed all the assumptions and preconceived ideas that go along with blackness to her. She felt sad about the lack of validation, yet she was also resigned to the fact that there would always be a chasm between her self-identification (as biracial) and society's identification of her (as black).[31]

While people like Anthony whose physical appearance is racially ambiguous (some combination of lighter skin, lighter eye color, curly or straight hair, European facial features, for example) may have their biracial self-identification accepted, legitimized, and validated by others, those whose physical characteristics are quickly recognizable by others as Black do not experience the external validation of their self-identification as biracial. More than half of the respondents in the Rockquemore study who claimed a border identity were *unvalidated* by others (acquaintances, strangers, and society at large), though like Chris, they may well be validated by those closest to them (family members and intimate friends). Because they are treated by most others as Black, members of the unvalidated group "are more likely to report their cultural, political, physical and bureaucratic identity (i.e., the identity they select on forms) as 'black' rather than 'biracial.'"[32]

Those who claim what Rockquemore and Brunsma call a "protean" identity are chameleon-like in the fluidity of their identity expression. Only 6.5 percent of the respondents in their study described themselves in this way. Mike is one of them. He grew up in a small midwestern town where his parents were the only interracial couple in the area, and Mike was the only person of color at school and in his social network in the town. But he also spent a lot of time with his Black extended family, and he feels like he is an "insider" whether he is in the company of Black people or with Whites or as a biracial person in a racially mixed group.

For Mike, any social situation must be assessed for what identity will "work," and then that particular identity will be presented. Does he view this shape-shifting as problematic? On the contrary, he views his ability to effectively possess and present different identities and have them accepted as authentic by different groups of people as "the gift of being biracial."

> [For] respondents like Mike . . . their racial identities are directly tied to their ability to cross boundaries between black, white and biracial, which is possible because they possess black, white and biracial identities. These individuals feel endowed with a degree of cultural savvy in several social worlds and understand their mixed-race status as the way in which they are accepted, however conditionally, in varied interactional settings. . . . This contextual shifting leads individuals to form a belief that their multiple racial backgrounds are but one piece of a complex self that is composed of assorted identifications that are not culturally integrated. When the topic of racial identification was initially broached with Mike, he said: "Well shit, it depends on what day it is and where I'm goin'."[33]

Though what is called here a "protean identity" was not a common way of self-identifying—in fact, it was the least frequent—it is of particular interest to researchers because it requires "a complex mastery of various cultural norms and values and an ongoing awareness and monitoring of one's presentation of self."[34] Those who self-identify this way report feeling close to both Blacks and Whites and are distinguished from the other identity groups previously described by the fact that they have racially mixed social networks and had lots of experience in both Black and White communities during their growing-up years. In that sense, they are truly multicultural "border-crossers," shifting from one identity to another with relative ease and psychological comfort, just as some multilingual people can switch between languages as needed.[35]

The last type of self-identification that Rockquemore and Brunsma described is the transcendent or "non-racial" identity. Approximately 15 percent of the study respondents expressed this self-understanding, essentially refusing to participate in the racial categorization process in any way other than as "human." The following quote captures the transcendent perspective:

> I'm just John, you know. I never thought this was such a big deal to be identified, I just figured I'm a good guy, just like me for that, you know. But when I came here [to college] it was like I was almost forced to look at people as being white, black, Asian or Hispanic. And so now, I'm still trying to go, "I'm just John" but uh, you gotta be something.[36]

Most, but not all, of the "transcendents" were perceived by others as White based on their physical appearance. In that sense, they may not claim "Whiteness" as Michelle did, but they are viewed and treated by others as if that were their self-identification. It is not uncommon to hear monoracial White people say that they don't think about race, and if one is perceived as White, it is relatively easy to move through the world without having one's self-identification as "non-racial" questioned. However, it would seem to be quite difficult to assume a "non-racial" stance if your physical appearance marked you as Black, yet a small number did. For all of the participants in this category,

> their status as mixed-race provided them with the perspective of the "stranger." They perceived their detached, outsider's perspective as enabling them to objectively articulate the social meaning placed on race and discount it as a "master status" altogether. . . . Experiences of discrimination, perceived from the standpoint of the stranger, neither reinforce nor negate their existing sense of self. Our respondents who have a transcendent identity seemed content to be at the periphery of a racially divided America, annoyed by the inconveniences, but playing their role when necessary.[37]

What is abundantly clear from the results of the Rockquemore and Brunsma study is that there is no unified racial identity known as "multiracial" or singular understanding as to what it means in one's daily life. It is also clear that while physical appearance plays a role in how one's self-understanding evolves, it is not the only determining factor. Socioeconomic status plays a role because the higher the social status of the parents, the more likely the child is to have access to White social networks through the schools they attend and the neighborhoods in which they reside. Having a more White-like appearance and high exposure to White social networks increases the likelihood of developing a border identity that will be validated and reduces the likelihood of developing a singular Black identity. Mixed-race individuals who grow up in predominantly Black communities, regardless of physical appearance, are likely to be validated as "Black" by their Black neighbors, who themselves vary in phenotype, and in that context mixed-race individuals are more likely to choose an exclusively Black identity because of their community acceptance.[38] But it is not always that straightforward.

It seems to be the quality of interaction within those social networks that makes the difference. "What occurs within those networks and the type of interactions that individuals have within those settings affect their choices of racial identity. We conceptualize these as push and pull factors where individuals, located within particular types of social networks, may feel pulled toward one racial identity option because of positive experiences with one group and/or may feel pushed away from another racial identity because of negative experiences."[39]

Building on the findings of Rockquemore and Brunsma, social scientist Nikki Khanna also noted the "push-pull" phenomena that mixed-race youth experience in her qualitative interview study of forty individuals (average age of twenty-four) living at the time of the interviews in metropolitan Atlanta. She found that the majority of biracial respondents in her study felt pulled toward identifying as Black because of the general acceptance of the Black community and pushed away from claiming a White identity because of a sense of rejection from Whites who perceived them as Black, or at least "not White."[40]

However, she describes what she calls the "gendered rejection" that mixed-race women experience in both White and Black communities.

Social exclusion appeared more pronounced for women than men in this study within the context of dating in adolescence and young adulthood. While biracial men in this study described feeling desired by white female peers in dating relationships, biracial women told a markedly different story. White males, they argued, ignored and overlooked them as potential romantic partners, leaving those who grew up in predominantly white communities feeling unattractive and socially isolated.[41]

Biracial girls are often considered beautiful objects of curiosity because of their "exotic" looks, but this attention does not necessarily translate into dating partners if they live in White communities. Conversely, biracial girls in predominantly Black environments may be actively sought after by Black boys and consequently become objects of resentment by monoracial Black girls because of the legacy of colorism in Black communities, conferring favored status to those with light skin, straight or wavy hair, and European features. Indeed, the biracial women in Khanna's study reported encountering hostility from Black women who seemed jealous of their physical appearance and popularity with Black males. This was a dynamic that biracial males did not encounter. "When asked whether they ever faced hostility or negative treatment from black people, 61.3 percent of women said yes, while only one biracial male agreed."[42] Despite the dynamic of colorism within the Black community, which was a factor in biracial women's sense of acceptance, most of the men and women in Khanna's study still felt more strongly identified as Black as overall they felt more accepted in Black communities.

To further probe how mixed-race youth come to understand where they "belong" racially, Khanna makes use of social comparison theory to look at how adolescents form their internalized racial identities. "Fundamental questions facing black-white biracial people such as 'Who am

I racially?' may be answered by comparing themselves to black, white, and other black-white biracial people on several dimensions, including 1) phenotype (i.e., how they look); 2) culture (e.g., how they dress, what they eat, how they speak); and 3) experiences of privilege, prejudice and discrimination."[43]

The first social comparison the mixed-race child is likely to make is with other family members. Biracial children, like all children, begin to develop their racial awareness during the preschool years. They notice physical differences between themselves, their parents, and others. Skin color and hair texture are likely to be commented on from an early age. As discussed earlier, these observations can catch parents off guard. Maureen Reddy, the author of *Crossing the Color Line: Race, Parenting, and Culture*, relates her son's efforts to understand both gender and race simultaneously at the age of three.[44] Her son had observed that he and his Black father both had penises, but his White mother did not. Attributing the difference to race rather than gender, he asked, "Why do White people have vaginas?" Such questions reflect the child's efforts to make sense of the world and to create categories, as all children do. Racial awareness seems to develop earlier among biracial children than it does among White children, probably due to their early exposure to different racial groups in the context of their own family. In this regard, their experiences may be similar to monoracial Black children growing up in families where one parent is light-skinned and the other dark.

If the child's look is significantly different from that of the same-sex parent, the child may express a desire for sameness at an early age. For example, if the mother's skin is light and her daughter's is dark, the daughter may wish for lighter skin like Mom's. This wish in itself is not necessarily a sign of low self-esteem but a natural expression of a desire to be identified with the parent. In fact, in the following example, it was the mother that the five-year-old child wished to change, not herself. As a mother and daughter were riding in the car together, the child was playing with a "magic wand." The White mother asked, "If you really had magic, what would you do?" Without any hesitation, the Black daughter replied, "I would turn your skin brown."[45]

The fact that the child and parent don't match may be a cause for unwanted attention from others who ask if the child is adopted or assume that the parent is a babysitter. Particularly if the parent appears Black and the child appears White, White adults may even question the parent's right to be with the child. For example, one Black mother of a White-looking child took her infant to a public gathering several weeks after her birth, one of their first outings together. An older White woman saw her carrying the child and asked accusingly, "Where did you get that baby?" While the infant surely doesn't remember this event, similar scenes are repeated during the preschool years and later, heightening the child's awareness of the physical differences between family members.

The impact of physical social comparisons within the family is captured in this quote from one of Khanna's participants, Lauren, who internally identifies as Black:

> I think in some instances when I was younger [being with my white family members] made me acutely aware that I was different. . . . You know, because when I'd go in these situations with my [white] mom and . . . her family, I mean there was me and there was everybody else with their blonde-haired and blue-eyed kids. And then there's me. . . . It was just kind of filtered into my brain that I was different. It makes it easier for me to identify with being black. I look at [black] people [and] I'm like, "Okay, you look like me. So obviously I'm one of you if I look like you and you look like me.[46]

Biracial children within the same family can have different phenotypes and consequently make different social comparisons. Kate, who identifies internally as White, says, "I don't really feel like I look really black compared to black people that I know. Or even like biracial people. I don't even look anything like my [biracial] sister. She has, like, the black person hair and I have the white person hair and I look really different. . . . I look more like my [white] mom."[47]

While social comparisons regarding physical appearance are usually based on *realistic* comparisons—that is, comparisons to real people in the person's social network (e.g., family members or school peers)—other kinds of social comparisons (perceived cultural differences, for example) may be based on *constructive* comparisons—that is, comparisons based on imagined differences, often stereotypes. "In the case of black-white biracial people, they may rely on constructed comparisons when real (black or white) referents are underrepresented in their social networks, and hence, when real referents are unavailable for direct comparison."[48] For example, in Khanna's study, biracial youth who grew up in predominantly White racial networks tended to compare themselves against negative racial stereotypes of Blacks, and consequently, there was a desire to differentiate themselves from the negative stereotype by identifying as White or biracial. There was also a tendency for some biracial respondents to conflate race and class in the social comparisons they made, "equating being middle class with having a White identity."[49] Says Kate, also quoted above, who grew up in a small, predominantly White community:

I think of that African American English and very hip-hop culture. Usually, like, lower class, but then again I know black people who aren't any of those stereotypes . . . one of my favorite professors. She is black and her [black] husband is a physician, but I wouldn't think of that first. I really don't identify with being black because I'm not into the, like, hip-hop culture and the bling-bling with the jerseys.[50]

By contrast, biracial youth who have racially mixed social networks with numerous real referents (both Black and White family, friends, and peers) are more likely to rely on realistic social comparisons than constructed ones, and consequently are less impacted by the limited negative stereotypes about Black people. Khanna concludes that "social networks provide both *opportunities for* and *limitations* to the types of social comparisons that individuals can make with others (realistic or constructive), and as a consequence, the types of comparisons they make influence their racial identities."[51] In Khanna's study, most of the biracial respondents in racially mixed social networks identified internally as Black, while few of those in predominantly White social networks identified internally as Black.

## The Socializing Role of Parents

The importance of the parents' role in helping children make sense of the social comparisons they are making, as well as other race-related experiences they are having, cannot be overemphasized. As shown here, the choices parents make about where they live and where their children go to school has implications for identity development. Their own racial ideology will also influence how they socialize their children. All parents, regardless of their own racial group membership, send messages to their children, directly or indirectly, about race. As discussed in previous chapters, learning about race begins at an early age, but both the process and content is different for Blacks and other people of color than for Whites. "In contrast to the explicit racial socialization strategies used by black families, the process in white families is both subtler and different in content."[52] When interracial couples have children, they bring to the parenting experience different racial socialization histories, and unless one of them is a mixed-race person, neither of them has had the experience of growing up as a biracial child. Because the rates of Black-White marriage are higher for Black men than for Black women (25 percent versus 12 percent in 2013),[53] and mothers are usually the primary caretakers in families, the most common scenario is for the White mother to be the primary caretaker of the children.[54] If parents are not in agreement about the racial socialization strategies, this may be a source of tension.

For example, during the preschool years children begin to learn racial labels. Some parents may intentionally choose "Black" as the child's label, recognizing that if the child looks Black, he or she will be treated as such. Emphasizing the child's Black heritage in a positive way may be viewed as a strategy to counteract the devaluing messages of the dominant society.[55] Such a choice may be a point of conflict, however, for the White parent, who may feel left out by this choice.

If the parents have separated and the custodial parent is White, what meaning will a Black or biracial identity have for the child? While it is certainly possible for a White parent to actively promote a positive sense of Blackness—seeking out culturally relevant books and toys, developing a Black or biracial friendship network, seeking out multiracial environments—it may not always be recognized as important to do so. If Blackness is devalued by either parent or within either extended family, if the Black parent is disparaged in front of the child, or if there are no positive ties to a Black community, then it will be very difficult for the child to value his or her Black heritage. There will be no buffer against the negative messages about Blackness in the wider society, posing a threat to the child's developing self-esteem. Of course, it is also important that the White parent not be disparaged in racial terms, but in the context of the wider culture that is less likely to happen because Whiteness is more highly valued.[56]

Some parents choose to teach their children to label themselves as biracial, hoping to affirm both identities. But the concept of "both" is a complex one for preschoolers to understand, simply because of their cognitive immaturity. They may learn the "biracial" label, with little grasp of its social meaning initially, though that will change as they get older. Psychologists Robin Lin Miller and Mary-Jane Rotheram-Borus recommend that if parents are going to encourage a biracial identity, they need to provide substantial positive exposure to both racial groups to help the child understand what it means to be a participant in both cultures.[57] The research of Khanna as well as Rockquemore and Brunsma illustrate the benefits to young adults who have had such experiences.

The challenge for parents of preschoolers, regardless of the chosen label, is to affirm who the child is and to help the child see him or herself positively reflected in the environment around them. Necessity is sometimes the mother of invention. One grandmother, unable to find a doll that matched her biracial grandchild's complexion, made a Raggedy Ann–style doll for her, choosing fabric of just the right shade. A wonderful book depicting a multiracial family consisting of a White father and a Black mother, *Black, White, Just Right!*, was written by a grandmother who wanted to offer her grandchildren that kind of positive reflection.[58] A Google search will reveal a growing list of children's books specifically written with multiracial families in mind.

Parents who have a "color-blind" ideology may be reluctant to talk to their children about potential encounters with racism, hoping perhaps that if they don't mention it, it won't be a problem.[59] Talking about the possibility of such interactions and providing children with appropriate responses they might use in such situations is one way to inoculate children against the stress of this kind of racism. Several of the biracial adults profiled by Lise Funderburg expressed a wish that their parents had prepared them better for the situations they would encounter. Said one, "I thought my parents should have talked to me about it or tried to figure it out, but I don't think they knew themselves, so they just didn't try at all." This respondent, now a parent herself, is being more proactive with her own racially mixed child.[60]

## Identity in Adoptive Families Considered

In 2013 more than 40 percent of adoptions in the US were transracial in nature, up from 28 percent in 2004.[61] In considering the identity development of children of color adopted by White parents, issues similar to those experienced by nonadopted biracial children emerge relative to the question, "Where do I fit racially?" However, some issues are unique to children adopted into White families. In particular, the absence of an adult of color in the family to serve as a racial role model may make adolescent identity development more difficult. In addition, the identity process is often complicated by the adolescent's questions and feelings about the adoption itself. "Who are my biological parents? What were the circumstances of my birth? Why did my birth mother give me up for adoption?" These questions add another layer to the complex process of identity development in adolescence.

However, as in the case of nonadopted biracial children, the role of the caregivers is critical in easing this process. Race-conscious parents who openly discuss racism, who seek to create a multiracial community of friends and family (perhaps adopting more than one child of color so there will be siblings with a shared experience), who seek out racially mixed schools, who, in short, take seriously the identity needs of their adopted children of color and try to provide for those needs, increase the likelihood that their adopted children of color will grow to adulthood feeling good about themselves and their adoptive parents.

Consider the case of Alan, a dark-skinned Black male raised by White parents in a predominantly White community. In an interview with me, he remarked that his Black friends were often surprised to learn that his parents were White. How was it possible that a Black guy with White parents could be so "cool"? He attributed his social success to the fact that his parents always sought out integrated neighborhoods and placed him in racially mixed schools. They encouraged his involvement in athletics, where he made strong connections with other Black boys. In junior high school, when the identity process often begins to unfold, Alan felt most comfortable with those Black boys. He explained, "Whenever I went out with my [Black] friends or played my sports . . . that's where I liked to be. That's where I found myself." When his parents wanted to leave the city on vacation, he found himself less and less willing to leave his network of Black friends. Their idea of getting away meant social isolation for him. As he got older he realized that he didn't want to go on vacation to a place "where there's three Black people in the whole town."

While it does not seem that he ever rejected his parents in his adolescence, as a young adult he has put some distance between himself and his extended family members. He is the only Black person among a large extended family, and his mother's relatives live in a rural area in a state with a very small Black population. Whenever Alan goes to visit them, he feels very self-conscious, very aware of his visibility in that environment. His parents, respectful of his feelings, do not insist that he accompany them on those family visits. Alan has considered a search for his biological mother but has not yet pursued it. His parents have responded to the possibility in a supportive way.

Alan's experience is contrasted with the experiences of several Korean adoptees I have taught over the years. In all of these cases, the young women grew up in White families that considered their daughters' racial category irrelevant to their child-rearing. No particular effort was made to affirm their Korean heritage, beginning with the choice of their first names, which typically reflected the parents' European heritage rather than the children's Korean heritage.

The names themselves often led to encounters with racism. For example, one young woman told me of an experience she had cashing a check. The White male clerk looked at her face and then looked down at the surname on the check and asked, "What kind of name is that?" She identified its European origin. The clerk looked dumbfounded and said rudely, "What are you doing with a name like that?!" Such experiences remind these adoptees of their outsider status in White communities.

In one instance, a young woman reported that when she was a child a Korean family friend had offered to take her to Korean cultural events, but her parents had declined the offers, encouraging instead her complete assimilation into her adoptive culture. Unfortunately, *complete* assimilation was not possible because she did not look the part. Her Asian features continually set her apart, but with no cultural connection to any Asian community she had no one to share these experiences with and no help in learning how to cope with the racism she encountered. In college she began to realize her need for some connection to an Asian community and began to explore how to make those connections. In reflecting on the choices her parents made, she said, "In a way I think my parents messed up and that they taught me to hate what I really was. Maybe if they hadn't ignored my racial heritage so much I would have an easier time accepting that I am an Asian and that I always will be." At least, that is the way she believes the world will always see her.

In a mixed-method study, Godon, Green, and Ramsey surveyed 109 transracial adoptees (TRAs) and interviewed a subset of eleven. The backgrounds of the study participants, all of whom had been adopted by White families, represented fifteen different birth countries, but most were from South Korea. The average age of the participants overall was twenty-six; the subset of interviewees were a bit younger, with an average age of twenty-one. My Korean student's experience was echoed in the narratives of the study participants. Though all ultimately viewed their adoptions as positive, many reported feeling racially isolated growing up and felt discomfort at being visibly different from their White adoptive families.[62]

One participant described her frustration when she joined the Asian American Association in high school: "I totally did not fit in. . . . It kind of made me mad because I looked like them, so I felt like I identified with them, but once I got in, I learned I really don't at all." Caught between the expectations of two groups, TRAs often felt rejected by White people due to physical differences and by people of their birth ethnicity due to lack of language and cultural knowledge.[63]

As with biracial youth, adoptive parents who attend to the identity development needs of their children for a same-experience peer group can reduce the isolation and discomfort for their children. In the case of Eunliz, a twenty-year old Korean adopted while still an infant, she and her parents lived in an area with many Korean adoptees. Her parents encouraged her to learn about Korean culture and provided the opportunity for her to attend Korean culture camp every summer, allowing her to develop sustaining connections with other Korean adoptees. She eventually studied the Korean language and traveled to South Korea, a trip she described as one of the best experiences of her life. Clearly her adoptive parents took a race-conscious approach to her socialization, which has contributed to her self-confidence and comfort with her ethnic identity.

By contrast, twenty-two-year old Selma, also adopted from South Korea as an infant, grew up in a family that had a color-blind ideology. They discouraged her from actively exploring her Korean identity by learning about her cultural background and minimized her experiences with racism.

When she told her parents about her classmates' racist comments, her mother advised her to "stop being the victim." Her father refused to acknowledge even the possibility that she could have a different perspective: "My dad, being a Christian, he sees humans as of one blood. He tells me all the time, 'Stop it, stop it, you're not Korean, you know you're American . . . ' He couldn't fathom what it's like to be a minority." Even though her father seemed to have good intentions, he adhered to the color-blind approach to race and thereby negated a central aspect of Selma's identity.[64]

When Selma found her own way to a Korean American church, finally, in a room full of Asians, she realized what she had been missing. "I never realized how uncomfortable I was until I was comfortable. . . . I felt for the first time that I didn't have to explain."[65]

Journalist Mark Hagland, himself a Korean adoptee and adoption literacy advocate, insists that "parents who believe they can raise their child color-blind are making a terrible mistake. And it's shocking how many people I meet still think this way. If there's a single thing I can share with white adoptive parents [it's to] look at the adult adoptees who have committed suicide, or who have substance abuse problems. Love was not enough for them."[66] He and other adult transracial adoptees argue that teaching children to cope with the racism they will inevitably encounter is a necessary part of the White adoptive parent's responsibility. Abigail, a twenty-one-year old Chinese female adoptee, said, "I think every adoptee inevitably is going to go through a period where the shock of race is real. . . . It can happen when you're 8 or 13 or 28. And when you're really depressed and feel really different, you don't want to hear *love is enough.*" For Abigail, the best thing that her mother did when she felt depressed was to "listen to her pain, rather than dismiss her with excuses or denials."[67]

In some instances, preparing children for encounters with racism can be a matter of life and death. Karen Valby, writer and adoptive White parent of two Black girls, acknowledges that "many adoptive parents, including me, feel tremendous anxiety about introducing concepts of racism to their children." Hagland, the adoption literacy advocate, has a response for her and others: "Are you not going to teach your child how to cross the street? [Are you going to say] 'I could never talk about being hit by a car because then my child would fear it.' Well guess what? Part of your role as a parent is teaching your child how to safely cross the street."[68]

Alex Landau, a Black transracial adoptee, had such a life-threatening encounter in 2009, when he was just nineteen. Stopped by the police and accused of making an illegal left turn, he was ordered out of his car and searched. Landau's White father had never had "the talk" that is a rite of passage in African American families—when Black parents explain to their teenage sons how to behave if stopped by the police. Landau asserted his rights with the three police officers present and asked to see a warrant before they searched his car. The officers responded by punching him in the face. He was knocked to the ground and remembers hearing one of the officers saying, "Where's your warrant now, you f—ing n—?" When his mother arrived at the jail, she was horrified to find her son there with forty-five stitches in his face. Though the officers were cleared of any misconduct, the City of Denver awarded Landau a $795,000 settlement. He and his mother are now working to educate other transracial families. Landau says, "I know my mother wishes she could have had the insight herself to prepare me for the ugly realities that can occur."[69]

Almost twenty years ago I was invited to moderate a panel of adoptive parents who were sharing their experiences with interracial adoption with an audience of prospective parents considering the same option. The White panelists spoke of ways they had tried to affirm the identities of their adopted children of color. One parent, the mother of a Central American adoptee, spoke of how she had become involved in a support group of parents who had adopted Latinx children as a way of providing her son with playmates who had a shared experience. She also described her efforts to find Latinx adults who might serve as role models for her child. There were very few Latinx families in her mostly White community, but she located a Latinx organization in a nearby town and began to do volunteer work for it as a way of building a Latinx friendship network.

During the question-and-answer period that followed, a White woman stood up and explained that she was considering adopting a Latinx child but lived in a small rural community that was entirely White. She was impressed by the mother's efforts to create a Latinx network for her child but expressed doubts that she herself could do so. She said she would feel too uncomfortable placing herself in a situation where she would be one of few Whites. She didn't think she could do it.

I thought this was an amazing statement. How could this White adult seriously consider placing a small child in a situation where the child would be in the minority *all* the time, while the idea of spending a few hours as a "minority" was too daunting for her? Had I been the social worker doing the home study in that case, I would not have recommended an interracial placement. The prospective mother was apparently not ready to risk the discomfort required to help a child of color negotiate a racist environment. The kind of reluctance to engage in diverse communities that that prospective parent expressed back then is still being articulated today.

Transracial adoptee Chad Goller-Sojourner is a playwright and solo performer who writes and speaks about his identity development journey. "In college he began what he calls a 'descent into blackness and out of whiteness.' He describes it as a journey, giving up the privileges he claimed as a child of white parents and learning to accept his identity independent of them. He added Sojourner to his name."[70]

Adopted in 1972, he gives his parents credit for doing the best they could to prepare him for his life as a Black man. They were among the first in his community to adopt transracially; in that sense they were pioneers. He says today's adoptive parents can and should do better. "I don't have a checklist," he says, "but if I did, it would sound something like this: if you don't have any close friends or people who look like your kid before you adopt a kid, then why are you adopting that kid? Your child should not be your first black friend."[71]

The successful adoption of children of color by White parents requires those parents to be willing to experience the close encounters with racism that their children—and they as parents—will have, and to be prepared to talk to their children about them. Ultimately they need to examine their own identities as White people, going beyond the idea of raising a child of color in a White family to a new understanding of themselves and their children as members of a multiracial family.

The creation of well-adjusted multiracial families, whether through adoption or through the union of parents of different racial backgrounds, is clearly possible, but it's not automatic. Considerable examination of one's own racial identity is required. Adults willing to do the personal work required to confront racism and stretch their own cultural boundaries increase the possibility that they will have the reward of watching their children emerge into adulthood with a positive sense of their identities intact.

# PART V

## Breaking the Silence

# TEN

# Embracing a Cross-Racial Dialogue

*"We were struggling for the words."*

SOME PEOPLE SAY THERE IS TOO MUCH TALK ABOUT RACE AND RACISM in the United States. I say that there is not enough. The twenty-year history I recounted in the prologue and the many examples throughout the preceding chapters highlight the pervasiveness of our problem. We need to continually break the silence about racism whenever we can.[1] We need to talk about it at home, at school, in our houses of worship, in our workplaces, in our community groups. But talk does not mean idle chatter. It means meaningful, productive dialogue to raise consciousness and lead to effective action and social change. But how do we start? This is the question my students and workshop participants ask me. "How do I engage in meaningful dialogue about racial issues? How do I get past my fear? How do I get past my anger? Am I willing to take the risk of speaking up? Can I trust that there will be others to listen and support me? Will it even make a difference? Is it worth the effort?"

## The Paralysis of Fear

Fear is a powerful emotion, one that immobilizes, traps words in our throats, and stills our tongues. Like a deer on the highway, frozen in the panic induced by the lights of an oncoming car, when we are afraid it seems that we cannot think, we cannot speak, we cannot move.

What do we fear? Isolation from friends and family, ostracism for speaking of things that generate discomfort, rejection by those who may be offended by what we have to say, the loss of privilege or status for speaking in support of those who have been marginalized by society, physical harm caused by the irrational wrath of those who disagree with your stance? My students readily admitted their fears in their journals and essays. Some White students were afraid of their own ignorance, afraid that because of their limited experience with people of color they might ask a naive question or make an offensive remark that could provoke the anger of the people of color around them.

"Yes, there is fear," one White woman wrote, "the fear of speaking is overwhelming. I do not feel, for me, that it is fear of rejection from people of my race, but anger and disdain from people of color. The ones who I am fighting for." In my response to this woman's comment, I explained that she needs to fight for herself, not for people of color. After all, she has been damaged by the cycle of racism, too, though perhaps this is less obvious. If she speaks because she needs to speak, perhaps then it would be less important whether the people of color are appreciative of her comments. She seemed to understand my comment, but the fear remained.

Another student, a White woman in her late thirties, wrote about her fears when trying to speak honestly about her understanding of racism.

> Fear requires us to be honest with not only others, but with ourselves. Often this much honesty is difficult for many of us, for it would permit our insecurities and ignorance to surface, thus opening the floodgate to our vulnerabilities. This position is difficult for most of us when [we are] in the company of entrusted friends and family. I can imagine fear heightening when [we are] in the company of those we hardly know. Hence, rather than publicly admit our weaknesses, we remain silent.

These students are not alone in their fear-induced silence. Christine Sleeter, a White woman who has written extensively about multicultural

education and antiracist teaching, writes in her classic 1994 autobiographical essay:

> I first noticed White silence about racism about 15 years ago, al-
> though I was not able to name it as such. I recall realizing after hav-
> ing shared many meals with African American friends while teaching
> in Seattle, that racism and race-related issues were fairly common
> topics of dinner-table conversation, which African Americans talked
> about quite openly. It struck me that I could not think of a single
> instance in which racism had been a topic of dinner-table conversa-
> tion in White contexts. Race-related issues sometimes came up, but
> not racism.[2]

Instead, Sleeter argues, White people often speak in a kind of racial
code, using communication patterns with each other that encourage a
kind of White racial bonding. These communication patterns include
race-related asides in conversations, strategic eye contact, jokes, and other
comments that assert an "us-them" boundary. Sleeter observes, "These
kinds of interactions seem to serve the purpose of defining racial lines,
and inviting individuals to either declare their solidarity or mark themselves as deviant. Depending on the degree of deviance, one runs the risk
of losing the other individual's approval, friendship and company."[3]

The fear of the isolation that comes from this kind of deviance is
a powerful silencer. My students, young and old, often talked about
this kind of fear, experienced not only with friends but with colleagues
or employers in work settings. For instance, Lynn struggled when her
employer casually used racial slurs in conversation with her. It was especially troubling to Lynn because her employer's young children were
listening to their conversation. Though she was disturbed by the interaction, Lynn was afraid and then embarrassed by her own silence: "I
was completely silent following her comment. I knew that I should say
something, to point out that she was being completely inappropriate
(especially in front of her children) and that she had really offended me.
But I just sat there with a stupid forced half-smile on my face."

How could she respond to this, she asked? What would it cost her to speak? Would it mean momentary discomfort or could it really mean losing her job? And what did her silence cost her on a personal level?

Because of the White culture of silence about racism, my White students often had little experience engaging in dialogue about racial issues. They had not had much practice at overcoming their inhibitions to speak. They noticed that the students of color spoke about racism more frequently, and they assumed they did so more easily. One White woman observed,

> In our class discussion when White students were speaking, we sounded so naive and so "young" about what we were discussing. It was almost like we were struggling for the words to explain ourselves and were even speaking much slower than the students of color. The students of color, on the other hand, were extremely well aware of what to say and of what they wanted to express. It dawned on me that these students had dealt with this long before I ever thought about racism. Since last fall, racism has been a totally new concept to me, almost like I was hearing about it for the first time. For these students, however, the feelings, attitudes and terminology came so easily.

This woman was correct in her observation that most of the people of color in that classroom were more fluent in the discourse of racism and more aware of its personal impact on their lives than perhaps she was. But she was wrong that their participation was easy. They were also afraid.

I am reminded of an article I read when my own children were in school. It was written by Kirsten Mullen, a Black parent who needed to speak to her child's White teachers about issues of racial insensitivity at his school. She wrote, "I was terrified the first time I brought up the subject of race at my son's school. My palms were clammy, my heart was racing, and I could not have done it without rehearsing in the bathroom mirror."[4] She was afraid, but who would advocate for her son if she didn't? She could not afford the cost of silence.

An Asian American woman in my class also wrote about the difficulty of speaking:

> The process of talking about this issue is not easy. We people of color can't always make it easier for White people to talk about race relations because sometimes they need to break away from that familiar and safe ground of being neutral or silent. . . . I understand that [some are] trying but sometimes they need to take bigger steps and more risks. As an Asian in America, I am always taking risks when I share my experiences of racism; however, the dominant culture expects it of me. They think I like talking about how my parents are laughed at at work or how my older sister is forced to take [cancer-causing] birth control pills because she is on welfare. Even though I am embarrassed and sometimes get too emotional about these issues, I talk about them because I want to be honest about how I feel.

She had fears, but who would tell her story if she didn't? For many people of color, learning to break the silence is a survival issue. To remain silent would be to disconnect from her own experience, to swallow and internalize her own oppression. The cost of silence is too high.

Sometimes we fear our own anger and frustration, the chance of losing control or perhaps collapsing into despair should our words, yet again, fall on deaf ears. A Black woman wrote:

> One thing that I struggle with as an individual when it comes to discussions about race is the fact that I tend to give up. When I start to think, "He or she will never understand me. What is the point?" I have practically defeated myself. No human can ever fully understand the experiences and feelings of another, and I must remind myself that progress, although often slow and painful, can be made.

A very powerful example of racial dialogue between a multiracial group of men can be seen in the award-winning video *The Color of*

*Fear.*[5] One of the most memorable moments in the film is when Victor, an African American man, begins to shout angrily at David, a White man, who continually invalidates what Victor has said about his experiences with racism. After viewing the video in my class, several students of color wrote about how much they identified with Victor's anger and how relieved they were to see that it could be expressed without disastrous consequences. An Asian American woman wrote:

> I don't know if I'll ever see a more powerful, moving, on-the-money movie in my life! . . . Victor really said it all. He verbalized all I've ever felt or will feel so eloquently and so convincingly. When he first started speaking, he was so calm and I did not expect anything remotely close to what he exhibited. When he started shouting, my initial reaction was of discomfort. Part of that discomfort stemmed from watching him just going nuts on David. But there was something else that was embedded inside of me. I kept thinking throughout the whole movie and I finally figured it out at the end. Victor's rage and anger was mine as well. Those emotions that I had hoped to keep inside forever and ever because I didn't know if I was justified in feeling that way. I had no words or evidence, solid evidence, to prove to myself or others that I had an absolute RIGHT to scream and yell and be angry for so many things.

The anger and frustration of people of color, even when received in smaller doses, is hard for some White people to tolerate. One White woman needed to vent her own frustrations before she could listen to the frustration and anger of people of color. She wrote:

> Often I feel that because I am White, my feelings are disregarded or looked down upon in racial dialogues. I feel that my efforts are unappreciated. . . . I also realize that it is these feelings which make me want to withdraw from the fight against racism altogether. . . . [However,] I acknowledge the need for White students to listen to minority students when they express anger against the system which has failed them without taking this communication as a personal attack.

Indeed, this is what one young woman of color hoped for: "When I'm participating in a cross-racial dialogue, I prefer that the people I'm interacting with understand why I react the way that I do. When I say that I want understanding, it does not mean that I'm looking for sympathy. I merely want people to know why I'm angry and not to be offended by it."

In order for there to be meaningful dialogue, fear, whether of anger or isolation, must eventually give way to risk and trust. A leap of faith must be made. It is not easy, and it requires being willing to push past one's fear. Wrote one student, "At times it feels too risky . . . but I think if people remain equally committed, it can get easier. It's a very stressful process, but I think the consequences of not exploring racial issues are ultimately far more damaging."

## The Psychological Cost of Silence

As a society, we pay a price for our silence. Unchallenged personal, cultural, and institutional racism results in the loss of human potential, lowered productivity, and a rising tide of fear and violence in our society. Individually, racism stifles our own growth and development. It clouds our vision and distorts our perceptions. It alienates us not only from others but also from ourselves and our own experiences.

Jean Baker Miller's paper "Connections, Disconnections and Violations" offers a helpful framework for seeing how this self-alienation takes place.[6] As Miller describes, when we have meaningful experiences, we usually seek to share those experiences with someone else. In doing so, we hope to be heard and understood, to feel validated by the other. When we do not feel heard, we feel invalidated, and a relational disconnection has taken place. We may try again, persisting in our efforts to be heard, or we may choose to disconnect from that person. If there are others available who will listen and affirm us, disconnection from those who won't may be the best alternative. But if disconnection means what Miller calls "condemned isolation," then we will do whatever we have to in order to remain in connection with others. That may mean denying our own experiences of racism, selectively screening things out of our consciousness so that we can continue our relationships with reduced discomfort. As a person of color, to remain silent and deny my own experience with racism may be an important coping strategy in some contexts, but it may also lead to the self-blame and self-doubt of internalized oppression.[7]

The consequences are different but also damaging for Whites. As we have seen, many Whites have been encouraged by their culture of silence to disconnect from their racial experiences. When White children make racial observations, they are often silenced by their parents, who feel uncomfortable and unsure of how to respond. With time, the observed contradictions between parental attitudes and behaviors or between societal messages about meritocracy and visible inequities become difficult to process in a culture of silence. In order to prevent chronic discomfort, Whites may learn not to notice.

But in not noticing, one loses opportunities for greater insight into oneself and one's experience. A significant dimension of who one is in the world, one's Whiteness, remains uninvestigated and perceptions of daily experience are routinely distorted. Privilege goes unnoticed, and all but the most blatant acts of racial bigotry are ignored. Not noticing requires energy. Exactly how much energy is used up in this way becomes apparent with the opportunity to explore those silenced perceptions. It is as though a blockage has been removed and energy is released.

According to Miller, when a relationship is growth-producing, it results in five good things: increased zest, a sense of empowerment, greater knowledge, an increased sense of self-worth, and a desire for more connection. In interviews done with White teachers who were leading discussions with others about racism, there was abundant evidence of these benefits. Said one, "The thing that's happened for me is that I'm no longer afraid to bring [race] up. I look to bring it up; I love bringing it up." This educator now brings these issues up regularly with her colleagues, and they, like she, seem to feel liberated by the opportunity for dialogue. Describing a discussion group in which participants talked about racial issues, she said, "It was such a rich conversation and it just flowed the whole time. It was exciting to be a part of it. Everybody contributed and everybody felt the energy and the desire."

Another participant described the process of sharing the new information she had learned with her adult son and said, "There's a lot of energy that's going on in all sorts of ways. It feels wonderful." Yet another described her own exploration of racial issues as "renewal at midlife." The increased self-knowledge she experienced was apparent as she said, "I'm continuing to go down the path of discovery for myself about what I think and what I believe and the influences I've had in my life. . . . It impacts me almost every moment of my waking hours." These benefits of self-discovery are made available to them as the silence about racism is broken.

It is important to say that even as good things are generated, the growth process is not painless. One of the White teachers interviewed described the early phase of her exploration of racism as "hell," a state of constant dissonance. Another commented, "I get really scared at some of the things that come up. And I've never been so nervous in my life as I have been facilitating that antiracist study group." A third said, "How do I feel about the fact that I might be influencing large groups of people? Well, in a way, I'm proud of it. I'm scared about it [too] because it puts me out in the forefront. It's a vulnerable position." The fear is still there, but these pioneers are learning to push past it.[8]

## Finding Courage for Social Change

Breaking the silence undoubtedly requires courage. How can we find the courage we need? This is a question I ask myself a lot, because I too struggle with fear. I am aware of my own vulnerability even as I write this book. What will writing it mean for my life? Will it make me a target for attack? How will readers respond to what I have to say? Have I really said anything helpful? Silence feels safer, but in the long run, I know that it is not. So I, like so many others, need courage.

I look for it in the lives of others, seeking role models for how to be an effective agent of change. As a person of faith, I find that the Bible is an important source of inspiration for me. It is full of stories of change agents whose lives inspire me. Moses and Esther are two favorites. Because I am a Black woman, I am particularly interested in the lives of other Black women who have been agents of change. I find strength in learning about the lives of Harriet Tubman, Sojourner Truth, Ida B. Wells, Zora Neale Hurston, Fannie Lou Hamer, Rosa Parks, Coretta Scott King, Angela Davis, to name a few. I also want to know about the lives of my White allies, past and present: Angelina and Sarah Grimké, Clarence Jordan, Virginia Foster Durr, Lois Stalvey, Mab Segrest, Bill Bradley, Morris Dees, Gloria Steinem, for example. What about Black men and other men and women of color, Asian, Latinx, Native? W. E. B. Du Bois, Thurgood Marshall, Derald Wing Sue, Maxine Hong Kingston, Cesar Chavez, Wilma Mankiller, Joel Spring, Mitsuye Yamada, Gloria Anzaldúa? Yes, those examples and many unnamed others are important, too. I am still filling in the gaps in my education as quickly as I can.

I have heard many people say, "But I don't know enough! I don't even recognize most of those names. I don't have enough of the facts to be able to speak up about racism or anything else!" They are not alone. We have all been miseducated in this regard. Educating ourselves and others is an essential step in the process of change. Few of us have been taught to think critically about issues of social injustice. We have been taught not to notice or to accept our present situation as a given, "the way it is." But we can learn the history we were not taught, we can watch the documentaries we never saw in school, and we can read about the lives of change agents, past and present. We can discover another way. We are surrounded by a "cloud of witnesses" who will give us courage if we let them.

Do you feel overwhelmed by the task? When my students begin to recognize the pervasiveness of racism in the culture and our institutions, they begin to despair, feeling powerless to effect change. Sometimes I feel overwhelmed, too. The antidote I have found is to focus on my own sphere of influence. I can't fix everything, but some things are within my control. While many people experience themselves as powerless, everyone has some sphere of influence in which they can work for change, even if it is just in their own personal network of family and friends. Ask yourself, "Whose lives do I affect and how? What power and authority do I wield in the world? What meetings do I attend? Who do I talk to in the course of a day?" Identify your strengths and use them.

If you are a parent, what conversations have you had with your children about these issues? What books are sitting on their bookshelves? Do you know what discussions are taking place at your child's school? If you are a teacher, what dialogue is taking place in your classroom? Regardless of your subject matter, there are ways to engage students in critical thinking about racism that are relevant to your discipline. Have you considered what they might be? If you like to write letters to friends, have you written any letters to the editor, adding to the public discourse about dismantling racism? Have you written to broadcasters protesting programming that reinforces racial stereotypes? If you are an extrovert, have you used your people skills to gather others together for dialogue about racism? If you are an athlete, what language and behavior do you model in the locker room? If you are a board member, what questions do you raise at the meetings? Who sits on the board with you? What values and perspectives are represented there? If you are an employer, who is missing from your work force? What are you doing about it?

"What if I make a mistake?" you may be thinking. "Racism is a volatile issue, and I don't want to say or do the wrong thing." In almost forty years of teaching and leading workshops about racism, I have made many mistakes. I have found that a sincere apology and a genuine desire to learn from one's mistakes are usually rewarded with forgiveness. If we wait for perfection, we will never break the silence. The cycle of racism will continue uninterrupted.

We all want to do the right thing, but each of us must determine what our own right thing is. The right thing for me, writing this book, may not be the right thing for you. Parker Palmer offers this wisdom about doing the "right thing": "Right action requires only that we respond faithfully to our own inner truth and to the truth around us. . . . If an action is rightly taken, taken with integrity, its outcomes will achieve whatever is possible—which is the best that anyone can do."[9]

You may be saying, "I am a change agent. I am always the one who speaks up at the meetings, but I'm tired. How do I keep going?" This is an important question, because a genuine commitment to interrupting racism is a long-term commitment. How can we sustain ourselves for the long haul? One thing I have learned is that we need a community of support. We all need community to give us energy, to strengthen our voices, and to offer constructive criticism when we stray off course. We need to speak up against racism and other forms of oppression, but we do not have to speak alone. Look for like-minded others. Organize a meeting for friends or colleagues concerned about racial issues. Someone else will come. Attend the meetings others have organized. Share your vision. Others will be drawn to you. Your circle of support does not have to be big. It may be only two or three other people with whom you can share the frustrations of those meetings and the joys of even the smallest victories. Even those who seem to be solo warriors have a support network somewhere. It is essential. If you don't have such a network now, start thinking about how to create one. In the meantime, learn more about that cloud of witnesses. Knowing that history can sustain you as well.

We all have a sphere of influence. Each of us needs to find our own sources of courage so that we will begin to speak. There are many problems to address, and we cannot avoid them indefinitely. We cannot continue to be silent. We must begin to speak, knowing that words alone are insufficient. But I have seen that meaningful dialogue can lead to effective action. Change is possible.

# Signs of Hope, Sites of Progress

As I was writing the prologue for the twentieth-anniversary edition of this book, I was struck by how much bad news there was in it. The events of the last two decades (1997–2017) have done little to improve the quality of life for those most negatively impacted by the structural racism of our society. Recognizing and acknowledging the persistence of residential and school segregation; the economic inequality that grows from limited access to socioeconomically diverse social networks and high-quality education as well as continued discrimination in the workplace; and the stranglehold of mass incarceration, unequal justice, and growing voter disenfranchisement left me feeling disheartened. But I am an optimist by nature *and* I have lived long enough to know that meaningful change *is* possible. I was determined not to give in to a sense of despair but rather to actively seek out signs of hope—stories of people making a difference and promising practices that could move others to meaningful action. I found that these signs of hope are everywhere. I found them daily on my Twitter feed, in the conversations I had as I traveled around the country doing my speaking engagements, and in some of the materials I read in preparation for the book. My intention in this epilogue is to share some of what I found in hopes that the examples will uplift you as they uplifted me.

When I was growing up in the Northeast and the cold of winter was dragging on for what seemed like far too long, I was always excited by the first signs of spring—the sighting of a robin in the yard or an early crocus pushing up through melting snow. Such evidence of spring coming always lifted my spirits. I believe deeply that the winter of the social-political climate of 2017—the time at which I am writing this epilogue—can give way to spring, but it is the collective *actions* of people committed to social justice that will bring about the thaw. Here are some of the signs of hope—both large and small—that I have found in the journey of writing this new edition.

In March 2016 I was in Texas, speaking on the campus of Texas A&M. By coincidence, a few weeks before I arrived there had been a racial incident. A group of Black teenagers from an urban high school in Texas were touring the campus. During the tour they were approached by a small group of students who yelled racial slurs at them and told them to go back where they came from. "What's hopeful about that?" you might be asking yourself. Nothing. What gave me hope is what happened next. The student body president, a young White man named Joseph Benigno, a member of the Class of 2016, issued a statement on YouTube, just three and a half minutes long but clear, concise, and courageous.[1] He began by challenging those who were trying to deny that the incident had happened, implicitly or directly accusing the students and their chaperones of fabricating the story, to do one thing: "Stop!" "An attitude of denial is dangerous," he said, recognizing that "it inhibits our ability to learn from what happened." Then, acknowledging that he himself had been silent in the face of racist, sexist, and homophobic jokes and passing comments, often made behind closed doors, he made clear that his and others' silence gave permission for the hateful remarks to be made publicly. "I feel that silence in response to these comments camouflages the genuinely hateful and empowers them in the development of their beliefs. . . . Our silence fosters hate. Our silence enables the hateful to feel comfortable and welcome," he said, urging his fellow students to join him in taking responsibility for making a change. I was very impressed with it. This student government president clearly recognized his sphere of influence, and he was using it effectively. With the power of social media, he was able to amplify his message in a powerful way. His example of leadership was for me a sign of hope.

Another hopeful glimmer came to me in my adopted hometown of Atlanta. The Atlanta Friendship Initiative (AFI) was started in the fall of 2016 by two business leaders in Atlanta, Bill Nordmark, who is White, and John Grant, who is Black.[2] It was Bill's idea. He was at a meeting of the Rotary Club of Atlanta when he heard philanthropist and retired Georgia-Pacific CEO Pete Correll talking about racial issues that still plague the city. Troubled by what he heard, Bill decided to do something. He reached out to John, with whom he was only casually acquainted, and asked if they could take their acquaintanceship to the next level and become friends as the first step toward his vision of the Atlanta Friendship Initiative. Bill explained the concept—to pair up two people from different racial or ethnic backgrounds and have them become friends. The pairs would agree to get together at least once a quarter, and once a year they would bring their families together in fellowship. John's response was immediately positive. In an interview with the *Atlanta Business Chronicle,* the two men recalled that first meeting and its impact:

> "John didn't even blink. . . . He said, 'I'm in. Bill, I feel God's hand in what you're saying today, and I'm in.' I said, 'Take another day or two to think about this.' He looked at me and said, 'What don't you understand about "I'm in"?' I knew then that this was a friendship I wanted forever." Since that visit in September, Grant said, "We have been talking almost every day." They also have been reaching out to other "friends" to join their cause. "It's refreshing to see the responses," Grant said. "To a person, no one has said no. The responses have been 'thank you for doing this.'"[3]

In the first three months of the initiative, eighty friendship pairs have been formed across lines of racial, gender, and/or ethnic difference. The AFI is apolitical, but I know from my own experience (I have a friendship partner) that the pairs cross political party lines as well. Can new cross-racial friendships change the racial climate of a city or the structural racism that is baked into its historical foundation and the map of its neighborhoods? There's no guarantee that it will, but it could. Institutional policies and practices are created and carried out by individuals, and when those individuals have homogeneous social networks, they too often lack empathy for those whose lives are outside their own frame of reference. I believe opening social networks and closing the empathy gap is a step toward bringing about positive change.

In February 2017 the first gathering of the newly formed friendship pairs took place, and several partners spoke to those present about the personal impact of their new relationships and the richness of their conversations. For example, two men, one Black and one White, natives of the same city, found that their early lives in their community were separated not only by race but also by class. The Black partner, who grew up in a low-income Black neighborhood, said with feeling about his partner from an affluent White family, "I've learned a lot. It's helped me get past that chip on my shoulder." His White partner agreed, "We started with race, but that has led to very rich conversations." Another pair is meeting monthly, and after sharing how much they were enjoying those meetings, they said to the group, "Now what's our homework?" While the AFI does not yet (and may never) have a specific action agenda, the cofounders believe that the pairs, all community leaders in their own social networks, will find ways to work together in coalition for the betterment of the community. As John Grant has said, "Friendships can change a lot of things." Says Bill Nordmark, "We hope it doesn't stay in Atlanta," expecting that the AFI will be replicated in other communities, and it seems that has already begun to happen as he is receiving inquiries from around the country about how to start similar programs.

A community initiative that has at least twenty years of history behind it can be found in the community of South Orange / Maplewood, New Jersey. Two neighboring towns that twenty years ago were faced with the specter of "white flight," turning what was an integrated suburb into a racially segregated one, formed the Community Coalition on Race with this mission statement: "To achieve and sustain the benefits of a thriving, racially integrated and truly inclusive community that serves as a model for the nation."[4] Collectively, they were successful in curbing the "white flight" phenomenon and have maintained a very diverse community. Their challenge now is to keep it affordable for all who live there, as they are attracting more high-income White New

Yorkers who are drawn to the suburban diversity they offer, and housing prices are now escalating.

I had the privilege of speaking in South Orange / Maplewood in 1999 and returned to speak again in May 2016, and I was greeted that evening by a standing-room-only crowd that was truly racially, ethnically, and religiously diverse, young and old, ready to engage in dialogue about this effort to be a truly inclusive community. It was quite inspiring to see! I am sure it is not perfect. In fact, while I was visiting, I learned that there had been a few recent race-related incidents in the schools, a reminder to the Community Coalition that the work is not done but has to be revisited continually, particularly as new families come into the community. The most hopeful thing is that there is a community of committed citizens still doing that work. Twenty years later, they know that persistence is important!

In early 2016 I was contacted by Barry Yeoman, a journalist working on a story about conversation across racial lines. His topic was something called The Welcome Table. I didn't know what it was then, but I was delighted to find out that it was a signature program of the William Winter Institute for Racial Reconciliation at the University of Mississippi. The institute has an inspiring vision statement:

> Envision[ing] a world where people honestly engage in their history in order to live more truthfully in the present; where the inequities of the past no longer dictate the possibilities of the future. We envision a world where people of all identities are treated equally; where equality of and access to opportunity are available and valued by all; where healing and reconciliation are commonplace and social justice is upheld and honored. We acknowledge and recognize that it is not enough for us to be intentional, but we must be purposeful in making this vision a reality—not only for Mississippi, but for all people.[5]

The Welcome Table, a community-building program of the institute, is part of that purposeful action.

The idea for the Welcome Table can be traced back to Philadelphia, Mississippi, in 2004, when the fortieth anniversary of the Mississippi

Freedom Summer of 1964 was approaching. In June 1964, three civil rights workers were murdered—James Chaney, Andrew Goodman, and Michael Schwerner—one Black Mississippian and two White students from the North. Though a local Klan leader bragged about ordering the killings, no one was ever charged with the crime. With that historical backdrop, the community was in disagreement about how to commemorate the town's role in the struggle for civil rights. Two community leaders, the NAACP president, who was Black, and the newspaper editor, who was White, joined together and reached out to the Winter Institute for help. The executive director, Dr. Susan Glisson, responded by helping to facilitate community storytelling sessions where participants were able to build trust among each other and to create an oral history project for the town. Importantly, they decided to work together to lobby local officials to prosecute the Klan leader, who after forty years was eventually brought to justice. The institute did similar reconciliation work in McComb, Mississippi, known as "the bombing capital of the world" because of the anti–civil rights violence perpetrated there during that era.[6]

The lessons learned from those experiences led to the Welcome Table framework in use today. The three phases include: (1) a period of trust building across racial lines, accomplished through a series of monthly meetings and a weekend retreat built around a curriculum of structured storytelling activities; (2) a period of planning and implementing a community-building group project, such as an oral history, after-school mentoring program, or community garden, while monthly workshops still continue; and (3) developing an equity action plan, specifically focused on addressing a structural issue (a policy or practice) that is perpetuating inequity in the community. Participants say that the face-to-face nature of the interaction is a welcome antidote to the disconnection many people feel in our digitally driven society, and connection offers hope for action. "When you have a group that has some commitment to each other, the group becomes aware of so much in our culture that needs to be worked on. It's like, 'I was blind to all of this and now I see it.' It compels people to action."[7] Dr. Glisson, the executive director, believes that "Mississippi is going to lead the nation in dealing with race. We want to be a part of providing the tools for people to be able to do that."[8]

William F. Winter, a former governor of Mississippi (1980–1984), for whom the William Winter Institute for Racial Reconciliation is named, and Deval Patrick, former governor of Massachusetts (2007–2015), now serve together as honorary cochairs of the Truth, Racial Healing, and Transformation (TRHT) Enterprise of the W. K. Kellogg Foundation, one of the most hopeful and ambitious projects I have learned about during my book-writing process.

The Kellogg Foundation is one of the nation's largest private foundations, and between 2007 and 2016 it has invested more than $200 million in organizations working to heal racial divisions in the United States. Drawing upon the lessons learned from those investments, in 2016 the foundation launched its Truth, Racial Healing, and Transformation (TRHT) Enterprise, described on its website as "a multi-year, national and community-based effort to engage communities, organizations and individuals from multiple sectors across the United States in racial healing and addressing present-day inequities linked to historic and contemporary beliefs in a hierarchy of human value."[9] Partnering with more than a hundred national and local organizations, diverse and broad in scope, ranging from the American Library Association and the Boys & Girls Clubs of America to the Council of State Governments, the National Association of Community and Restorative Justice, Sundance Institute, and the YWCA USA, to name just a few, the THRT will bring together "the intellectual power and resources of foundations, communities, government, nonprofits, and corporations in efforts to dismantle racism."[10]

At the core of their mission is the recognition that it will be necessary to rid ourselves of the belief in a racial hierarchy of human value and replace it with the belief in a shared common humanity, a task much easier said than done.

Jettisoning belief in a hierarchy of human value—a belief that has been well established in America for four centuries—will require a multipronged, strategic effort to heal the racial wounds of the past and to transform our socioeconomic institutions. These two goals are intimately connected, because belief in racial hierarchy translates into values and principles that influence public, personal, and corporate practices and, thereby, perpetuate biases and inequities based on race and ethnicity.[11]

The TRHT effort is based on lessons learned from the Truth and Reconciliation Commissions (TRCs) that have been effective in resolving deeply rooted conflicts around the world, but the US model emphasizes *transformation* rather than *reconciliation*, because the root cause of racial hierarchy is not the result of conflict between groups; rather, it is built into the foundational governance structures of the nation. It has always been there, and it must be rooted out for lasting progress to take place. Gail Christopher, the vice president for Truth, Racial Healing, and Transformation and senior adviser at the Kellogg Foundation, delineates seven guiding principles that have been developed to undergird this transformational work:

1. *There must be an accurate recounting of history, both local and national.* Truth-telling requires that there be an atmosphere of forgiveness and people of *all* racial, ethnic and ancestral backgrounds have the opportunity "to tell their stories without fear of recrimination, but with a sense that justice will be served."

2. *A clear and compelling vision, accompanied by a set of ambitious but achievable goals, both long term and short term, must be developed, and progress must be regularly assessed.*

3. *The process must be expansive and inclusive in all respects, and there must be a deep and unyielding commitment to a) understanding the different cultures, experiences, and perspectives that coexist in a community; b) recognizing and acknowledging the interdependence of the variety of approaches to seeking enduring racial equity; c) reaching out to nontraditional allies in order to broaden support for meaningful change; and d) giving every*

*participant an opportunity to tell his or her story in a respectful and supportive setting.*

4. *The process of healing requires a building of trust and must be viewed as a "win-win" process.* Ultimately we all share a common fate. Substantial and enduring progress toward racial equity and healing benefits all of us.

5. *There must be a commitment to some form of reparative or restorative justice and to policies that can effectively foster systemic change.*

6. *A thoughtful and comprehensive communications strategy must be designed to keep the entire community informed, even those who are neither involved in, nor supportive of, the process.*

7. *There must be a broadly understood way of dealing with the tensions that inevitably will arise.* If organizations can anticipate "teachable moments," it is possible to keep moving forward and not become derailed by the tensions of the moment.[12]

One of the institutional partners for the TRHT initiative is the Association of American Colleges and Universities (AAC&U). AAC&U president Lynn Pasquerella has articulated the role of higher education in advancing these principles, especially the first one, not only in making the telling of American history more complete but also in developing the capacity of students to listen deeply to another person's perspective.

It is the cultivation of the capacity to listen that is central to the practice of dialogue. It is on the campuses of colleges and universities that are taking full advantage of their diverse learning environments to create communities of dialogue that I see sites of progress. For example, in October 2016 I visited Franklin and Marshall College, a small liberal arts college in Lancaster, Pennsylvania, increasingly known for its commitment to expanding access for student talent from all racial, ethnic, and socioeconomic backgrounds. President Dan Porterfield invited me to join him in a conversation about the importance of dialogue as the kickoff event for "A Day of Dialogue" on the campus. He explained that after the college had spent the previous school year "participating in a national conversation about inclusiveness and discrimination, about identity and community, about who we are and who we hope to become," the faculty had suggested that classes be canceled for a day to allow time for the community to "center ourselves . . . and listen to one another, where we set a goal to be able to go forward as a community in diversity—not have *one* day of dialogue but *catalyze* deeper inquiry together as a part of who we are, our very core."[13]

The schedule for the day was full, and students were actively engaged in the conversations offered on various topics. Every session room I saw was full, and students were listening to each other intently. At lunchtime, students were randomly assigned to eat lunch with other students in student spaces that they might not otherwise enter. I joined a group of students having lunch in one of the fraternity houses. Many of the students had never been in it before, and the young White man who served as one of the hosts acknowledged that he too had avoided spaces on campus that felt unfamiliar to him. For example, he had never entered the Black Cultural Center, though he had been invited to programs there, or attended a Hillel event, though he had a number of Jewish friends, or made the time to attend the weekly International Student Coffee Hour. Student enthusiasm for the opportunity to connect was genuine. Building on the day's momentum for sustained engagement is their challenge now.

The University of Michigan is widely acknowledged as the intellectual home of intergroup dialogue programs on college campuses, an initiative that has been in place at Michigan since 1988. In October 2016 the university was the site of the Second Biennial Difficult Dialogues in Higher Education Conference, a project of the Difficult Dialogues National Resource Center (DDNRC). Founded in 2011, the goal of the DDNRC is to ensure that college and university campuses remain places where freedom of expression is protected, academic freedom is sustained, pluralism is promoted, and opportunities for constructive communication across different perspectives are expanded.[14] The diverse gathering of faculty and administrative leaders from across the country to share best practices for engaging both faculty and students in dialogue about challenging social-justice issues in and out of classrooms was in itself a hopeful sign.

But what was most encouraging to me was the time I spent with David Schoem, the founding faculty director of the Michigan Community Scholars Program (MCSP), and a group of his students. In October 2016, the country was immersed in the negativity of the presidential election season, and the toxicity of campaign rhetoric was being felt on college campuses across the country. My visit with the Michigan Community Scholars Program (MCSP), a model undergraduate residential learning community at the University of Michigan, was a source of hope during that bleak month. It is definitely a site of progress.

Established in 1999, MCSP has an inspiring mission statement:

> The Michigan Community Scholars Program is a residential learning community emphasizing deep learning, engaged community, meaningful civic engagement/community service learning, and intercultural understanding and dialogue. Students, faculty, community partners and staff think critically about issues of community, seek to model a just, diverse, and democratic community, and wish to make a difference throughout their lives as participants and leaders involved in local, national and global communities.[15]

The learning community is made up of 120 first-year students and their resident advisers, as well as ten to fifteen faculty members linked to the program. An intentionally diverse community, MCSP interrupts the experience of segregated residential communities from which the students typically come. MCSP uniquely brings together service-learning, diversity, and dialogue in a powerful way. David Schoem explains, "Groups of students across different backgrounds are brought together from their first day on campus to build bonds and begin the process of engaging one another in substantive issues."[16] Unlike the typical residence hall experience where students from different backgrounds might pass each other in the hallway without really engaging one another, at the core of the MCSP experience is the opportunity, indeed the requirement, for intergroup dialogue. As part of the residential experience, the students take a seminar together and participate in various structured dialogues in the residence hall.

In the focus group conversation I had with participating students, past and present, I heard all speak eloquently about how much they had gained from the program, and also about how different their experience was from those of their classmates who are not part of such a program. The students are deeply engaged with each other, across lines of difference, and learning how to talk *with* one another about hard topics rather than talking *past* one another or avoiding interaction altogether.

The value of those cross-group connections was made more salient by racist acts on the campus during the fall 2016 semester. White supremacist posters with explicitly anti-Black content were posted around the Michigan campus, creating a hostile environment for Black students, who were feeling under attack. One young African American woman, still in her first year, said, "It's hard to focus [on your schoolwork] when there's so much hateful stuff. . . . It's hard to know who to trust. . . . It takes energy to reach out to Whites without knowing if they are 'safe.' MCSP helps with that." A White woman in her cohort was quick to second that sentiment, even though as a White student she is not the target of hateful rhetoric. She said, "MCSP is the only place where I've constantly felt supported, listened to, and understood."

In a study of the impact of the MCSP on students' growth relative to social-justice outcomes, Rebecca Christensen found that nineteen out of twenty-two participants exhibited greater cognitive, affective, and behavioral empathy toward others and were actively engaged in educating others and speaking out against injustice. They had heightened motivation to "create small-scale change in their everyday lives" and to "incorporate social justice into their future careers." Of the various curricular, cocurricular, and informal MCSP-affiliated activities that facilitated their growth, students identified the dialogues both in and outside of the classroom as the most influential.[17]

Though only a small number of students (relative to the thousands who attend the University of Michigan) will participate in the residential MCSP program, it serves as an excellent model that could be expanded at Michigan and certainly replicated on other campuses. Alternatively, Michigan students have the opportunity to register for one of the dialogue courses offered by the Program on Intergroup Relations (IGR).

The first program of its kind in the nation, the Program on Intergroup Relations is a social-justice education program founded in 1988. Unique in its partnership between Student Life and the College of Literature, Science and the Arts, IGR blends theory and experiential learning to facilitate students' learning about social group identity, social inequality, and intergroup relations. It is intentional in its effort to prepare students to live and work in a diverse world and educate them in making choices that advance equity, justice, and peace.[18] What exactly are the dialogues? Defined by Zúñiga, Nagda, Chesler, and Cytron, an intergroup dialogue is a facilitated face-to-face encounter that seeks to foster meaningful engagement between members of two or more social identity groups that have a history of conflict (e.g. Whites and people of color, Arabs and Jews).[19] According to the Michigan website,

Intergroup Dialogues are three-credit courses carefully structured to explore social group identity, conflict, community, and social justice. Each dialogue involves identity groups defined by race, ethnicity, religion, socioeconomic class, gender, sexual orientation, (dis)ability status, or national origin.

Each identity group is represented in the dialogue by a balanced number of student participants, usually five to seven participants from each group. We also offer dialogues where only participants from the same identity groups are placed in the dialogues. These are called intragroup dialogues.[20]

The course structure emphasizes both process and content, using a four-stage model that provides a developmental sequence for the dialogue. "The stages are: creating a shared meaning of dialogue; identity, social relations, and conflict; issues of social justice; and alliances and empowerment."[21]

Opportunities for this kind of engagement are life-changing and hope-producing as we consider the impact on the next generation. Here's what students have to say about their experience, as quoted on the Michigan website:[22]

*Vishnu:* I think that IGR gave me the ability to speak about a great deal of issues that I had been dealing with for a long time and taught me how progress can be made if we are able to talk about those issues in intra and inter group settings. The program gave me the ability to have conversations across differences about the things that are causing those differences, which to me is incredibly important. IGR gave me that. And for it, I am eternally grateful.

*Ariel:* I have been involved with IGR since my freshman year, and it is by far the best thing I've done while at college. From my first dialogue class onward, all I wanted was to study Intergroup Relations, and to devote my time at school to learning about diversity and social justice. I am delighted to declare an IGR minor, so that I can continue learning about dialogue, communication, and social change!

It's not just the students who are transformed. Their instructors (the dialogue facilitators) are changed as well. Said one,

I have had the great honor of accompanying this remarkable group of students as they practice and hone their facilitations skills. As they prepare themselves for leading their own dialogues next term and taking what we have learned beyond the classroom, I can't help but feel inspired to do the same and think about how I can integrate this dialogic pedagogy into my future teaching. Whenever we do go-arounds and reflect as a class on how the day's activities went, I always feel a sense of gratitude for the students and the ways that together we are transformed through dialogue. I am confident that feeling will remain with me for many semesters to come.[23]

Does dialogue lead to social action? The research evidence suggests the answer is yes! Both White students and students of color demonstrate attitudinal and behavioral changes, including: increased self-awareness about issues of power and privilege, greater awareness of the institutionalization of race and racism in the US, better cross-racial interaction, less fear of race-related conflict, and greater participation in social-change actions during and after college.[24]

The fact that the Michigan IGR program has been in existence for almost thirty years and is providing students with the inspiration and the tools they need to be change agents after graduation is hopeful by itself, but even more encouraging is that dialogue programs are spreading to other campuses.

Dr. Ximena Zúñiga, who was one of the original architects of the Michigan IGR program, now teaches at the University of Massachusetts in the Social Justice Education program, where she is training graduate students who want to become expert in dialogue facilitation and related research. Like Michigan, they offer intergroup dialogue courses. I had the opportunity to sit in on two dialogue group sessions in November 2016, just ten days after the presidential election. It was powerful to hear students talking about how they had been able to use their dialogic skills outside of class to have difficult conversations with peers about the election at a time when so many of their elders were struggling to have such conversations themselves.

The ripple effects of the Michigan and UMass models can be seen at Skidmore College, where Dr. Kristie Ford, associate professor of sociology, is now the director of the Skidmore Intergroup Relations Program, where they have adapted the Michigan model to suit their small campus. In 2012 Skidmore became the first college or university in the US to offer a minor in intergroup relations. (Even though it is the leader in intergroup dialogue, University of Michigan did not establish its intergroup relations minor until 2015.) Unlike UMass or the

University of Michigan, Skidmore is a liberal arts college and does not have a ready supply of graduate students to serve as dialogue facilitators. Instead, Skidmore has an intentional focus on developing peer facilitators to lead the dialogue groups. They are selected based on their academic performance, developmental maturity, leadership potential, and demonstrated facilitation ability. They take at least three courses over a three-semester period as preparation, and they are provided ongoing support and supervision from a faculty member during their peer-facilitation experience. It is hard to imagine a more powerful leadership development experience that a college student might have.[25]

In her book *Facilitating Change Through Intergroup Dialogue: Social Justice Advocacy in Practice,* Ford documents the postgraduate effects on those undergraduates who learned to be facilitators. Their commitment to social justice is evidenced in their career choices and their continued growth as White allies and as empowered people of color.[26]

It has been said that to teach is to touch the future.[27] Helping students to see the past more clearly, to understand and communicate with others more fully in the present, and to imagine the future more justly is to transform the world.

There is nothing more hopeful than that. I started this book with the question, Is it better? My answer is: Not yet, but it could be. It's up to us to make sure it is. I remain hopeful.

# NOTES

## Prologue: "Why Are All the Black Kids *Still* Sitting Together in the Cafeteria?" and Other Conversations About Race in the Twenty-First Century

1. Steve Phillips, *Brown Is the New White: How the Demographic Revolution Has Created a New American Majority* (New York: The New Press, 2016), 7.

2. I am choosing to use the term *Latinx,* rather than *Latino* or *Latina,* as a gender-inclusive, nonbinary way of referring to people of Latin American descent.

3. Marta Tienda, "Diversity as a Strategic Advantage: A Sociodemographic Perspective," in *Our Compelling Interests: The Value of Diversity for Democracy and a Prosperous Society,* ed. Earl Lewis and Nancy Cantor (Princeton, NJ: Princeton University Press, 2016), 204.

4. US Census Bureau, "Annual Estimates of the Resident Population by Sex, Age, Race, and Hispanic Origin for the United States and States: April 1, 2010 to July 1, 2015," American FactFinder, May 2015, https://factfinder.census.gov/faces/tableservices /jsf/pages/productview.xhtml.

5. Pew Research Center, *The Rise of Asian Americans,* June 19, 2012, updated April 4, 2013, http://www.pewsocialtrends.org/2012/06/19/the-rise-of-asian-americans/.

6. Besheer Mohamed, "A New Estimate of the U.S. Muslim Population," *Fact Tank,* Pew Research Center, January 6, 2016, http://www.pewresearch.org/fact -tank/2016/01/06/a-new-estimate-of-the-u-s-muslim-population/.

7. Pew Research Center, *Multiracial in America,* June 11, 2015, http://www .pewsocialtrends.org/2015/06/11/multiracial-in-america/.

8. Carl Kaestle, "Federalism and Inequality in Education: What Can History Tell Us?," in *The Dynamics of Opportunity in America: Evidence and Perspectives,* ed. Irwin Kirsch and Henry Braun (Princeton, NJ: Educational Testing Service, 2016).

9. Thomas J. Sugrue, "Less Separate, Still Unequal: Diversity and Equality in 'Post-Civil Rights' America," in *Our Compelling Interests: The Value of Diversity for Democracy and a Prosperous Society,* ed. Earl Lewis and Nancy Cantor (Princeton, NJ: Princeton University Press, 2016).

10. For a detailed discussion of the Supreme Court rulings that set the stage for school resegregation, see Beverly Daniel Tatum, "The Resegregation of Our Schools and

the Affirmation of Identity," in *Can We Talk About Race? and Other Conversations in an Era of School Resegregation* (Boston: Beacon Press, 2007).

11. Gary Orfield et al., *Brown at 62: School Segregation by Race, Poverty and State* (Los Angeles: Civil Rights Project, University of California at Los Angeles, 2016).

12. Daria Roithmayr, *Reproducing Racism: How Everyday Choices Lock In White Advantage* (New York: NYU Press, 2014), Kindle edition, location 732.

13. Douglas S. Massey and Nancy A. Denton, *American Apartheid: Segregation and the Making of the Underclass* (Cambridge, MA: Harvard University Press, 1993), 53.

14. Ibid., 55.

15. Roithmayr, *Reproducing Racism,* location 736.

16. National Fair Housing Alliance, *Unequal Opportunity—Perpetuating Housing Segregation in America,* April 5, 2006, http://nationalfairhousing.org/wp-content/uploads/2017/04/trends2006.pdf.

17. Douglas S. Massey and Jonathan Tannen, "Segregation, Race and the Social Worlds of Rich and Poor," in *The Dynamics of Opportunity in America: Evidence and Perspectives,* ed. Irwin Kirsch and Henry Baum (Princeton, NJ: Educational Testing Service, 2016).

18. William H. Frey, "The 'Diversity Explosion' Is America's Twenty-First-Century Baby Boom," in *Our Compelling Interests: The Value of Diversity for Democracy and a Prosperous Society,* ed. Earl Lewis and Nancy Cantor (Princeton, NJ: Princeton University Press, 2016).

19. Camille Zubrinsky Charles, *Won't You Be My Neighbor? Race, Class and Residence in Los Angeles* (New York: Russell Sage Foundation, 2006).

20. Sugrue, "Less Separate, Still Unequal," 51.

21. John Iceland, Daniel H. Weinberg, and Erika Steinmetz, "The Residential Segregation of American Indians and Alaska Natives: 1980–2000," in *Racial and Ethnic Residential Segregation in the United States: 1980–2000,* US Census Bureau, August 2002, https://www.census.gov/hhes/www/housing/resseg/pdf/ch3.pdf.

22. Eduardo Bonilla-Silva, *Racism Without Racists: Color-Blind Racism and the Persistence of Racial Inequality in America,* 4th ed. (Lanham, MD: Rowman and Littlefield Publishers, 2014), 241.

23. Sugrue, "Less Separate, Still Unequal," 49.

24. Massey and Tannen, "Segregation, Race and the Social Worlds of Rich and Poor," 31.

25. Roithmayr, *Reproducing Racism,* location 916.

26. "Remarks by the President at Howard University Commencement Ceremony" (press release), The White House, Office of the Press Secretary, May 7, 2016, https://www.whitehouse.gov/the-press-office/2016/05/07/remarks-president-howard-university-commencement-ceremony.

27. Drew DeSilver, "Supreme Court Says States Can Ban Affirmative Action; 8 Already Have," *Fact Tank,* Pew Research Center, April 22, 2014, http://www.pewresearch.org/fact-tank/2014/04/22/supreme-court-says-states-can-ban-affirmative-action-8-already-have/.

28. Brief for 39 Undergraduate and Graduate Student Organizations Within the University of California as Amicus Curiae, *Fisher v. University of Texas at Austin,* http://www.scotusblog.com/wp-content/uploads/2015/11/14-981_amicus_resp_39Undergraduateand GraduateStudentOrganizations.authcheckdam.pdf.

29. William C. Kidder, "The Salience of Racial Isolation: African Americans' and Latinos' Perceptions of Climate and Enrollment Choices with and Without Proposition 209," Civil Rights Project at UCLA / Proyecto Derechos Civiles, October 2012.

30. Brief for the University of Michigan as Amicus Curiae, *Fisher v. University of Texas at Austin,* http://www.scotusblog.com/wp-content/uploads/2015/11/FILED-14 -981-bsac-U.-Michigan-11-2-15.pdf.

31. *Fisher v. University of Texas at Austin,* 579 US (2016), https://www.supreme-court.gov/opinions/15pdf/14-981_4g15.pdf.

32. Barbara Ehrenreich and Dedrick Muhammad, "The Destruction of the Black Middle Class," *Huffington Post,* September 3, 2009 (updated May 25, 2011), http://www.huffingtonpost.com/barbara-ehrenreich/the-destruction-of-the-bl_b_250828 .html.

33. Bureau of Labor Statistics, "Labor Force Statistics from the Current Population Survey," retrieved October 7, 2016, https://www.bls.gov/cps/.

34. Anthony Carnevale and Nicole Smith, "The Economic Value of Diversity," in *Our Compelling Interests: The Value of Diversity for Democracy and a Prosperous Society,* ed. Earl Lewis and Nancy Cantor (Princeton, NJ: Princeton University Press, 2016), 127.

35. Robert Kelchen, "Financial Need and Aid Volatility Among Students with Zero Expected Family Contribution," *Journal of Student Financial Aid* 44, no. 3 (2015): 190, http://publications.nasfaa.org/jsfa/vol44/iss3/2/.

36. Ibid.

37. Hope Yen, "80 Percent of U.S. Adults Face Near-Poverty, Unemployment: Survey," *Huffington Post,* July 28, 2013, http://conservativeread.com/80-percent-of-u-s -adults-face-near-poverty-unemployment-survey/.

38. Carol Anderson, *White Rage: The Unspoken Truth of Our Racial Divide* (New York: Bloomsbury, 2016).

39. Equal Justice Initiative, *Lynching in America: Confronting the Legacy of Racial Terror* (Montgomery, AL: Equal Justice Initiative, 2015).

40. For compelling oral histories of the African American Great Migration and the efforts to circumvent threats of violence and/or imprisonment by White southerners desperate to keep the Black labor force intact, see Isabel Wilkerson, *The Warmth of Other Suns: The Epic Story of America's Great Migration* (New York: Random House, 2010).

41. Anderson, *White Rage,* 103.

42. For an in-depth discussion of the strategic use of racism in the form of dog whistle politics, see Ian Haney López, *Dog Whistle Politics: How Coded Racial Appeals Have Reinvented Racism and Wrecked the Middle Class* (New York: Oxford University Press, 2014).

43. Michelle Alexander, *The New Jim Crow* (New York: The New Press, 2010), 180.

44. The Sentencing Project, *Fact Sheet: Incarcerated Women and Girls,* November 2015, http://www.sentencingproject.org/wp-content/uploads/2016/02/Incarcerated-Women-and-Girls.pdf.

45. The Sentencing Project, *Fact Sheet: Trends in U.S. Corrections,* 2016, http://sentencingproject.org/wp-content/uploads/2016/01/Trends-in-US-Corrections.pdf.

46. Lauren E. Glaze and Laura M. Maruschak, *Parents in Prison and Their Minor Children,* US Department of Justice, Bureau of Justice Statistics, March 30, 2010, https://www.bjs.gov/content/pub/pdf/pptmc.pdf.

47. Alexander, *The New Jim Crow,* 58.

48. "Obama's Victory on Newspaper Front Pages," *Huffington Post,* December 6, 2008, http://www.huffingtonpost.com/2008/11/05/obamas-victory-on-newspap_n_141 311.html.

49. Susan Page, "Poll: Hopes Are High for Race Relations," *USA Today,* weekend edition, November 7–9, 2008, https://usatoday30.usatoday.com/news/politics/election 2008/2008-11-06-poll_N.htm#.

50. López, *Dog Whistle Politics,* 150.

51. Anderson, *White Rage,* 138.

52. Rosalind S. Helderman and Jon Cohen, "As Republican Convention Emphasizes Diversity, Racial Incidents Intrude," *Washington Post,* August 29, 2012, http://www.washingtonpost.com/politics/2012/08/29/b9023a52-f1ec-11e1-892d-bc92fee603a7_story.html.

53. Anderson, *White Rage,* 150.

54. Voting Rights Act of 1965, Pub. L. 89-110, 79 Stat. 437.

55. Shelby County v. Holder, 570 U.S. (2013), https://www.supremecourt.gov/opinions/12pdf/12-96_6k47.pdf.

56. Anderson, *White Rage,* 151.

57. Jane Mayer, "The Voter-Fraud Myth," *New Yorker,* October 29, 2012, http://www.newyorker.com/magazine/2012/10/29/the-voter-fraud-myth.

58. Anderson, *White Rage,* 152.

59. Ibid.

60. Veasey et al. v. Perry et al., 574 U.S. (2014), Ginsburg, J., dissenting), https://www.supremecourt.gov/opinions/14pdf/14a393_08m1.pdf.

61. Anderson, *White Rage,* 153.

62. López, *Dog Whistle Politics,* 151.

63. Seth Stephens-Davidowitz, "The Data of Hate," *New York Times,* July 12, 2014, https://nyti.ms/1kifZ4t.

64. Tina Nguyen, "Suspected Church Shooter Allegedly Said He Wanted to Start a Race War," *Vanity Fair,* June 19, 2015, http://www.vanityfair.com/news/2015/06/charleston-church-shooter-confesses-dylan-roof.

65. *DBR MTV Bias Survey Full Report II,* April 2014, http://www.lookdifferent.org/about-us/research-studies/1-2014-mtv-david-binder-research-study.

66. *DBR MTV Bias Survey Summary,* April 2014, http://www.lookdifferent.org/about-us/research-studies/1-2014-mtv-david-binder-research-study.

67. Mahzarin. R. Banaji and Anthony G. Greenwald, *Blindspot: Hidden Biases of Good People* (New York: Delacorte Press, 2013), Kindle edition, location 3105–3107.

68. "Trayvon Martin Shooting Fast Facts," CNN.com, http://www.cnn.com /2013/06/05/us/trayvon-martin-shooting-fast-facts/, retrieved October 20, 2016; Dan Barry, Serge F. Kovaleski, Campbell Robertson, and Lizette Alvarez, "Race, Tragedy and Outrage Collide After a Shot in Florida," *New York Times*, April 1, 2012, http:// www.nytimes.com/2012/04/02/us/trayvon-martin-shooting-prompts-a-review-of -ideals.html.

69. "Statement by the President" (press release), The White House, Office of the Press Secretary, July 14, 2013, https://www.whitehouse.gov/the-press-office/2013/07/14 /statement-president.

70. Wesley Lowery, *They Can't Kill Us All: Ferguson, Baltimore, and a New Era in America's Racial Justice Movement* (New York: Little, Brown & Company, 2016), 169.

71. Collier Meyerson. "The Founders of Black Lives Matter: 'We Gave Tongue to Something That We All Knew Was Happening,'" *Glamour*, November 1, 2016, http:// www.glamour.com/story/women-of-the-year-black-lives-matter-founders.

72. Jenna Wortham. "Black Tweets Matter," *Smithsonian*, September 2016, 22.

73. Keeanga-Yamahtta Taylor, *From #BlackLivesMatter to Black Liberation* (Chicago: Haymarket Books, 2016), 151.

74. Nicholas Quah and Laura E. Davis, "Here's a Timeline of Unarmed Black People Killed by Police over Past Year," *BuzzFeed*, May 1, 2015, https://www.buzzfeed.com /nicholasquah/heres-a-timeline-of-unarmed-black-men-killed-by-police-over?utm _term=.mxzKnEJLO#.hypOZzjkd.

75. Joe Coscarelli, "No Charges Against Ohio Police in John Crawford III Walmart Shooting, Despite Damning Security Video," *New York*, September 24, 2014, http:// nymag.com/daily/intelligencer/2014/09/no-charges-john-crawford-iii-walmart -shooting-video.html.

76. Taylor, *From #BlackLivesMatter to Black Liberation*, 154.

77. Ibid., 153.

78. Lowery, *They Can't Kill Us All*, 27–28.

79. Ibid., 28.

80. Jelani Cobb, "The Matter of Black Lives," *The New Yorker*, March 14, 2016, http:// www.newyorker.com/magazine/2016/03/14/where-is-black-lives-matter-headed.

81. Taylor, *From #BlackLivesMatter to Black Liberation*, 156.

82. Lowery, *They Can't Kill Us All*, 186.

83. Taylor, *From #BlackLivesMatter to Black Liberation*, 155.

84. Theodore M. Shaw, introduction to *The Ferguson Report: Department of Justice Investigation of the Ferguson Police Department*, by US Department of Justice, Civil Rights Division (New York: The New Press, 2015), ix.

85. US Department of Justice, Civil Rights Division, *The Ferguson Report: Department of Justice Investigation of the Ferguson Police Department* (New York: The New Press, 2015), 2–3.

86. Lowery, *They Can't Kill Us All*, 44.

87. US Department of Justice, *The Ferguson Report*, 84.

88. Ibid., 104.

89. Ibid., 52.

90. Lowery, *They Can't Kill Us All*, 53.

91. US Department of Justice, *The Ferguson Report*, 47–48.

92. Ibid., 8.

93. Ibid., 102.

94. Ibid., 8.

95. Brad Heath, "Racial Gap in U.S. Arrest Rates: 'Staggering Disparity,'" *USA Today*, November 18, 2014, http://www.usatoday.com/story/news/nation/2014/11/18/ferguson-black-arrest-rates/19043207/.

96. Matt Zapotowsky, "Justice Department Report Blasts San Francisco Police," *Washington Post*, October 12, 2016, https://www.washingtonpost.com/world/national-security/justice-department-report-blasts-san-francisco-police/2016/10/12/becb841c-90a2-11e6-a6a3-d50061aa9fae_story.html.

97. Johnetta Elzie, "'When I Close My Eyes at Night, I See People Running from Tear Gas,'" *Ebony*, September 8, 2014, http://www.ebony.com/news-views/ferguson-forward-when-i-close-my-eyes-at-night-i-see-people-running-from-tear-ga#ixzz4RSXl9KJj.

98. Taylor, *From #BlackLivesMatter to Black Liberation*, 159.

99. Ibid., 160–161.

100. Joel Anderson, "Ferguson's Angry Young Men," *BuzzFeed*, August 22, 2014, https://www.buzzfeed.com/joelanderson/who-are-fergusons-young-protesters?utm_term=.mvqJZa3Wm#.ee3apJ4dO.

101. Taylor, *From #BlackLivesMatter to Black Liberation*, 169.

102. Ibid., 162.

103. Ibid., 170.

104. Ibid., 173.

105. Noah Bertlatsky, "Hashtag Activism Isn't a Cop-Out," *The Atlantic*, January 7, 2015, http://www.theatlantic.com/politics/archive/2015/01/not-just-hashtag-activism-why-social-media-matters-to-protestors/384215/.

106. Lowery, *They Can't Kill Us All*, 74.

107. "Why Freddie Gray Ran," *Baltimore Sun*, April 25, 2015, http://www.baltimoresun.com/news/opinion/editorial/bs-ed-freddie-gray-20150425-story.html.

108. Lowery, *They Can't Kill Us All*, 167.

109. Taylor, *From #BlackLivesMatter to Black Liberation*, 176.

110. Ibid., 165.

111. Ibid.

112. Ibid., 166.

113. Cobb, "The Matter of Black Lives."

114. Kimberlé Williams Crenshaw and Andrea J. Ritchie, *Say Her Name: Resisting Police Brutality Against Black Women* (New York: African American Policy Forum, July 2015), http://static1.squarespace.com/static/53f20d90e4b0b80451158d8c/t/560c068ee4b0af26f72741df/1443628686535/AAPF_SMN_Brief_Full_singles-min.pdf.

115. Ibid., 11.

116. Lowery, *They Can't Kill Us All*, 208.

117. Beth McMurtrie, "I Believe I Can Leave This Place Better Than I Found It," *Chronicle of Higher Education*, January 3, 2016, http://www.chronicle.com/article/What -Its-Like-to-Be-Black-at/234771.

118. Lowery, *They Can't Kill Us All*, 208–209.

119. Ibid., 211.

120. McMurtrie, "I Believe I Can Leave This Place Better Than I Found It."

121. Lowery, *They Can't Kill Us All*, 212.

122. Emma Vandelinder, "Racial Climate at MU: A Timeline of Incidents This Fall," *Columbia Missourian*, November 6, 2015 (updated November 9, 2015), http://www .columbiamissourian.com/news/higher_education/racial-climate-at-mu-a-timeline-of -incidents-this-fall/article_0c96f986-84c6-11e5-a38f-2bd0aab0bf74.html.

123. Ibid.

124. Lowery, *They Can't Kill Us All*, 214.

125. Vandelinder, "Racial Climate at MU."

126. Sarah Brown, "Activist Group Unites via Social Media," *Chronicle of Higher Education*, April 10, 2016, http://www.chronicle.com/article/Activist-Group-Unites -via/235993.

127. We the Protesters, *The Demands*, http://www.thedemands.org.

128. Hollie Chessman and Lindsay Wayt, "What Are Students Demanding?," *Higher Education Today*, American Council on Education, January 13, 2016, https:// higheredtoday.org/2016/01/13/what-are-students-demanding/.

129. Vandelinder, "Racial Climate at MU."

130. Lorelle Espinosa, Hollie Chessman, and Lindsay Wayt, "Racial Climate on Campus: A Survey of College Presidents," *Higher Education Today*, http://higheredtoday .org/2016/03/08/racial-climate-on-campus-a-survey-of-college-presidents/.

131. McMurtrie, "I Believe I Can Leave This Place Better Than I Found It."

132. Robert P. Jones, "Self-Segregation: Why It's So Hard for Whites to Understand Ferguson," *The Atlantic*, August 21, 2014, http://www.theatlantic.com/national /archive/2014/08/self-segregation-why-its-hard-for-whites-to-understand-ferguson /378928/.

133. Marcia Chatelain, "What Mizzou Taught Me," *Chronicle of Higher Education*, November 12, 2015, http://www.chronicle.com/article/What-Mizzou-Taught -Me/234180.

134. Stephanie Woodard, "The Police Killings No One Is Talking About: A Special Investigation," *In These Times*, October 17, 2016, http://inthesetimes.com/features /native_american_police_killings_native_lives_matter.html.

135. Ibid.

136. For more information, see Lakota People's Law Project, *Native Lives Matter*, February 2015, http://www.docs.lakotalaw.org/reports/Native%20Lives%20Matter%20 PDF.pdf.

137. Woodard, "The Police Killings No One Is Talking About."

138. Chessman and Wayt, "What Are Students Demanding?"

139. Amherst College Demands, November 12, 2015. Retrieved from http://www .thedemands.org/.

140. Cullen Murphy, "Home: Some Thoughts on the Frost Library Protest," *Amherst* magazine, August 1, 2016, https://www.amherst.edu/amherst-story/magazine/issues/2016-summer/home.

141. Ibid.

142. Amherst Uprising, "A Letter of Clarification for Amherst Alumni, Family, and Friends," November 15, 2015, http://amherstuprising.com/demands.html.

143. Murphy, "Home."

144. Biddy Martin, "President Martin's Statement on Campus Protests," November 15, 2015, https://www.amherst.edu/amherst-story/president/statements/node/620480.

145. Amherst Uprising, "A Letter of Clarification."

146. Murphy, "Home."

147. Derald Wing Sue, *Microaggressions in Everyday Life: Race, Gender, and Sexual Orientation* (New Jersey: John Wiley and Sons, 2010), 5.

148. Michael Luo, "An Open Letter to the Woman Who Told My Family to Go Back to China," *New York Times,* October 10, 2016, http://www.nytimes.com/2016/10/10/nyregion/to-the-woman-who-told-my-family-to-go-back-to-china.html.

149. Michael Luo, "'Go Back to China': Readers Respond to Racist Insults shouted at a New York Times Editor," *New York Times,* October 10, 2016, http://www.nytimes.com/2016/10/11/nyregion/go-back-to-china-readers-respond-to-racist-insults-shouted-at-a-new-york-times-editor.html.

150. Sue, *Microaggressions in Everyday Life,* 6.

151. "Here's Donald Trump's Presidential Announcement Speech," Time.com, June 16, 2015, http://time.com/3923128/donald-trump-announcement-speech/.

152. Ashley Parker and Steve Eder, "Inside the Six Weeks Donald Trump Was a Nonstop 'Birther,'" *New York Times,* July 2, 2016, http://nyti.ms/29o4pbq.

153. Donald Trump, "Full Text: Donald Trump 2016 RNC Draft Speech Transcript, July 21, 2016," *Politico,* http://www.politico.com/story/2016/07/full-transcript-donald-trump-nomination-acceptance-speech-at-rnc-225974.

154. Nicholas Confessore, "For Whites Sensing Decline, Donald Trump Unleashes Words of Resistance," *New York Times,* July 13, 2016, https://www.nytimes.com/2016/07/14/us/politics/donald-trump-white-identity.html.

155. Ibid.

156. Ibid.

157. Ibid.

158. "Alternative Right," Southern Poverty Law Center, https://www.splcenter.org/fighting-hate/extremist-files/ideology/alternative-right.

159. "'New York Times' Executive Editor on the New Terrain of Covering Trump," *Fresh Air,* NPR, December 8, 2016, http://www.npr.org/templates/transcript/transcript.php?storyId=504806512.

160. Joseph Goldstein, "Alt-Right Gathering Exults in Trump Election with Nazi-Era Salute," *New York Times,* November 20, 2016, http://www.nytimes.com/2016/11/21/us/alt-right-salutes-donald-trump.html.

161. Confessore, "For Whites Sensing Decline, Donald Trump Unleashes Words of Resistance."

162. Jenna Johnson, "Inside Donald Trump's Strategic Decision to Target Muslims," *Washington Post,* June 21, 2016, https://www.washingtonpost.com/politics/inside-donald -trumps-strategic-decision-to-target-muslims/2016/06/20/d506411e-3241-11e6-8758 -d58e76e11b12_story.html.

163. Robert Samuels, "Donald Trump Keeps Attacking Muslims. They Plan to Fight Back at the Ballot Box," *Washington Post,* June 15, 2016, https://www.washingtonpost .com/politics/election-rhetoric-spurs-political-awakening-among-muslims-in-new -jersey/2016/06/14/01734464-3237-11e6-8ff7-7b6c1998b7a0_story.html.

164. Johnson, "Inside Donald Trump's Strategic Decision to Target Muslims."

165. Jenna Johnson, "Donald Trump to African American and Hispanic Voters: 'What Do You Have to Lose?'," *Washington Post,* August 22, 2016, https:// www.washingtonpost.com/news/post-politics/wp/2016/08/22/donald-trump-to -african-american-and-hispanic-voters-what-do-you-have-to-lose/.

166. Dara Lind, "The Problem with Violence at Trump Rallies Starts with Trump Himself," *Vox,* March 13, 2016, http://www.vox.com/2016/3/11/11202540/trump -violent.

167. Carl Bialik, "How the Republican Field Dwindled from 17 to Donald Trump," *FiveThirtyEight,* May 5, 2016, http://fivethirtyeight.com/features/how-the -republican-field-dwindled-from-17-to-donald-trump/.

168. Jelani Cobb, "After Dallas, the Future of Black Lives Matter," *The New Yorker,* July 10, 2016, http://www.newyorker.com/news/news-desk/after-dallas-the-future-of-black -lives-matters.

169. Richard Fausset, Richard Pérez-Peña, and Campbell Robertson, "Alton Sterling Shooting in Baton Rouge Prompts Justice Dept. Investigation," *New York Times,* July 6, 2016, http://nyti.ms/29xqUea.

170. Christina Capecchi and Mitch Smith, "Officer Who Shot Philando Castile Is Charged with Manslaughter," *New York Times,* November 16, 2016, http://nyti.ms /2eGcSf4.

171. Manny Fernandez, Richard Pérez-Peña, and Jonah Engel Bromwich, "Five Dallas Officers Were Killed as Payback, Police Chief Says," *New York Times,* July 8, 2016, http://www.nytimes.com/2016/07/09/us/dallas-police-shooting.html.

172. Lizette Alvarez and Richard Pérez-Peña, "Orlando Gunman Attacks Gay Nightclub, Leaving 50 Dead," *New York Times,* June 12, 2016, http://nyti.ms/28u5TJ6.

173. Amy Chozick, "Hillary Clinton and Donald Trump Strike Different Tones After Dallas Shooting," *New York Times,* July 8, 2016, http://www.nytimes .com/2016/07/09/us/politics/clinton-trump-shooting-reaction.html.

174. Jelani Cobb, "Honoring the Police and Their Victims," *The New Yorker,* July 25, 2016, http://www.newyorker.com/magazine/2016/07/25/baton-rouge-st-paul-and-dallas.

175. Cobb, "After Dallas, the Future of Black Lives Matter."

176. Cobb, "Honoring the Police and Their Victims."

177. Timothy Williams and Michael Wines, "Shootings Further Divide a Nation Torn over Race," *New York Times,* July 8, 2016, http://www.nytimes.com/2016/07/09 /us/shootings-further-divide-a-nation-torn-over-race.html.

178. Trump, "Full Text: Donald Trump 2016 RNC Draft Speech Transcript."

179. Cobb, "Honoring the Police and Their Victims."

180. Trump, "Full Text: Donald Trump 2016 RNC Draft Speech Transcript."

181. Danielle Kurtzleben et al., "FACT CHECK: Hillary Clinton's Speech to the Democratic Convention, Annotated," July 28, 2016, http://www.npr.org/2016 /07/28/487817725/fact-check-hillary-clintons-speech-to-the-democratic-convention -annotated.

182. David A. Fahrenthold, "Trump Recorded Having Extremely Lewd Conversation About Women in 2005," *Washington Post,* October 8, 2016, https://www .washingtonpost.com/politics/trump-recorded-having-extremely-lewd-conversation -about-women-in-2005/2016/10/07/3b9ce776-8cb4-11e6-bf8a-3d26847eeed4_story .html.

183. Aaron Blake, "Three Dozen Republicans Have Now Called for Trump to Drop Out," *Washington Post,* October 9, 2016, https://www.washingtonpost.com /news/the-fix/wp/2016/10/07/the-gops-brutal-responses-to-the-new-trump-video -broken-down/.

184. Sam Frizell, "FBI Director James Comey Under Fire After Hillary Clinton Email Investigation Announcement," *Time,* October 29, 2016, http://time.com/4550453 /hillary-clinton-james-comey-fbi-emails/.

185. Matt Apuzzo, Michael S. Schmidt, and Adam Goldman, "Emails Warrant No New Action Against Hillary Clinton, F.B.I. Director Says," *New York Times*, November 6, 2016, http://nyti.ms/2edtN8v.

186. "Presidential Election Results: Donald J. Trump Wins," *New York Times,* December 8, 2016, http://www.nytimes.com/elections/results/president.

187. Alec Tyson and Shiva Maniam, "Behind Trump's Victory: Divisions by Race, Gender, Education," *Fact Tank,* Pew Research Center, November 9, 2016, http://www.pewresearch.org/fact-tank/2016/11/09/behind-trumps-victory-divisions -by-race-gender-education/.

188. Laura Morgan Roberts and Robin J. Ely, "Why Did So Many White Women Vote for Donald Trump?," *Fortune,* November 17, 2016, http://fortune.com /2016/11/17/donald-trump-women-voters-election/.

189. Sheryl Estrada, "CNN's Van Jones: 'White-lash' Against a Changing U.S. Led to Trump's Win," *DiversityInc,* November 10, 2016, http://www.diversityinc.com/news /cnns-van-jones-white-lash-changing-u-s-led-trumps-win/.

190. Jeffrey Toobin, "The Real Voting Scandal of 2016," *The New Yorker,* December 12, 2016, http://www.newyorker.com/magazine/2016/12/12/the-real-voting-scandal -of-2016.

191. Ari Berman, "The GOP War on Voting," *Rolling Stone,* August 30, 2011, http:// www.rollingstone.com/politics/news/the-gop-war-on-voting-20110830.

192. Ari Berman, "Did Republicans Rig the Election?," *The Nation,* November 15, 2016. https://www.thenation.com/article/did-republicans-rig-the-election/.

193. Ari Berman, "The GOP's Attack on Voting Rights Was the Most Under-Covered Story of 2016," *The Nation,* November 9, 2016, https://www.thenation.com /article/the-gops-attack-on-voting-rights-was-the-most-under-covered-story-of-2016/.

194. Toobin, "The Real Voting Scandal of 2016."

195. Alan Rappeport and Noah Weiland, "White Nationalists Celebrate 'an Awakening' After Donald Trump's Victory," *New York Times,* November 19, 2016, http://nyti.ms/2fc6vve.

196. Caitlin Dickerson and Stephanie Saul, "Campuses Confront Hostile Acts Against Minorities After Donald Trump's Election," *New York Times,* November 10, 2016, http://nyti.ms/2eFAM5v.

197. Southern Poverty Law Center, *Ten Days After: Harassment and Intimidation in the Aftermath of the Election* (November 2016), https://www.splcenter.org/sites/default/files/com_hate_incidents_report_final.pdf.

198. Ibid., 4.

199. Ibid., 6.

200. Nadia Dreid and Shannon Najambadi, "Here's a Rundown of the Latest Campus-Climate Incidents Since Trump's Election," *Chronicle of Higher Education,* December 6, 2016, http://www.chronicle.com/blogs/ticker/heres-a-rundown-of-the-latest-campus-climate-incidents-since-trumps-election/.

201. Sarah Maslin Nir, "Finding Hate Crimes on the Rise, Leaders Condemn Vicious Acts," *New York Times,* December 5, 2016, http://nyti.ms/2h9hmYg.

202. Ibid.

203. Southern Poverty Law Center, *Ten Days After,* 5.

204. Alan Rappeport, "Civil Rights Groups Call on Trump to Denounce Racism of Alt-Right," *New York Times,* November 21, 2016, http://mobile.nytimes.com/2016/11/21/us/politics/alt-right-trump.html.

205. Southern Poverty Law Center, *Ten Days After,* 5.

206. Ari Berman, "Jeff Sessions, Trump's Pick for Attorney General, Is a Fierce Opponent of Civil Rights," *The Nation,* November 18, 2016, https://www.thenation.com/article/jeff-sessions-trumps-pick-for-attorney-general-is-a-fierce-opponent-of-civil-rights/.

207. Eric Lichtblau, "Jeff Sessions, as Attorney General, Could Overhaul Department He's Skewered," *New York Times,* November 18, 2016, http://www.nytimes.com/2016/11/19/us/politics/jeff-sessions-donald-trump-attorney-general.html.

208. Katherine Mangan, "With Trump's Rise, Undocumented Students Fear for Their Futures," *Chronicle of Higher Education,* November 11, 2016, http://www.chronicle.com/article/With-Trump-s-Rise/238387.

209. Immaculée Ilibagiza, *Left to Tell: Discovering God Amidst the Rwandan Holocaust* (Carlsbad, CA: Hay House, 2006).

## Introduction: A Psychologist's Perspective

1. J. H. Katz, *White Awareness: Handbook for Anti-Racism Training* (Norman: University of Oklahoma Press, 1978). A revised and expanded edition was released in 2003.

2. For more information about the Psychology of Racism course, see Beverly Daniel Tatum, "Talking About Race, Learning About Racism: An Application of Racial Identity Development Theory in the Classroom," *Harvard Educational Review* 62, no. 1 (1992): 1–24.

3. For a description of the professional development course for educators, see Sandra M. Lawrence and Beverly Daniel Tatum, "White Educators as Allies: Moving from Awareness to Action," in *Off White: Readings on Race, Power, and Society,* ed. Michelle Fine, Lois Weis, Linda Powell Pruitt, and April Burns (New York: Routledge, 2004), 362–372.

4. Tatum, "Talking About Race, Learning About Racism."

5. I was honored to serve as president of Spelman College, the oldest historically Black college for women in the United States, from 2002 to 2015; however, I did not teach any courses there.

# Chapter 1: Defining Racism

1. C. O'Toole, "The Effect of the Media and Multicultural Education on Children's Perceptions of Native Americans" (senior thesis, Department of Psychology and Education, Mount Holyoke College, 1990).

2. For an extended discussion of this point, see David Wellman, "Prejudiced People Are Not the Only Racists in America," chap. 1 in *Portraits of White Racism* (Cambridge: Cambridge University Press, 1977), 1–44. A second edition was published in 1993. See also Eduardo Bonilla-Silva, "The Strange Enigma of Race in Contemporary America," chap. 1 in *Racism Without Racists: Color-Blind Racism and the Persistence of Racial Inequality in America,* 4th ed. (Lanham, MD: Rowman and Littlefield, 2013), 1–24.

3. For specific statistical information, see Tim Sullivan et al., *State of the Dream 2012: The Emerging Majority* (United for a Fair Economy, 2012), http://www.faireconomy.org/dream12. It measures the impacts of the past thirty years of public policy on the racial divide and offers thirty-year projections, from 2012 to 2042, based on data trends since the Reagan presidency.

4. Peggy McIntosh, "White Privilege: Unpacking the Invisible Knapsack," *Peace and Freedom,* July/August 1989, 10–12. Now available at http://nationalseedproject.org/peggy-mcintosh-s-white-privilege-papers.

5. For further discussion of the concept of "belief in a just world," see Melvin Lerner, "Social Psychology of Justice and Interpersonal Attraction," in *Foundations of Interpersonal Attraction,* ed. Ted L. Huston (New York: Academic Press, 1974), 331–351.

6. For a brief historical overview of the institutionalization of racism and sexism in our legal system, see "Part VII: How It Happened: Race and Gender Issues in U.S. Law," in *Race, Class, and Gender in the United States: An Integrated Study,* 9th ed., ed. Paula S. Rothenberg (New York: Worth Publishers, 2014). See also Daria Roithmayr, *Reproducing Racism: How Everyday Choices Lock In White Advantage* (New York: New York University Press, 2014).

7. Phyllis A. Wentworth, "The Identity Development of Non-Traditionally Aged First-Generation Women College Students: An Exploratory Study" (master's thesis, Department of Psychology and Education, Mount Holyoke College, 1994).

8. Ta-Nehisi Coates, *Between the World and Me* (New York: Penguin Random House, 2015), 144.

9. Walter L. Updegrave, "Race and Money," *Money,* December 1989, 152–172.

10. See Ani Turner, *The Business Case for Racial Equity*, (Battle Creek, MI: W. K. Kellogg Foundation and Altarum Institute, 2013), http://www.wkkf.org/resource-directory/resource/2013/10/the-business-case-for-racial-equity.

11. For further discussion of the impact of racism on Whites, see Benjamin P. Bowser and Raymond G. Hunt, eds., *Impacts of Racism on White Americans*, 2nd ed. (Thousand Oaks, CA: Sage, 1996); Joseph Barndt, *Understanding and Dismantling Racism: The Twenty-First Century Challenge to White America* (Minneapolis: Fortress Press, 2007); Paul Kivel, *Uprooting Racism: How White People Can Work for Racial Justice*, 3rd ed. (Philadelphia: New Society Publishers, 2011); and Jim Wallis, *America's Original Sin: Racism, White Privilege, and a Bridge to a New America* (Grand Rapids, MI: Brazos Press, 2016).

12. Wendell Berry, *The Hidden Wound* (San Francisco: North Point Press, 1989), 3–4.

13. It is important to note here that these groups are not necessarily mutually exclusive. For example, people of Latin American descent may have European, African, and Native American ancestors. The politics of racial categorization has served to create artificial boundaries between groups with shared ancestry.

14. It is difficult to know which is the preferred term because different subgroups have different preferences that may change over time. According to Amado Padilla, younger US-born, university-educated individuals of Mexican ancestry prefer *Chicano/a* to *Mexican American* or *Hispanic*. On the other hand, *Latino/a* is preferred by others of Mexican ancestry or other Latin American origin. Those of Cuban ancestry may prefer *Cuban American* to *Latino*, whereas recent immigrants from Central America would rather be identified by their nationality (e.g., *Guatematecos* or *Salvadoreños*). See Amado Padilla, ed., *Hispanic Psychology* (Thousand Oaks, CA: Sage, 1995).

15. For an expanded discussion of the social construction of race, see Michael Omi and Howard Winant, *Racial Formation in the United States*, 3rd ed. (New York: Routledge, 2015).

16. Pierre L. van den Berghe, *Race and Racism: A Comparative Perspective* (New York: Wiley, 1967).

17. See Richard Alba, *Ethnic Identity: The Transformation of White America* (New Haven, CT: Yale University Press, 1990).

18. In the year 2000 the US Census Bureau began allowing people to choose more than one racial category to describe themselves. For a discussion of the census classification debate that led to the policy change and the history of racial classification in the United States, see Lawrence Wright, "One Drop of Blood," *The New Yorker*, July 25, 1994, 46–55.

## Chapter 2: The Complexity of Identity

1. See Charles Cooley, *Human Nature and the Social Order* (New York: Scribner, 1922). George H. Mead expanded on this idea in his book *Mind, Self, and Society* (Chicago: University of Chicago Press, 1934).

2. Abigail J. Stewart and Joseph M. Healy, "Linking Individual Development and Social Changes," *American Psychologist* 44, no. 1 (1989): 30–42.

3. Erik. H. Erikson, *Identity, Youth, and Crisis* (New York: W. W. Norton, 1968), 22.

4. For a discussion of the Western biases in the concept of the self and individual identity, see Alan Roland, "Identity, Self, and Individualism in a Multicultural Perspective," in *Race, Ethnicity, and Self: Identity in Multicultural Perspective,* ed. Elizabeth Pathy Salett and Diane R. Koslow (Washington, DC: National MultiCultural Institute, 1994), 11–23.

5. Becky Thompson and Sangeeta Tyagi, eds., *Names We Call Home: Autobiography on Racial Identity* (New York: Routledge, 1996).

6. Ibid., xi.

7. *Anti-Semitism* is a term commonly used to describe the oppression of Jewish people. However, other Semitic peoples (Arab Muslims, for example) are also subject to oppressive treatment on the basis of ethnicity as well as religion. For that reason, the terms *Jewish oppression* and *Arab oppression* are sometimes used to specify the particular form of oppression under discussion.

8. Audre Lorde, "Age, Race, Class, and Sex: Women Redefining Difference," in *Sister Outsider: Essays and Speeches* (Freedom, CA: Crossing Press, 1984), 115.

9. Jean Baker Miller, "Domination and Subordination," in *Toward a New Psychology of Women* (Boston: Beacon Press, 1976), 3–9.

10. Ibid., 8.

11. Valerie Adams-Bass, Keisha L. Bentley-Edwards, and Howard C. Stevenson, "That's Not Me I See on TV . . . : African American Youth Interpret Media Images of Black Females," *Women, Gender and Families of Color* 2, no. 1 (Spring 2014): 79–100.

12. Susan T. Fiske, "Controlling Other People: The Impact of Power on Stereotyping," *American Psychologist* 48, no. 6 (1993): 624.

13. Richard Wright, "The Ethics of Living Jim Crow: An Autobiographical Sketch," in *Uncle Tom's Children* (New York: Harper and Brothers, 1938; New York: Harper Collins, 2009), Kindle edition, location 401.

14. An article in the popular weekly magazine *People* chronicled the close encounters of famous Black men with White police officers. Despite their fame, these men were treated as potential criminals. Highlighted in the article is the story of Jonny Gammage, who was beaten to death by White police officers in 1995 following a routine traffic stop in Pittsburgh. Thomas Fields-Meyer, "Under Suspicion," *People,* January 15, 1996, 40–47, http://people.com/archive/under-suspicion-vol-45-no-2/. These incidents are strikingly similar to some of the twenty-first-century examples provided in the prologue of this book.

15. Miller, "Domination and Subordination," 10.

16. Herbert Kohl, "I Won't Learn from You," in *I Won't Learn from You, and Other Thoughts on Creative Maladjustment,* 2nd ed. (New York: The New Press, 1995), 6.

17. Miller, "Domination and Subordination," 12.

18. Audre Lorde, "There Is No Hierarchy of Oppression," in *I Am Your Sister: Collected and Unpublished Writings of Audre Lorde,* ed. Rudolph P. Byrd, Johnnetta Betsch Cole, and Beverly Guy-Sheftall (New York: Oxford University Press, 2009), 219–220.

## Chapter 3: The Early Years

1. For an in-depth discussion of preschool children's recognition and understanding of racial differences, see Louise Derman-Sparks and Julie Olsen Edwards, "Learning About Racial Identity and Fairness," chap. 7 in *Anti-Bias Education for Young Children and Ourselves,* (Washington, DC: National Association for the Education of Young Children, 2010), 77–89.

2. For an expanded discussion of the role of Black families in the positive socialization of their children, see Beverly Daniel Tatum, *Assimilation Blues: Black Families in a White Community* (New York: Basic Books, 1999).

3. See Patricia G. Ramsey, "The Context of Race," in *Teaching and Learning in a Diverse World: Multicultural Education for Young Children,* 4th ed. (New York: Teachers College Press, 2015), Kindle edition, locations 1684–2073.

4. For other examples of good responses to preschoolers' questions, order the helpful brochure "Teaching Young Children to Resist Bias: What Parents Can Do," available from the National Association for the Education of Young Children, https://store .naeyc.org/store/teaching-young-children-resist-bias-what-parents-can-do. The flyers are very inexpensive and can be ordered in bulk to be given to parents at school meetings and other educational forums. They are also available in Spanish.

5. In terms of Piaget's model of cognitive development, preschool children are considered to be in the preoperational stage. For more information about the preoperational stage as it relates to children's understanding of racial and other forms of difference, see Ramsey, *Teaching and Learning in a Diverse World.* For a clear discussion of the cognitive characteristics of children at various stages of development, see Barry J. Wadsworth, *Piaget's Theory of Cognitive and Affective Development: Foundations of Constructivism,* 5th ed. (Boston: Allyn & Bacon, 2003).

6. Sandra M. Lawrence and Beverly Daniel Tatum, "Teachers in Transition: The Impact of Anti-Racist Professional Development on Classroom Practice," *Teachers College Record* 99 (Fall 1997), 169.

7. Faith Ringgold, *Aunt Harriet's Underground Railroad in the Sky* (New York: Crown, 1992).

8. Jeanette Winter, *Follow the Drinking Gourd* (New York: Dragonfly Books, 1988).

9. See Louise Derman-Sparks, Carol Tanaka Higa, and Bill Sparks, "Children, Race, and Racism: How Race Awareness Develops," *Interracial Books for Children Bulletin* 11, no. 3–4 (1980), 6, https://www.teachingforchange.org/wp-content/uploads/2012/08 /ec_childrenraceracism_english.pdf.

10. Ibid.

11. For a more in-depth discussion of the impact of colorism, see Kathy Russell, Midge Wilson, and Ronald Hall, *The Color Complex* (San Diego: Harcourt Brace Jovanovich, 1992). See also David Knight, "What's Colorism?," *Teaching Tolerance,* no. 51 (Fall 2015), http://www.tolerance.org/magazine/number-51-fall-2015/feature/what -s-colorism.

12. Nancy Boyd-Franklin, *Black Families in Therapy: A Multisystems Approach* (New York: Guilford, 1989), 34.

13. bell hooks, *Sisters of the Yam: Black Women and Self-Recovery* (Boston: South End Press, 1993), 95.

14. John Steptoe, *Mufaro's Beautiful Daughters: An African Tale* (New York: Scholastic, 1989).

15. The first book in this series by Gertrude Chandler Warner is *The Boxcar Children* (Niles, IL: Albert Whitman, 1942). Other books in the series include *Surprise Island, The Yellow House Mystery, Mystery Ranch,* and many others.

16. Janie Victoria Ward, "Raising Resisters: The Role of Truth Telling in the Psychological Development of African-American Girls," in *Urban Girls: Resisting Stereotypes, Creating Identities,* ed. Bonnie J. Ross Leadbeater and Niobe Way (New York: New York University Press, 1996), 85–99. See also Janie Victoria Ward, "Uncovering Truths, Recovering Lives," in *Urban Girls Revisited: Building Strengths,* ed. Bonnie J. Ross Leadbeater and Niobe Way (New York: New York University Press, 2007), 190–207.

17. For a useful set of guidelines for analysis of media, see Council on Interracial Books for Children, "Ten Quick Ways to Analyze Children's Books for Racism and Sexism," in *Rethinking Our Classrooms,* vol. 1, rev. ed., (Milwaukee, WI: Rethinking Schools, 2007), 10–11.

18. Derman-Sparks and Edwards, "Learning About Racial Identity and Fairness."

19. "Kids Pluck Arrow from Pilgrim's Hat," United Press International, November 23, 1989, http://www.upi.com/Archives/1989/11/23/kids-pluck-arow-from-Pilgrims -hat/4156627800400.

20. Louise Derman-Sparks and the ABC Task Force, *Anti-Bias Curriculum: Tools for Empowering Young Children* (Washington, DC: National Association for the Education of Young Children, 1989), 77.

## Chapter 4: Identity Development in Adolescence

1. James E. Marcia, "Development and Validation of Ego Identity Status," *Journal of Personality and Social Psychology* 3, no. 5 (1966), 551–558.

2. For a review of the research on ethnic identity in adolescents, see Jean S. Phinney, "Ethnic Identity in Adolescents and Adults: Review of Research," *Psychological Bulletin* 108, no. 3 (1990): 499–514. See also "Part I: Identity Development" in *Urban Girls: Resisting Stereotypes, Creating Identities,* ed. Bonnie J. Ross Leadbeater and Niobe Way (New York: New York University Press, 1996). See also Sabine Elizabeth French et al., "The Development of Ethnic Identity During Adolescence," *Developmental Psychology* 42, no.1 (2006): 1–10.

3. William E. Cross Jr., *Shades of Black: Diversity in African-American Identity* (Philadelphia: Temple University Press, 1991).

4. William E. Cross and T. Binta Cross, "Theory, Research, and Models," in *Handbook of Race, Racism, and the Developing Child,* ed. Stephen M. Quintana and Clark McKown (Hoboken, NJ: Wiley and Sons, 2008), 156.

5. Ibid., 158.

6. Ibid., 156.

7. For an expanded discussion of "race-conscious" parenting, see Beverly Daniel Tatum, "Making Choices," chap. 6 in *Assimilation Blues: Black Families in a White Community* (New York: Basic Books, 1999), 111–130.

8. Adriana J. Umaña-Taylor et al., "Ethnic and Racial Identity During Adolescence and into Young Adulthood: An Integrated Conceptualization," *Child Development* 85, no. 1 (2014): 21–39.

9. Ibid., 27.

10. Jean S. Phinney and Steve Tarver, "Ethnic Identity Search and Commitment in Black and White Eighth Graders," *Journal of Early Adolescence* 8, no. 3 (1988): 265–77. See also French et al., "The Development of Ethnic Identity During Adolescence."

11. Umaña-Taylor et al., "Ethnic and Racial Identity During Adolescence and into Young Adulthood."

12. See Beverly Daniel Tatum, "African-American Identity, Academic Achievement, and Missing History," *Social Education* 56, no. 6 (1992): 331–334; Beverly Daniel Tatum, "Racial Identity and Relational Theory: The Case of Black Women in White Communities," *Work in Progress*, no. 63 (Wellesley, MA: Stone Center Working Papers, 1992); Beverly Daniel Tatum, "Out There Stranded? Black Youth in White Communities," in *Black Families*, 3rd ed., ed. Harriet Pipes McAdoo (Thousand Oaks, CA: Sage, 1996), 214–233.

13. For an in-depth discussion of the negative effects of tracking in schools, see Jeannie Oakes, *Keeping Track: How Schools Structure Inequality* (New Haven, CT: Yale University Press, 1985). See also Sonali Kholi, "Modern-Day Segregation in Public Schools," *The Atlantic*, November 18, 2014, http://www.theatlantic.com/education /archive/2014/11/modern-day-segregation-in-public-schools/382846/.

14. Roslyn Arlin Mickelson and Anne E. Velasco, "Bring It On! Diverse Responses to 'Acting White' Among Academically Able Black Adolescents," chap. 1 in *Beyond Acting White: Reassessments and New Directions in Research on Black Students and School Success*, ed. Erin McNamara Horvat and Carla O'Connor (New York: Rowman and Littlefield, 2006), 27–57.

15. Catherine E. Lhamon, "Dear Colleague Letter: Resource Comparability," version 1.02, October 10, 2014, US Department of Education, Office of Civil Rights. http://www2.ed.gov/about/offices/list/ocr/letters/colleague-resourcecomp-201410.pdf.

16. For further discussion of the social dynamics for Black youth in White communities, see Tatum, "Out There Stranded?"

17. Leadbeater and Way, *Urban Girls*, 5. See also Bonnie J. Ross Leadbeater and Niobe Way, eds., *Urban Girls Revisited: Building Strengths* (New York: New York University Press, 2007).

18. Valerie Adams-Bass, Keisha L. Bentley-Edwards, and Howard C. Stevenson, "That's Not Me I See on TV . . . : African American Youth Interpret Media Images of Black Females," *Women, Gender and Families of Color* 2, no. 1 (Spring 2014): 81.

19. Ibid., 88.

20. Ibid., 90.

21. Lawrence Otis Graham, "I Taught My Black Kids That Their Elite Upbringing Would Protect Them from Discrimination. I Was Wrong," *Washington Post*, November 6,

2014, https://www.washingtonpost.com/posteverything/wp/2014/11/06/i-taught-my-black-kids-that-their-elite-upbringing-would-protect-them-from-discrimination-i-was-wrong/.

22. Malcolm X with Alex Haley, *The Autobiography of Malcolm X* (New York: Grove Press, 1965), 36.

23. William E. Cross Jr., "The Psychology of Nigrescence: Revising the Cross Model," in *Handbook of Multicultural Counseling,* ed. Joseph G. Ponterotto et al. (Thousand Oaks, CA: Sage, 1995), 93–122.

24. See page 25 for a discussion of the Trayvon Martin case. Jordan Davis was a seventeen-year-old teenager who was shot and killed by Michael Dunn, a forty-seven-year-old White man, at a Jacksonville, Florida, gas station on November 23, 2012. Dunn told Davis and his friends in the car that they were playing their music too loud. Words were exchanged between Dunn and the teens inside the car, and Dunn responded by shooting ten shots into the car, killing Davis. The shots missed the other passengers. The case took on additional national significance because it occurred just a few months after the killing of Trayvon Martin. Unlike George Zimmerman, the man who shot Trayvon Martin, Michael Dunn was eventually convicted of first-degree murder for the killing of Jordan Davis.

25. Mary Madden et al., *Teens and Technology 2013,* Pew Research Center, March 13, 2013, http://www.pewinternet.org/2013/03/13/teens-and-technology-2013/.

26. Brendesha M. Tynes, "Online Racial Discrimination: A Growing Problem for Adolescents," Science Brief. *Psychological Science Agenda,* December 2015, http://www.apa.org/science/about/psa/2015/12/online-racial-discrimination.aspx.

27. Ibid.

28. Susan Svrluga, "Black UPenn Freshmen Added to Racist Social Media Account with 'Daily Lynching' Calendar," *Washington Post,* November 11, 2016, https://www.washingtonpost.com/news/grade-point/wp/2016/11/11/black-upenn-freshmen-added-to-racist-social-media-account-with-daily-lynching-calendar/.

29. Tynes, "Online Racial Discrimination."

30. Signithia Fordham and John U. Ogbu, "Black Students' School Success: Coping with the Burden of 'Acting White,'" *Urban Review* 18 (1986): 176–206.

31. Ibid., 181.

32. Ivory A. Toldson, "The 'Acting White' Theory Doesn't Add Up," *The Root,* January 30, 2013, http://www.theroot.com/articles/politics/2013/01/acting_white_theory_black_academic_achievement_based_on_other_factors/.

33. Brian K. Bridges, Janet T. Awokoya, and Frances Messano, *Done to Us, Not with Us: African American Parent Perceptions of K–12 Education* (Washington, DC: Frederick Patterson Research Institute, United Negro College Fund), https://www.uncf.org/pages/FDPRI-Reports.

34. Renee Stepler, "Hispanic, Black Parents See College Degree as Key for Children's Success," *Fact Tank,* Pew Research Center, February 24, 2016, http://www.pewresearch.org/fact-tank/2016/02/24/hispanic-black-parents-see-college-degree-as-key-for-childrens-success/.

35. Karolyn Tyson, William Darity Jr., and Domini R. Castellino, "It's Not 'A Black Thing': Understanding the Burden of Acting White and Other Dilemmas of High Achievement," *American Sociological Review* 70, no. 4 (August 2005): 582–605.

36. Mickelson and Velasco, "Bring It On!"

37. Karolyn Tyson, "The Making of a 'Burden': Tracing the Development of a 'Burden of Acting White' in Schools," in Horvat and O'Connor, *Beyond Acting White*, 61.

38. Mickelson and Velasco, "Bring It On!," 41.

39. Tyson, "The Making of a 'Burden,'" 85.

40. Ibid.

41. Signithia Fordham, "Racelessness as a Factor in Black Students' School Success: Pragmatic Strategy or Pyrrhic Victory?" *Harvard Educational Review* 58, no. 1 (1988): 54–84.

42. Graham, "I Taught My Black Kids That Their Elite Upbringing Would Protect Them from Discrimination. I Was Wrong."

43. For further discussion of this point, see Richard L. Zweigenhaft and G. William Domhoff, *Blacks in the White Establishment? A Study of Race and Class in America* (New Haven, CT: Yale University Press, 1991), 155.

44. Ibid.

45. Mickelson and Velasco, "Bring It On!," 42.

46. Lori A. Barker, "Presidents, Stereotypes, and Prototypes, Oh My!: Understanding the Psychological Impact of Obama," in *Obama on Our Minds: The Impact of Obama on the Psyche of America* (New York: Oxford University Press, 2016), 17.

47. Hollie Chessman and Lindsay Wayt, "What Are Students Demanding?," *Higher Education Today*, January 13, 2016, https://higheredtoday.org/2016/01/13/what-are-students-demanding/.

48. Chester Pierce, "Mundane Extreme Environment and Its Effects on Learning," in *Learning Disabilities: Issues and Recommendations for Research*, ed. Suzanne Gage Brainard (Washington, DC: National Institute of Education, 1975), 111–118.

49. Daphna Oyserman, Daniel Brickman, and Marjorie Rhodes, "Racial-Ethnic Identity: Content and Consequences for African American, Latino and Latina Youths," in *Contesting Stereotypes and Creating Identities: Social Categories, Social Identities, and Educational Participation*, ed. Andrew J. Fuligni (New York: Russell Sage Foundation, 2007), 91–114.

50. See Mary C. Waters, "The Intersection of Gender, Race, and Ethnicity in Identity Development of Caribbean American Teens," in Leadbeater and Way, *Urban Girls*, 65–84. See also Sherri-Ann P. Butterfield, "To Be Young, Gifted, Black, and Somewhat Foreign: The Role of Ethnicity in Black Student Achievement," in Horvat O'Connor, *Beyond Acting White*, 133–155.

51. Tina Q. Richardson et al., "African and Afro-Caribbean American Identity Development," in Ponterotto et al., *Handbook of Multicultural Counseling*, 232.

52. Waters, "The Intersection of Gender, Race, and Ethnicity in Identity Development of Caribbean American Teens."

53. The METCO program was established in 1966 under the state's Racial Imbalance Act, passed by the Massachusetts General Court in 1965. METCO was established to

provide (1) the opportunity for an integrated public school education for urban Black children and other children of color from racially imbalanced schools in Boston by placing them in suburban schools, (2) a new learning experience for suburban children, and (3) a closer understanding and cooperation between urban and suburban parents and other citizens in the Boston metropolitan area. Thirty-four suburban communities participate in the METCO program.

54. For a more complete description of the program and its evaluation, see B. D. Tatum et al., "Student Efficacy Training: An Evaluation of One Middle School's Programmatic Response to the Eastern Massachusetts Initiative" (presentation at the annual meeting of the American Educational Research Association, New York, April 9, 1996).

55. Claude M. Steele, "Thin Ice: Stereotype Threat and Black College Students," *Atlantic Monthly*, August 1999, 44–54.

56. Geoffrey L. Cohen and Claude M. Steele, "A Barrier of Mistrust: How Negative Stereotypes Affect Cross-Race Mentoring," in *Improving Academic Achievement: Impact of Psychological Factors on Education,* ed. Joshua Aronson (San Diego, CA: Academic, 2002).

57. Claude M. Steele, *Whistling Vivaldi and Other Clues to How Stereotypes Affect Us* (New York: W. W. Norton & Co., 2010).

58. Catherine Good, Carol S. Dweck, and Joshua Aronson, "Social Identity, Stereotype Threat, and Self-Theories," in Fuligni, *Contesting Stereotypes and Creating Identities,* 115–135.

59. Ibid.

60. Claude M. Steele, "Stereotype Threat and African-American Student Achievement," in *Young, Gifted and Black: Promoting High Achievement Among African-American Students,* ed. Theresa Perry, Claude Steele, and Asa Hilliard III (Boston: Beacon Press, 2003), 121.

61. Claude M. Steele and Joshua Aronson, "Stereotype Threat and the Intellectual Test Performance of African-Americans," *Journal of Personality and Social Psychology* 69, no. 5 (1995): 797–811.

62. Good, Dweck, and Aronson, "Social Identity, Stereotype Threat, and Self-Theories."

63. Ibid.

64. Spelman College has been recognized by the National Science Foundation as the leading undergraduate institution for graduating Black women who go on to earn PhDs in the sciences.

65. Steele, "Thin Ice," 51.

66. Steele, "Stereotype Threat and African-American Student Achievement," 126–127.

67. Ibid., 126.

68. Jeff Howard, *Getting Smart: The Social Construction of Intelligence* (Waltham, MA: Efficacy Institute, 1992).

69. Carol Dweck, "Messages That Motivate: How Praise Molds Students' Beliefs, Motivation, and Performance (In Surprising Ways)," in Aronson, *Improving Academic Achievement,* 38–60.

70. Joshua Aronson, Carrie B. Fried, and Catherine Good, "Reducing the Effects of Stereotype Threat on African American College Students by Shaping Theories of Intelligence," *Journal of Experimental Social Psychology* 38, no. 2 (2002): 113–125.

71. Lisa S. Blackwell, Kali H. Trzesniewski, and Carol Sorich Dweck, "Implicit Theories of Intelligence Predict Achievement Across an Adolescent Transition," *Child Development* 78, no. 1 (January–February 2007): 246–263.

72. Good, Dweck, and Aronson, "Social Identity, Stereotype Threat, and Self-Theories," 131.

## Chapter 5: Racial Identity in Adulthood

1. Over the years I have met White classmates at Wesleyan reunions and have had conversations about how it was that our paths did not intersect meaningfully when we were in college. Though in classes together, we were living parallel lives.

2. Adriana J. Umaña-Taylor et al., "Ethnic and Racial Identity During Adolescence and into Young Adulthood: An Integrated Conceptualization," *Child Development* 85, no. 1 (2014): 21–39.

3. Ibid., 25.

4. For more information, see Walter R. Allen, Edgar G. Epps, and Nesha Z. Haniff, eds., *College in Black and White: African American Students in Predominantly White and in Historically Black Public Universities* (Albany: State University of New York Press, 1991). See also Frank W. Hale Jr., *How Black Colleges Empower Black Students: Lessons for Higher Education* (Sterling, VA: Stylus Publishing, 2006).

5. Mark K. Fiegener and Steven L. Proudfoot, "Baccalaureate Origins of U.S.-Trained S&E Doctorate Recipients," *InfoBrief,* National Center for Science and Engineering Statistics, National Science Foundation, April 2013, NSF 13-323, https://www.nsf.gov/statistics/infbrief/nsf13323/nsf13323.pdf.

6. Walter R. Allen, "The Color of Success: African-American College Student Outcomes at Predominantly White and Historically Black Public Colleges and Universities," *Harvard Educational Review* 62, no. 1 (1992): 26–44. The National Study of Black College Students (NSBCS) surveyed more than 2,500 Black college students attending a total of sixteen public universities (eight predominantly White and eight historically Black) about their college experiences and outcomes.

7. Jake New, "Survey Finds Big Differences Between Black HBCU Graduates, Those Who Attended Other Institutions," *Inside Higher Ed,* October 28, 2015, https://www.insidehighered.com/news/2015/10/28/survey-finds-big-differences-between-black-hbcu-graduates-those-who-attended-other.

8. Though overall the percentage of Black students attending college has risen, the percentage choosing to attend HBCUs has declined from 18 percent in 1976 to 8 percent in 2014, according to the National Center for Education Statistics. "Historically Black Colleges and Universities," *Fast Facts,* National Center for Education Statistics, https://nces.ed.gov/fastfacts/display.asp?id=667.

9. An example of that kind of help can be found in a discussion of White students' responses to learning about the racial identity development process of students of color.

See Beverly Daniel Tatum, "Talking About Race, Learning About Racism: An Application of Racial Identity Development Theory in the Classroom," *Harvard Educational Review* 62, no. 1 (1992): 1–24.

10. Margarita Azmitia, Moin Syed, and Kimberly Radmacher, "On the Intersection of Personal and Social Identities: Introduction and Evidence from a Longitudinal Study of Emerging Adults," *New Directions for Child and Adolescent Development: The Intersections of Personal and Social Identities* 2008, no. 120 (Summer 2008): 1–16.

11. Malcolm X with Alex Haley, *The Autobiography of Malcolm X* (New York: Grove Press, 1965), 174.

12. Michael E. Dyson, *Race Rules: Navigating the Color Line* (Boston: Beacon Press, 1996), 151.

13. Melanie Eversley, "Thousands Pack D.C. for 20th Anniversary of Million Man March," *USA Today,* October 10, 2015, http://www.usatoday.com/story/news/nation/2015/10/10/washington-dc-million-man-march-20th-anniversary/73728720/.

14. Patricia Hill Collins, *Black Feminist Thought: Knowledge, Consciousness, and the Politics of Empowerment* (London: HarperCollins Academic, 1990), 96.

15. The National Survey of Black Americans (NSBA) was the first in a series of major research projects undertaken by social scientists at the Institute for Social Research at the University of Michigan to collect and analyze high-quality national survey data on the social, psychological, economic, and political behaviors of Black Americans. The NSBA and the major studies that followed it are all part of the Program for Research on Black Americans (PRBA) at the Institute for Social Research. The PRBA has involved thousands of Black participants in both face-to-face and telephone interviews. The findings of the PRBA are reported in James S. Jackson, ed., *Life in Black America* (Thousand Oaks, CA: Sage, 1991).

16. See Robert Joseph Taylor and Linda M. Chatters, "Religious Life," in Jackson, *Life in Black America,* 105–123.

17. For an in-depth discussion of alternative patterns of Black REC-identity development, see William E. Cross Jr. and Peony Fhagen-Smith, "Patterns of African American Identity Development: A Life Span Perspective," in *New Perspectives on Racial Identity Development: A Theoretical and Practical Anthology,* ed. Charmaine L. Wijeyesinghe and Bailey W. Jackson III (New York: New York University Press, 2001), 243–270.

18. Azmitia, Syed, and Radmacher, "On the Intersection of Personal and Social Identities," 13.

19. Thomas A. Parham, "Cycles of Psychological Nigrescence," *The Counseling Psychologist* 17, no. 2 (1989): 187–226.

20. Daniel J. Levinson, *The Seasons of a Man's Life* (New York: Knopf, 1978).

21. Parham, "Cycles of Psychological Nigrescence," 202.

22. Beverly Daniel Tatum, *Assimilation Blues: Black Families in a White Community* (New York: Basic Books, 1999), 85.

23. Parham, "Cycles of Psychological Nigrescence," 196.

24. Tatum, *Assimilation Blues,* 99.

25. Ibid., 108.

26. Adia Harvey Wingfield, "Being Black—but Not Too Black—in the Workplace," *The Atlantic,* October 14, 2015, http://www.theatlantic.com/business/archive/2015/10/being-black-work/409990/.

27. Tatum, *Assimilation Blues,* 79.

28. William E. Cross and T. Binta Cross, "Theory, Research, and Models," in *Handbook of Race, Racism, and the Developing Child,* ed. Stephen M. Quintana and Clark McKown (Hoboken, NJ: Wiley and Sons, 2008), 176.

29. Parham, "Cycles of Psychological Nigrescence," 204.

30. Gerald Early, introduction to *Lure and Loathing: Essays on Race, Identity, and the Ambivalence of Assimilation* (New York: Penguin, 1993), xxiii.

31. See Erik Erikson, chap. 8 in *Childhood and Society* (New York: W. W. Norton, 1950).

32. Rose C. Gibson, "Retirement," in Jackson, *Life in Black America,* 179–198.

33. W. E. Cross, "The Psychology of Nigrescence: Revising the Cross Model," in *Handbook of Multicultural Counseling,* ed. Joseph G. Ponterotto et al. (Thousand Oaks, CA: Sage, 1995), 116.

34. The concept of tokenism is explored in Rosabeth Moss Kanter, *Men and Women of the Corporation* (New York: Basic Books, 1977). See also *A Tale of O* (video), prod. Barry A. Stein (Cambridge, MA: Goodmeasure, 1979); and Rosabeth Moss Kanter with Barry A. Stein, *A Tale of "O": On Being Different in an Organization* (New York: Harper Colophon, 1980).

35. Erin Osterhaus, "Survey: Employee Resource Groups Help Engage Gen Y Workers," *New Talent Times,* July 28, 2014, http://new-talent-times.softwareadvice.com/employee-resource-groups-engage-gen-y-0714/.

## Chapter 6: The Development of White Identity

1. Sandra M. Lawrence and Beverly Daniel Tatum, "White Educators as Allies: Moving from Awareness to Action," in *Off White: Readings on Race, Power, and Society,* ed. Michelle Fine et al. (New York: Routledge, 2004), 333.

2. Debby Irving, *Waking Up White and Finding Myself in the Story of Race* (Cambridge, MA: Elephant Room Press, 2014), xi.

3. Janet E. Helms, ed., *Black and White Racial Identity: Theory, Research, and Practice* (Westport, CT: Greenwood, 1990).

4. Paul Kivel, *Uprooting Racism: How White People Can Work for Racial Justice,* 3rd ed. (Gabriola Island, BC, Canada: New Society Publishers, 2011), 10–11.

5. There are other models of White racial identity development; however, Helms' model is used here because it is the most commonly cited of the White identity models and is the one most often used in empirical investigations of White racial identity. For more information, see Lisa B. Spanierman and Jason R. Soble, "Understanding Whiteness: Previous Approaches and Possible Directions in the Study of White Racial Attitudes and Identity," in *Handbook of Multicultural Counseling,* 3rd ed., ed. Joseph G. Ponterotto et al. (Los Angeles: Sage, 2010), 283–299.

6. Janet Helms has changed her terminology from *stages* to *statuses* in describing this six-part model. Helms discusses the change in terminology in her article "An Update of Helms' White and People of Color Racial Identity Models," in Ponterotto et al., *Handbook of Multicultural Counseling*, 181–198.

7. Peggy McIntosh, "White Privilege: Unpacking the Invisible Knapsack," *Peace and Freedom*, July/August 1989, 12.

8. Sonia Scherr, "Children of Extremists Denounce Parents' Beliefs," *Intelligence Report*, Southern Poverty Law Center, November 30, 2009, https://www.splcenter.org/fighting-hate/intelligence-report/2009/children-extremists-denounce-parents'-beliefs.

9. Robert T. Carter, "Is White a Race? Expressions of White Racial Identity," in Fine et al., *Off White*, 201.

10. Jill Robbins, "How I Finally 'Got' the Meaning of White Privilege," *Huffington Post*, July 8, 2016, http://www.huffingtonpost.com/jill-robbins/what-white-privilege-means_b_10874218.html.

11. *Ethnic Notions*, produced and directed by Marlon Riggs (San Francisco: Resolution/California Newsreel, 1986), video.

12. Robin DiAngelo, *What Does It Mean to Be White? Developing White Racial Literacy*, rev. ed. (New York: Peter Lang, 2016), 247.

13. This interview was conducted by my graduate student, Elizabeth Knaplund, as part of a study we conducted on the relational impact of antiracist activity on the lives of White women. See Beverly Daniel Tatum and Elizabeth G. Knaplund, "Outside the Circle: The Relational Implications for White Women Working Against Racism," *Work in Progress*, no. 78 (Wellesley, MA: Stone Center Working Paper Series, 1996).

14. McIntosh, "White Privilege," 11.

15. See Nancie Zane, "Interrupting Historical Patterns: Bridging Race and Gender Gaps Between Senior White Men and Other Organizational Groups," in Fine et al., *Off White*, 349.

16. Jews are a multiracial group, including Jews of African descent. For a helpful discussion of the complexity of Jewish racial identity, see Melanie Kaye/Kantrowitz, "Jews in the U.S.: The Rising Costs of Whiteness," in *Names We Call Home: Autobiography on Racial Identity*, ed. Becky Thompson and Sangeeta Tyagi (New York: Routledge, 1996), 121–138. See also Warren J. Blumenfeld, "Inside and Outside: How Being an Ashkenazi Jew Illuminates and Complicates the Binary of Racial Privilege," chap. 12 in *Everyday White People Confront Racial and Social Injustice: 15 Stories*, ed. Eddie Moore Jr., Marguerite W. Penick-Parks, and Ali Michael (Sterling, VA: Stylus, 2015).

17. Heather W. Hackman, "Calling Out the Wizard Behind the Curtain," chap. 5 in Moore, *Everyday White People Confront Racial and Social Injustice*.

18. Lawrence and Tatum, "White Educators as Allies."

19. Lois Stalvey, *The Education of a WASP* (Madison: University of Wisconsin Press, [1970] 1989), 151.

20. Ruth Frankenberg, *White Women, Race Matters: The Social Construction of Whiteness* (Minneapolis: University of Minnesota Press, 1993).

21. Ruth Frankenberg, "'When We Are Capable of Stopping, We Begin to See': Being White, Seeing Whiteness," in Thompson and Tyagi, *Names We Call Home*, 14.

22. Ibid.

23. Morris Dees with Steve Fiffer, *A Season of Justice: A Lawyer's Own Story of Victory over America's Hate Groups* (New York: Touchstone, 1991).

24. Mab Segrest, *Memoir of a Race Traitor* (Boston: South End Press, 1994).

25. Virginia Foster Durr, *Outside the Magic Circle: The Autobiography of Virginia Foster Durr,* ed. Hollinger F. Barnard (Tuscaloosa: University of Alabama Press, 1985). An excerpt of this oral history can also be found in Anne Colby and William Damon, *Some Do Care: Contemporary Lives of Moral Commitment* (New York: Free Press, 1992).

26. Stalvey, *The Education of a WASP.*

27. Becky Thompson, *A Promise and a Way of Life: White Antiracist Activism* (Minneapolis: University of Minneapolis Press, 2001).

28. Bernestine Singley, *When Race Becomes Real: Black and White Writers Confront Their Personal Histories* (Chicago: Lawrence Hill Books, 2002).

29. Tim Wise, *White Like Me: Reflections on Race from a Privileged Son—The Remix,* rev. ed (Berkeley, CA: Soft Skull Press, 2011).

30. Debby Irving, *Waking Up White and Finding Myself in the Story of Race* (Cambridge, MA: Elephant Room Press, 2014).

31. Shelly Tochluk, *Witnessing Whiteness: The Need to Talk About Race and How to Do It,* 2nd ed. (Lanham, MD: Rowman and Littlefield Education, 2010).

32. Mark R. Warren, *Fire in the Heart: How White Activists Embrace Racial Justice* (New York: Oxford University Press, 2010).

33. Eddie Moore Jr., Marguerite W. Penick-Parks, and Ali Michael, eds., *Everyday White People Confront Racial and Social Injustice: 15 Stories* (Sterling, VA: Stylus, 2015).

34. Warren, *Fire in the Heart,* x.

35. Andrea Ayvazian, "Interrupting the Cycle of Oppression: The Role of Allies as Agents of Change," *Fellowship,* January/February 1995, 7–10.

36. For an example of such a group in process, see Becky Thompson and White Women Challenging Racism, "Home/Work: Antiracism Activism and the Meaning of Whiteness," in Fine et al., *Off White,* 354–366.

37. For more information about Showing Up for Racial Justice (SURJ) and their commitment to working with the poor and working-class, visit www.showingupforracial justice.org/about and http://www.showingupforracialjustice.org/pwc_commitment.

38. For a discussion of the value of Whites-only support groups, see Becky Thompson, "Time Traveling and Border Crossing: Reflections on White Identity," in Thompson and Tyagi, *Names We Call Home,* 104–105.

39. Ibid., 104.

40. Clayton P. Alderfer, "A White Man's Perspective on the Unconscious Process Within Black-White Relations in the United States," in *Human Diversity,* ed. Edison J. Trickett, Roderick J. Watts, and Dina Birman (San Francisco: Jossey-Bass, 1994), 202.

41. Helms, *Black and White Racial Identity,* 66.

42. Tochluk, *Witnessing Whiteness,* 47–48.

43. For more information about AWARE-LA, see https://www.awarela.org.

44. Tochluk, *Witnessing Whiteness,* 49.

45. Ibid., 105.

## Chapter 7: White Identity, Affirmative Action, and Color-Blind Racial Ideology

1. For more information about Whiteness Project and its creator, Whitney Dow, visit http://whitenessproject.org/.

2. Betsy Cooper et al., *Anxiety, Nostalgia, and Mistrust: Findings from the 2015 American Values Survey,* Public Religion Research Institute, http://www.prri.org/research/survey-anxiety-nostalgia-and-mistrust-findings-from-the-2015-american-values-survey/.

3. Ibid., 38.

4. Lee Anne Bell et al., "Racism and White Privilege," in *Teaching for Diversity and Social Justice,* 3rd ed., ed. Maurianne Adams et al. (New York: Taylor and Francis, 2016), Kindle edition, locations 4543–4552.

5. Ibid.

6. Monique W. Morris, *Black Stats: African Americans by the Numbers in the Twenty-First Century* (New York: The New Press, 2014), Kindle edition, location 3269.

7. Pew Research Center, *On Views of Race and Inequality, Blacks and Whites Are Worlds Apart,* June 27, 2016, http://www.pewsocialtrends.org/2016/06/27/on-views-of-race-and-inequality-blacks-and-whites-are-worlds-apart/.

8. Ruy Teixeira and John Halpin, *Building an All-In Nation: A View from the American Public,* Center for American Progress, October 22, 2013, 3, https://www.americanprogress.org/issues/race/reports/2013/10/22/77665/building-an-all-in-nation/.

9. Ibid., 5.

10. Arlie Russell Hochschild, *Strangers in Their Own Land: Anger and Mourning on the American Right* (New York: The New Press, 2016), Kindle edition, location 2306.

11. For more information about the history of affirmative action, see Frances A. Holloway, "What Is Affirmative Action?" and Dalmas A. Taylor, "Affirmative Action and Presidential Executive Orders," both in *Affirmative Action in Perspective,* ed. Fletcher A. Blanchard and Faye J. Crosby (New York: Springer-Verlag, 1989).

12. See Jerome Karabel, *The Chosen: The Hidden History of Admission and Exclusion at Harvard, Yale, and Princeton* (New York: Mariner Books, 2006).

13. Faye J. Crosby and Alison M. Konrad, "Affirmative Action in Employment," *Diversity Factor* 10, no. 2 (Winter 2002): 5–9.

14. Ibid.

15. Faye J. Crosby, *Affirmative Action Is Dead; Long Live Affirmative Action* (New Haven, CT: Yale University Press, 2004), 6.

16. Faye J. Crosby, "Understanding Affirmative Action," *Basic and Applied Social Psychology* 15, no. 1–2 (1994): 13–41.

17. Crosby, *Affirmative Action Is Dead; Long Live Affirmative Action,* 5.

18. I have borrowed this phrase from Stephen Carter, who argues that when candidates of color are "too good to ignore," affirmative action programs should be unnecessary. See Stephen Carter, *Reflections of an Affirmative Action Baby* (New York: Basic Books, 1991).

19. For a discussion of the American preference for process-oriented affirmative action, see Crosby, *Affirmative Action Is Dead; Long Live Affirmative Action,* chap. 3.

20. Marianne Bertrand and Sendhil Mullainathan, "Are Emily and Greg More Employable Than Lakisha and Jamal? A Field Experiment on Labor Market Discrimination," *American Economic Review* 94, no. 4 (September 2004): 991–1013.

21. Devah Pager, "The Mark of a Criminal Record," *American Journal of Sociology* 108, no. 5 (March 2003): 937–975.

22. Devah Pager, Bruce Western, and Bart Bonikowski, "Discrimination in a Low-Wage Labor Market: A Field Experiment," *American Sociological Review* 74 (2009): 777–799.

23. Ibid., 787.

24. John F. Dovidio, Jeffrey Mann, and Samuel L. Gaertner, "Resistance to Affirmative Action: The Implications of Aversive Racism," in Blanchard and Crosby, *Affirmative Action in Perspective,* 86.

25. John F. Dovidio and Samuel L. Gaertner, "Aversive Racism," *Advances in Experimental Social Psychology* 36 (2004), 4.

26. Ibid., 17.

27. Ibid., 18.

28. This description of the IAT is taken from the Project Implicit website's "Frequently Asked Questions" section, https://implicit.harvard.edu/implicit/faqs.html#faq2.

29. Mahzarin R. Banaji and Anthony G. Greenwald, *Blindspot: Hidden Biases of Good People* (New York: Random House Publishing Group. 2013), Kindle edition, locations 707–710.

30. Ibid., locations 729–732.

31. Ibid., locations 755–758.

32. Institute of Medicine, *Unequal Treatment: Confronting Racial and Ethnic Disparities in Healthcare* (Washington, DC: National Academy of Sciences, 2002).

33. Banaji and Greenwald, *Blindspot,* locations 2386–2398.

34. Ibid., locations 2976–2977.

35. Ibid., locations 3083–3091

36. See "Frequently Asked Questions," Project Implicit, https://implicit.harvard.edu/implicit/faqs.html. Retrieved January 18, 2017.

37. Eduardo Bonilla-Silva, *Racism Without Racists: Color-Blind Racism and the Persistence of Racial Inequality in America,* 4th ed. (Lanham, MD: Rowman and Littlefield, 2014), 3.

38. Ruth Frankenberg, *White Women, Race Matters: The Social Construction of Whiteness* (Minneapolis: University of Minneapolis Press, 1993).

39. Helen Neville, Miguel Gallardo, and Derald Wing Sue, eds., *The Myth of Racial Color Blindness: Manifestations, Dynamics and Impact* (Washington, DC: American Psychological Association, 2016,) Kindle edition, locations 216–218.

40. Ibid., locations 247–248.

41. Ian Haney López, *Dog Whistle Politics: How Coded Racial Appeals Have Reinvented Racism and Wrecked the Middle Class* (New York: Oxford University Press, 2014), 137.

42. Lee Anne Bell, "Telling on Racism: Developing a Race-Conscious Agenda," in Neville, Gallardo, and Wing Sue, *The Myth of Racial Color Blindness,* locations 2297–2298.

43. John F. Dovidio, "Changing the Course of Race Relations in America: From Prevention of Discrimination to Promotion of Racial Equality," in *Obama on Our Minds: The Impact of Obama on the Psyche of America,* ed. Lori A. Barker (New York: Oxford University Press, 2016), 103.

44. Drew DeSilver, "Supreme Court Says States Can Ban Affirmative Action; 8 Already Have," *Fact Tank,* Pew Research Center, April 22, 2014, http://www .pewresearch.org/fact-tank/2014/04/22/supreme-court-says-states-can-ban-affirmative -action-8-already-have/.

45. Scott E. Page, *The Difference: How the Power of Diversity Creates Better Groups, Firms, Schools, and Societies* (Princeton, NJ: Princeton University Press, 2007).

46. Crosby, *Affirmative Action Is Dead; Long Live Affirmative Action,* 112.

47. For a discussion of how the concept of aversive racism might apply to discriminatory treatment of Hispanics, see John. F. Dovidio et al., "Cognitive and Motivational Bases of Bias: Implications of Aversive Racism for Attitudes Toward Hispanics," in *Hispanics in the Workplace,* ed. Stephen B. Knouse, Paul Rosenfeld, and Amy L. Culbertson (Newbury Park, CA: Sage, 1992), 75–106. For a discussion of affirmative action as it relates to other groups, see George E. Curry, ed., *The Affirmative Action Debate,* chap. 5, "Beyond Black and White" (Reading, MA: Addison-Wesley, 1996).

48. Audrey J. Murrell et al., "Aversive Racism and Resistance to Affirmative Action: Perceptions of Justice Are Not Necessarily Color Blind," *Basic and Applied Social Psychology* 15, no. 1–2 (1994): 81.

49. Of course the evaluation of scores on such standardized tests as the SAT and the GRE must be done with the understanding that the predictive validity of such tests varies among racial and gender groups. For an interesting investigation of the impact of racial variables on test performance, see Claude M. Steele and Joshua Aronson, "Stereotype Threat and the Intellectual Test Performance of African-Americans," *Journal of Personality and Social Psychology* 69, no. 5 (1995): 797–811.

50. Fletcher A. Blanchard, "Effective Affirmative Action Programs," in Blanchard and Crosby, *Affirmative Action in Perspective,* 193–207.

51. See the prologue for discussion of the most recent Supreme Court rulings regarding affirmative action and college admissions.

52. Faye J. Crosby, "Confessions of an Affirmative Action Mama," in Fine et al., *Off White,* 185.

## Chapter 8: Critical Issues in Latinx, Native, Asian and Pacific Islander, and Middle Eastern / North African Identity Development

1. Sonia Nieto and Patty Bode, *Affirming Diversity: The Sociopolitical Context of Multicultural Education,* 6th ed. (Boston: Allyn & Bacon, 2012), 250.

2. *Skin Deep: College Students Confront Racism,* produced and directed by Frances Reid (San Francisco: Resolution/California Newsreel, 1995), video.

3. Ibid.

4. Amani Al-Khatahtbeh, *Muslim Girl: A Coming of Age* (New York: Simon & Schuster, 2016), Kindle edition, location 36.

5. An excellent source for a multicultural history of these and other groups in the United States is Ronald Takaki, *A Different Mirror: A History of Multicultural America* (Boston: Little, Brown, 1993).

6. Jean Phinney, "A Three-Stage Model of Ethnic Identity Development in Adolescence," in *Ethnic Identity: Formation and Transmission Among Hispanics and Other Minorities*, ed. Martha E. Bernal and George P. Knight (Albany: State University of New York Press, 1993), 61–79.

7. An excellent source for detailed discussions of identity development for these and other groups is Joseph G. Ponterotto et al., eds., *Handbook of Multicultural Counseling* (Thousand Oaks, CA: Sage, 1995). Subsequent editions of the *Handbook* are also very helpful.

8. US Census Bureau, "Hispanic Heritage Month 2016," *Facts for Features,* October 12, 2016, https://www.census.gov/newsroom/facts-for-features/2016/cb16-ff16.html.

9. Jens Manuel Krogstad, "Key Facts About How the U.S. Hispanic Population Is Changing," *Fact Tank,* Pew Research Center, September 8, 2016, http://www.pew research.org/fact-tank/2016/09/08/key-facts-about-how-the-u-s-hispanic-population -is-changing/.

10. Renee Stepler and Anna Brown, *Statistical Portrait of Hispanics in the United States,* Pew Research Center, April 19, 2016, http://www.pewhispanic.org/2016/04/19 /statistical-portrait-of-hispanics-in-the-united-states-key-charts/.

11. Eileen Patten, *The Nation's Latino Population Is Defined by Its Youth,* Pew Research Center, April 20, 2016, http://www.pewhispanic.org/files/2016/04/PH_2016 -04-20_LatinoYouth-Final.pdf.

12. US Census Bureau, "Hispanic Heritage Month 2016."

13. Joel Spring, *Deculturalization and the Struggle for Equality: A Brief History of the Education of Dominated Cultures in the United States*, 8th ed. (New York: Routledge, 2016), 92.

14. Ibid., 95.

15. Ibid., 96.

16. Patten, *The Nation's Latino Population Is Defined by Its Youth.*

17. Seth Motel and Eileen Patten, *Hispanics of Mexican Origin in the United States, 2010: Statistical Profile,* Pew Research Center, June 27, 2012, http://www.pewhispanic .org/2012/06/27/hispanics-of-mexican-origin-in-the-united-states-2010/.

18. Roberto A. Ferdman, "The Great American Hispanic Wealth Gap," *Washington Post,* July 1, 2014, https://www.washingtonpost.com/news/wonk/wp/2014/07/01 /hispanics-make-up-more-than-16-of-the-u-s-population-but-own-less-than-2-3-of -its-wealth/?utm_term=.f2f3abfad331.

19. Spring, *Deculturalization and the Struggle for Equality,* chap. 5.

20. Nieto and Bode, *Affirming Diversity,* 179.

21. Gustavo López and Eileen Patten, *Hispanics of Puerto Rican Origin in the United States, 2013: Statistical Profile,* Pew Research Center, September 15, 2015, http://www.pew hispanic.org/2015/09/15/hispanics-of-puerto-rican-origin-in-the-united-states-2013/.

22. Eduardo Bonilla-Silva, *Racism Without Racists: Color-Blind Racism and the Persistence of Racial Inequality in America* (Lanham, MD: Rowman & Littlefield, 2014), 240.

23. US Census Bureau, "Hispanic Heritage Month 2016."

24. Gustavo López, *Hispanics of Cuban Origin in the United States, 2013: Statistical Profile,* Pew Research Center, September 15, 2015, http://www.pewhispanic.org/2015/09/15/hispanics-of-cuban-origin-in-the-united-states-2013/.

25. Gerardo Marín and Barbara VanOss Marín, *Research with Hispanic Populations* (Newbury Park, CA: Sage, 1991).

26. Sylvia Rusin, Jie Zong, and Jeanne Batalova, "Cuban Immigrants in the United States," *Migration Information Source,* Migration Policy Institute, April 7, 2015, http://www.migrationpolicy.org/article/cuban-immigrants-united-states.

27. Ibid.

28. Julie Hirschfeld Davis and Frances Robles, "Obama Ends Exemption for Cubans Who Arrive Without Visas," *New York Times,* January 12, 2017, https://nyti.ms/2ipHEc5.

29. Rusin, Zong, and Batalova, "Cuban Immigrants in the United States."

30. López, *Hispanics of Cuban Origin in the United States, 2013.*

31. Marín and Marín, *Research with Hispanic Populations.*

32. Aaron Terrazas, "Salvadoran Immigrants in the United States," *Migration Information Source,* Migration Policy Institute, January 5, 2010, http://www.migrationpolicy.org/article/salvadoran-immigrants-united-states.

33. Gustavo López, *Hispanics of Salvadoran Origin in the United States, 2013: Statistical Profile,* Pew Research Center, September 15, 2015, http://www.pewhispanic.org/2015/09/15/hispanics-of-salvadoran-origin-in-the-united-states-2013/.

34. Mark Hugo Lopez, Ana Gonzalez-Barrera, and Danielle Cuddington, *Diverse Origins: The Nation's 14 Largest Hispanic-Origin Groups,* Pew Research Center, June 19, 2013, http://www.pewhispanic.org/2013/06/19/diverse-origins-the-nations-14-largest-hispanic-origin-groups/.

35. Marie L. Miville, "Latina/o Identity Development: Updates on Theory, Measurement, and Counseling Implications," in Ponterotto et al., *Handbook of Multicultural Counseling,* 3rd ed.

36. For a discussion of *racismo* in Latino communities, see Lillian Comas-Díaz, "LatiNegra," in *The Multiracial Experience: Racial Borders as the New Frontier,* ed. Maria P. P. Root (Thousand Oaks, CA: Sage, 1996), 167–190.

37. Miguelina Germán, Nancy A. Gonzales, and Larry Dumka, "Familism Values as a Protective Factor for Mexican-Origin Adolescents Exposed to Deviant Peers," *Journal of Early Adolescence* 29, no. 1 (2009): 17.

38. Nydia Garcia-Preto, "Latino Families: An Overview," in *Ethnicity and Family Therapy,* 3rd ed., ed. Monica McGoldrick, Joe Giordano, and Nydia Garcia-Preto (New York: Guilford Press, 2005), 153–165.

39. Carola Suárez-Orozco and Marcelo Suárez-Orozco, *Transformations: Immigration, Family Life, and Achievement Motivation Among Latino Adolescents* (Stanford, CA: Stanford University Press, 1995), 136.

40. Fabio Sabogal et al., "Hispanic Familism and Acculturation: What Changes and What Doesn't?" *Hispanic Journal of Behavioral Sciences* 9, no. 4 (1987): 397–412.

41. Anthony D. Ong, Jean S. Phinney, and Jessica Dennis, "Competence Under Challenge: Exploring the Protective Influence of Parental Support and Ethnic Identity in Latino College Students," *Journal of Adolescence* 29, no. 6 (2006): 961–979; Germán, Gonzales, and Dumka, "Familism Values as a Protective Factor for Mexican-Origin Adolescents Exposed to Deviant Peers."

42. Suárez-Orozco and Suárez-Orozco, *Transformations,* 52.

43. For further discussion of these four options and their connection to Tajfel's social identity theory, see Jean S. Phinney, Bruce T. Lochner, and Rodolfo Murphy, "Ethnic Identity Development and Psychological Adjustment in Adolescence," in *Ethnic Issues in Adolescent Mental Health,* ed. Arlene Rubin Stiffman and Larry E. Davis (Newbury Park, CA: Sage, 1990), 53–72.

44. Richard Rodriguez, *Hunger of Memory: The Education of Richard Rodriguez* (New York: Bantam, 1982), 23.

45. Maria Zavala, "Who Are You If You Don't Speak Spanish? The Puerto Rican Dilemma," (presentation at the annual meeting of the American Educational Research Association, New York, April 1996).

46. Maria Zavala, "A Bridge over Divided Worlds: An Exploration into the Nature of Bilingual Puerto Rican Youths' Ethnic Identity Development" (master's thesis, Mount Holyoke College, 1995).

47. Zavala, "Who Are You If You Don't Speak Spanish?," 9.

48. Ibid.

49. Ibid., 11.

50. Edward Fergus, "The Relevance of Skin Color in the Construction of an Ethnic Identification Among Mexican and Puerto Rican Boys," in *Invisible No More: Understanding the Disenfranchisement of Latino Men and Boys,* ed. Pedro Noguera, Aída Hurtado, and Edward Fergus (New York: Routledge, 2012), 228.

51. Vasti Torres, "Influences on Ethnic Identity Development of Latino College Students in the First Two Years of College," *Journal of College Student Development* 44, no. 4 (2003), 542.

52. Ibid.

53. Mark Hugo Lopez, "Is Speaking Spanish Necessary to Be Hispanic? Most Hispanics Say No," *Fact Tank,* Pew Research Center, February 19, 2016, http://www .pewresearch.org/fact-tank/2016/02/19/is-speaking-spanish-necessary-to-be-hispanic -most-hispanics-say-no/.

54. Nieto and Bode, *Affirming Diversity,* 227.

55. Ibid., 224.

56. Ibid., 226.

57. Natalia Molina, "How Mexican-Americans Assimilate into U.S. Culture," *San Diego Union-Tribune,* November 23, 2016, http://www.sandiegouniontribune.com /opinion/commentary/sd-mexican-americans-molina-20161123-story.html.

58. Katie Reilly, "Kids Are Stressed About Donald Trump. So Los Angeles Schools Launched a Hotline," *Time,* December 8, 2016, http://time.com/4595309 /los-angeles-school-counselors-donald-trump/.

59. Jens Manuel Krogstad, Jeffrey S. Passel, and D'Vera Cohn, "5 Facts About Illegal Immigration in the U.S.," *Fact Tank,* Pew Research Center, November 3, 2016, http:// www.pewresearch.org/fact-tank/2016/11/03/5-facts-about-illegal-immigration-in -the-u-s/.

60. Jie Zong and Jeanne Batalova, "Frequently Requested Statistics on Immigrants and Immigration in the United States," *Migration Information Source,* Migration Policy Institute, April 14, 2016, http://www.migrationpolicy.org/article /frequently-requested-statistics-immigrants-and-immigration-united-states.

61. Krogstad, Passel, and Cohn, "5 Facts About Illegal Immigration in the U.S."

62. Ibid.

63. J. Manuel Casas, "Caution: Immigration May Be Harmful to Your Health," in *Handbook of Multicultural Counseling,* 4th ed., ed. J. Manuel Casas et al. (Los Angeles: Sage, 2017), 348–359.

64. Hirokazu Yoshikawa and Jenya Kholoptseva, *Unauthorized Immigrant Parents and Their Children's Development,* Migration Policy Institute, March 2013, http://www .migrationpolicy.org/research/unauthorized-immigrant-parents-and-their-childrens -development.

65. Ibid.

66. Roberto G. Gonzales, "Learning to Be Illegal: Undocumented Youth and Shifting Legal Contexts in the Transition to Adulthood," *American Sociological Review* 76, no. 4 (2011): 602–619.

67. Ibid., 605–608.

68. Ibid., 610.

69. Ibid.

70. Ibid., 605.

71. Ibid., 615.

72. Ibid., 617.

73. Jens Manuel Krogstad, "Unauthorized Immigrants Covered by DACA Face Uncertain Future," *Fact Tank,* Pew Research Center, January 5, 2017, http:// www.pewresearch.org/fact-tank/2017/01/05/unauthorized-immigrants-covered-by -daca-face-uncertain-future/.

74. Gonzales, "Learning to Be Illegal," 614.

75. Molina, "How Mexican-Americans Assimilate into U.S. Culture."

76. Lewis Lord, "How Many People Were Here Before Columbus?" *U.S. News & World Report,* August 18–25, 1997, 68–70, http://www.bxscience.edu/ourpages /auto/2009/4/5/34767803/Pre-Columbian%20population.pdf.

77. US Census Bureau, "American Indian and Alaska Native Heritage Month: November 2016," *Facts for Features,* November 2016, http://www.census.gov/content /dam/Census/newsroom/facts-for-features/2016/cb26-ff22_aian.pdf.

78. R. D. Herring, "Native American Indian Identity: A People of Many Peoples," in *Race, Ethnicity, and Self: Identity in Multicultural Perspective,* ed. Elizabeth Pathy Salett and Diane R. Koslow (Washington, DC: National MultiCultural Institute, 1994), 170–197.

79. C. Matthew Snipp, "American Indian Studies," in *Handbook on Research on Multicultural Education*, 2nd ed., ed. James A. Banks and Cherry A. McGee Banks (San Francisco: Jossey Bass, 2004), 315–331.

80. Ibid., 318.

81. K. Tsianina Lomawaima, "Educating Native Americans," in Banks and Banks, *Handbook on Research on Multicultural Education*, 442.

82. Timothy Williams, "Quietly, Indians Reshape Cities and Reservations," *New York Times*, April 13, 2013, http://www.nytimes.com/2013/04/14/us/as-american-indians-move-to-cities-old-and-new-challenges-follow.html.

83. "2010 Census Shows Nearly Half of American Indians and Alaska Natives Report Multiple Races" (press release), US Census Bureau, January 25, 2012, https://www.census.gov/newsroom/releases/archives/2010_census/cb12-cn06.html.

84. US Census Bureau, "American Indian and Alaska Native Heritage Month: November 2016."

85. CharlesEtta T. Sutton and Mary Anne Broken Nose, "American Indian Families: An Overview," in McGoldrick, Giordano, and Garcia-Preto, *Ethnicity and Family Therapy*, 43–54.

86. Spring, *Deculturalization and the Struggle for Equality*, 13.

87. Nadine Tafoya and Ann Del Vecchio, "Back to the Future: An Examination of the Native American Holocaust Experience," in McGoldrick, Giordano, and Garcia-Preto, *Ethnicity and Family Therapy*, 55–64.

88. Spring, *Deculturalization and the Struggle for Equality*, 119–120.

89. Sutton and Broken Nose, "American Indian Families," 46; Snipp, "American Indian Studies," 322.

90. Tafoya and Del Vecchio, "Back to the Future." Note that a shorter version of this quote appears in the third edition. However, I am using the longer version that appeared in the 1996 edition of *Ethnicity and Family Therapy*.

91. Spring, *Deculturalization and the Struggle for Equality*, 120.

92. See "History," Diné College, http://www.dinecollege.edu/about/history.php.

93. Kevin K. Washburn, "What's at Stake for Tribes? The U.S. Department of Justice Office of Legal Counsel Opinion on Internet Gaming, Testimony of Dean Kevin K. Washburn, Oversight Hearing Before the United States Senate Committee on Indian Affairs, 112th Congress, Second Session," UNM School of Law Research Paper No. 2012-04, February 9, 2012, https://papers.ssrn.com/sol3/papers.cfm?abstract_id=1999813.

94. Indian Gaming Regulatory Act, 25 U.S.C. § 2701 et seq. (1988).

95. Washburn, "What's at Stake for Tribes?"

96. Robin J. Anderson, "Tribal Casino Impacts on American Indians' Well-Being: Evidence from Reservation-Level Census Data," *Contemporary Economic Policy* 31, no. 2 (2013): 291–300, doi: 10.1111/j.1465-7287.2011.00300.x.

97. Matthew A. King, "Indian Gaming and Native Identity," *Chicano-Latino Law Review* 30, no. 1 (2011), https://ssrn.com/abstract=2018751.

98. Ibid., 18.

99. Ibid., 32.

100. "Have You Ever Seen a Real Indian? American Indian College Fund Advertising Campaign Challenges Stereotypes" (press release), American Indian College Fund, *PRNewswire*, March 2, 2001, http://www.prnewswire.com/news-releases/have-you-ever-seen-a-real-indian-american-indian-college-fund-advertising-campaign-challenges-stereotypes-71520017.html.

101. Lee Little Soldier, "Is There an 'Indian' in Your Classroom? Working Successfully with Urban Native American Students," *Phi Delta Kappan* 78, no. 8 (April 1997): 650–653.

102. Donald Andrew Grinde Jr., "Place and Kinship: A Native American's Identity Before and After Words," in *Names We Call Home: Autobiography on Racial Identity*, ed. Becky Thompson and Sangeeta Tyagi (New York: Routledge, 1996), 66.

103. Nieto and Bode, *Affirming Diversity*, 152.

104. Stephanie A. Fryberg et al., "Of Warrior Chiefs and Indian Princesses: The Psychological Consequences of American Indian Mascots," *Basic and Applied Social Psychology* 30, no 3 (2008): 208–218.

105. Angela R. Riley and Kristen A. Carpenter, "Owning *Red*: A Theory of Indian (Cultural) Appropriation," *Texas Law Review* 94 (2016): 859–931.

106. Victoria Phillips and Erik Stegman, *Missing the Point: The Real Impact of Native Mascots and Team Names on American Indian and Alaska Native Youth* (Washington, DC: Center for American Progress, 2014), http://digitalcommons.wcl.american.edu/cgi/viewcontent.cgi?article=1003&context=fasch_rpt.

107. "Statement of U.S. Commission on Civil Rights on the Use of Native American Images and Nicknames as Sports Symbols" (press release), US Commission on Civil Rights, 2001, http://www.usccr.gov/press/archives/2001/041601st.htm.

108. Phillips and Stegman, *Missing the Point*.

109. Ibid., 5.

110. Ibid., 8.

111. Fryberg et al., "Of Warrior Chiefs and Indian Princesses," 216.

112. Ibid.

113. Nieto and Bode, *Affirming Diversity*, 70–72.

114. Paul Ongtooguk, "Remarks of Mr. Paul Ongtooguk," Alaska Native Education Summit, November 30, 2001, Anchorage, AK. http://www.alaskool.org/native_ed/PO-ANES-speech.htm.

115. Paul Ongtooguk, "Their Silence About Us: The Absence of Alaska Natives in the Curriculum" (presentation at the annual meeting of the American Educational Research Association, Atlanta, GA, April 1993).

116. Ibid.

117. Elizabeth M. Hoeffel et al., *The Asian Population: 2010*, C2010BR-11, US Census Bureau, March 2012, https://www.census.gov/prod/cen2010/briefs/c2010br-11.pdf.

118. Evelyn Lee and Matthew R. Mock, "Asian Families: An Overview," in McGoldrick, Giordano, and Garcia-Preto, *Ethnicity and Family Therapy*, 269–289.

119. Min Zhou and Jennifer Lee, "Introduction: The Making of Culture, Identity, and Ethnicity Among Asian American Youth," in *Asian American Youth: Culture, Identity and Ethnicity* (New York: Routledge, 2004), 11.

120. Min Zhou and Jennifer Lee, *The Asian American Achievement Paradox* (New York: Russell Sage Foundation, 2015).

121. Pew Research Center, *The Rise of Asian Americans,* updated ed., April 4, 2013, http://www.pewsocialtrends.org/2012/06/19/the-rise-of-asian-americans/.

122. Hoeffel et al., *The Asian Population: 2010.*

123. US Census Bureau, "Asian/Pacific American Heritage Month: May 2016," *Facts for Features,* April 21, 2016, http://www.census.gov/newsroom/facts-for-features/2016/cb16-ff07.html.

124. Pew Research Center, *The Rise of Asian Americans.*

125. Ibid.

126. Spring, *Deculturalization and the Struggle for Equality,* 72.

127. Ibid.

128. Zhou and Lee, *The Asian American Achievement Paradox,* 23.

129. Takaki, *A Different Mirror,* 188.

130. Zhou and Lee, *The Asian American Achievement Paradox.*

131. Spring, *Deculturalization and the Struggle for Equality,* 76.

132. Zhou and Lee, *The Asian American Achievement Paradox,* 24.

133. Ibid.

134. Tazuko Shibusawa, "Japanese Families," in McGoldrick, Giordano, and Garcia-Preto, *Ethnicity and Family Therapy,* 339–348.

135. Spring, *Deculturalization and the Struggle for Equality,* chap. 4.

136. Shibusawa, "Japanese Families."

137. Pew Research Center, *The Rise of Asian Americans.*

138. Bok-Lim C. Kim and Eunjung Ryu, "Korean Families," in McGoldrick, Giordano, and Garcia-Preto, *Ethnicity and Family Therapy,* 349–362.

139. Pew Research Center, *The Rise of Asian Americans.*

140. Ibid.

141. Maria P. P. Root, "Filipino Families," in McGoldrick, Giordano, and Garcia-Preto, *Ethnicity and Family Therapy,* 319–331.

142. Lee and Mock, "Asian Families: An Overview," 271.

143. Pew Research Center, *The Rise of Asian Americans.*

144. Ibid.

145. Quoted in Spring, *Deculturalization and the Struggle for Equality,* 75.

146. Ibid., 77.

147. Pew Research Center, *The Rise of Asian Americans.*

148. Migration Policy Institute, *The Pakistani Diaspora in the United States,* rev. ed., June 2015, www.migrationpolicy.org/sites/default/files/publications/RAD-Pakistan.pdf.

149. Karthick Ramakrishnan and Farah Z. Ahmad, *State of Asian Americans and Pacific Islanders Series: A Multifaceted Portrait of a Growing Population,* Center for American Progress, September 2014, http://aapidata.com/wp-content/uploads/2015/10/AAPIData-CAP-report.pdf.

150. US Census Bureau, "Asian/Pacific American Heritage Month: May 2016."

151. Quoted in David Mura, "A Shift in Power, a Sea Change in the Arts: Asian American Constructions," in *The State of Asian America: Activism and Resistance in the 1990s,* ed. Karin Aguilar-San Juan (Boston: South End Press, 1994), 183–204.

152. Kenyon S. Chan and Shirley Hune, "Racialization and Panethnicity: From Asians in America to Asian Americans," in *Toward a Common Destiny: Improving Race and Ethnic Relations in America,* ed. Willis D. Hawley and Anthony W. Jackson (San Francisco: Jossey-Bass, 1995), 210.

153. Ibid., 215.

154. Ibid., 218.

155. *Skin Deep.*

156. William Petersen, "Success Story, Japanese-American Style," *New York Times Magazine,* January 9, 1966; "Success Story of One Minority in the U.S.," *U.S. News and World Report,* December 26, 1966, 73–78.

157. Chan and Hune, "Racialization and Panethnicity," 222.

158. Zhou and Lee, *The Asian American Achievement Paradox,* 65.

159. Ibid.

160. Ibid., 31.

161. Ibid., 32.

162. Ibid., 29.

163. Ibid., 9.

164. Ibid., 37.

165. Ibid., 6.

166. Ibid.

167. Ibid., 125.

168. Ibid., 126.

169. Ibid., 120.

170. Ibid., 7.

171. Ibid., 143.

172. Ibid., 172.

173. Ibid., 174.

174. Ibid., 42.

175. National Center for Education Statistics, "Indicator 16 Snapshot: High School Status Dropout Rates for Racial/Ethnic Subgroups," August 2016, https://nces.ed.gov /programs/raceindicators/indicator_rdcs.asp.

176. National Center for Education Statistics, "Indicator 18 Snapshot: College Participation Rates for Racial/Ethnic Subgroups," August 2016, https://nces.ed.gov/programs /raceindicators/indicator_reas.asp.

177. Lisa Delpit, *Other People's Children: Cultural Conflict in the Classroom* (New York: The New Press, 2006), 171.

178. Nieto and Bode, *Affirming Diversity,* 195.

179. Valerie Ooka Pang, Peter N. Kiang, and Yoon K. Pak, "Asian Pacific American Students: Challenging a Biased Educational System," in J. A. Banks and C. M. Banks, *Handbook on Research on Multicultural Education,* 542–563.

180. Mitsuye Yamada, "Invisibility Is an Unnatural Disaster: Reflections of an Asian American Woman," in *This Bridge Called My Back: Writings by Radical Women of Color,* ed. Cherríe Moraga and Gloria Anzaldúa (New York: Kitchen Table Press, 1981), 35–40.

181. Ibid., 35.

182. Peter Nien-chu Kiang, "We Could Shape It: Organizing for Asian Pacific American Student Empowerment," in *Struggling to Be Heard: The Unmet Needs of APA Children*, ed. Valerie Ooka Pang and Li-Rong Lilly Cheng (Albany: State University of New York Press, 1998), 243–264.

183. Ibid., 249.

184. Ibid., 259.

185. Ibid.

186. Ibid.

187. Lucy Tse, "Finding a Place to Be: Asian Americans in Ethnic Identity Exploration," *Adolescence* 34, no. 133 (Spring 1999): 121–138.

188. Traci G. Lee, "Gangs of Atlanta: New Film Upends Asian 'Model Minority Myth,'" NBCNews.com, March 11, 2015, http://www.nbcnews.com/news/asian-america/gangs -atlanta-new-film-upends-asian-model-minority-myth-n321421.

189. Ibid.

190. Chan and Hune, "Racialization and Panethnicity," 208.

191. Phinney, "A Three-Stage Model of Ethnic Identity Development in Adolescence."

192. Tara Bahrampour, "A U.S. Census Proposal to Add Category for People of Middle Eastern Descent Makes Some Uneasy," *Washington Post*, October 21, 2016, https:// www.washingtonpost.com/local/social-issues/a-proposal-to-add-a-us-census-category -for-people-of-middle-eastern-descent-makes-some-uneasy/2016/10/20/8e9847a0 -960e-11e6-bb29-bf2701dbe0a3_story.html.

193. Ibid.

194. Nuha Abudabbeh, "Arab Families: An Overview," in McGoldrick, Giordano, and Garcia-Preto, *Ethnicity and Family Therapy*, 423–436.

195. Jie Zong and Jeanne Batalova, "Middle Eastern and North African Immigrants in the United States," *Migration Information Source*, Migration Policy Institute, June 3, 2015, http://www.migrationpolicy.org/article/middle-eastern-and-north -african-immigrants-united-states.

196. Ibid.

197. Ibid.

198. "American Muslims in the United States," Teaching Tolerance, Southern Poverty Law Center, http://www.tolerance.org/publication/american-muslims-united-states

199. Eboo Patel, introduction to Andrew Garrod and Robert Kilkenny, eds., *Growing Up Muslim: Muslim College Students in America Tell Their Life Stories* (Ithaca, NY: Cornell University Press, 2014), Kindle edition, location 148.

200. Ibid., location 490.

201. Ibid., location 1418.

202. Amir Marvasti and Karyn D. McKinney, *Middle Eastern Lives in America* (Lanham, MD: Rowman and Little, 2004).

203. Al-Khatahtbeh, *Muslim Girl,* location 36.

204. Ibid., location 241.

205. Ibid., location 261.

206. Ibid., location 503.

207. Ibid., location 506.

208. Ibid., location 518.

209. Ibid., location 542.

210. Ibid., location 985.

211. Ibid., location 998.

212. Garrod and Kilkenny, *Growing Up Muslim,* location 501.

213. Ibid., location 582.

214. Eric Lichtblau, "U.S. Hate Crimes Surge 6%, Fueled by Attacks on Muslims," *New York Times,* November 14, 2016, https://nyti.ms/2ezOFXH.

215. Al-Khatahtbeh, *Muslim Girl,* location 1451.

216. Peter Baker, "Travelers Stranded and Protests Swell over Trump Order," *New York Times,* January 29, 2017, https://nyti.ms/2jFy45B.

217. Al-Khatahtbeh, *Muslim Girl,* location 1433.

## Chapter 9: Identity Development in Multiracial Families

1. Pew Research Center, *Multiracial in America: Proud, Diverse and Growing in Numbers,* June 2015, http://www.pewsocialtrends.org/2015/06/11/multiracial-in-america/.

2. Charmaine L. Wijeyesinghe, "The Intersectional Model of Multiracial Identity: Integrating Multiracial Identity Theories and Intersectional Perspectives on Social Identity," in *New Perspectives on Racial Identity Development: Integrating Emerging Frameworks,* 2nd ed., ed. Charmaine L. Wijeyesinghe and Bailey W. Jackson III (New York: New York University Press, 2012), 81–107.

3. Charles A. Gallagher, "Color Blindness: An Obstacle to Racial Justice?," in *Mixed Messages: Multiracial Identities in the "Color-Blind" Era,* ed. David L. Brunsma (Boulder, CO: Lynne Rienner Publishers, 2006), 103–116.

4. Maria P. P. Root, ed., *Racially Mixed People in America* (Thousand Oaks, CA: Sage, 1992).

5. This chapter will be focused primarily on biracial Black-White identity development. For information regarding Black-Japanese identity, see Christine Catherine Iijima Hall, "The Ethnic Identity of Racially Mixed People: A Study of Black-Japanese" (doctoral dissertation, University of California, Los Angeles, 1980). For information regarding Asian-White experiences, see George Kitahara Kich, "The Developmental Process of Asserting a Biracial, Bicultural Identity," in Root, *Racially Mixed People in America,* 304–317.

6. Maria P. P. Root, "Within, Between, and Beyond Race," in Root, *Racially Mixed People in America,* 3–11.

7. Paul R. Spickard, "The Illogic of American Racial Categories," in Root, *Racially Mixed People in America,* 15.

8. See F. James Davis, chap. 1, "The Nation's Rule," and chap. 2, "Miscegenation and Beliefs," in *Who Is Black? One Nation's Definition* (University Park: Pennsylvania State University Press, 1991), 17–30.

9. Kerry Ann Rockquemore and David L. Brunsma, *Beyond Black: Biracial Identity in America* (Lanham, MD: Rowman & Littlefield, 2008), 18.

10. Lise Funderberg, *Black, White, Other: Biracial Americans Talk About Race and Identity* (New York: Quill, 1994), 186.

11. Davis, *Who Is Black?*, 12.

12. For more details, see Davis, *Who Is Black?*, 10–11.

13. Rockquemore and Brunsma, *Beyond Black*, Kindle edition, location 91.

14. Frank Newport, "In U.S., 87% Approve of Black-White Marriage, vs. 4% in 1958," Gallup, July 25, 2013, http://www.gallup.com/poll/163697/approve-marriage-blacks-whites.aspx.

15. Pew Research Center, chap. 4 of *The Rise of Asian Americans*, updated ed., April 4, 2013, http://www.pewsocialtrends.org/2012/06/19/the-rise-of-asian-americans/.

16. Newport, "In U.S., 87% Approve of Black-White Marriage, vs. 4% in 1958."

17. Erica Chito Childs, "Black and White: Family Opposition to Becoming Multiracial," in Brunsma, *Mixed Messages*, 233–246.

18. *Imitation of Life* was released in 1934 and remade in 1959. It follows the lives of two women, one White and one Black, and their daughters. The Black mother is heartbroken when her light-skinned daughter disavows her and chooses to pass for White.

19. Jewelle Taylor Gibbs, "Biracial Adolescents," in *Children of Color: Psychological Interventions with Minority Youth*, ed. Jewelle Taylor Gibbs and Larke Nahme Huang (San Francisco: Jossey-Bass, 1989), 322–350.

20. Ana Mari Cauce et al., "Between a Rock and a Hard Place: Social Adjustment of Biracial Youth," in Root, *Racially Mixed People in America*, 207–222.

21. Ibid., 220.

22. For a review of the 1980s and 1990s literature, see Jewelle Taylor Gibbs and Alice M. Hines, "Negotiating Ethnic Identity: Issues for Black-White Biracial Adolescents," in Root, *Racially Mixed People in America*, 223–238. See also Lynda D. Field, "Piecing Together the Puzzle: Self-Concept and Group Identity in Biracial Black/White Youth," in *The Multiracial Experience: Racial Borders as the New Frontier*, ed. Maria P. P. Root (Thousand Oaks, CA: Sage, 1996), 211–226.

23. Rockquemore and Brunsma, *Beyond Black*, 36.

24. Ibid., 39.

25. Ibid.

26. Maria P. P. Root, "The Multiracial Experience: Racial Borders as a Significant Frontier in Race Relations," in Root, *The Multiracial Experience*, xiii–xxviii.

27. Rockquemore and Brunsma, *Beyond Black*.

28. Ibid., 41.

29. Ibid.

30. Ibid., 43.

31. Ibid., 44.

32. Ibid., 45.

33. Ibid., 47.

34. Ibid., 69.

35. Ibid., 95.

36. Ibid., 49.

37. Ibid., 49–50.

38. Ibid., 60.

39. Ibid.

40. Nikki Khanna, *Biracial in America: Forming and Performing Racial Identity* (Lanham, MD: Lexington Books, 2011).

41. Ibid., 82.

42. Ibid., 75.

43. Ibid., 85.

44. See Maureen T. Reddy, *Crossing the Color Line: Race, Parenting, and Culture* (New Brunswick, NJ: Rutgers University Press, 1994), chap. 3.

45. Robin Lin Miller and Mary-Jane Rotheram-Borus, "Growing Up Biracial in the United States," in *Race, Ethnicity, and Self: Identity in Multicultural Perspective,* ed. Elizabeth Pathy Salett and Diane R. Koslow (Washington, DC: National Multicultural Institute, 1994), 143–169.

46. Khanna, *Biracial in America,* 85.

47. Ibid., 88.

48. Ibid., 100.

49. Ibid., 109.

50. Ibid., 104.

51. Ibid., 111.

52. Kerry Ann Rockquemore, Tracy Laszloffy, and Julia Noveske, "It All Starts at Home: Racial Socialization in Multiracial Families," in Brunsma, *Mixed Messages,* 206.

53. Wendy Wang, "Interracial Marriage: Who Is 'Marrying Out'?," *Fact Tank,* Pew Research Center, June 12, 2015, http://www.pewresearch.org/fact-tank/2015/06/12/interracial-marriage-who-is-marrying-out/.

54. Rockquemore, Laszloffy, and Noveske, "It All Starts at Home."

55. Miller and Rotheram-Borus, "Growing Up Biracial in the United States."

56. Even when White people are demeaned as "nigger lovers," it is the association with Blackness that is the source of the insult, not Whiteness itself.

57. Miller and Rotheram-Borus, "Growing Up Biracial in the United States," 156.

58. Marguerite Davol, *Black, White, Just Right!* (Morton Grove, IL: A. Whitman, 1993).

59. Rockquemore, Laszloffy, and Noveske, "It All Starts at Home," 210.

60. Funderburg, *Black, White, Other,* 367.

61. Karen Valby, "The Realities of Raising a Kid of a Different Race," Time.com, 2015, http://time.com/the-realities-of-raising-a-kid-of-a-different-race/.

62. Danielle E. Godon, Whitney F. Green, and Patricia G. Ramsey, "Transracial Adoptees: The Search for Birth Family and the Search for Self," *Adoption Quarterly* 17, no. 1 (2014): 1–27.

63. Ibid., 14.

64. Ibid., 17.

65. Ibid.

66. Valby, "The Realities of Raising a Kid of a Different Race."

67. Ibid.

68. Ibid.

69. Ibid.

70. "Growing Up 'White,' Transracial Adoptee Learned to Be Black," *Weekend Edition Sunday*, NPR, January 26, 2014, http://www.npr.org/2014/01/26/266434175/growing-up-white-transracial-adoptee-learned-to-be-black.

71. Ibid.

## Chapter 10: Embracing a Cross-Racial Dialogue

1. In the same way, we need to break the silence about sexism, anti-Semitism, heterosexism and homophobia, classism, ageism, and ableism. In my experience, once we learn to break the silence about one ism, the lessons learned transfer to other isms.

2. Christine Sleeter, "White Racism," *Multicultural Education* 1, no. 4 (Spring 1994): 6.

3. Ibid., 8.

4. Kirsten Mullen, "Subtle Lessons in Racism," *USA Weekend*, November 6–8, 1992, 10–11.

5. *The Color of Fear*, produced and directed by Lee Mun Wah (Oakland, CA: Stir-Fry Productions, 1994), video.

6. Jean Baker Miller, "Connections, Disconnections, and Violations," *Work in Progress*, no. 33 (Wellesley, MA: Stone Center Working Paper Series, 1988).

7. Beverly Daniel Tatum, "Racial Identity and Relational Theory: The Case of Black Women in White Communities," *Work in Progress*, no. 63 (Wellesley, MA: Stone Center Working Paper Series, 1992).

8. An in-depth discussion of the relational implications of working against racism for these female educators can be found in Beverly Daniel Tatum and Elizabeth G. Knaplund, "Outside the Circle: The Relational Implications for White Women Working Against Racism," *Work in Progress*, no. 78 (Wellesley, MA: Stone Center Working Paper Series, 1996).

9. Parker Palmer, *The Active Life: Wisdom for Work, Creativity, and Caring* (New York: HarperCollins, 1990), 115.

## Epilogue: Signs of Hope, Sites of Progress

1. "A Statement from Joseph Benigno '16 Student Body President," TAMU Student Government Association, February 11, 2016, https://www.youtube.com/watch?v=Yo9sZlmdzBU.

2. See https://www.atlantafriendshipinitiative.com for more information.

3. Maria Saporta, "Business Leaders Launch Atlanta Friendship Initiative," *Atlanta Business Chronicle*, October 28, 2016, http://www.bizjournals.com/atlanta/news/2016/10/28/business-leaders-launch-atlanta-friendship.html.

4. See www.twotowns.org for more information.

5. See www.winterinstitute.org for more information.

6. Barry Yeoman, "Telling Stories, Breaking Barriers," *Mindful*, August 11, 2016, 58.

7. Ibid., 62.

8. See http://winterinstitute.org/community-relations/the-welcome-table/ for a video interview with Dr. Glisson.

9. See http://www.racialequityresourceguide.org/TRHTSummit for more information and a resource guide.

10. La June Montgomery Tabron, "The W. K. Kellogg Foundation's Deepening Commitment to Racial Equity," *Liberal Education* 102, no. 4 (Fall 2016): 22–45.

11. Ibid., 28.

12. Gail C. Christopher, "The Time for Truth, Racial Healing and Transformation Is Now," *Liberal Education* 102, no. 4 (Fall 2016): 8–15.

13. "Day of Dialogue Welcome Ceremony," fandmcollege, October 6, 2016, https://www.youtube.com/watch?v=-azgbWIWFjk.

14. See http://www.difficultdialogues.org for more information.

15. "Mission, History, Goals & Highlights," Michigan Community Scholars Program, University of Michigan, https://lsa.umich.edu/mcsp/about-us/mission-history-goals-highlights.html.

16. David Schoem and Penny A. Pasque, "The Michigan Community Scholars Program: Engaging the Whole of Service-Learning, Diversity, and Learning Communities," in Joseph A. Galura et al., *Engaging the Whole of Service-Learning, Diversity, and Learning Communities* (Ann Arbor, MI: OCSL Press at the University of Michigan, 2004), 33–50.

17. Rebecca Dora Christensen, "'Making a Difference': Residential Learning Community Students' Trajectories Toward Promoting Social Justice" (doctoral dissertation, University of Michigan, 2016).

18. See https://igr.umich.edu/about for more information.

19. Ximena Zúñiga et al., *Intergroup Dialogue in Higher Education: Meaningful Learning About Social Justice,* ASHE Higher Education Report Series, vol. 32, no. 4 (San Francisco, CA: Jossey-Bass, 2007).

20. "Intergroup Dialogues," The Program on Intergroup Relations, University of Michigan, https://igr.umich.edu/article/intergroup-dialogues.

21. Kelly E. Maxwell, Aaron Traxler-Ballew, and K. Foula Dimopoulos, "Intergroup Dialogue and the Michigan Community Scholars Program: A Partnership for Meaningful Engagement," in Galura et al., *Engaging the Whole of Service-Learning, Diversity, and Learning Communities,* 122.

22. "Students Talk About the Minor in Intergroup Relations Education," The Program on Intergroup Relations, University of Michigan, https://igr.umich.edu/article/students-talk-about-minor-intergroup-relations.

23. "Reflections from IGR's Graduate Student Instructors," The Program on Intergroup Relations, University of Michigan, https://igr.umich.edu/article/reflections-igrs-graduate-student-instructors.

24. Kristie A. Ford, ed., *Facilitating Change Through Intergroup Dialogue: Social Justice Advocacy in Practice* (New York: Routledge, forthcoming), chap. 1.

25. Ibid., chap. 2.

26. Ibid.

27. I am paraphrasing the quote "I touch the future. I teach," which is attributed to Christa McAuliffe, the first American educator selected to travel to outer space on a NASA mission in 1986. Tragically, the space vessel exploded shortly after liftoff and she and the other astronauts on board were killed.

# BIBLIOGRAPHY

Abudabbeh, Nuha. "Arab Families: An Overview." In McGoldrick, Giordano, and Garcia-Preto, *Ethnicity and Family Therapy*, 423–436.

Adams-Bass, Valerie, Keisha L. Bentley-Edwards, and Howard C. Stevenson. "That's Not Me I See on TV . . . : African American Youth Interpret Media Images of Black Females." *Women, Gender and Families of Color* 2, no. 1 (Spring 2014): 79–100.

Alba, Richard. *Ethnic Identity: The Transformation of White America.* New Haven, CT: Yale University Press, 1990.

Alderfer, Clayton P. "A White Man's Perspective on the Unconscious Process Within Black-White Relations in the United States." In *Human Diversity,* edited by Edison J. Trickett, Roderick J. Watts, and Dina Birman, 201–229. San Francisco: Jossey-Bass, 1994.

Alexander, Michelle. *The New Jim Crow.* New York: The New Press, 2010.

Al-Khatahtbeh, Amani. *Muslim Girl: A Coming of Age.* New York: Simon & Schuster, 2016, Kindle edition.

Allen, Walter R. "The Color of Success: African-American College Student Outcomes at Predominantly White and Historically Black Public Colleges and Universities." *Harvard Educational Review* 62, no. 1 (1992): 26–44.

Allen, Walter R., Edgar G. Epps, and Nesha Z. Haniff, eds. *College in Black and White: African American Students in Predominantly White and in Historically Black Public Universities.* Albany: State University of New York Press, 1991.

"Alternative Right." Southern Poverty Law Center. https://www.splcenter.org/fighting -hate/extremist-files/ideology/alternative-right.

Alvarez, Lizette, and Richard Pérez-Peña. "Orlando Gunman Attacks Gay Nightclub, Leaving 50 Dead." *New York Times,* June 12, 2016. http://nyti.ms/28u5TJ6.

"American Muslims in the United States." Teaching Tolerance, Southern Poverty Law Center. http://www.tolerance.org/publication/american-muslims-united-states.

Amherst College Demands. November 12, 2015. Retrieved from http://www.the demands.org/.

Amherst Uprising. "A Letter of Clarification for Amherst Alumni, Family and Friends." November 15, 2015. http://amherstuprising.com/demands.html.

Anderson, Carol. *White Rage: The Unspoken Truth of Our Racial Divide.* New York: Bloomsbury, 2016.

Anderson, Joel. "Ferguson's Angry Young Men." *BuzzFeed*, August 22, 2014. http://www .buzzfeed.com/joelanderson/who-are-fergusons-young-protestors?utm_term= .mvqJZa3Wm#.ee3apJ4dO.

Anderson, Robin J. "Tribal Casino Impacts on American Indians' Well-Being: Evidence from Reservation-Level Census Data." *Contemporary Economic Policy,* 31, no. 2 (2013): 291–300. doi: 10.1111/j/1465-7287.2011.00300.x.

Apuzzo, Matt, Michael S. Schmidt, and Adam Goldman. "Emails Warrant No New Action Against Hillary Clinton, F.B.I. Director Says." *New York Times,* November 6, 2016. http://nyti.ms/2edtN8v.

Aronson, Joshua, ed. *Improving Academic Achievement: Impact of Psychological Factors on Education.* San Diego: Academic, 2002.

Aronson, Joshua, Carrie B. Fried, and Catherine Good. "Reducing the Effects of Stereotype Threat on African American College Students by Shaping Theories of Intelligence." *Journal of Experimental Social Psychology* 38, no. 2 (2002): 1–13.

Ayvazian, Andrea. "Interrupting the Cycle of Oppression: The Role of Allies as Agents of Change." *Fellowship*, January/February 1995, 7–10.

Azmitia, Margarita, Moin Syed, and Kimberly Radmacher, "On the Intersection of Personal and Social Identities: Introduction and Evidence from a Longitudinal Study of Emerging Adults." *New Directions for Child and Adolescent Development: The Intersections of Personal and Social Identities* 2008, no. 120 (Summer 2008): 1–16.

Bahrampour, Tara. "A U.S. Census Proposal to Add Category for People of Middle Eastern Descent Makes Some Uneasy." *Washington Post*, October 21, 2016. https://www .washingtonpost.com/local/social-issues/a-proposal-to-add-a-us-census-category -for-people-of-middle-eastern-descent-makes-some-uneasy/2016/10/20/8e 9847a0-960e-11e6-bb29-bf2701dbe0a3_story.html.

Baker, Peter. "Travelers Stranded and Protests Swell over Trump Order." *New York Times*, January 29, 2017. https://nyti.ms/2jFy45B.

Banks, James A., and Cherry A. McGee Banks, eds. *Handbook of Research on Multicultural Education.* 2nd ed. New York: Simon & Schuster, 1995.

Barker, Lori A. "Presidents, Stereotypes, and Prototypes, Oh My!: Understanding the Psychological Impact of Obama." In Barker, *Obama on Our Minds*, 3–27.

———, ed. *Obama on Our Minds: The Impact of Obama on the Psyche of America.* New York: Oxford University Press, 2016.

Banaji, Mahzarin R., and Anthony G. Greenwald. *Blindspot: Hidden Biases of Good People.* New York: Delacorte Press, 2013. Kindle edition.

Barndt, Joseph. *Understanding and Dismantling Racism: The Twenty-First Century Challenge to White America.* Minneapolis: Fortress Press, 2007.

Barry, Dan, Serge F. Kovaleski, Campbell Robertson, and Lizette Alvarez. "Race, Tragedy and Outrage Collide After a Shot in Florida." *New York Times,* April 1, 2012. http://www.nytimes.com/2012/04/02/us/trayvon-martin-shooting-prompts-a -review-of-ideals.html.

Bell, Lee Anne. "Telling on Racism: Developing a Race-Conscious Agenda." In Neville, Gallardo, and Wing Sue, *The Myth of Racial Color Blindness,* locations 2297–2298.

Bell, Lee Anne, Michael S. Funk, Khyati Y. Joshi, and Marjorie Valdivia. "Racism and White Privilege." In *Teaching for Diversity and Social Justice,* edited by Maurianne Adams and Lee Anne Bell, with Diane J. Goodman and Khyati Y. Joshi, Kindle locations 4543–4552. New York: Taylor and Francis, 2016. Kindle edition.

Benigno, Joseph. "A Statement from Joseph Benigno '16 Student Body President." TAMU Student Government Association, February 11, 2016, https://www.you tube.com/watch?v=Yo9sZlmdzBU.

Berman, Ari. "Jeff Sessions, Trump's Pick for Attorney General, Is a Fierce Opponent of Civil Rights." *The Nation,* November 18, 2016. https://www.thenation.com /article/jeff-sessions-trumps-pick-for-attorney-genearl-is-a-fierce-opponent-of -civil-rights/.

———. "Did Republicans Rig the Election?" *The Nation,* November 15, 2016. https:// www.thenation.com/article/did-republicans-rig-the-election/.

———. "The GOP's Attack on Voting Rights Was the Most Under-Covered Story of 2016." *The Nation,* November 9, 2016. https://www.thenation.com/article /the-gops-attack-on-voting-rights-was-the-most-under-covered-story-of-2016/.

———. "The GOP War on Voting." *Rolling Stone,* August 30, 2011. http://www.rolling stone.com/politics/news/the-gop-war-on-voting.

Berry, Wendell. *The Hidden Wound.* San Francisco: North Point Press, 1989.

Bertlatsky, Noah. "Hashtag Activism Isn't a Cop-Out." *The Atlantic,* January 7, 2015. http://www.theatlantic.com/politics/archive/2015/01/not-just-hashtag-activism -why-social-media-matters-to-protestors/384215/.

Bertrand, Marianne, and Sendhil Mullainathan. "Are Emily and Greg More Employable Than Lakisha and Jamal? A Field Experiment on Labor Market Discrimination." *American Economic Review* 94, no. 4 (September 2004): 991–1013.

Bialik, Carl. "How the Republican Field Dwindled from 17 to Donald Trump." *FiveThirty Eight,* May 5, 2016. http://fivethirtyeight.com/features/how-the-republican-field -dwindled-from-17-to-donald-trump/.

Blackwell, Lisa S., Kali H. Trzesniewski, and Carol Sorich Dweck. "Implicit Theories of Intelligence Predict Achievement Across an Adolescent Transition." *Child Development* 78, no. 1 (2007): 246–263.

Blake, Aaron. "Three Dozen Republicans Have Now Called for Trump to Drop Out." *Washington Post,* October 9, 2016. https://www.washingtonpost.com/news/the -fix/wp/2016/10/07/the-gops-brutal-responses-to-the-new-trump-video-broken -down/.

Blanchard, Fletcher A. "Effective Affirmative Action Programs." In Blanchard and Crosby, *Affirmative Action in Perspective,* 193–207.

Blanchard, Fletcher A., and Faye J. Crosby, eds. *Affirmative Action in Perspective.* New York: Springer-Verlag, 1989.

Blumenfeld, Warren J. "Inside and Outside: How Being an Ashkenazi Jew Illuminates and Complicates the Binary of Racial Privilege." In Moore, Penick-Parks, and Michael, *Everyday White People Confront Racial and Social Injustice,* chap. 12.

Bonilla-Silva, Eduardo. *Racism Without Racists: Color-Blind Racism and the Persistence of Racial Inequality in America.* 4th ed. Lanham, MD: Rowman and Littlefield, 2013.

Bowser, Benjamin P., and Raymond G. Hunt, eds. *Impacts of Racism on White Americans.* 2nd ed. Thousand Oaks, CA: Sage, 1996.

Boyd-Franklin, Nancy. *Black Families in Therapy: A Multisystems Approach.* New York: Guilford, 1989.

Bridges, Brian K., Janet T. Awokoya, and Frances Messano. *Done to Us, Not with Us: African American Parent Perceptions of K–12 Education.* Washington, DC: Frederick Patterson Research Institute, UNCF, 2012.

Brief for 39 Undergraduate and Graduate Student Organizations Within the University of California as Amicus Curiae. *Fisher v. University of Texas at Austin.* http://www.scotusblog.com/wp-content/uploads/2015/11/14-981_amicus_resp_39UndergraduateandGraduateStudentOrganizations.authcheckdam.pdf

Brief for the University of Michigan as Amicus Curiae. *Fisher v. University of Texas at Austin.* http://www.scotusblog.com/wp-content/uploads/2015/11/FILED-14-981-bsac-U-Michigan-11-12-15.pdf.

Brown, Sarah. "Activist Group Unites via Social Media." *Chronicle of Higher Education,* April 10, 2016. http://www.chronicle.com/article/Activist-Group-Unites-via/235993.

Brunsma, David L., ed. *Mixed Messages: Multiracial Identities in the "Color-Blind" Era.* Boulder, CO: Lynne Rienner Publishers, 2006.

Bureau of Labor Statistics. "Labor Force Statistics from the Current Population Survey," retrieved October 7, 2016. https://www.bls.gov/cps/.

Butterfield, Sherri-Ann P. "To Be Young, Gifted, Black, and Somewhat Foreign: The Role of Ethnicity in Black Student Achievement." In Horvat and O'Connor, *Beyond Acting White,* 133–155.

Capecchi, Christina, and Mitch Smith. "Officer Who Shot Philando Castile Is Charged with Manslaughter." *New York Times,* November 16, 2016. http://nyti.ms/2eGeSf4/.

Carnevale, A. and N. Smith. "The Economic Value of Diversity." In Lewis and Cantor, *Our Compelling Interests,* 106–157.

Carter, Robert. "Is White a Race? Expressions of White Racial Identity." In Fine et al., *Off White,* 198–209.

Carter, Stephen. *Reflections of an Affirmative Action Baby.* New York: Basic Books, 1991.

Casas, J. M. "Caution: Immigration May Be Harmful to Your Health." In *Handbook of Multicultural Counseling,* 4th ed., edited by J. Manuel Casas, Lisa A. Suzuki, Charlene M. Alexander, and Margo A. Jackson, 348–359. Los Angeles: Sage, 2017.

Cauce, Ana Mari, Yumi Hiraga, Craig Mason, Tanya Aguilar, Nydia Ordonez, and Nancy Gonzales. "Between a Rock and a Hard Place: Social Adjustment of Biracial Youth." In Root, *Racially Mixed People in America,* 207–222.

Chan, Kenyon S., and Shirley Hune. "Racialization and Panethnicity: From Asians in America to Asian Americans." In *Toward a Common Destiny: Improving Race and Ethnic Relations in America,* edited by Willis D. Hawley and Anthony W. Jackson, 205–233. San Francisco: Jossey-Bass, 1995.

Charles, Camille Zubrinsky. *Won't You Be My Neighbor? Race, Class and Residence in Los Angeles.* New York: Russell Sage Foundation, 2006.

Chatelain, Marcia. "What Mizzou Taught Me." *Chronicle of Higher Education,* November 12, 2015. http://www.chronicle.com/article/What-Mizzou-Taught-Me/234180.

Chessman, Hollie, and Lindsay Wayt. "What Are Students Demanding?" *Higher Education Today,* American Council on Education, January 13, 2016. https://higher edtoday.org/2016/01/13/what-are-students-demanding/.

Childs, Erica Chito. "Black and White: Family Opposition to Becoming Multiracial." In Brunsma, *Mixed Messages,* 233–246.

Chozick, Amy. "Hillary Clinton and Donald Trump Strike Different Tones After Dallas Shooting." *New York Times,* July 8, 2016. http://www.nytimes.com/2016/07/09 /us/politics/clinton-trump-shooting-reaction.html.

Christensen, Rebecca Dora. "'Making a Difference': Residential Learning Community Students' Trajectories Toward Promoting Social Justice." Doctoral diss., University of Michigan, 2016.

Christopher, Gail C. "The Time for Truth, Racial Healing, and Transformation Is Now," *Liberal Education* 102, no. 4 (Fall 2016): 8–15.

CNN.com, "Trayvon Martin Shooting Fast Facts," June 5, 2013. http://www.cnn .com/2013/06/05/us/trayvon-martin-shooting-fast-facts.

Coates, Ta-Nehisi. *Between the World and Me.* New York: Penguin Random House, 2015.

Cobb, Jelani. "Honoring the Police and Their Victims," *The New Yorker,* July 25, 2016. http://www.newyorker.com/2016/07/25/baton-rouge-st-paul-and-dallas.

———. "After Dallas, the Future of Black Lives Matter." *The New Yorker,* July 10, 2016. http://www.newyorker.com/news/news-desk/after-dallas-the-future-of-black -lives-matters.

———. "The Matter of Black Lives." *The New Yorker,* March 14, 2016. http://www. thenewyorker.com/magazine/2016/03/14/where-is-black-lives-matter-headed.

Cohen, Geoffrey L., and Claude M. Steele. "A Barrier of Mistrust: How Negative Stereotypes Affect Cross-Race Mentoring." In Aronson, *Improving Academic Achievement,* 303–328.

Colby, Anne, and William Damon, *Some Do Care: Contemporary Lives of Moral Commitment* (New York: Free Press, 1992).

Collins, Patricia Hill. *Black Feminist Thought: Knowledge, Consciousness, and the Politics of Empowerment.* London: HarperCollins Academic, 1990.

*The Color of Fear,* produced and directed by Lee Mun Wah (Oakland, CA: Stir-Fry Productions, 1994), video.

Comas-Díaz, Lillian. "LatiNegra." In Root, *The Multiracial Experience,* 167–190.

Confessore, Nicholas. "For Whites Sensing Decline, Donald Trump Unleashes Words of Resistance." *New York Times,* July 13, 2016. http://nyti.ms/29WCu51.

Cooley, Charles. *Human Nature and the Social Order.* New York: Scribner, 1922.

Cooper, Betsy, Daniel Cox, Rachel Lienesch, and Robert P. Jones. *Anxiety, Nostalgia, and Mistrust: Findings from the 2015 American Values Survey.* Washington, DC: Public Religion Research Institute. http://www.prri.org/research/survey-anxiety -nostalgia-and-mistrust-findings-from-the-2015-american-values-survey/.

Coscarelli, Joe. "No Charges Against Ohio Police in John Crawford III Walmart Shooting, Despite Damning Security Video." *New York,* September 24, 2014. http://nymag .com/daily/intelligencer/2014/09/no-charges-john-crawford-iii-walmart-shooting -video.html.

Council on Interracial Books for Children. "Ten Quick Ways to Analyze Children's Books for Racism and Sexism." In *Rethinking Our Classrooms.* Rev. ed., vol.1. Milwaukee, WI: Rethinking Schools, 2007.

Crenshaw, Kimberlé Williams, and Andrea J. Ritchie. *Say Her Name: Resisting Police Brutality Agsainst Black Women.* African American Policy Forum, July 2015. http://www.aapf.org/sayhername/.

Crosby, Faye J. *Affirmative Action Is Dead; Long Live Affirmative Action.* New Haven, CT: Yale University Press, 2004.

———. "Confessions of an Affirmative Action Mama." In Fine et al., *Off White,* 179–186.

———. "Understanding Affirmative Action." *Basic and Applied Social Psychology* 15, nos. 1–2 (1994): 13–41.

Crosby, Faye J., and Alison M. Konrad. "Affirmative Action in Employment." *Diversity Factor* 10, no. 2 (Winter 2002): 5–9.

Cross, William E., Jr. "The Psychology of Nigrescence: Revising the Cross Model." In Ponterotto et al., *Handbook of Multicultural Counseling,* 1st ed., 93–122.

Cross, William E., Jr. *Shades of Black: Diversity in African-American Identity.* Philadelphia: Temple University Press, 1991.

Cross, William E., and T. Binta Cross. "Theory, Research, and Models." In *Handbook of Race, Racism, and the Developing Child,* edited by Stephen M. Quintana and Clark McKown, 154–180. Hoboken, NJ: Wiley and Sons, 2008.

Cross, William E., Jr., and Peony Fhagen-Smith. "Patterns of African American Identity Development: A Life Span Perspective." In *New Perspectives on Racial Identity Development: A Theoretical and Practical Anthology,* edited by Charmaine J. Wijeyesinghe and Bailey W. Jackson III, 243–270. New York: New York University Press, 2001.

Curry, George E., ed. *The Affirmative Action Debate.* Reading, MA: Addison-Wesley, 1996.

Davis, F. James. *Who Is Black? One Nation's Definition.* University Park: Pennsylvania State University Press, 1991.

Davis, Julie Hirschfeld, and Frances Robles. "Obama Ends Exemption for Cubans Who Arrive Without Visas." *New York Times,* January 12, 2017. https://nyti.ms/2ip HEc5.

Davol, Marguerite. *Black, White, Just Right!* Morton Grove, IL: A. Whitman, 1993.

*DBR MTV Bias Survey Full Report II.* MTV and David Binder Research, April 2014. http://www.lookdifferent.org/about-us/research-studies/1-2014-mtv-david -binder-research-study.

*DBR MTV Bias Survey Summary.* MTV and David Binder Research, April 2014. http:// www.lookdifferent.org/about-us/research-studies/1-2014-mtv-david-binder-research -study.

Dees, Morris, with Steve Fiffer. *A Season of Justice: A Lawyer's Own Story of Victory over America's Hate Groups.* New York: Touchstone Books, 1991.

Delpit, Lisa. *Other People's Children: Cultural Conflict in the Classroom.* New York: The New Press, 2006.

Derman-Sparks, Louise, and the ABC Task Force. *Anti-Bias Curriculum: Tools for Empowering Young Children.* Washington, DC: National Association for the Education of Young Children, 1989.

Derman-Sparks, Louise, and Julie Olsen Edwards. "Learning About Racial Identity and Fairness." In *Anti-Bias Education for Young Children and Ourselves,* 77–89. Washington, DC: National Association for the Education of Young Children, 2010.

Derman-Sparks, Louise, Carol Tanaka Higa, and Bill Sparks. "Children, Race, and Racism: How Race Awareness Develops." *Interracial Books for Children Bulletin* 11, no. 3–4, (1980): 3–9. https://www.teachingforchange.org/wp-content/uploads/2012/08/ec_childrenraceracism_english.pdf.

DeSilver, Drew. "Supreme Court Says States Can Ban Affirmative Action; 8 Already Have." *Fact Tank,* Pew Research Center, April 22, 2014. http://www.pewresearch.org/fact-tank/2014/04/22/supreme-court-says-states-can-ban-affirmative-action-8-already-have/.

DiAngelo, Robin. *What Does It Mean to Be White? Developing White Racial Literacy.* Rev. ed. New York: Peter Lang, 2016.

Dickerson, Caitlin, and Stephanie Saul. "Campuses Confront Hostile Acts Against Minorities After Donald Trump's Victory." *New York Times,* November 10, 2016. http://nyti.ms/2eFAM5v.

Dovidio, John F. "Changing the Course of Race Relations in America: From Prevention of Discrimination to Promotion of Racial Equality." In Barker, *Obama on Our Minds,* 93–107.

Dovidio, John F., Jeffrey Mann, and Samuel L. Gaertner. "Resistance to Affirmative Action: The Implications of Aversive Racism." In Blanchard and Crosby, *Affirmative Action in Perspective,* 83–102.

Dovidio, John F., and Samuel L. Gaertner. "Aversive Racism." *Advances in Experimental Social Psychology* 36 (2004): 1–52.

Dovidio, John F., Samuel L. Gaertner, Phyllis A. Anastasio, and Rasyid Sanitioso. "Cognitive and Motivational Bases of Bias: Implications of Aversive Racism for Attitudes Toward Hispanics." In *Hispanics in the Workplace,* edited by Stephen B. Knouse, Paul Rosenfeld, and Amy L. Culbertson, 75–106. Newbury Park, CA: Sage, 1992.

Dreid, Nadia, and Shannon Najambadi. "Here's a Rundown of the Latest Campus-Climate Incidents Since Trump's Election." *Chronicle of Higher Education,* December 6, 2016. http://www.chronicle.com/blogs/ticker/heres-a-rundown-of-the-latest-campus-climate-incidents-since-trumps-election/.

Durr, Virginia Foster. *Outside the Magic Circle: The Autobiography of Virginia Foster Durr.* Edited by Hollinger F. Barnard. Tuscaloosa: University of Alabama Press, 1985.

Dweck, Carol. "Messages That Motivate: How Praise Molds Students' Beliefs, Motivation, and Performance (In Surprising Ways)." In Aronson, *Improving Academic Achievement*, 38–60.

Dyson, Michael E. *Race Rules: Navigating the Color Line*. Boston: Beacon Press, 1996.

Early, Gerald. *Lure and Loathing: Essays on Race, Identity, and the Ambivalence of Assimilation*. New York: Penguin, 1993.

Ehrenreich, Barbara, and Dedrick Muhammad. "The Destruction of the Black Middle Class." *Huffington Post*, September 3, 2009 (updated May 25, 2011). http://www.huffingtonpost.com/barbara-ehrenreich/the-destruction-of-the-bl_b_250828.html.

Elzie, Johnetta. "When I Close My Eyes at Night, I See People Running from Tear Gas." *Ebony*, September 8, 2014. http://www.ebony.com/news-views-ferguson-forward-when-i-close-my-eyes-at-night-i-see-people-running-from-tear-ga#ix zz4RSX19KJj.

Equal Justice Initiative. *Lynching in America: Confronting the Legacy of Racial Terror*. Montgomery, AL: Equal Justice Initiative, 2015.

Erikson, Erik H. *Identity, Youth, and Crisis*. New York: W. W. Norton, 1968.

———. *Childhood and Society*. New York: W. W. Norton, 1950.

Espinosa, Lorelle, Hollie Chessman, and Lindsay Wayt. "Racial Climate on Campus: A Survey of College Presidents." *Higher Education Today*, March 8, 2016. http://higheredtoday.org/2016/03/08/racial-climate-on-campus-a-survey-of-college-presidents/.

Estrada, Sheryl. "CNN's Van Jones: 'White-lash' Against a Changing U.S. Led to Trump's Win." *DiversityInc*, November 10, 2016. http://www.diversityinc.com/news/cnns-van-jones-white-lash-changing-u-s-led-trumps-win/.

*Ethnic Notions*. Produced and directed by Marlon Riggs. San Francisco, CA: Resolution/California Newsreel, 1986. Video.

Eversley, Melanie. "Thousands Pack D.C. for 20th Anniversary of Million Man March." *USA Today*, October 10, 2015. http://www.usatoday.com/story/news/nation/2015/10/10/washington-dc-million-man-march-20th-anniversary/73728720/.

Fahrenthold, David A. "Trump Recorded Having Extremely Lewd Conversation About Women in 2005." *Washington Post*, October 8, 2016. https://www.washingtonpost.com/politics/trump-recorded-having-extremely-lewd-conversation-about-women-in-2005/2016/10/07/3b9ce776-8cb4-11e6-bf8a-3d26847eeed4_story.html.

Fausset, Richard, Richard Pérez-Peña, and Campbell Robertson. "Alton Sterling Shooting in Baton Rouge Prompts Justice Dept. Investigation." *New York Times*, July 6, 2016. http://nyti.ms/2eGcSf4.

Ferdman, Roberto A. "The Great American Hispanic Wealth Gap." *Washington Post*, July 1, 2014. https://www.washingtonpost.com/news/wonk/wp/2014/07/01/hispanics-of-mexican-origin-in-the-united-states-2010.

Fergus, Edward. "The Relevance of Skin Color in the Construction of an Ethnic Identification Among Mexican and Puerto Rican Boys." In *Invisible No More: Understanding the Disenfranchisement of Latino Men and Boys*, edited by Pedro Noguera, Aída Hurtado, and Edward Fergus, 229–245. New York: Routledge, 2012.

Fernandez, Manny, Richard Pérez-Peña, and Jonah Engel Bromwich. "Five Dallas Officers Were Killed as Payback, Police Chief Says." *New York Times*, July 8, 2016. http://www.nytimes.com/2016/07/09/us/dallas-police-shooting.html.

Fiegener, Mark K., and Steven L. Proudfoot. "Baccalaureate Origins of U.S.-Trained S&E Doctorate Recipients." *InfoBrief*, National Center for Science and Engineering Statistics, National Science Foundation, April 2013, NSF 13-323. https://www.nsf.gov/statistics/infbrief/nsf13323/nsf13323.pdf.

Field, Lynda D. "Piecing Together the Puzzle: Self-Concept and Group Identity in Biracial Black/White Youth." In Root, *The Multiracial Experience*, 211–226.

Fields-Meyer, Thomas. "Under Suspicion." *People*, January 15, 1996, 40–47. http://people.com/archive/under-suspicion-vol-45-no-2/.

Fine, Michelle, Lois Weis, Linda Powell Pruitt, and April Burns, eds. *Off White: Readings on Race, Power, and Society*. New York: Routledge, 2004.

Fiske, Susan. T. "Controlling Other People: The Impact of Power on Stereotyping." *American Psychologist* 48, no. 6 (1993): 621–628.

Ford, Kristie A., ed. *Facilitating Change Through Intergroup Dialogue: Social Justice Advocacy in Practice*. New York: Routledge, forthcoming.

Fordham, Signithia. "Racelessness as a Factor in Black Students' School Success: Pragmatic Strategy or Pyrrhic Victory?" *Harvard Educational Review* 58, no. 1 (1988): 54–84.

Fordham, Signithia, and John U. Ogbu. "Black Students' School Success: Coping with the Burden of 'Acting White.'" *Urban Review* 18 (1986): 176–206.

Frankenberg, Ruth. "'When We Are Capable of Stopping, We Begin to See': Being White, Seeing Whiteness." In Thompson and Tyagi, *Names We Call Home*, 3–17.

———. *White Women, Race Matters: The Social Construction of Whiteness*. Minneapolis: University of Minnesota Press, 1993.

French, Sabine Elizabeth, Edward Seidman, LaRue Allen, and J. Lawrence Aber. "The Development of Ethnic Identity During Adolescence." *Developmental Psychology* 42, no. 1 (2006): 1–10.

Frey, William H. "The 'Diversity Explosion' Is America's Twenty-First-Century Baby Boom." In Lewis and Cantor, *Our Compelling Interests*, 16–35.

Frizell, Sam. "FBI Director James Comey Under Fire After Hillary Clinton Email Investigation Announcement." *Time*, October 29, 2016. http://time.com/4550453/hillary-clinton-james-comey-fbi-emails/.

Fryberg, Stephanie A., Hazel Rose Markus, Daphna Oyserman, and Joseph M. Stone. "Of Warrior Chiefs and Indian Princesses: The Psychological Consequences of American Indian Mascots." *Basic and Applied Social Psychology*, 30, no. 3 (2008): 208–218.

Fuligni, Andrew J., ed. *Contesting Stereotypes and Creating Identities*. New York: Russell Sage Foundation, 2007.

Funderberg, Lise. *Black, White, Other: Biracial Americans Talk About Race and Identity*. New York: Quill, 1994.

Gallagher, Charles A. "Color Blindness: An Obstacle to Racial Justice?" In Brunsma, *Mixed Messages,* 103–116.

Galura, Joseph A., Penny A. Pasque, David Schoem, and Jeffrey Galura Howard, eds. *Engaging the Whole of Service-Learning, Diversity, and Learning Communities.* Ann Arbor, MI: OCSL Press at the University of Michigan, 2004.

Garcia-Preto, Nydia. "Latino Families: An Overview." In McGoldrick, Giordano, and Garcia-Preto, *Ethnicity and Family Therapy,* 153–165.

Garrod, Andrew, and Robert Kilkenny, eds. *Growing Up Muslim: Muslim College Students in America Tell Their Life Stories.* Ithaca, NY: Cornell University Press, 2014. Kindle edition.

Germán, Miguelina, Nancy A. Gonzales, and Larry Dumka. "Familism Values as a Protective Factor for Mexican-Origin Adolescents Exposed to Deviant Peers." *Journal of Early Adolescence* 29, no. 1 (2009): 16–42.

Gibbs, Jewelle Taylor. "Biracial Adolescents." In *Children of Color: Psychological Interventions with Minority Youth,* edited by Jewelle Taylor Gibbs and Larke Nahme Huang, 322–350. San Francisco: Jossey-Bass, 1989.

Gibbs, Jewelle Taylor, and Alice M. Hines. "Negotiating Ethnic Identity: Issues for Black-White Biracial Adolescents." In Root, *Racially Mixed People in America,* 223–238.

Gibson, Rose C. "Retirement." In Jackson, *Life in Black America,* 179–198.

Glaze, Lauren E., and Laura M. Maruschak. *Parents in Prison and Their Minor Children* US Bureau of Justice Statistics, March 30, 2010. https://www.bjs.gov/content /pub/pdf/pptmc.pdf/.

Godon, Danielle E., Whitney F. Green, and Patricia G. Ramsey. "Transracial Adoptees: The Search for Birth Family and the Search for Self." *Adoption Quarterly* 17, no. 1 (2014): 1–27.

Goldstein, Joseph. "Alt-Right Gathering Exults in Trump Election with Nazi-Era Salute." *New York Times,* November 20, 2016. http://www.nytimes.com/2016/11/21/us /alt-right-salutes-donald-trump.html.

Gonzales, Roberto G. "Learning to Be Illegal: Undocumented Youth and Shifting Legal Contexts in the Transition to Adulthood." *American Sociological Review* 76, no. 4 (2011): 602–619.

Good, Catherine, Carol S. Dweck, and Joshua Aronson. "Social Identity, Stereotype Threat, and Self-Theories." In Fuligni, *Contesting Stereotypes and Creating Identities,* 115–135.

Graham, Lawrence Otis. "I Taught My Black Kids That Their Elite Upbringing Would Protect Them from Discrimination. I Was Wrong." *Washington Post,* November 6, 2014. https://www.washingtonpost.com/posteverything/wp2014/11/06/i-taught-my -black-kids-that-their-elite-upbringing-would-protect-them-from-discrimination -i-was-wrong/.

Grinde, Donald Andrew, Jr. "Place and Kinship: A Native American's Identity Before and After Words." In Thompson and Tyagi, *Names We Call Home,* 63–72.

"Growing Up 'White,' Transracial Adoptee Learned to Be Black." *Weekend Edition Sunday,* NPR, January 26, 2014. http://www.npr.org/2014/01/26/266434175/growing -up-white-transracial-adoptee-learned-to-be-black.

Hackman, Heather W. "Calling Out the Wizard Behind the Curtain." In Moore, Penick-Parks, and Michael, *Everyday White People Confront Racial and Social Injustice,* location 1275–1489.

Hale, Frank W., Jr. *How Black Colleges Empower Black Students: Lessons for Higher Education.* Sterling, VA: Stylus Publishing, 2006.

Hall, Christine Catherine Iijima. "The Ethnic Identity of Racially Mixed People: A Study of Black-Japanese." Doctoral diss., University of California, Los Angeles, 1980.

"Have You Ever Seen a Real Indian? American Indian College Fund Advertising Campaign Challenges Stereotypes." Press release. American Indian College Fund, *PRNewswire,* March 2, 2001. http://www.prnewswire.com/news-releases/have-you-ever-seen -a-real-indian-american-indian-college-fund-advertising-campaign-challenges -stereotypes-71520017.html.

Heath, Brad. "Racial Gap in U.S. Arrest Rates: 'Staggering Disparity.'" *USA Today,* November 18, 2014. http://www.usatoday.com/story/news/nation/2014/11/18 /ferguson-black-arrest-rates/19043207/.

Helderman, Rosalind S., and Jon Cohen. "As Republican Convention Emphasizes Diversity, Racial Incidents Intrude." *Washington Post,* August 29, 2012. http:// www.washingtonpost.com/politics/2012/08/29/b9023a52-f1ec-11-1-892d -bc92fee603a7_story.html.

Helms, Janet E. "An Update of Helms's White and People of Color Racial Identity Models." In Ponterotto et al., *Handbook of Multicultural Counseling,* 1st ed., 181–198.

———, ed. *Black and White Racial Identity: Theory, Research, and Practice.* Westport, CT: Greenwood, 1990.

"Here's Donald Trump's Presidential Announcement Speech." Time.com, June 16, 2015. http://time.com/3923128/donald-trump-announcement-speech/.

Herring, R. D. "Native American Indian Identity: A People of Many Peoples." In Salett and Koslow, *Race, Ethnicity, and Self,* 170–197.

"Historically Black Colleges and Universities." *Fast Facts,* National Center for Education Statistics. https://nces.ed.gov/fastfacts/display.asp?id=667.

Hochschild, Arlie Russell. *Strangers in Their Own Land: Anger and Mourning on the American Right.* New York: The New Press, 2016. Kindle edition.

Hoeffel, Elizabeth M., Sonya Rastogi, Myoung Ouk Kim, and Hasan Shield. *The Asian Population: 2010.* C2010BR-11, US Census Bureau. March 2012. https://www .census.gov/prod/cen2010/briefs/c2010br-11.pdf.

Holloway, Frances A. "What Is Affirmative Action?" In Blanchard and Crosby, *Affirmative Action in Perspective,* 9–19.

hooks, bell. *Sisters of the Yam: Black Women and Self-Recovery.* Boston: South End Press, 1993.

Horvat, Erin McNamara, and Carla O'Connor. *Beyond Acting White: Reassessments and New Directions in Research on Black Students and School Success.* New York: Rowman and Littlefield, 2006.

Howard, Jeff. *Getting Smart: The Social Construction of Intelligence.* Waltham, MA: The Efficacy Institute, 1992.

Iceland, John, Daniel H. Weinberg, and Erika Steinmetz. "The Residential Segregation of American Indians and Alaska Natives: 1980–2000." In *Racial and Ethnic*

*Residential Segregation in the United States: 1980–2000,* US Census Bureau, August 2002. https://www.census.gov/hhes/www/housing/resseg/pdf/ch3.pdf.

Ilibagiza, Immaculeé. *Left to Tell: Discovering God Amidst the Rwandan Holocaust.* Carlsbad, CA: Hay House, 2006.

Institute of Medicine. *Unequal Treatment: Confronting Racial and Ethnic Disparities in Healthcare.* Washington, DC: National Academy of Sciences.

Irving, Debby. *Waking Up White and Finding Myself in the Story of Race.* Cambridge, MA: Elephant Room Press, 2014.

Jackson, James S., ed. *Life in Black America.* Thousand Oaks, CA: Sage, 1991.

Johnson, Jenna. "Donald Trump to African American and Hispanic Voters: 'What Do You Have to Lose?'" *Washington Post,* August 22, 2016. https://www.washington post.com/news/post-politics/wp/2016/08/22/donald-trump-to-african-american -and-hispanic-voters-what-do-you-have-to-lose/.

———. "Inside Donald Trump's Strategic Decision to Target Muslims," *Washington Post,* June 21, 2016. https://www.washingtonpost.com/politics/inside-donald-trumps -strategic-decision-to-target-muslims/2016/06/20/d506411e-3241-11e6-8758 -d58e76e11b12_story.html?tid=a_inl&utm_term=.513d88de3cc3.

Jones, Robert P. "Self-Segregation: Why It's So Hard for Whites to Understand Ferguson." *The Atlantic,* August 21, 2014. http://www.theatlantic.com/nationa/archive/2014 /08/self-segregation-why-its-hard-for-whites-to-understand-ferguson/378928/.

Kaestle, Carl. "Federalism and Inequality in Education: What Can History Tell Us?" In Kirsch and Braun, *The Dynamics of Opportunity in America,* 35–96.

Kanter, Rosabeth Moss. *Men and Women of the Corporation.* New York: Basic Books, 1977.

Kanter, Rosabeth Moss, with Barry A. Stein, *A Tale of "O": On Being Different in an Organization.* New York: Harper Colophon, 1980.

Karabel, Jerome. *The Chosen: The Hidden History of Admission and Exclusion at Harvard, Yale, and Princeton.* New York: Mariner Books, 2006.

Kaye/Kantrowitz, Melanie. "Jews in the U.S.: The Rising Costs of Whiteness." In Thompson and Tyagi, *Names We Call Home,* 121–138.

Katz, J. H. *White Awareness: Handbook for Anti-Racism Training.* Norman: University of Oklahoma Press, 1978.

Kelchen, Robert. "Financial Need and Aid Volatility Among Students with Zero Expected Family Contribution." *Journal of Student Financial Aid* 44, no. 3 (2015). http://publications.nasfaa.org/jsfa/vol44/iss3/2/.

Khanna, Nikki. *Biracial in America: Forming and Performing Racial Identity.* Lanham, MD: Lexington Books, 2011.

Kholi, Sonali. "Modern-Day Segregation in Public Schools." *The Atlantic,* November 18, 2014. http://www.theatlantic.com/education/archive/2014/11/modern-day -segregation-in-public-schools/382846/.

Kiang, Peter Nien-chu. "We Could Shape It: Organizing for Asian Pacific American Student Empowerment." In *Struggling to Be Heard: The Unmet Needs of APA Children,* edited by Valerie Ooka Pang and Li-Rong Lilly Cheng, 243–264. Albany, NY: State University of New York Press, 1998.

Kich, George Kitahara. "The Developmental Process of Asserting a Biracial, Bicultural Identity." In Root, *Racially Mixed People in America*, 304–317.

Kidder, William C. "The Salience of Racial Isolation: African Americans' and Latinos' Perceptions of Climate and Enrollment Choices With and Without Proposition 209." Civil Rights Project at UCLA / Proyecto Derechos Civiles, October 2012.

Kim, Bok-Lim C., and Eunjung Ryu. "Korean Families." In McGoldrick, Giordano, and Garcia-Preto, *Ethnicity and Family Therapy*, 349–362.

King, Matthew A. "Indian Gaming and Native Identity." *Chicano-Latino Law Review* 30, no. 1 (2011). https://ssrn.com/abstract=2018751.

Kirsch, Irwin, and Henry Braun, eds. *The Dynamics of Opportunity in America: Evidence and Perspectives*. Princeton, NJ: Educational Testing Service, 2016.

Kivel, Paul. *Uprooting Racism: How White People Can Work for Racial Justice*. 3rd ed. Gabriola Island, BC, Canada: New Society Publishers, 2011.

Knight, David. "What's Colorism?" *Teaching Tolerance*, no. 51 (Fall 2015). http://www.tolerance.org/magazine/number-51-fall-2015/feature/what-s-colorism.

Kohl, Herbert. *I Won't Learn from You, and Other Thoughts on Creative Maladjustment*. 2nd ed. New York: The New Press, 1995.

Krogstad, Jens Manuel. "Unauthorized Immigrants Covered by DACA Face Uncertain Future." *Fact Tank*, Pew Research Center, January 5, 2017. http://www.pewresearch.org/fact-tank/2017/01/05/unauthorized-immigrants-covered-by-daca-face-uncertain-future/.

———. "Key Facts About How the U.S. Hispanic Population Is Changing." *Fact Tank*, Pew Research Center, September 8, 2016. http://www.pewresearch.org/fact-tank/2016/09/08/key-facts-about-how-the-u-s-hispanic-population-is-changing/.

Krogstad, Jens Manuel, Jeffrey S. Passel, and D'Vera Cohn. "5 Facts About Illegal Immigration in the U.S." *Fact Tank*, Pew Research Center, November 3, 2016. http://www.pewresearch.org/fact-tank/2016/11/03/5-facts-about-illegal-immigration-in-the-u-s/.

Kurtzleben, Danielle, Tamara Keith, Arnie Seipel, Peter Overby, Matt Katz, and Scott Horsley. "FACT CHECK: Hillary Clinton's Speech to the Democratic Convention, Annotated." NPR, July 28, 2016. http://www.npr.org/2016/07/28/487817725/fact-check-hillary-clintons-speech-to-the-democratic-convention-annotated.

Lawrence, Sandra, and Beverly Daniel Tatum. "Teachers in Transition: The Impact of Anti-Racist Professional Development on Classroom Practice." *Teachers College Record* 99 (Fall 1997): 162–178.

———. "White Educators as Allies: Moving from Awareness to Action." In Fine et al., *Off White*, 362–372.

Leadbeater, Bonnie J. Ross, and Niobe Way, eds. *Urban Girls: Resisting Stereotypes, Creating Identities*. New York: New York University Press, 1996.

———. *Urban Girls Revisited: Building Strengths*. New York: New York University Press, 2007.

Lee, Evelyn, and Matthew R. Mock, "Asian Families: An Overview." In McGoldrick, Giordano, and Garcia-Preto, *Ethnicity and Family Therapy*, 269–289.

Lee, Traci G. "Gangs of Atlanta: New Film Upends Asian 'Model Minority' Myth." NBCNews.com, March 11, 2015. http://www.nbcnews.com/news/asian-america /gangs-atlanta-new-film-upends-asian-model-minority-myth-n321421.

Lerner, Melvin. "Social Psychology of Justice and Interpersonal Attraction." In *Foundations of Interpersonal Attraction,* edited by Ted L. Huston, 331–351. New York: Academic Press, 1974.

Levinson, Daniel. *The Seasons of a Man's Life.* New York: Knopf, 1978.

Lewis, Earl, and Nancy Cantor. *Our Compelling Interests: The Value of Diversity for Democracy and a Prosperous Society.* Princeton, NJ: Princeton University Press, 2016.

Lhamon, Catherine E. "Dear Colleague Letter: Resource Comparability." Version 1.02, October 10, 2014. US Department of Education, Office of Civil Rights. http:// www2.ed.gov/about/offices/list/ocr/letters/colleague-resourcecomp-201410.pdf.

Lichtblau, Eric. "Jeff Sessions, as Attorney General, Could Overhaul Department He's Skewered." *New York Times,* November 18, 2016. http://www.nytimes .com/2016/11/19/us/politics/jeff-sessions-donald-trump-attorney-general.html.

———. "U.S. Hate Crimes Surge 6%, Fueled by Attacks on Muslims." *New York Times,* November 14, 2016. https://nyti.ms/2ezOFXH.

Lind, Dara. "The Problem with Violence at Trump Rallies Starts with Trump Himself." *Vox,* March 13, 2016. http://www.vox.com/2016/3/11/11202540/trump-violent.

Little Soldier, Lee. "Is There an 'Indian' in Your Classroom? Working Successfully with Urban Native American Students." *Phi Delta Kappan* 78, no. 8 (April 1997): 650–653.

Lomawaima, K. Tsianina. "Educating Native Americans." In Banks and Banks, *Handbook of Research on Multicultural Education,* 441–461.

López, Gustavo. *Hispanics of Cuban Origin in the United States, 2013: Statistical Profile.* Pew Research Center, September 15, 2015. http://www.pewhispanic .org/2015/09/15/hispanics-of-cuban-origin-in-the-united-states-2013/.

———. *Hispanics of Salvadoran Origin in the United States, 2013: A Statistical Profile.* Pew Research Center, September 15, 2015. http://www.pewhispanic.org /2015/09/15/hispanics-of-salvadoran-origin-in-the-united-states-2013/.

López, Gustavo and Eileen Patten. *Hispanics of Puerto Rican Origin in the United States, 2013: Statistical Profile.* Pew Research Center, September 15, 2015. http://www .pewhispanic.org/2015/09/15/hispanics-of-puerto-rican-origin-in-the-united -states-2013/.

López, Ian Haney. *Dog Whistle Politics: How Coded Racial Appeals Have Reinvented Racism and Wrecked the Middle Class.* New York: Oxford University Press, 2014. Kindle edition.

Lopez, Mark Hugo. "Is Speaking Spanish Necessary to Be Hispanic? Most Hispanics Say No." *Fact Tank,* Pew Research Center, February 19, 2016. http://www.pew research.org/fact-tank/2016/02/19/is-speaking-spanish-necessary-to-be-hispanic -most-hispanics-say-no/.

Lopez, Mark Hugo, Ana Gonzalez-Barrera, and Danielle Cuddington. *Diverse Origins: The Nation's 14 Largest Hispanic-Origin Groups.* Pew Research Center, June

19, 2013. http://www.pewhispanic.org/2013/06/19/diverse-origins-the-nations -14-largest-hispanic-origin-groups/.

Lord, Lewis. "How Many People Were Here Before Columbus?" *U.S. News & World Report*, August 18–25, 1997, 68–70. http://www.bxscience.edu/ourpages/ auto/2009/4/5/34767803/Pre-Columbian%20population.pdf.

Lorde, Audre. "Age, Race, Class, and Sex: Women Redefining Difference." In *Sister Outsider: Essays and Speeches*, 114–123. Freedom, CA: Crossing Press, 1984.

———. "There Is No Hierarchy of Oppression." In *I Am Your Sister: Collected and Unpublished Writings of Audre Lorde*, edited by Rudolph P. Byrd, Johnnetta B. Cole, and Beverly Guy-Sheftall, 219–220. New York: Oxford University Press, 2009.

Lowery, Wesley. *They Can't Kill Us All: Ferguson, Baltimore, and a New Era in America's Racial Justice Movement*. New York: Little, Brown & Company.

Luo, Michael. "An Open Letter to the Woman Who Told My Family to Go Back to China." *New York Times*, October 10, 2016. http://www.nytimes.com/2016 /10/10/nyregion/to-the-woman-who-told-my-family-to-go-back-to-china.html.

———. "'Go Back to China': Readers Respond to Racist Insults Shouted at a New York Times Editor." *New York Times*, October 10, 2016. http://www.nytimes .com/206/10/11/nyregion/go-back-to-china-readers-respond-to-racist-insults -shouted-at-a-new-york-times-editor.html.

Madden, Mary, Amanda Lenhart, Maeve Duggan, Sandra Cortesi, and Urs Gasser. *Teens and Technology 2013*. Pew Research Center, March 13, 2013. http://www .pewinternet.org/2013/03/13/teens-and-technology-2013/.

Malcolm X with Alex Haley. *The Autobiography of Malcolm X*. New York: Grove Press, 1965.

Mangan, Katherine. "With Trump's Rise, Undocumented Students Fear for Their Futures." *Chronicle of Higher Education*, November 11, 2016. http://www.chronicle .com/article/With-Trump-s-rise/238387.

Marcia, James E. "Development and Validation of Ego Identity Status." *Journal of Personality and Social Psychology* 3, no. 5 (1966): 551–558.

Marín, Gerardo, and Barbara VanOss Marín. *Research with Hispanic Populations*. Newbury Park, CA: Sage, 1991.

Martin, Biddy. "President Martin's Statement on Campus Protests." November 15, 2015. https://www.amherst.edu/amherst-story/president/statements/node/620480.

Marvasti, Amir, and Karyn D. McKinney. *Middle Eastern Lives in America*. Lanham, MD: Rowman and Littlefield, 2004.

Massey, Douglas S., and Nancy A. Denton. *American Apartheid: Segregation and the Making of the Underclass*. Cambridge, MA: Harvard University Press, 1993.

Massey, Douglas S., and Jonathan Tannen. "Segregation, Race and the Social Worlds of Rich and Poor." In Kirsch and Braun, *The Dynamics of Opportunity in America*, 13–33.

Maxwell, Kelly E., Aaron Traxler-Ballew, and K. Foula Dimopoulos. "Intergroup Dialogue and the Michigan Community Scholars Program: A Partnership for Meaningful Engagement." In Galura et al., *Engaging the Whole of Service-Learning, Diversity, and Learning Communities*, 121–133.

Mayer, Jane. "The Voter-Fraud Myth." *The New Yorker,* October 29, 2012. http://www
.thenewyorker.com/magazine/2012/10/29/the-voter-fraud-myth.

McGoldrick, Monica, Joe Giordano, and Nydia Garcia-Preto, eds. *Ethnicity and Family
Therapy.* 3rd ed. New York: Guilford Press, 2005.

McIntosh, Peggy. "White Privilege: Unpacking the Invisible Knapsack." *Peace and Freedom,* July/August 1989, 10–12. http://nationalseedproject.org/peggy-mcintosh
-s-white-privilege-papers.

McMurtrie, Beth. "I Believe I Can Leave This Place Better Than I Found It." *Chronicle
of Higher Education,* January 8, 2016. http://www.chronicle.com/article/What
-Its-Like-to-Be-Black-at/234771.

Mead, George H. *Mind, Self, and Society.* Chicago: University of Chicago Press, 1934.

Meyerson, Collier. "The Women Behind Black Lives Matter: 'We Gave Tongue to
Something We All Knew Was Happening.'" *Glamour,* November 1, 2016. http://
www.glamour.com/story/women-of-the-year-black-lives-matter-founders.

Mickelson, Roslyn Arlin, and Anne E. Velasco. "Bring It On! Diverse Responses to
'Acting White' Among Academically Able Black Adolescents." In Horvat and
O'Connor, *Beyond Acting White,* 27–57.

Migration Policy Institute. *The Pakistani Diaspora in the United States,* rev. ed., June
2015. www.migrationpolicy.org/sites/default/files/publications/RADPakistan.pdf.

Miller, Jean Baker. "Connections, Disconnections, and Violations." *Work in Progress,*
no. 33. Wellesley, MA: Stone Center Working Paper Series, 1988.

———. "Domination and Subordination." In *Toward a New Psychology of Women,* 3–9.
Boston: Beacon Press, 1976.

Miller, Robin Lin, and Mary-Jane Rotheram-Borus. "Growing Up Biracial in the
United States." In Salett and Koslow, *Race, Ethnicity, and Self,* 143–169.

Miville, Marie L. "Latina/o Identity Development: Updates on Theory, Measurement,
and Counseling Implications." In Ponterotto et al., *Handbook of Multicultural
Counseling,* 241–252.

Mohamed, Besheer. "A New Estimate of the U.S. Muslim Population." *Fact Tank,* Pew
Research Center, January 9, 2016. http://www.pewresearch.org/fact-tank/2016
/01/06/a-new-estimate-of-the-u-s-muslim-population/.

Molina, Natalia. "How Mexican-Americans Assimilate into U.S. Culture." *San Diego
Union Tribune,* November 23, 2016. http://www.sandiegotribune.com/opinion
/commentary/sd-mexican-americans-molina-20161123-story.html

Moore, Eddie, Jr., Marguerite W. Penick-Parks, and Ali Michael, eds. *Everyday White
People Confront Racial and Social Injustice: 15 Stories.* Sterling, VA: Stylus, 2015.
Kindle edition.

Morris, Monique W. *Black Stats: African Americans by the Numbers in the Twenty-First
Century.* New York: The New Press, 2014. Kindle edition.

Motel, Seth, and Eileen Patten. *Hispanics of Mexican Origin in the United States, 2010:
Statistical Profile.* Pew Research Center, June 27, 2012. http://www.pewhispanic
.org/2012/06/27/hispanics-of-mexican-origin-in-the-united-states-2010/.

Mullen, Kirsten. "Subtle Lessons in Racism." *USA Weekend,* November 6–8, 1992,
10–11.

Mura, David. "A Shift in Power, a Sea Change in the Arts: Asian American Construc- tions." In *The State of Asian America: Activism and Resistance in the 1990s,* edited by Karin Aguilar-San Juan, 183–204. Boston: South End Press, 1994.

Murphy, Cullen. "Home: Some Thoughts on the Frost Library Protest." *Amherst,* August 1, 2016. https://www.amherst.edu/amherst-story/magazine/issues/2016-summer /home.

Murrell, Audrey J., Beth L. Dietz-Uhler, John F. Dovidio, Samuel L. Gaertner, and Cheryl Drout. "Aversive Racism and Resistance to Affirmative Action: Percep- tions of Justice Are Not Necessarily Color Blind." *Basic and Applied Social Psychol- ogy* 15, no. 1–2 (1994): 71–86.

National Center for Education Statistics. "Indicator 16 Snapshot: High School Status Dropout Rates for Racial/Ethnic Subgroups." August 2016. https://nces.ed.gov /programs/raceindicators/indicator_rdcs.asp.

National Center for Education Statistics. "Indicator 18 Snapshot: College Participation Rates for Racial/Ethnic Subgroups." August 2016. https://nces.ed.gov/programs /raceindicators/indicator_reas.asp.

National Fair Housing Alliance. *Unequal Opportunity—Perpetuating Housing Segrega- tion in America.* April 5, 2006. http://nationalfairhousing.org/wp-content/uploads /2017/04/trends2006.pdf.

Neville, Helen, Miguel Gallardo, and Derald Wing Sue, eds. *The Myth of Racial Color Blindness: Manifestations, Dynamics and Impact.* Washington, DC: American Psychological Association, 2016. Kindle edition.

New, Jake. "Survey Finds Big Differences Between Black HBCU Graduates, Those Who Attended Other Institutions." *Inside Higher Ed,* October 28, 2015. https://www .insidehighered.com/news/2015/10/28/survey-finds-big-differences-between -black-hbcu-graduates-those-who-attended-other.

Newport, Frank. "In U.S., 87% Approve of Black-White Marriage, vs. 4% in 1958." Gallup, July 25, 2013. http://www.gallup.com/poll/163697/approve-marriage-blacks -whites.aspx.

"New York Times Executive Editor on the New Terrain of Covering Trump." *Fresh Air,* NPR, December 8, 2016. http://www.npr.org/templates/transcript/transcript .php?storyId=504806512.

Nguyen, Tina. "Suspected Church Shooter Allegedly Said He Wanted to Start a Race War." *Vanity Fair,* June 19, 2015. http://www.vanityfair.com/news/2015/06 /Charleston-church-shooter-confesses-dylan-roof.

Nieto, Sonia, and Patty Bode. *Affirming Diversity: The Sociopolitical Context of Multicul- tural Education.* 6th ed. Boston: Allyn & Bacon, 2012.

Nir, Sarah Maslin. "Finding Hate Crimes on the Rise, Leaders Condemn Vicious Acts." *New York Times,* December 5, 2016. http://nyti.ms/2h9hmYg.

Oakes, Jeannie. *Keeping Track: How Schools Structure Inequality.* New Haven, CT: Yale University Press, 1985.

Obama, Barack. "Remarks by the President at Howard University Commencement Cer- emony." Press release. The White House, Office of the Press Secretary, May 7, 2016. https://www.whitehouse.gov/the-press-office/2016/05/07/remarks-president -howard-university-commencement-ceremony.

————. "Statement by the President." Press release. The White House, Office of the Press Secretary, July 14, 2013. https://www.whitehouse.gov/the-press-office/2013 /07/14/statement-president.

"Obama's Victory on Newspaper Front Pages." *Huffington Post,* December 6, 2008. http://www.huffingtonpost.com/2008/11/05/obamas-victory-on-newspaper_n _141311.html.

Omi, Michael, and Howard Winant. *Racial Formation in the United States.* 3rd ed. New York: Routledge, 2015.

Ong, Anthony D., Jean S. Phinney, and Jessica Dennis. "Competence Under Challenge: Exploring the Protective Influence of Parental Support and Ethnic Identity in Latino College Students." *Journal of Adolescence* 29, no. 6 (2006): 961–979.

Ongtooguk, Paul. "Remarks of Mr. Paul Ongtooguk." Alaska Native Education Summit, November 30, 2001, Anchorage, AK. http://www.alaskool.org/native_ed/PO -ANES-speech.html.

————. "Their Silence About Us: The Absence of Alaska Natives in the Curriculum." Presentation at the annual meeting of the American Educational Research Association, Atlanta, GA, April 1993.

Orfield, Gary, Jongyeon Ee, Erica Frankenberg, and Genevieve Siegel-Hawley. *Brown at 62: School Segregation by Race, Poverty and State.* Los Angeles: Civil Rights Project, University of California, Los Angeles, 2016.

Osterhaus, Erin. "Survey: Employee Resource Groups Help Engage Gen Y Workers." *New Talent Times,* July 28, 2014. http://new-talent-times.softwareadvice.com /employee-resource-groups-engage-gen-y-0714/.

O'Toole, C. "The Effect of the Media and Multicultural Education on Children's Perceptions of Native Americans." Senior thesis, Department of Psychology and Education, Mount Holyoke College, May 1990.

Oyserman, Daphna, Daniel Brickman, and Marjorie Rhodes. "Racial-Ethnic Identity: Content and Consequences for African American, Latino and Latina Youths." In Fuligni, *Contesting Stereotypes and Creating Identities,* 91–114.

Padilla, Amado, ed. *Hispanic Psychology.* Thousand Oaks, CA: Sage, 1995.

Page, Scott E. *The Difference: How the Power of Diversity Creates Better Groups, Firms, Schools, and Societies.* Princeton, NJ: Princeton University Press, 2007.

Page, Susan. "Poll: Hopes Are High for Race Relations." *USA Today,* weekend edition, November 7–9, 2008. https://usatoday30.usatoday.com/news/politics/election 2008/2008-11-06-poll_N.htm#.

Pager, Devah. "The Mark of a Criminal Record." *American Journal of Sociology* 108, no. 5 (March 2003): 937–975.

Pager, Devah, Bruce Western, and Bart Bonikowski. "Discrimination in a Low-Wage Labor Market: A Field Experiment." *American Sociological Review* 74 (2009): 777–799.

Palmer, Parker. *The Active Life: Wisdom for Work, Creativity, and Caring.* New York: HarperCollins, 1990.

Pang, Valerie Ooka, Peter N. Kianga, and Yoon K. Pak. "Asian Pacific American Students: Challenging a Biased Educational System." In Banks and Banks, *Handbook of Research on Multicultural Education,* 542–563.

Parham, Thomas A. "Cycles of Psychological Nigrescence." *The Counseling Psychologist* 17, no. 2 (1989): 187–226.

Parker, Ashley, and Steve Eder. "Inside the Six Weeks Donald Trump Was a Nonstop 'Birther.'" *New York Times,* July 2, 2016. http://nyti.ms/29WCu51.

Patel, Eboo. Introduction to Garrod and Kilkenny, *Growing Up Muslim,* locations 137–365.

Patten, Eileen. *The Nation's Latino Population Is Defined By Its Youth.* Pew Research Center, April 20, 2016. http://www.pewhispanic.org/files/2016/04/PH_2016-04 -20_LatinoYouth-Final.pdf.

Petersen, William. "Success Story, Japanese-American Style." *New York Times Magazine,* January 9, 1966.

Pew Research Center. *On Views of Race and Inequality, Blacks and Whites Are Worlds Apart.* June 27, 2016. http://www.pewsocialtrends.org/2016/06/27/on-views-of -race-and-inequality-blacks-and-whites-are-worlds-apart/.

———. *Multiracial in America: Proud, Diverse and Growing in Numbers.* June 11, 2015. http://www.pewsocialtrends.org/2015/06/11/multiracial-in-america/.

———. *The Rise of Asian Americans.* Updated ed. April 4, 2013. http://www.pew socialtrends.org/2012/06/19/the-rise-of-asian-americans/.

Phillips, Steve. *Brown Is the New White: How the Demographic Revolution Has Created a New American Majority.* New York: The New Press, 2016.

Phillips, Victoria, and Erik Stegman. *Missing the Point: The Real Impact of Native Mascots and Team Names on American Indian and Alaska Native Youth.* Washington, DC: Center for American Progress, 2014. http://digitalcommons.wcl.american .edu/cgi/viewcontent.cgi?article=1003&context=fasch_rpt.

Phinney, Jean S. "Ethnic Identity in Adolescents and Adults: Review of Research." *Psychological Bulletin* 108, no. 3 (1990): 499–514.

———. "A Three-Stage Model of Ethnic Identity Development in Adolescence." In *Ethnic Identity: Formation and Transmission Among Hispanics and Other Minorities,* edited by Martha E. Bernal and George P. Knight, 61–79. Albany: State University of New York Press, 1993.

Phinney, Jean S., Bruce T. Lochner, and Rodolfo Murphy. "Ethnic Identity Development and Psychological Adjustment in Adolescence." In *Ethnic Issues in Adolescent Mental Health,* edited by Arlene Rubin Stiffman and Larry. E. Davis, 53–72. Newbury Park, CA: Sage, 1990.

Phinney, Jean S., and Steve Tarver. "Ethnic Identity Search and Commitment in Black and White Eighth Graders." *Journal of Early Adolescence* 8, no. 3 (1988): 265–277.

Pierce, Chester. "Mundane Extreme Environment and Its Effects on Learning." In *Learning Disabilities: Issues and Recommendations for Research,* edited by Suzanne Gage Brainard, 111–118. Washington, DC: National Institute of Education, 1975.

Ponterotto, Joseph G., J. Manuel Casas, Lisa A. Suzuki, and Charlene M. Alexander, eds. *Handbook of Multicultural Counseling.* 3rd ed. Thousand Oaks, CA: Sage, 2010.

———, eds. *Handbook of Multicultural Counseling.* 1st ed. Thousand Oaks, CA: Sage, 1995.

"Presidential Election Results: Donald J. Trump Wins." *New York Times,* December 8, 2016. http://www.nytimes.com/elections/results/president.

Quah, Nicholas, and Laura E. Davis. "Here's a Timeline of Unarmed Black People Killed by Police over Past Year." *BuzzFeed,* May 1, 2015. https://www.buzzfeed .com/nicholasquah/heres-a-timeline-of-unarmed-black-men-killed-by-police -over?utm_term=.mxzKnEJLO#.hypOZzjkd.

Ramakrishnan, Karthick, and Farah Z. Ahmad. *State of Asian Americans and Pacific Islanders Series: A Multifaceted Portrait of a Growing Population.* Center for American Progress, April 2014. http://aapidata.com/wp-content/uploads/2015/10 /AAPIData-CAP-report.pdf.

Ramsey, Patricia G. *Teaching and Learning in a Diverse World: Multicultural Education for Young Children.* 4th ed. New York: Teachers College Press, 2015.

Rappeport, Alan. "Civil Rights Groups Call on Trump to Denounce Racism of Alt-Right." *New York Times,* November 21, 2016. http://mobile.nytimes.com/2016 /11/21/us/politics/alt-right-trump.html.

Rappeport, Alan, and Noah Wieland. "White Nationalists Celebrate 'an Awakening' After Donald Trump's Victory." *New York Times,* November 19, 2016. http://nyti .ms/2fc6vve.

Reddy, Maureen T. *Crossing the Color Line: Race, Parenting, and Culture.* New Brunswick, NJ: Rutgers University Press, 1994.

"Reflections from IGR's Graduate Student Instructors." The Program on Intergroup Relations, University of Michigan, https://igr.umich.edu/article/reflections-igrs -graduate-student-instructors.

Reilly, Katie. "Kids Are Stressed About Donald Trump. So Los Angeles Schools Launched a Hotline." *Time,* December 8, 2016. http://time.com/4595309/los -angeles-school-counselors-donald-trump/.

Richardson, Tina Q., Angela R. Bethea, Charlayne C. Hayling, and Claudette Williamson-Taylor. "African and Afro-Caribbean American Identity Development." In Ponterotto et al., *Handbook of Multicultural Counseling,* 227–240.

Riley, Angela R., and Kristen A. Carpenter. "Owning *Red*: A Theory of Indian (Cultural) Appropriation." *Texas Law Review* 94 (2016): 859–931.

Ringgold, Faith. *Aunt Harriet's Underground Railroad in the Sky.* New York: Crown, 1992.

Robbins, Jill. "How I Finally 'Got' the Meaning of White Privilege." *Huffington Post,* July 8, 2016. http://www.huffingtonpost.com/jill-robbins/what-white-privilege -means_b_10874218.html.

Roberts, Laura Morgan, and Robin J. Ely. "Why Did So Many White Women Vote for Donald Trump?" *Fortune,* November 17, 2016. http://fortune.com/2016/11/17 /donald-trump-women-voters-election/.

Rockquemore, Kerry Ann and David Brunsma. *Beyond Black: Biracial Identity in America.* Lanham, MD: Rowman and Littlefield, 2008.

Rockquemore, Kerry Ann, Tracey Laszloffy, and Julia Noveske. "It All Starts at Home: Racial Socialization in Multiracial Families." In Brunsma, *Mixed Messages,* 203–216.

Rodriguez, Richard. *Hunger of Memory: The Education of Richard Rodriguez.* New York: Bantam, 1982.

Roithmayr, Daria. *Reproducing Racism: How Everyday Choices Lock In White Advantage.* New York: New York University Press, 2014.

Roland, Alan. "Identity, Self, and Individualism in a Multicultural Perspective." In Salett and Koslow, *Race, Ethnicity, and Self,* 11–23.

Root, Maria P. P. "Filipino Families." In McGoldrick, Giordano, and Garcia-Preto, *Ethnicity and Family Therapy,* 319–331.

———. "Within, Between, and Beyond Race." In Root, *Racially Mixed People in America,* 3–11.

———, ed. *The Multiracial Experience: Racial Borders as the New Frontier.* Thousand Oaks, CA: Sage, 1996

———, ed. *Racially Mixed People in America.* Thousand Oaks, CA: Sage, 1992.

Rothenberg, Paula S., ed. *Race, Class, and Gender in the United States: An Integrated Study.* 9th ed. New York: Worth Publishers / Macmillan Learning, 2016.

Rusin, Sylvia, Jie Zong, and Jeanne Batalova. "Cuban Immigrants in the United States." *Migration Information Source,* Migration Policy Institute, April 2015. http://www.migrationpolicy.org/article/cuban-immigrants-united-states.

Russell, Kathy, Midge Wilson, and Ronald Hall. *The Color Complex.* San Diego: Harcourt Brace Jovanovich, 1992.

Sabogal, Fabio, Gerardo Marín, Regina Otero-Sabogal, Barbara Vanoss Marín, and Eliseo J. Perez-Stable. "Hispanic Familism and Acculturation: What Changes and What Doesn't?" *Hispanic Journal of Behavioral Sciences* 9, no. 4 (1987): 397–412.

Salett, Elizabeth Pathy, and Diane R. Koslow, eds. *Race, Ethnicity, and Self: Identity in Multicultural Perspective.* Washington, DC: National MultiCultural Institute, 1994.

Samuels, Robert. "Donald Trump Keeps Attacking Muslims. They Plan to Fight Back at the Ballot Box." *Washington Post,* June 15, 2016. https://www.washingtonpost.com/politics/election-rhetoric-spurs-political-awakening-among-muslims-in-new-jersey/2016/06/14/01734464-3237-11e6-8ff7-7b6c1998b7a0_story.html.

Saporta, Maria. "Business Leaders Launch Atlanta Friendship Initiative." *Atlanta Business Chronicle,* October 28, 2016. http://www.bizjournals.com/atlanta/news/2016/10/28/business-leaders-launch-atlanta-friendship.html.

Scherr, Sonia. "Children of Extremists Denounce Parents' Beliefs." *Intelligence Report,* Southern Poverty Law Center, November 30, 2009. https://www.splcenter.org/fighting-hate/intelligence-report/2009/children-extremists-denounce-parents'-beliefs.

Schoem, David, and Penny A. Pasque. "The Michigan Community Scholars Program: Engaging the Whole of Service-Learning, Diversity, and Learning Communities." In Galura et al., *Engaging the Whole of Service-Learning, Diversity, and Learning Communities,* 33–50.

Segrest, Mab. *Memoir of a Race Traitor.* Boston: South End Press, 1994.

Shaw, Theodore. Introduction to *The Ferguson Report: Department of Justice Investigation of the Ferguson Police Department,* by US Department of Justice, Civil Rights Division. New York: The New Press, 2015.

Shibusawa, Tazuko. "Japanese Families." In McGoldrick, Giordano, and Garcia-Preto, *Ethnicity and Family Therapy,* 339–348.

Singley, Bernestine. *When Race Becomes Real: Black and White Writers Confront Their Personal Histories.* Chicago: Lawrence Hill Books, 2002.

*Skin Deep: College Students Confront Racism,* produced and directed by Frances Reid (San Francisco: Resolution/California Newsreel, 1995), video.

Sleeter, Christine. "White Racism." *Multicultural Education* 1, no. 4 (Spring 1994): 5–8, 39.

Snipp, C. Matthew. "American Indian Studies." In Banks and Banks, *Handbook on Research on Multicultural Education,* 315–331.

Southern Poverty Law Center. *Ten Days After: Harassment and Intimidation in the Aftermath of the Election.* November 2016. https://www.splcenter.org/sites/default /files/com_hate_incidents_report_final.pdf.

Spanierman, Lisa B., and Jason R. Soble. "Understanding Whiteness: Previous Approaches and Possible Directions in the Study of White Racial Attitudes and Identity." In Ponterotto et al., *Handbook of Multicultural Counseling,* 283–299.

Spickard, Paul R. "The Illogic of American Racial Categories." In Root, *Racially Mixed People in America,* 12–23.

Spring, Joel. *Deculturalization and the Struggle for Equality: A Brief History of the Education of Dominated Cultures in the United States.* 8th ed. New York: Routledge, 2016.

Stalvey, Lois. *The Education of a WASP.* Madison: University of Wisconsin Press, [1970] 1989.

Steele, Claude. "Stereotype Threat and African-American Student Achievement." In *Young, Gifted and Black: Promoting High Achievement Among African American Students,* edited by Theresa Perry, Claude Steele, and Asa Hilliard III, 109–130. Boston: Beacon Press, 2003.

———. "Thin Ice: Stereotype Threat and Black College Students." *Atlantic Monthly,* August 1999, 44–54.

———. *Whistling Vivaldi and Other Clues to How Stereotypes Affect Us.* New York: W. W. Norton, 2010.

Steele, Claude, and Joshua Aronson. "Stereotype Threat and the Intellectual Test Performance of African-Americans." *Journal of Personality and Social Psychology* 69, no. 5 (1995): 797–811.

Stephens-Davidowitz, Seth. "The Data of Hate." *New York Times,* July 12, 2014. https://nyti.ms/1kifZ4t.

Stepler, Renee. "Hispanic, Black Parents See College Degree as Key for Children's Success." *Fact Tank,* Pew Research Center, February 24, 2016. http://www.pew research.org/fact-tank/2016/02/24/hispanic-black-parents-see-college-degree-as -key-for-childrens-success/.

Stepler, Renee, and Anna Brown. *Statistical Portrait of Hispanics in the United States.* Pew Research Center, April 19, 2016. http://www.pewhispanic.org/2016/04/19 /statistical-portrait-of-hispanics-in-the-united-states-key-charts/.

Steptoe, John. *Mufaro's Beautiful Daughters: An African Tale.* New York: Scholastic, 1989.

Stewart, Abigail J., and Joseph M. Healy. "Linking Individual Development and Social Changes." *American Psychologist* 44, no. 1 (1989): 30–42.

"Students Talk About the Minor in Intergroup Relations Education." The Program on Intergroup Relations, University of Michigan, https://igr.umich.edu/article/students-talk-about-minor-intergroup-relations.

Suárez-Orozco, Carola, and Marcelo Suárez-Orozco. *Transformations: Immigration, Family Life, and Achievement Motivation Among Latino Adolescents.* Stanford, CA: Stanford University Press, 1995.

"Success Story of One Minority in the U.S." *U.S. News and World Report,* December 26, 1966, 73–78.

Sue, Derald Wing. *Microaggressions in Everyday Life: Race, Gender, and Sexual Orientation.* Hoboken, NJ: John Wiley & Sons, 2010.

Sugrue, Thomas J. "Less Separate, Still Unequal: Diversity and Equality in 'Post-Civil Rights' America." In Lewis and Cantor, *Our Compelling Interests,* 39–70.

Sullivan, Tim, Wanjiku Mwangi, Brian Miller, Dedrick Muhammad, and Colin Harris. *State of the Dream 2012: The Emerging Majority.* United for a Fair Economy, 2012. http://www.faireconomy.org/dream12.

Sutton, CharlesEtta T., and Mary Anne Broken Nose. "American Indian Families: An Overview." In McGoldrick, Giordano, and Garcia-Preto, *Ethnicity and Family Therapy,* 43–54.

Svrluga, Susan. "Black UPenn Freshman Added to the Racist Social Media Account with 'Daily Lynching' Calendar." *Washington Post,* November 11, 2016. https://www.washingtonpost.com/news/grade-point/wp/2016/11/11/black-upenn-freshmen-added-to-racist-social-media-account-with-daily-lynching-calendar/

Tabron, La June Montgomery. "The W. K. Kellogg Foundation's Deepening Commitment to Racial Equity." *Liberal Education* 102, no. 4 (Fall 2016): 22–45.

Tafoya, Nadine, and Ann Del Vecchio. "Back to the Future: An Examination of the Native American Holocaust Experience." In McGoldrick, Giordano, and Garcia-Preto, *Ethnicity and Family Therapy,* 55–64.

Takaki, Ronald. *A Different Mirror: A History of Multicultural America.* Boston: Little, Brown, 1993.

Tatum, Beverly Daniel. "African-American Identity, Academic Achievement, and Missing History." *Social Education* 56, no. 6 (1992): 331–334.

———. *Assimilation Blues: Black Families in a White Community.* New York: Basic Books, 2002.

———. *Can We Talk About Race? and Other Conversations in an Era of School Resegregation.* Boston: Beacon Press, 2007.

———. "Out There Stranded? Black Youth in White Communities." In *Black Families,* 3rd ed., edited by Harriet Pipes McAdoo, 214–233. Thousand Oaks, CA: Sage, 1996.

———. "Racial Identity and Relational Theory: The Case of Black Women in White Communities." *Work in Progress,* no. 63. Wellesley, MA: Stone Center Working Papers, 1992.

———. "Talking About Race, Learning About Racism: An Application of Racial Identity Development Theory in the Classroom." *Harvard Educational Review* 62, no. 1 (1992): 1–24.

————. "Teaching White Students About Racism: The Search for White Allies and the Restoration of Hope." *Teachers College Record* 95, no. 4 (1994): 462–476.

Tatum, Beverly Daniel, and Elizabeth G. Knaplund. "Outside the Circle: The Relational Implications for White Women Working Against Racism." *Work in Progress*, no. 78. Wellesley, MA: Stone Center Working Paper Series, 1996.

Tatum, Beverly Daniel, Phyllis C. Brown, Paula Elliott, and Travis Tatum. "Student Efficacy Training: An Evaluation of One Middle School's Programmatic Response to the Eastern Massachusetts Initiative." Presentation at the annual meeting of the American Educational Research Association, New York, April 9, 1996.

Taylor, Dalmas. "Affirmative Action and Presidential Executive Orders." In Blanchard and Crosby, *Affirmative Action in Perspective*, 21–29.

Taylor, Keeanga-Yamahtta. *From #BlackLivesMatter to Black Liberation*. Chicago: Haymarket Books, 2016.

Taylor, Robert Joseph, and Linda M. Chatters. "Religious Life." In Jackson, *Life in Black America*, 105–123.

Teixeira, Ruy, and John Halpin, *Building an All-In Nation: A View from the American Public*. Center for American Progress, October 2013. https://www.american progress.org/issues/race/reports/2013/10/22/77665/building-an-all-in-nation/.

Terrazas, Aaron. "Salvadoran Immigrants in the United States." *Migration Information Source*, Migration Policy Institute, January 2010. http://www.migrationpolicy .org/article/salvadoran-immigrants-united-states.

The Sentencing Project. *Fact Sheet: Incarcerated Women and Girls*. November 2015. http://www.sentencingproject.org/wp-content/uploads/2016/02/Incarcerated -Women-and-Girls.pdf.

The Sentencing Project. *Fact Sheet: Trends in U.S. Corrections*. 2016. http://sentencing project.org/wp-content/uploads/2016/01/Trends-in-US-Corrections.pdf.

Thompson, Becky. *A Promise and a Way of Life: White Antiracist Activism*. Minneapolis: University of Minneapolis Press.

————. "Time Traveling and Border Crossing: Reflections on White Identity." In Thompson and Tyagi, *Names We Call Home*, 93–109.

Thompson, Becky, and Sangeeta Tyagi, eds. *Names We Call Home: Autobiography on Racial Identity*. New York: Routledge, 1996.

Thompson, Becky, and White Women Challenging Racism. "Home/Work: Antiracism Activism and the Meaning of Whiteness." In Fine et al., *Off White*, 354–366.

Tienda, Marta. "Diversity as a Strategic Advantage: A Sociodemographic Perspective." In Lewis and Cantor, *Our Compelling Interests*, 192–205.

Tochluk, Shelly. *Witnessing Whiteness: The Need to Talk About Race and How to Do It*. 2nd ed. Lanham, MD: Rowman and Littlefield Education, 2010.

Toldson, Ivory A. "The 'Acting White' Theory Doesn't Add Up." *The Root*, January 30, 2013. http://www.theroot.com/articles/politics/2013/01/acting_white_theory_black _academic_achievement_based_on_other_factors.

Toobin, Jeffrey. "The Real Voting Scandal of 2016." *The New Yorker*, December 12, 2016. http://www.newyorker.com/magazine/2016/12/12/the-real-voting-scandal -of-2016.

Torres, Vasti. "Influences on Ethnic Identity Development of Latino College Students in the First Two Years of College." *Journal of College Student Development* 44, no. 4 (2003): 532–547.

Trump, Donald. "Full Text: Donald Trump 2016 RNC Draft Speech Transcript, July 21, 2016." http://www.politico.com/story/2016/07/full-transcript-donald-trump-nomination-acceptance-speech-at-rnc-225974.

Tse, Lucy. "Finding a Place to Be: Asian Americans in Ethnic Identity Exploration." *Adolescence* 34, no. 133 (Spring 1999):121–138.

Turner, Ani. *The Business Case for Racial Equity.* W. K. Kellogg Foundation and Altarum Institute, 2013. http://www.wkkf.org/resource-directory/resource/2013/10/the-business-case-for-racial-equity.

Tynes, Brendesha M. "Online Racial Discrimination: A Growing Problem for Adolescents." Science Brief, *Psychological Science Agenda*, December 2015. American Psychological Association. http://www.apa.org/science/about/psa/2015/12/online-racial-discrimination.aspx.

Tyson, Alec, and Shiva Maniam. "Behind Trump's Victory: Divisions by Race, Gender, Education." *Fact Tank,* Pew Research Center, November 9, 2016. http://www.pewresearch.org/fact-tank/2016/11/09/behind-trumps-victory-divisions-by-race-gender-education.

Tyson, Karolyn. "The Making of A 'Burden': Tracing the Development of a 'Burden of Acting White' in Schools." In Horvat and O'Connor, *Beyond Acting White,* 57–88.

Tyson, Karolyn, William Darity Jr., and Domini R. Castellino. "It's Not 'A Black Thing': Understanding the Burden of Acting White and Other Dilemmas of High Achievement." *American Sociological Review* 70, no. 4 (August 2005): 582–605.

Umaña-Taylor, Adriana J., Stephen Quintana, Richard M. Lee, William E. Cross Jr., Deborah Rivas-Drake, Seth J. Schwartz, Moin Syed, Tiffany Yip, Eleanor Seaton, and Ethnic and Racial Identity in the 21st Century Study Group. "Ethnic and Racial Identity During Adolescence and into Young Adulthood: An Integrated Conceptualization." *Child Development* 85, no. 1 (2014): 21–39.

United States Census Bureau. "2010 Census Shows Nearly Half of American Indians and Alaska Natives Report Multiple Races." Press release. January 25, 2012. https://www.census.gov/newsroom/releases/archives/2010_census/cb 12-cn06.html.

———. "American Indian and Alaska Native Heritage Month: November 2016." *Facts for Features,* November 2016. www.census.gov/content/dam/Census/newsroom/facts-for-features/2016/cb26-ff22_aian.pdf.

———. "Annual Estimates of the Resident Population by Sex, Age, Race Alone or in Combination, and Hispanic Origin for the United States and States: April 1, 2010 to July 1, 2015." American FactFinder, May 2015. https://factfinder.census.gov/bkmk/table/1.0/en/PEP/2015/PEPASR5H.

———. "Asian/Pacific American Heritage Month: May 2016." *Facts for Features,* April 21, 2016 http://www.census.gov/newsroom/facts-for-features/2016/cb16-ff07.

———. "Hispanic Heritage Month 2016." *Facts for Features,* October 12, 2016. www.census.gov/newsroom/facts-for-features/2016/cb16-ff16.html.

United States Commission on Civil Rights. "Statement of U.S. Commission on Civil Rights on the Use of Native American Images and Nicknames as Sports Symbols." Press release. 2001. http://www.usccr.gov/press/archives/2001/041601st.htm.

United States Department of Justice, Civil Rights Division. *The Ferguson Report: Department of Justice Investigation of the Ferguson Police Department.* New York: The New Press, 2015.

United States Supreme Court. *Fisher v. University of Texas at Austin et al.* Syllabus. 579 US ___ (2016). https://www.supremecourt.gov/opinions/15pdf/14-981_4g15.pdf.

Updegrave, Walter L. "Race and Money." *Money,* December 1989, 152–172.

Valby, Karen. "The Realities of Raising a Kid of a Different Race." Time.com, 2015. http://time.com/the-realities-of-raising-a-kid-of-a-different-race.

van den Berghe, Pierre L. *Race and Racism: A Comparative Perspective.* New York: Wiley, 1967.

Vandelinder, Emma. "Racial Climate at MU: A Timeline of Incidents This Fall." *Columbia Missourian,* November 6, 2015 (updated November 9, 2015). http://www.columbiamissourian.com/news/higher_education/racial-climate-at-mu-a-timeline-of-incidents-this-fall/article_0c96f986-84c6-11e5-a38f-2bd0aab0bf74.html.

*Veasey et al. v. Perry et al.* 574 U.S. _2014 (Ginsburg, J., dissenting). https://www.supremecourt.gov/opinions/14pdf/14a393_08m1.pdf.

Voting Rights Act of 1965. Pub. L. 89-110, 79 Stat. 437.

Wadsworth, Barry J. *Piaget's Theory of Cognitive and Affective Development: Foundations of Constructivism.* 5th ed. Boston: Allyn and Bacon, 2003.

Wallis, Jim. *America's Original Sin: Racism, White Privilege, and a Bridge to a New America.* Grand Rapids, MI: Brazos Press, 2016.

Wang, Wendy. "Interracial Marriage: Who Is 'Marrying Out'?" *Fact Tank,* Pew Research Center, June 12, 2015. http://www.pewresearch.org/fact-tank/2015/06/12/interracial-marriage-who-is-marrying-out/.

Ward, Janie Victoria. "Uncovering Truths, Recovering Lives." In Leadbeater and Way, *Urban Girls Revisited,* 190–207.

———. "Raising Resisters: The Role of Truth Telling in the Psychological Development of African-American Girls." In Leadbeater and Way, *Urban Girls,* 85–99. New York: New York University Press, 1996.

Warner, Gertrude Chandler. *The Boxcar Children.* Niles, IL: Albert Whitman, 1942.

Warren, Mark R. *Fire in the Heart: How White Activists Embrace Racial Justice.* New York: Oxford University Press, 2010.

Washburn, Kevin K. "What's at Stake for Tribes? The U.S. Department of Justice Office of Legal Counsel Opinion on Internet Gaming, Testimony of Dean Kevin K. Washburn, Oversight Hearing Before the United States Senate Committee on Indian Affairs, 112th Congress, Second Session." UNM School of Law Research Paper No. 2012-04, February 9, 2012. http://lawschool.unm.edu/news/archives/2012/feb/washburn-testimony.pdf.

Waters, Mary C. "The Intersection of Gender, Race, and Ethnicity in Identity Development of Caribbean American Teens." In Leadbeater and Way, *Urban Girls,* 65–81.

Wellman, David. *Portraits of White Racism.* Cambridge: Cambridge University Press, 1977.

Wentworth, Phyllis A. "The Identity Development of Non-Traditionally Aged First-Generation Women College Students: An Exploratory Study." Master's thesis, Department of Psychology and Education, Mount Holyoke College, 1994.

"Why Freddie Gray Ran." *Baltimore Sun,* April 25, 2015. http://www.baltimoresun.com/news/opinion/editorial/bs-ed-freddie-gray-20150425-story.html.

Wijeyesinghe, Charmaine. "The Intersectional Model of Multiracial Identity: Integrating Multiracial Identity Theories and Intersectional Perspectives on Social Identity." In *New Perspectives on Racial Identity Development: Integrating Emerging Frameworks,* 2nd ed., edited by Charmaine L. Wijeyesinghe and Bailey W. Jackson III, 81–107. New York: New York University Press, 2012.

Wilkerson, Isabel. *The Warmth of Other Suns: The Epic Story of America's Great Migration.* New York: Random House, 2010.

Williams, Timothy. "Quietly, Indians Reshape Cities and Reservations." *New York Times,* April 13, 2013. http://www.nytimes.com/2013/04/14/us/as-american-indians-move-to-cities-old-and-new-challenges-follow.html.

Williams, Timothy, and Michael Wines. "Shootings Further Divide a Nation Torn over Race." *New York Times,* July 8, 2016. http://www.nytimes.com/2016/07/09/us/shootings-further-divide-a-nation-torn-over-race.html.

Wingfield, Adia Harvey. "Being Black—But Not Too Black—in the Workplace." *The Atlantic,* October 14, 2015. http://www.theatlantic.com/business/archive/2015/10/being-black-work/409990/.

Winter, Jeanette. *Follow the Drinking Gourd.* New York: Dragonfly Books, 1988.

Wise, Tim. *White Like Me: Reflections on Race from a Privileged Son—The Remix.* Rev. ed. Berkeley, CA: Soft Skull Press, 2011.

Woodward, Stephanie. "The Police Killings No One Is Talking About: A Special Investigation." *In These Times,* October 17, 2016. http://inthesetimes.com/features/native_american_police_killings_native_lives_matter.html.

Wortham, Jenna. "Black Tweets Matter." *Smithsonian,* September 2016.

Wright, Lawrence. "One Drop of Blood." *The New Yorker,* July 25, 1994, 46–55.

Wright, Richard. "The Ethics of Living Jim Crow: An Autobiographical Sketch." In *Uncle Tom's Children,* 1–15. New York: Harper and Brothers, 1938; New York: HarperCollins, 2009.

Yamada, Mitsuye. "Invisibility Is an Unnatural Disaster: Reflections of an Asian American Woman." In *This Bridge Called My Back: Writings by Radical Women of Color,* edited by Cherríe Moraga and Gloria Anzaldúa, 35–40. New York: Kitchen Table Press, 1981.

Yen, Hope. "80 Percent of U.S. Adults Face Near-Poverty, Unemployment: Survey." *Huffington Post,* July 28, 2013. http://www.huffingtonpost.com/2013/07/28/poverty-unemployment-rates_n_3666594.html.

Yeoman, Barry. "Telling Stories, Breaking Barriers." *Mindful,* August 11, 2016, 58.

Yoshikawa, Hirokazu, and Jenya Kholoptseva. *Unauthorized Immigrant Parents and Their Children's Development: A Summary of the Evidence.* Migration Policy Institute,

March 2013. http://www.migrationpolicy.org/research/unauthorized-immigrant -parents-and-their-childrens-development.

Zane, Nancie. "Interrupting Historical Patterns: Bridging Race and Gender Gaps Between Senior White Men and Other Organizational Groups." In Fine et al., *Off White,* 343–353.

Zapotowsky, Matt. "Justice Department Report Blasts San Francisco Police." *Washington Post,* October 12, 2016. https://www.washingtonpost.com/world/national-security /justice-department-report-blasts-san-francisco-police/2016/10/12/becb841c-90 a2-11e6-a6a3-d50061aa9fae_story.html.

Zavala, Maria. "A Bridge over Divided Worlds: An Exploration into the Nature of Bilingual Puerto Rican Youths' Ethnic Identity Development." Master's thesis, Mount Holyoke College, 1995.

———. "Who Are You If You Don't Speak Spanish? The Puerto Rican Dilemma." Presentation at the annual meeting of the American Educational Research Association, New York, April 1996.

Zhou, Min, and Jennifer Lee. "Introduction: The Making of Culture, Identity and Ethnicity Among Asian American Youth." In *Asian American Youth: Culture, Identity and Ethnicity,* edited by Min Zhou and Jennifer Lee, 1–30. New York: Routledge, 2004.

———. *The Asian American Achievement Paradox.* New York: Russell Sage Foundation, 2015.

Zong, Jie, and Jeanne Batalova. "Frequently Requested Statistics on Immigrants and Immigration in the United States." *Migration Information Source,* Migration Policy Institute, April 14, 2016. http://www.migrationpolicy.org/article/frequently-requested -statistics-immigrants-and-immigration-united-states.

———. "Middle Eastern and North African Immigrants in the United States." *Migration Information Source,* Migration Policy Institute, June 3, 2015. http:// www.migrationpolicy.org/article/middle-eastern-and-north-african-immigrants -united-states.

Zúñiga, Ximena, Biren (Ratnesh) A. Nagda, Mark Chesler, and Adena Cytron-Walker. *Intergroup Dialogue in Higher Education: Meaningful Learning About Social Justice.* ASHE Higher Education Report Series, vol. 32, no. 4. San Francisco, CA: Jossey-Bass, 2007.

Zweigenhaft, Richard L., and G. William Domhoff. *Blacks in the White Establishment? A Study of Race and Class in America.* New Haven, CT: Yale University Press, 1991.

# ACKNOWLEDGMENTS

When I retired from the presidency of Spelman College in July 2015, I did not know that I would spend the next fourteen months taking care of dying parents. Two weeks after I left my job, my mother was diagnosed with pancreatic cancer, and she passed away in November of that year at the age of eighty-nine, leaving behind her husband of sixty-four years, my father. Though my dad suffered from dementia, he never forgot that I was his daughter Beverly, and he often asked me, encouragingly, "Are you working on your book?" He passed away peacefully in September 2016, just a few days after his ninetieth birthday. It is with deep gratitude for the gift of such loving and supportive parents that I dedicate this book to them. I thank my siblings, Patricia Daniel Keenan, Kevin Daniel, and Eric Daniel, for their help and support during that difficult time.

To begin this book revision, I sought out feedback from faculty and students who had been using the earlier edition in their courses to see what concepts had been most useful and remained most relevant for them, in addition to other questions I had. I hired Creative Research Solutions, a research evaluation firm, to help me with that data collection. The fact that my oldest son, Travis Jonathan Tatum, and his wife, Shanesha Brooks-Tatum, lead Creative Research Solutions made that collaboration especially wonderful. Thank you, Travis J. and Shanesha, for your assistance! Thanks as well to all of those who responded to their survey and interview requests. I hope you see the positive impact of your comments in this new edition.

So much of the original version of my book was informed by my teaching career at Mount Holyoke College that it seemed only fitting to return to MHC to talk with current students taking the Psychology of Racism course I created, now being taught by Jen Daigle-Matos. Thank you, Jen, for opening up your classroom to me, and to Dr. Sandra Lawrence, for connecting me back to Jen. Thanks as well to Pat Romney and Patty Ramsey, who also shared reference materials and words of encouragement as I pushed forward on this revision. Thanks, too, to Susan Kennedy Marx, for her enthusiasm for my project and the many ways she has put my work to good use in her own antiracist teaching and consultation. Susan, your encouragement and affirmation are much appreciated!

The years I spent living in Northampton, Massachusetts, were enriched by my friendships with Five College faculty colleagues, some of whom are or have been associated with the Social Justice Education program of the Graduate School of Education at the University of Massachusetts. Thanks to Charmaine Wijeyesinghe, Maurianne Adams, and Rhonda Cobham-Sander for your insights. In particular, I want to thank Ximena Zúñiga and her Social Justice Education students: Eun Y. Lee, William Syldor-Severino, Nina Tissi-Gassoway, Amer Ahmed, Shelly Perdomo, Dave Neely, Isaiah I. Iboko, Ro N. Sigle, Carol Huban, Rachel Card, Shady Kimsey, Itza Martinez, and Molly Keehn, for sharing your feedback and providing the opportunity to observe dialogue groups in session.

Thanks to Victoria Malaney for introducing me to Kristie Ford and the Intergroup Dialogue work being done at Skidmore College. Kristie, thanks for sharing the advance copy of your book, *Facilitating Change Through Intergroup Dialogue* (Routledge, forthcoming). Thanks to Mana Tahaie and Shelly Tochluk for our helpful conversation at NCORE.

Whenever I returned to Northampton, my friend Joan Rasool made space in her home for this writer's sanctuary. Our many conversations helped "prime the pump." Joan, thanks for your feedback on the new Chapter 8, especially. To my longtime friend and cofacilitator of many Unlearning Racism workshops, Andrea Ayvazian, thanks for keeping me lifted with your prayers. To Rita McDougald-Campbell, those "Are you finished yet?" text messages certainly helped me stay on task!

At the University of Michigan, David Schoem, an Intergroup Dialogue pioneer, generously hosted my meetings with U-M students who are participating in the Michigan Community Scholars Program. Thanks, David, for your many years of using the book and your insights about today's students. Thanks to Rebecca Christensen for sharing your dissertation on the impact of MCSP as well. Thanks, too, to Deborah Ball, former dean of the University of Michigan School of Education, for helping to identify faculty willing to share their feedback. It was invaluable!

Thanks to Basic Books publisher Lara Heimert for inviting me to do the twentieth-anniversary edition, and to my literary agent, Faith Childs, for helping me to bring this project to fruition. It was just the right opportunity for me to consider as I transitioned from the presidency at Spelman.

After the death of my father, when I needed a jump start to my writing, I spent two weeks in retreat at Rancho la Puerta in Tecate, Mexico. I wrote a tremendous amount in those two weeks and had the momentum I needed when I returned home. Thank you to the RLP staff for taking care of all of my needs during those weeks. It made all the difference!

As I put the finishing touches on the book in the spring of 2017, I had the wonderful opportunity to serve as the Mimi and Peter E. Haas Distinguished Visitor at the Haas Center for Public Service at Stanford University. I want to thank the Haas Center staff for providing such a warm welcome, and the Stanford faculty, staff, and students whose conversations helped me fine-tune this project.

A special thank-you to Gaye Theresa Johnson, Imani Romney-Rosa, and Kia Darling-Hammond for your very timely feedback about inclusive language.

To my youngest son, David, thanks for your careful reading and helpful feedback on the prologue, in particular. Your millennial perspective is important! Finally, to my dear husband, Travis the elder, who reads *every* word I write—you are truly the labor coach for yet another "baby." Thank you for your love and devotion. Life is so much sweeter because of you!

# INDEX

**Beverly Daniel Tatum, PhD,** is President Emerita of Spelman College and received in 2014 the Award for Outstanding Lifetime Contribution to Psychology, the highest honor presented by the American Psychological Association. She lives in Atlanta, Georgia.

*Photograph by J. D. Scott*